Introduction to Radio Engineering

T0179194

OTHER COMMUNICATIONS BOOKS FROM CRC PRESS

Advances in Communications-Based Train Control Systems
Edited by F. Richard Yu
ISBN 978-1-4822-5743-4

Advances in Mobile Cloud Computing Systems
Edited by F. Richard Yu and Victor Leung
ISBN 978-1-4987-1509-6

Analytical Evaluation of Nonlinear Distortion Effects on Multicarrier Signals
Theresa Araújo and Rui Dinis
ISBN 978-1-4822-1594-6

Cable and Wireless Networks: Theory and Practice
Mário Marques da Silva
ISBN 978-1-4987-4681-6

Cognitive Networks: Applications and Deployments
Edited by Jaime Lloret Mauri, Kayhan Zrar Ghafoor, Danda B. Rawat, and Javier Manuel Aguiar Perez
ISBN 978-1-4822-3699-6

Cognitive Radio Networks: Efficient Resource Allocation in Cooperative Sensing, Cellular Communications, High-Speed Vehicles
Tao Jiang, Zhiqiang Wang, and Yang Cao
ISBN 978-1-4987-2113-4

Cyber Physical Systems: Architectures, Protocols and Applications
Edited by Chi (Harold) Liu and Yan Zhang
ISBN 978-1-4822-0897-9

Cyber-Physical Systems: From Theory to Practice
Edited by Danda B. Rawat, Joel J.P.C. Rodrigues, and Ivan Stojmenovic
ISBN 978-1-4822-6332-9

Emerging Communication Technologies Based on Wireless Sensor Networks: Current Research and Future Applications
Edited by Mubashir Husain Rehmani and Al-Sakib Khan Pathan
ISBN 978-1-4987-2485-2

Handbook on Session Initiation Protocol: Networked Multimedia Communications for IP Telephony
Radhika Ranjan Roy
ISBN 978-1-4987-4770-7

Introduction to Communications Technologies: A Guide for Non-Engineers, Third Edition
Stephan Jones, Ronald J. Kovac, and Frank M. Groom
ISBN 978-1-4987-0293-5

Mobile Devices: Tools and Technologies
Lauren Collins and Scott R. Ellis
ISBN 978-1-4665-9416-6

Mobile Evolution: Insights on Connectivity and Service
Sebastian Thalanany
ISBN 978-1-4822-2480-1

Multi-Carrier Communication Systems with Examples in MATLAB®: A New Perspective
Emad Hassan
ISBN 978-1-4987-3532-2

Networked Filtering and Fusion in Wireless Sensor Networks
Magdi S. Mahmoud and Yuanqing Xia
ISBN 978-1-4822-5096-1

Opportunities in 5G Networks: A Research and Development Perspective
Edited by Fei Hu
ISBN 978-1-4987-3954-2

Radio Wave Propagation and Channel Modeling for Earth-Space Systems
Athanasios G. Kanatas and Athanasios D. Panagopoulos
ISBN 978-1-4822-4970-5

Securing Cyber-Physical Systems
Edited by Al-Sakib Khan Pathan
ISBN 978-1-4987-0098-6

Security and Privacy in Internet of Things (IoTs): Models, Algorithms, and Implementations
Edited by Fei Hu
ISBN 978-1-4987-2318-3

The Future of Wireless Networks: Architectures, Protocols, and Services
Edited by Mohesen Guizani, Hsiao-Hwa Chen, and Chonggang Wang
ISBN 978-1-4822-2094-0

The Future X Network: A Bell Labs Perspective
Marcus K. Weldon
ISBN 978-1-4987-7914-2

Understanding Spectrum Liberalisation
Martin Sims, Toby Youell, and Richard Womersley
ISBN 978-1-4987-0502-8

Wireless Network Performance Enhancement via Directional Antennas: Models, Protocols, and Systems
Edited by John D. Matyjas, Fei Hu, and Sunil Kumar
ISBN 978-1-4987-0753-4

Wireless Sensor Multimedia Networks: Architectures, Protocols, and Applications
Edited by Mohamed Mostafa A. Azim and Xiaohong Jiang
ISBN 978-1-4822-5311-5

TO ORDER: Call: 1-800-272-7737 • Fax: 1-800-374-3401 • E-mail: orders@crcpress.com

Introduction to Radio Engineering

Nathan Blaunstein
Christos Christodoulou
Mikhail Sergeev

CRC Press
Taylor & Francis Group
Boca Raton London New York

CRC Press is an imprint of the
Taylor & Francis Group, an **informa** business

CRC Press
Taylor & Francis Group
6000 Broken Sound Parkway NW, Suite 300
Boca Raton, FL 33487-2742

First issued in paperback 2020

ISBN 13: 978-0-367-57450-5 (pbk)
ISBN 13: 978-1-4987-6942-6 (hbk)

Library of Congress Cataloging-in-Publication Data

Names: Blaunstein, Nathan, author. | Christodoulou, Christos G., 1955- author. | Sergeev, Mikhail, 1982- author.
Title: Introduction to radio engineering / Nathan Blaunstein, Christos Christodoulou, and Mikhail Sergeev.
Description: Boca Raton : Taylor & Francis, a CRC title, part of the Taylor & Francis imprint, a member of the Taylor & Francis Group, the academic division of T&F Informa, plc, [2016] | Includes bibliographical references and index.
Identifiers: LCCN 2016016323 | ISBN 9781498769426 (alk. paper)
Subjects: LCSH: Radio--Equipment and supplies. | Radar--Equipment and supplies. | Electromagnetism.
Classification: LCC TK6560 .B53 2016 | DDC 621.384--dc23
LC record available at https://lccn.loc.gov/2016016323

Visit the Taylor & Francis Web site at
http://www.taylorandfrancis.com

and the CRC Press Web site at
http://www.crcpress.com

Contents

Preface

The book is intended to appeal to any practicing radio scientist or radio engineer who is concerned with the design, operation, and service of wired and wireless radio systems for resolving both the direct and the inverse problems of radio communication and radiolocation.

During the last 50 years, many radio elements, devices, and systems have been developed to satisfy the ever-increasing demand of modern radio engineering for wired and wireless communications and radar applications. It is well known that each completed radio system, wired or wireless, consists of several separate and independent "layers." The first "layer" deals with a wide range of electronic devices and circuits, such as generators, radiators, and radiation detectors. The second "layer" deals with signal processing, including various kinds of modulation and demodulation schemes. The last "layer" deals with antennas as elements of radiation and reception of radio signals sent through any communication link. To integrate all these "layers," an additional layer is introduced by the authors, referred to as the "physical and mathematical layer."

Therefore, all the aspects described in this book regarding radio engineering start from basic mathematical and physical explanations of matter, and then they progress to other, more complex engineering concepts, covering the three main radio "layers" mentioned above. Each engineering aspect is demonstrated with corresponding examples, giving the reader the ability to use the information obtained in the design of modern communications and radiolocation systems.

The main goal of this book is to introduce the main aspects of modern radio engineering and radio physics, in a way that has not been covered before in literature. The authors use the experience of many years of teaching courses in this area to undergraduate and graduate students.

The book is composed of fifteen chapters, divided into five sections. Section I, titled "Mathematical Foundations for Radio Engineering," consists of two chapters. Chapter 1 presents elements of basic mathematics, complex analysis, vector analysis, and tensor analysis. Chapter 2 covers differential and integral operators and formulas that are introduced for future explanation of fundamentals in classical electrodynamics, discussed in Chapters 3 through 5. These formulas and operators are also used during Chapters 6 through 14 to describe the operation of the basic aspects of guiding structures, antennas, and radars.

Section II, titled "Introduction to Classical Electrodynamics," consists of three chapters. In Chapter 3, the main laws of electrodynamics are presented in both differential and integral form. The main equations describing fundamental aspects of the propagation of electromagnetic waves and their characteristic distributions in the space and time domains are presented in this chapter. In Chapter 4, the propagation of electromagnetic waves, in plane, cylindrical, and spherical form, and their polarizations are described. Then, the propagation of a plane wave in various material media is discussed through the analysis of the corresponding wave and media characteristics. Various propagation media situations are discussed: propagation in nonideal dielectric media, ideal dielectric media, nonideal conductors, and ideal conductors. It is shown how to obtain the wave properties by knowing the various parameters and characteristics of the medium, and the possibility of resolving the inverse problem, that is, finding the parameters of the medium using knowledge of the parameters of the wave propagating through such a medium. Chapter 5 describes the boundary conditions if wave propagation occurs through the boundary of two different media. The corresponding formulas for the reflection and refraction coefficients for two types of wave polarization, vertical and horizontal, are presented. All the four chapters are accompanied by related examples.

Section III, titled "Guiding Structures and Guiding Waves," consists of four chapters. In Chapter 6, the main guiding structures that are used in most applications in practice today are described. The types of electromagnetic waves that can propagate in such structures are presented with the corresponding equations obtained from basic electrodynamics concepts mentioned in previous chapters. Chapter 7 emphasizes wave propagation in lossless two-wire transmission lines. In Chapter 8, the main characteristics and parameters of coaxial cables, as guiding wire structures, are described, and the corresponding types of propagating waves are presented. For each type of waves, several examples are presented to enhance the understanding of practical applications of coaxial cables. Separately, the leaky coaxial cable is described as a special case of coax lines.

Chapter 9 deals with various types of waveguide structures: plane, rectangular, and cylindrical. For all these types of guiding structures, the relations between characteristics of waves and the structures are presented and discussed.

Section IV, titled "Antenna Fundamentals," consists of only one chapter, Chapter 10, in which the basic antenna types and their characteristics are presented and discussed. The main equation of antennas in free space is presented, and it is shown how it is usually used and modified for different propagating media in wireless communications and radar systems. Finally, a brief description of types of antennas that are usually used in communication networks and radar systems is presented. Here, the authors describe not only the well-known types of antennas, such as dipole, loop, and antenna arrays, but also multibeam and phased-array antennas, which have become more attractive and effective in modern wired, wireless, and radar systems.

Section V, titled "Radar Fundamentals," consists of five chapters. Chapter 11 describes the basic characteristics and parameters of various types of radars, their classification associated with types of radiated signals, and their applications. Then, the path loss of the radar signals in various environments is briefly discussed: in free space, above terrain, and in the atmosphere and ionosphere, which characterize different kinds of radars, from ground based to atmospheric and ionospheric. The main radar equation is given by taking into consideration environmental and target effects. In Chapter 12, the main properties of active and passive millimeter wave radar are presented and discussed, accounting for clutter, environmental, and target effects. Chapter 13 deals with the description of ground-penetrating radars based on leaky coaxial cables, the main parameters and characteristics of which are covered in Chapter 8. The basic equation of such a radar operation, its regions of operation, and the radiation pattern and radiation characteristics for various types of ground-penetrating radar are presented and discussed. Next, various effects of clutter on buried leaky coaxial cables are discussed, and the corresponding comparison with experimental data is presented. In Chapter 14, the theoretical frameworks and models regarding ground-penetrating radars and remote sensing systems that are most applicable today are presented, with a brief coverage of the problems associated with their design and the influence of the subsoil or any clutter environment. Several recommendations are given for future practical applications. Chapter 15 introduces the methodology of ultra-wideband, extremely-short-pulse ground-penetrating radars and remote sensing systems, their operation, their description, and the corresponding operational problems and challenges. Then, the most important applications in practice of such ground-penetrating radars and remote sensing systems are briefly presented and compared with the corresponding theoretical prediction presented in Chapter 14.

Acknowledgments

The authors are grateful for the contributions of Professor Alexander Shepena with his insights on radar theory and radar applications, and also acknowledge the computational work of PhD student Vadim Nenashev in ground-to-air radar applications.

The authors also acknowledge the theoretical and experimental work of Mihael Mejibovsky in modeling radio propagation in subsoil media for ground-penetrating radar applications.

In addition, we thank Dr. Gregory Samelsohn for his contributions to the theoretical analysis of guiding radar systems based on leaky coaxial cables hidden in various clutter subsoil environments.

We are greatly indebted to the Taylor & Francis staff, the reviewers, and technical editors, for the presentation of this book with clarity and precision.

Authors

Nathan Blaunstein earned his MSc degree in radiophysics and electronics from Tomsk University, Tomsk, Russia, in 1972, and his PhD, DSc, and professor degrees in radiophysics and electronics from the Institute of Geomagnetism, Ionosphere, and Radiowave Propagation (IZMIR), Academy of Science USSR, Moscow, Russia, in 1985 and 1991, respectively.

From 1979 to 1984, he was an engineer and a lecturer, and then, from 1984 to 1992, a senior scientist, an associate professor, and a professor of Moldavian University, Beltsy, Moldova, former USSR.

From 1993 to 1998, Dr. Blaunstein was a scientist in the Department of Electrical and Computer Engineering and a visiting professor in the Wireless Cellular Communication Program at the Ben-Gurion University of the Negev, Beer Sheva, Israel. From 2001 to 2004, he was an associate professor, and from 2005, a full professor of the Department of Communication Systems Engineering.

His research interests include problems of radio-wave propagation, diffraction, and scattering in various media (subsoil and underwater media, terrestrial environments, the atmosphere, and the ionosphere) for the purposes of radiolocation, terrestrial, aircraft, and mobile-satellite wireless communications, remote sensing, and signal processing.

Christos Christodoulou earned his PhD degree in electrical engineering from North Carolina State University in 1985. He is a fellow member of the Institute of Electrical and Electronics Engineers, a member of Commission B of the Union Radio-Scientifique Internationale, and a distinguished professor at the University of New Mexico. Currently, he is the associate dean of research for the School of Engineering at the University of New Mexico. He is the recipient of the 2010 Institute of Electrical and Electronics Engineers John Krauss Antenna Award for his work on reconfigurable fractal antennas using micro-electro-mechanical system switches, the Lawton-Ellis Award, and the Gardner Zemke Professorship at the University of New Mexico.

Dr. Christodoulou has published over 500 papers in journals and conferences and 17 book chapters and has co-authored 6 books. His research interests are in the areas of modeling of electromagnetic systems, cognitive radio, machine learning in electromagnetics, high-power microwave antennas, and reconfigurable antennas for cognitive radio.

Mikhail Sergeev earned his PhD degree in automated data-processing equipment and management systems in 1989 and a Dr. Sc. (Technical Sciences) degree in 2001 from St. Petersburg State University of Aerospace Instrumentation, St. Petersburg, Russia. Currently, Dr. Sergeev is the director of the Institute of Computer Systems and Programming, head of the Department of Computing Systems and Networks of State University of Aerospace Instrumentation, and a professor.

He has published over 250 papers in journals and conferences and has co-authored 4 books. His research interests are in the areas of numerical methods, specialized processing systems of digital information, telecommunication systems, and simulation of electromagnetic systems.

He is editor-in-chief of the international journal *Information and Control Systems*, published by St. Petersburg State University of Aerospace Instrumentation, Russia.

Symbols and Abbreviations

A	arbitrary vectors of electromagnetic field
B	vector of induction of magnetic field component of the electromagnetic wave
$c = \dfrac{1}{\sqrt{\varepsilon_0 \mu_0}}$	velocity of light in free space
curl ≡ rot = $\nabla \times$	rotor of arbitrary vector field or the vector product of the operator Nabla
$\hat{C}$	capacity of the cable or transmission line normalized over their line
div ≡ $\nabla \cdot$	a flow of arbitrary vector or a scalar product ("Nabla dot") of the field
$d\mathbf{l}$	differential of the vector of line l
$d\mathbf{S}$	differential of the vector of surface S
$d\mathbf{V}$	differential of the vector of volume V
D	vector of induction of electric field component of the electromagnetic wave
E	vector of electric field component of the electromagnetic wave
$\tilde{\mathbf{E}}(z)$	phasor of the electrical component of the electromagnetic wave
$\mathbf{E}(z,t)$	2-D distribution of the vector of electrical component of the electromagnetic wave
grad $\Phi = \nabla \Phi$	gradient of arbitrary scalar field or effect of Nabla operator on the scalar field
$\hat{G}$	conductivity of the cable or transmission line normalized over their line
H	vector of magnetic field component of the electromagnetic wave
$\tilde{\mathbf{H}}(z)$	phasor of the magnetic component of the electromagnetic wave
$\mathbf{H}(z,t)$	2-D distribution of the vector of magnetic component of the electromagnetic wave
$i = \sqrt{-1}$	ort of imaginary part of the complex number

$\mathbf{i}_r, \mathbf{i}_\phi, \mathbf{i}_\theta$	unit vectors (orts) in spherical coordinate system
$\mathbf{i}_\rho, \mathbf{i}_\phi, \mathbf{i}_z$	unit vectors (orts) in cylindrical coordinate system
$\mathbf{i}_x, \mathbf{i}_y, \mathbf{i}_z$	unit vectors (orts) in Cartesian coordinate system
$I(z,t)$	wave of current in circuits, transmission lines, and cables
I_0	constant current in circuits, transmission lines, and cables
$\mathbf{j}$	vector of electric current density
$\mathbf{j}_c$	conductivity current density
$\mathbf{j}_d$	displacement current density
$\mathbf{J}$	vector of the full current in medium/circuit
$\hat{L}$	inductance of the cable or transmission line normalized over their line
$\mathbf{M}$	momentum of the magnetic ambient source
$\mathbf{P}$	vector of polarization
Q	full charge in circuit, material, or medium
$\{r, \varphi, \theta\}$	spherical coordinate system
$\hat{R}$	resistance of the cable or transmission line normalized over their line
S	area of arbitrary surface
T	coefficient of refraction (transfer of the wave into the medium)
v_{gr}	wave group velocity
v_{ph}	wave phase velocity
V	volume of arbitrary surface
VSWR	vertical standing-wave ratio
$V(z,t)$	the wave of voltage in circuits, transmission lines, and cables
V_0	constant voltage or potential difference
W	energy of arbitrary field
$\{x, y, z\}$	Cartesian coordinate system
$\hat{Y} = \hat{G} + i\omega\hat{C}$	full normalized complex conductivity of the cable or transmission line
$z = a + ib$	complex number: a, its real part; b, its imaginary part
$\hat{Z} = \hat{R} + i\omega\hat{L}$	full normalized complex impedance of the cable or transmission line
Z_c	intrinsic impedance of the transmission line or cable
Z_L	loading (shunt) impedance of the transmission line or cable
α	parameter of wave attenuation in arbitrary medium

β	parameter of phase velocity deviation in arbitrary medium
Γ	coefficient of reflection from boundary of two media
$\gamma = \alpha + i\beta$	parameter of propagation in arbitrary material medium
$\delta = \dfrac{1}{\alpha}$	skin layer in arbitrary material medium
$\Delta = \nabla^2$	Laplacian of the vector or scalar field
$\varepsilon = \varepsilon' + i\varepsilon''$	complex permittivity of arbitrary medium
$\varepsilon_r = \varepsilon_r' + i\varepsilon_r'' = \varepsilon_{Re}' + i\varepsilon_{Im}'''$	relative permittivity of arbitrary medium: $\varepsilon_{Re}' = \varepsilon'/\varepsilon_0$, its real part; $\varepsilon''' = \varepsilon'''/\varepsilon_0$, its imaginary part
$\varepsilon_0 = \dfrac{1}{36\pi}10^{-9}(\text{F/m})$	dielectric parameter of free space
η	wave impedance in arbitrary medium
$\eta_0 = 120\pi\,\Omega = 377\,\Omega$	wave impedance of free space
λ	wavelength in arbitrary medium
λ_g	wavelength in arbitrary waveguide structure
$\mu = \mu' + i\mu''$	complex permeability of arbitrary medium
$\mu_r = \mu_r' + i\mu_r'' = \mu_{Re}' + i\mu_{Im}'''$	relative permittivity of arbitrary medium: $\mu_{Re}' = \mu'/\mu_0$, its real part; $\mu_{Im}'' = \mu'''/\mu_0$, its imaginary part
$\mu_0 = 4\pi\times10^{-9}(\text{H/m})$	dielectric parameter of free space
ρ	charge density in medium
$\{\rho,\varphi,z\}$	cylindrical coordinate system
σ	conductivity of arbitrary medium or material
Ψ	flux of the electric or magnetic field
χ_e	electrical sensitivity
χ_m	magnetic sensitivity
∇	operator Nabla of arbitrary scalar field

MATHEMATICAL FOUNDATIONS FOR RADIO ENGINEERING

Chapter 1

Basic Definitions, Operations, and Differential Vectors

In our further description of mathematical foundations for classical and applied electrodynamics and electromagnetism, we will follow the excellent handbooks that were produced from the 1950s to the beginning of the twenty-first century [1–7].

1.1 Complex Values and Phasors

According to its definition, a complex value z has two parts: a real part a and an imaginary part b:

$$z = a + jb \tag{1.1}$$

Equation 1.1 is the rectangular form of the complex value presentation, and $j = \sqrt{-1}$ or $(\pm j)^2 = -1$. The exponential for of the complex value is defined as

$$z = Ae^{j\phi} = A(\cos\phi + j\sin\phi) \tag{1.2}$$

from which it follows that

$$a = A\cos\phi, b = A\sin\phi \tag{1.3a}$$

and

$$a^2 + b^2 = A^2, \tan\phi = \frac{b}{a} \tag{1.3b}$$

These definitions allow us to introduce the so-called *phasor technique*, which we use in our description of Maxwell's and wave equations in Chapters 3–5. Since

$$Ae^{j\phi} = A\cos\phi + jA\sin\phi,$$

we can write

$$A\cos\phi = \operatorname{Re}\left[Ae^{j\phi}\right] \tag{1.4}$$

where the notation "Re" stands for "real part of." In particular, if $\phi = \omega t + \theta$, then we have

$$A\cos(\omega t + \theta) = \operatorname{Re}\left[Ae^{j(\omega t+\theta)}\right]$$

$$= \operatorname{Re}\left[Ae^{j\theta}e^{j\omega t}\right] = \operatorname{Re}\left[\tilde{A}e^{j\omega t}\right] \tag{1.5}$$

where $\tilde{A} = Ae^{j\theta}$ is known as the *phasor*, that is, the complex number that is denoted as $\tilde{A}$, corresponding to $A\cos(\omega t + \theta)$. The phasor to a sine function can be obtained if we convert a sine into a cosine:

$$B\sin(\omega t + \theta) = B\cos\left(\omega t + \theta - \tfrac{\pi}{2}\right) = \operatorname{Re}\left[Ae^{j(\omega t+\theta-\frac{\pi}{2})}\right]$$

$$= \operatorname{Re}\left[Be^{j(\theta-\frac{\pi}{2})}e^{j\omega t}\right] = \operatorname{Re}\left[\tilde{B}e^{j\omega t}\right] \tag{1.6}$$

Hence, the phasor corresponding to $B\sin(\omega t + \theta)$ is $Be^{j(\theta-\frac{\pi}{2})} = Be^{j\theta}e^{-j\frac{\pi}{2}} = -jBe^{j\theta}$.

1.2 Vectors

Each vector **A** can be defined by its magnitude (or modules) and the direction. It can be determined by the use of unit vector **i**, that is, the vector of which the magnitude is equal to unity. A view of different kinds of vectors with different lengths (e.g., magnitudes) and directions is illustrated in Figure 1.1.

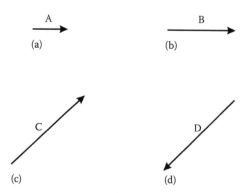

Figure 1.1 **(a–d) Types and directions of the vectors.**

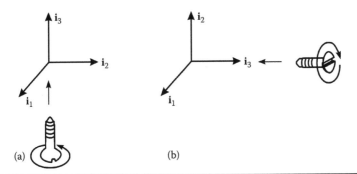

Figure 1.2 **Cartesian system of coordinates with two rotations of the vectors: (a) anti clockwise and (b) clockwise.**

We call these unit vectors *orts*. Thus, if according to the definition

$$\mathbf{A} = |\mathbf{A}|\mathbf{i} \tag{1.7}$$

it follows that

$$|\mathbf{i}| = \frac{\mathbf{A}}{|\mathbf{A}|} \equiv 1 \tag{1.8}$$

There are two kinds of coordinate systems presentation (see Figure 1.2) defined by the unit vectors: the right-handed and the left-handed.

If so, the Cartesian coordinate system can be presented by superposition of three orthogonal unit vectors, each of which determines the corresponding direction of the axis: x, y, or z.

This system is characterized by triple variables, which together create a system of equations:

$$x = \text{const}$$
$$y = \text{const} \tag{1.9}$$
$$z = \text{const}$$

If so, any arbitrary vector $\mathbf{r}$ with current coordinates (x, y, z) as variables can be presented through three orthogonal orts as

$$\mathbf{r} = x\mathbf{i}_x + y\mathbf{i}_y + z\mathbf{i}_z \tag{1.10}$$

and its magnitude or modules equal

$$\mathbf{r} = \sqrt{x^2 + y^2 + z^2} \tag{1.11}$$

Using these definitions, an expression for the arbitrary vector $\mathbf{R}_{12}$ joining two points, P_1 and P_2, which are determined by two vectors $\mathbf{r}_1$ and $\mathbf{r}_2$, respectively, from the origin (see Figure 1.3) is

$$\mathbf{R}_{12} = (x_2 - x_1)\mathbf{i}_x + (y_2 - y_1)\mathbf{i}_y + (z_2 - z_1)\mathbf{i}_z \tag{1.12}$$

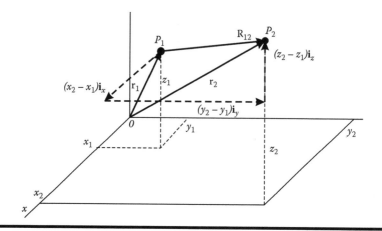

Figure 1.3   Presentation of arbitrary vector R$_{12}$ in the Cartesian coordinate system.

with modules

$$|\mathbf{R}_{12}| = \sqrt{(x_2 - x_1)^2 + (y_2 - y_1)^2 + (z_2 - z_1)^2} \qquad (1.13)$$

1.3 Vector and Scalar Operations

The sum (addition) of two any vectors, $\mathbf{r}_1$ and $\mathbf{r}_2$, is the sum of their parallel-like components, that is,

$$\mathbf{r}_1 + \mathbf{r}_2 = (x_1 \mathbf{i}_x + y_1 \mathbf{i}_y + z_1 \mathbf{i}_z) + (x_2 \mathbf{i}_x + y_2 \mathbf{i}_y + z_2 \mathbf{i}_z)$$
$$= (x_1 + x_2)\mathbf{i}_x + (y_1 + y_2)\mathbf{i}_y + (z_1 + z_2)\mathbf{i}_z \qquad (1.14)$$

In the same manner, the vector subtraction is a special case of addition:

$$\mathbf{r}_2 - \mathbf{r}_1 = (x_2 - x_1)\mathbf{i}_x + (y_2 - y_1)\mathbf{i}_y + (z_2 - z_1)\mathbf{i}_z \qquad (1.15)$$

Multiplication of any vector by a scalar m is the same as repeated addition of the vector. Thus,

$$m\mathbf{r} = m(x\mathbf{i}_x + y\mathbf{i}_y + z\mathbf{i}_z) = mx\mathbf{i}_x + my\mathbf{i}_y + mz\mathbf{i}_z \qquad (1.16)$$

Division by a scalar n is a special case of multiplication by a scalar $m = 1/n$ smaller than unity, but not equal to zero or infinity ($n \neq 0$, $n \neq \infty$), that is,

$$\frac{1}{n}\mathbf{r} = \frac{1}{n}(x\mathbf{i}_x + y\mathbf{i}_y + z\mathbf{i}_z) = \frac{x}{n}\mathbf{i}_x + \frac{y}{n}\mathbf{i}_y + \frac{z}{n}\mathbf{i}_z \qquad (1.17)$$

The *scalar* or *dot product* of two vectors is a scalar quantity equal to the magnitudes of these vectors and the cosine of the angle between them:

$$\mathbf{r}_1 \cdot \mathbf{r}_2 \equiv (\mathbf{r}_1, \mathbf{r}_2) = |\mathbf{r}_1||\mathbf{r}_2|\cos\alpha \qquad (1.18)$$

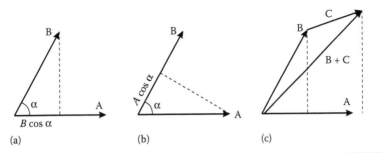

Figure 1.4 **(a–c) Geometrical presentation of the dot product and a vector sum C of the vectors A and B.**

Schematically, the sum, subtraction, and a scalar product (also called a dot product) for arbitrary vectors **A**, **B**, and **C**, are shown in Figure 1.4.

Properties of the dot product:

a. The dot product is a commutative operation, since

$$\mathbf{r}_2 \cdot \mathbf{r}_1 = |\mathbf{r}_2||\mathbf{r}_1|\cos\alpha = |\mathbf{r}_1||\mathbf{r}_2|\cos\alpha \equiv \mathbf{r}_1 \cdot \mathbf{r}_2$$

b. A more complicated product can be solved in the same manner:

$$\mathbf{r}_0(\mathbf{r}_1 + \mathbf{r}_2) = \mathbf{r}_0\mathbf{r}_1 + \mathbf{r}_0\mathbf{r}_2$$

Using these properties, we can define a dot product of two vectors in the Cartesian coordinate system according to Equation 1.10 as

$$\mathbf{r}_1 \cdot \mathbf{r}_2 = (x_1\mathbf{i}_x + y_1\mathbf{i}_y + z_1\mathbf{i}_z) \cdot (x_2\mathbf{i}_x + y_2\mathbf{i}_y + z_2\mathbf{i}_z)$$

$$= (x_1x_2)\mathbf{i}_x + (y_1y_2)\mathbf{i}_y + (z_1z_2)\mathbf{i}_z \tag{1.19}$$

If so, according to the definition of scalar product in Equation 1.18, we can obtain the important relationships between the unit vectors of a Cartesian coordinate system:

$$\mathbf{i}_x \cdot \mathbf{i}_x = 1, \mathbf{i}_x \cdot \mathbf{i}_y = 0, \mathbf{i}_x \cdot \mathbf{i}_z = 0$$

$$\mathbf{i}_y \cdot \mathbf{i}_x = 0, \mathbf{i}_y \cdot \mathbf{i}_y = 1, \mathbf{i}_y \cdot \mathbf{i}_z = 0 \tag{1.20}$$

$$\mathbf{i}_z \cdot \mathbf{i}_x = 0, \mathbf{i}_z \cdot \mathbf{i}_y = 0, \mathbf{i}_z \cdot \mathbf{i}_z = 1$$

The *vector or cross product* of any two vectors is a vector whose magnitude is equal to the product of the magnitudes of these vectors and the sine of the smaller angle between them, obtaining with these vectors the right-handed coordinate system (see Figure 1.5), that is,

$$\mathbf{A} \times \mathbf{B} = |\mathbf{A}||\mathbf{B}|\sin\alpha\mathbf{i}_N \tag{1.21a}$$

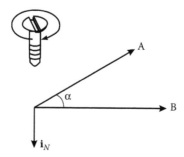

Figure 1.5   Geometrical presentation of the vector product of arbitrary vectors A and B and the vector i_N, normal to the plane (A, B).

and

$$|\mathbf{A} \times \mathbf{B}| = |\mathbf{A}||\mathbf{B}|\sin\alpha \tag{1.21b}$$

In contrast to the scalar product, this product is not commutative, since (in a Cartesian coordinate system)

$$\mathbf{r}_2 \times \mathbf{r}_1 = |\mathbf{r}_2||\mathbf{r}_1|\sin\alpha(-\mathbf{i}_N) = -|\mathbf{r}_2||\mathbf{r}_1|\sin\alpha\mathbf{i}_N = -\mathbf{r}_1 \times \mathbf{r}_2$$

From the above mentioned equation it follows that

$$\mathbf{i}_x \times \mathbf{i}_x = 0, \mathbf{i}_x \times \mathbf{i}_y = \mathbf{i}_z, \mathbf{i}_x \times \mathbf{i}_z = -\mathbf{i}_y$$
$$\mathbf{i}_y \times \mathbf{i}_x = -\mathbf{i}_z, \mathbf{i}_y \times \mathbf{i}_y = 0, \mathbf{i}_y \times \mathbf{i}_z = \mathbf{i}_x \tag{1.22}$$
$$\mathbf{i}_z \times \mathbf{i}_x = \mathbf{i}_y, \mathbf{i}_z \times \mathbf{i}_y = -\mathbf{i}_x, \mathbf{i}_z \times \mathbf{i}_z = 0$$

Using these properties, we have for the vector product in the Cartesian coordinate system

$$\mathbf{r}_1 \cdot \mathbf{r}_2 = (x_1\mathbf{i}_x + y_1\mathbf{i}_y + z_1\mathbf{i}_z) \times (x_2\mathbf{i}_x + y_2\mathbf{i}_y + z_2\mathbf{i}_z)$$
$$= (y_1z_2 - z_1y_2)\mathbf{i}_x + (z_1x_2 - x_1z_2)\mathbf{i}_y + (x_1y_2 - y_1x_2)\mathbf{i}_z \tag{1.23}$$

This definition can be presented in the following determinant form:

$$\mathbf{r}_1 \times \mathbf{r}_2 = \begin{vmatrix} \mathbf{i}_x & \mathbf{i}_y & \mathbf{i}_z \\ x_1 & y_1 & z_1 \\ x_2 & y_2 & z_2 \end{vmatrix} \tag{1.24}$$

The combination of scalar and vector product gives the scalar, which in the determinant form can be determined as

$$\mathbf{r}_0 \cdot \mathbf{r}_1 \times \mathbf{r}_2 = \begin{vmatrix} x_0 & y_0 & z_0 \\ x_1 & y_1 & z_1 \\ x_2 & y_2 & z_2 \end{vmatrix} = x_0(y_1 z_2 - y_2 z_1) +$$

$$+ y_0(x_2 z_1 - x_1 z_2) + z_0(x_1 y_2 - x_2 y_1) \tag{1.25}$$

Moreover, despite the fact that the vector product is not commutative and that

$$\mathbf{r}_0 \times (\mathbf{r}_1 \times \mathbf{r}_2) \neq (\mathbf{r}_0 \times \mathbf{r}_1) \times \mathbf{r}_2,$$

at the same time, the triple scalar-vector product can be changed in a cyclic manner:

$$\mathbf{r}_0 \cdot (\mathbf{r}_1 \times \mathbf{r}_2) = \mathbf{r}_1 \times (\mathbf{r}_2 \times \mathbf{r}_0) = \mathbf{r}_2 \times (\mathbf{r}_0 \times \mathbf{r}_1) \tag{1.26}$$

Moreover, for any arbitrary vector $\mathbf{r}_3$,

$$\mathbf{r}_3 \cdot \mathbf{r}_0 \times (\mathbf{r}_1 + \mathbf{r}_2) = \mathbf{r}_3 \cdot (\mathbf{r}_0 \times \mathbf{r}_1 + \mathbf{r}_0 \times \mathbf{r}_2) \tag{1.27}$$

1.4 Differential Vectors

1.4.1 Cartesian Coordinate System

The *differential length vector* is the vector drawn from a point $P(x,y,z)$ to a neighboring point $Q(x + dx, y + dy, z + dz)$ (see Figure 1.6), that is,

$$d\mathbf{l} = dx\mathbf{i}_x + dy\mathbf{i}_y + dz\mathbf{i}_z \tag{1.28}$$

The *differential surface vector* is a vector product of two differential vectors $d\mathbf{l}_1$ and $d\mathbf{l}_2$, which create a parallelogram having $d\mathbf{l}_1$ and $d\mathbf{l}_2$ as two of its adjacent sides (see Figure 1.7). The area of such a parallelogram is defined as dS, the magnitude of differential surface vector

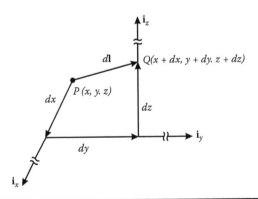

Figure 1.6 **Geometrical presentation of the differential length vector *dl*.**

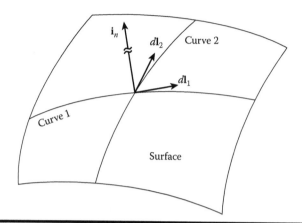

Figure 1.7 **Geometrical presentation of the differential surface vector *d*s.**

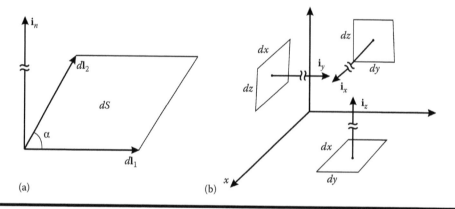

Figure 1.8 **(a) General view of presentation of the differential surface vector *d*s; (b) geometrical explanation of Formula 1.30.**

$$d\mathbf{s} = d\mathbf{l}_1 \times d\mathbf{l}_2 \tag{1.29a}$$

that is,

$$dS \equiv |d\mathbf{s}| = |d\mathbf{l}_1||d\mathbf{l}_2|\sin\alpha \tag{1.29b}$$

In the Cartesian coordinate system, the following useful expressions associated with each plane can be obtained from Equation 1.29 (see Figure 1.8):

$$\pm dy\mathbf{i}_y \times dz\mathbf{i}_z = \pm dydz\mathbf{i}_x$$

$$\pm dz\mathbf{i}_z \times dx\mathbf{i}_x = \pm dzdx\mathbf{i}_y \tag{1.30}$$

$$\pm dx\mathbf{i}_x \times dy\mathbf{i}_y = \pm dxdy\mathbf{i}_z$$

We notice that in Figure 1.8b, the corresponding vectors are shown for the plus signs in Equation 1.30.

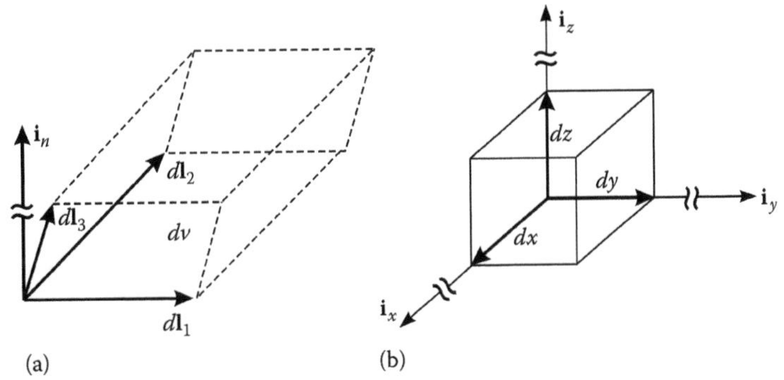

Figure 1.9 **(a,b) Geometrical presentation of the differential volume vector *dv*.**

The *differential volume vector* is produced by the arbitrary three differential length vectors $d\mathbf{l}_1 = da_1\mathbf{i}_1$, $d\mathbf{l}_2 = da_2\mathbf{i}_2$, and $d\mathbf{l}_3 = da_3\mathbf{i}_3$, accounting for the above definition $|\mathbf{i}_1| = |\mathbf{i}_2| = |\mathbf{i}_3| = 1$, which produces a parallelepiped with area $|d\mathbf{s}| = |d\mathbf{l}_1 \times d\mathbf{l}_2|$ and height $|d\mathbf{l}_n \times d\mathbf{l}_3|$ (see Figure 1.9a):

$$dv = |d\mathbf{l}_1 \times d\mathbf{l}_2||d\mathbf{l}_n \cdot d\mathbf{l}_3| \tag{1.31}$$

Because the normal vector to the horizontal surface can be defined through its length vectors $d\mathbf{i}_1$ and $d\mathbf{i}_2$ as

$$d\mathbf{l}_n = \frac{d\mathbf{l}_1 \times d\mathbf{l}_2}{|d\mathbf{l}_1 \times d\mathbf{l}_2|}, \tag{1.32}$$

for the Cartesian coordinate system $d\mathbf{l}_1 = dx\mathbf{i}_x$, $d\mathbf{l}_2 = dy\mathbf{i}_y$, $d\mathbf{l}_3 = dz\mathbf{i}_z$, finally we get (see Figure 1.9b)

$$dv = \frac{|d\mathbf{l}_1 \times d\mathbf{l}_2||d\mathbf{l}_3 \cdot d\mathbf{l}_1 \times d\mathbf{l}_2|}{|d\mathbf{l}_1 \times d\mathbf{l}_2|} = |d\mathbf{l}_3 \cdot d\mathbf{l}_1 \times d\mathbf{l}_2| \tag{1.33}$$

or

$$dv = dxdydz \tag{1.34}$$

1.4.2 Cylindrical Coordinate System

This system is characterized by the conditions

$$r = \text{const}$$

$$\phi = \text{const} \tag{1.35}$$

$$z = \text{const}$$

and is presented in Figure 1.10a.

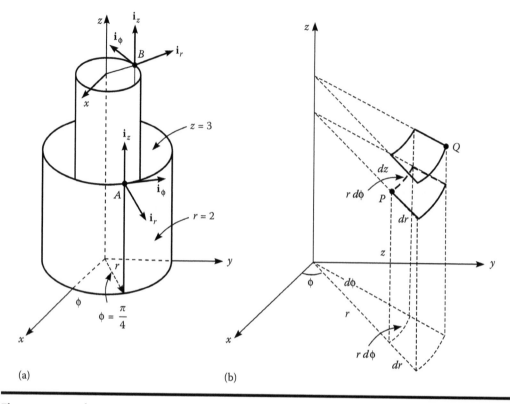

(a)   (b)

Figure 1.10   (a,b) Geometrical presentation of all differential vectors in a cylindrical coordinate system.

The *differential length vector* $d\mathbf{l}$ from point P to point Q (see Figure 1.10b) is given by

$$d\mathbf{l} = dr\mathbf{i}_r + d\phi\mathbf{i}_\phi + dz\mathbf{i}_z \tag{1.36}$$

The *differential surface vector* is defined by pairs of the differential length elements (see Figure 1.10b):

$$\pm rd\phi\mathbf{i}_\phi \times dz\mathbf{i}_z = \pm rd\phi dz\mathbf{i}_r,$$

$$\pm dz\mathbf{i}_z \times dr\mathbf{i}_r = \pm dzdr\mathbf{i}_\phi \tag{1.37}$$

$$\pm dr\mathbf{i}_r \times rd\phi\mathbf{i}_\phi = \pm rdrd\phi\mathbf{i}_z$$

These are associated with the $r = $ const, $\phi = $ const, and $z = $ const surfaces, respectively.

The *differential volume dv* is simply the volume of a box, which is defined by the following expression (see Figure 1.10b):

$$dv = (dr)(rd\phi)(dz) = rdrd\phi dz \tag{1.38}$$

1.4.3 Spherical Coordinate System

The spherical coordinate system is defined by the following conditions (see Figure 1.11a):

$$r = \text{const}$$
$$\theta = \text{const} \tag{1.39}$$
$$\phi = \text{const}$$

The *differential length vector* in such a system is defined as

$$d\mathbf{l} = dr\mathbf{i}_r + rd\theta\mathbf{i}_\theta + r\sin\theta d\phi\mathbf{i}_\phi \tag{1.40}$$

The *differential surface vector* is defined by pairs of the differential length elements:

$$\pm rd\theta\mathbf{i}_\theta \times r\sin\theta d\phi\mathbf{i}_\phi = \pm r^2\sin\theta d\theta d\phi\mathbf{i}_r$$
$$\pm r\sin\theta d\phi\mathbf{i}_\phi \times dr\mathbf{i}_r = \pm r\sin\theta drd\phi\mathbf{i}_\theta \tag{1.41}$$
$$\pm dr\mathbf{i}_r \times rd\theta\mathbf{i}_\theta = \pm rdrd\theta\mathbf{i}_\phi$$

The *Differential volume dv* formed by the three differential lengths is simply the volume of the box presented in Figure 1.11b:

$$dv = (dr)(rd\theta)(r\sin\theta d\phi) = r^2\sin\theta drd\theta d\phi \tag{1.42}$$

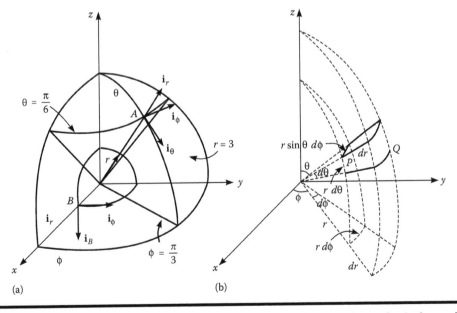

Figure 1.11 **(a,b) Geometrical presentation of all differential vectors in a spherical coordinate system.**

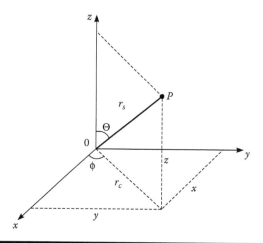

Figure 1.12 Illustration of the relations between Cartesian, cylindrical, and spherical coordinates.

1.5 Relationships between Coordinate Systems

1.5.1 Cartesian and Cylindrical Coordinate Systems

As follows from Figure 1.12, there are the following relationships between coordinates in these two systems:

$$x = r_c \cos\phi, \ y = r_c \sin\phi, \ z \equiv z \tag{1.43a}$$

$$r_c = \sqrt{x^2 + y^2}, \ \tan\phi = \frac{y}{x} \tag{1.43b}$$

Moreover, as follows from Figure 1.13, the unit vectors of both systems are related by

$$\mathbf{i}_{r_c} \cdot \mathbf{i}_x = \cos\varphi, \quad \mathbf{i}_{r_c} \cdot \mathbf{i}_y = \sin\varphi, \quad \mathbf{i}_{r_c} \cdot \mathbf{i}_z = 0$$

$$\mathbf{i}_{\varphi} \cdot \mathbf{i}_x = -\sin\varphi, \quad \mathbf{i}_{\varphi} \cdot \mathbf{i}_y = \cos\varphi, \quad \mathbf{i}_{\varphi} \cdot \mathbf{i}_z = 0 \tag{1.44}$$

$$\mathbf{i}_z \cdot \mathbf{i}_x = 0, \quad \mathbf{i}_z \cdot \mathbf{i}_y = 0, \quad \mathbf{i}_z \cdot \mathbf{i}_z = 1$$

Then,

$$\mathbf{i}_x = \cos\varphi \mathbf{i}_{r_c} - \sin\varphi \mathbf{i}_{\varphi}, \quad \mathbf{i}_y = \sin\varphi \mathbf{i}_{r_c} + \cos\varphi \mathbf{i}_{\varphi}, \quad \mathbf{i}_z = \mathbf{i}_z \tag{1.45}$$

1.5.2 Cartesian and Spherical Coordinate Systems

As follows from Figure 1.12, there are the following relationships between coordinates in these two systems:

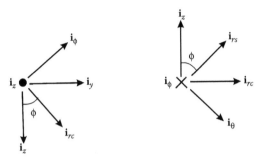

Figure 1.13   Geometrical presentation of relations between the unit vectors (orts).

$$x = r_s \sin\theta\cos\varphi, \ y = r_s \sin\theta\sin\varphi, \ z = r_s \cos\theta \tag{1.46a}$$

$$r_s = \sqrt{x^2 + y^2 + z^2}, \ \tan\theta = \frac{\sqrt{x^2 + y^2}}{z}, \ \tan\varphi = \frac{y}{x} \tag{1.46b}$$

Moreover, the unit vectors in both systems are related by (see Figure 1.13):

$$\mathbf{i}_{r_s}\cdot\mathbf{i}_x = \sin\theta\cos\varphi, \quad \mathbf{i}_{r_s}\cdot\mathbf{i}_y = \sin\theta\sin\varphi, \quad \mathbf{i}_{r_s}\cdot\mathbf{i}_z = \cos\theta$$

$$\mathbf{i}_\theta\cdot\mathbf{i}_x = \cos\theta\cos\varphi, \quad \mathbf{i}_\theta\cdot\mathbf{i}_y = \cos\theta\sin\varphi, \quad \mathbf{i}_\theta\cdot\mathbf{i}_z = -\sin\theta \tag{1.47}$$

$$\mathbf{i}_\varphi\cdot\mathbf{i}_x = -\sin\varphi, \quad \mathbf{i}_\varphi\cdot\mathbf{i}_y = \cos\varphi, \quad \mathbf{i}_\varphi\cdot\mathbf{i}_z = 0$$

Then,

$$\mathbf{i}_x = \sin\theta\cos\varphi\mathbf{i}_{r_s} + \cos\theta\cos\varphi\mathbf{i}_\theta - \sin\varphi\mathbf{i}_\varphi$$

$$\mathbf{i}_y = \sin\theta\sin\varphi\mathbf{i}_{r_s} + \cos\theta\sin\varphi\mathbf{i}_\theta + \cos\varphi\mathbf{i}_\varphi \tag{1.48}$$

$$\mathbf{i}_z = \cos\theta\mathbf{i}_{r_s} - \sin\theta\mathbf{i}_\theta$$

Having all these relations between vectors and operations on these vectors in various coordinate systems, we can explain in the next chapter all the differential-form and integral-form presentations of the differential and integral operators that are usually used in classical electrodynamics and electromagnetism.

PROBLEMS

Example 1.1: Given vectors $\mathbf{r}_1 = -2\mathbf{i}_x + 5\mathbf{i}_y + 3\mathbf{i}_z$ and $\mathbf{r}_2 = 4\mathbf{i}_x - \mathbf{i}_y - 7\mathbf{i}_z$.
   Find: (a) $\mathbf{r}_1 + \mathbf{r}_2$; (b) $\mathbf{r}_1 - \mathbf{r}_2$. Plot these two vectors graphically.
Example 1.2: Given vectors $\mathbf{r}_1 = 4\mathbf{i}_x + 3\mathbf{i}_y - \mathbf{i}_z$ and $\mathbf{r}_2 = 3\mathbf{i}_x - 5\mathbf{i}_y - 2\mathbf{i}_z$.
   Find: (a) $\mathbf{r}_1 \cdot \mathbf{r}_2$; (b) $\mathbf{r}_1 \times \mathbf{r}_2$. Plot these two vectors graphically.

Example 1.3: Given vectors $\mathbf{A} = 5\mathbf{i}_x \times 2\mathbf{i}_y + 3\mathbf{i}_z$ and $\mathbf{B} = 3\mathbf{i}_x - \mathbf{i}_y + 4\mathbf{i}_z$.
  Find: (a) scalar product $\mathbf{D} = \mathbf{A} \cdot \mathbf{B}$; (b) angle between vectors $\mathbf{A}$ and $\mathbf{B}$.
Example 1.4: Given vectors $\mathbf{A} = 5\mathbf{i}_x + 2\mathbf{i}_y + 3\mathbf{i}_z$ and $\mathbf{B} = 3\mathbf{i}_x - \mathbf{i}_y + 4\mathbf{i}_z$.
  Find: (a) scalar product of vectors $\mathbf{A}$ and $\mathbf{B}$; (b) angle between vectors $\mathbf{A}$ and $\mathbf{B}$.
Example 1.5: For the same vectors, as presented in Example 1.2,
  Find: (a) vector product $\mathbf{C}$ of vectors $\mathbf{A}$ and $\mathbf{B}$; (b) angle between vectors $\mathbf{A}$ and $\mathbf{B}$.
Example 1.6: Express the vector $\mathbf{A} = 5\mathbf{i}_x - 3\mathbf{i}_y + 4\mathbf{i}_z$ in cylindrical and spherical coordinates.
Example 1.7: Convert the vector $\mathbf{B} = 4\mathbf{i}_\rho + 2\mathbf{i}_\phi - 5\mathbf{i}_z$ from cylindrical coordinates into Cartesian coordinates.
Example 1.8: Convert the vector $\mathbf{B} = 2\mathbf{i}_x - 3\mathbf{i}_y + 4\mathbf{i}_z$ from spherical coordinates into Cartesian coordinates.
Example 1.9: For given vectors $\mathbf{A} = \mathbf{i}_x + 3\mathbf{i}_y + 5\mathbf{i}_z$, $\mathbf{B} = 2\mathbf{i}_x + 4\mathbf{i}_y + 6\mathbf{i}_z$, and $\mathbf{C} = 3\mathbf{i}_x + 4\mathbf{i}_y + 5\mathbf{i}_z$, show that $\mathbf{A} \times (\mathbf{B} \times \mathbf{C}) = \mathbf{B}(\mathbf{A} \cdot \mathbf{C}) - \mathbf{C}(\mathbf{A} \cdot \mathbf{B})$.
Example 1.10: For vectors given in Example 1.9, calculate: (a) $\mathbf{A} \cdot \mathbf{B}$, (b) $\mathbf{A} \times \mathbf{B}$, (c) $(\mathbf{A} \times \mathbf{B}) \cdot \mathbf{C}$, and (d) $\mathbf{A} \cdot (\mathbf{B} \times \mathbf{C})$.
Example 1.11: Express signal $s(t) = 30 \cos a(100\pi t - 60°)$ in phasor notations.
Example 1.12: Given voltage of the electric signal in phasor notations: $V = 10e^{j45°}$.
  Find: The harmonic presentation in the time domain of this voltage if the frequency equals 50 Hz.

References

1. Madelung, E., *Die Mathematischen Hilfsmittel des Physikers* (*Mathematical Apparatus of Physics*), Berlin: Springer, 1957.
2. Korn, G. and T. Korn, *Mathematical Handbook for Scientists and Engineers*, New York: McGraw-Hill, 1961.
3. Abramowitz, M. and I. A. Stegun, *Handbook of Mathematical Functions*, New York: Dover, 1965.
4. Dudley, D. G., *Mathematical Foundations for Electromagnetic Theory*, Piscataway, NJ: IEEE, 1994.
5. Tai, C. -T., *Generalized Vectors and Dyadic Analysis*, 2nd edn, Piscataway, NJ: IEEE, 1997.
6. Lindell, I. V., *Differential Forms in Electromagnetics*, Piscataway, NJ: IEEE, 2004.
7. Lonngren, K. E. and S. V. Savov, *Fundamentals of Electromagnetics with MATLAB*, 2nd edn, Raleigh, NC: SciTech, 2007.

Chapter 2

Differential Operators in Classical Electrodynamics

In this chapter, dealing with the description of differential operators and presenting also their integral form, we will again take as a basis the excellent handbooks that were produced from the 1950s to the beginning of the twenty-first century [1–7].

2.1 Gradient of the Scalar Field

Let us consider any arbitrary scalar field with the potential $\Phi = \Phi(P)$ (we consider the particular case of an electrostatic field with the potential Φ), where $P = P(x,y,z)$. The equal potential curves $\Phi(P) = \text{constant}$ describes changes of scalar field $\Phi = \Phi(P)$ in the space domain. The vector $\mathbf{i}_n$ is the normal vector to each virtual plane, as shown in Figure 2.1; the vector $d\mathbf{l}$ connects point P with each point Q_i, $i = 1, 2, 3\ldots$ (Figure 2.1b). The derivative of $\Phi(P)$ over $d\mathbf{l}$ can be defined as

$$\frac{\partial \Phi}{\partial l} = \frac{\partial \Phi}{\partial x}\cos(d\mathbf{l},\mathbf{i}_x) + \frac{\partial \Phi}{\partial y}\cos(d\mathbf{l},\mathbf{i}_y) + \frac{\partial \Phi}{\partial z}\cos(d\mathbf{l},\mathbf{i}_z) \tag{2.1}$$

where $\mathbf{i}_x$, $\mathbf{i}_y$, $\mathbf{i}_z$ were introduced in Chapter 1 as orthogonal unit vectors (orts) in the Cartesian coordinate system.

According to Definition 1.18 of the scalar product (see Chapter 1), we get

$$\cos(d\mathbf{l},\mathbf{i}_x) = \frac{d\mathbf{l}\cdot\mathbf{i}_x}{|d\mathbf{l}||\mathbf{i}_x|}, \cos(d\mathbf{l},\mathbf{i}_y) = \frac{d\mathbf{l}\cdot\mathbf{i}_y}{|d\mathbf{l}||\mathbf{i}_y|}, \cos(d\mathbf{l},\mathbf{i}_z) = \frac{d\mathbf{l}\cdot\mathbf{i}_z}{|d\mathbf{l}||\mathbf{i}_z|}$$

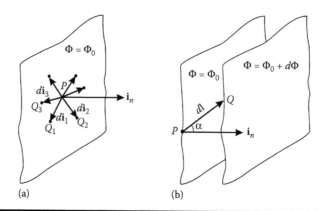

Figure 2.1 **(a,b) Geometrical explanation of the gradient of a scalar field.**

If so, then

$$\frac{\partial \Phi}{\partial dl} = \frac{1}{|dl|}\left(\frac{\partial \Phi}{\partial x}dl \cdot \mathbf{i}_x + \frac{\partial \Phi}{\partial y}dl \cdot \mathbf{i}_y + \frac{\partial \Phi}{\partial z}dl \cdot \mathbf{i}_z \right)$$

$$= \frac{1}{|dl|}dl \cdot \left(\frac{\partial \Phi}{\partial x}\mathbf{i}_x + \frac{\partial \Phi}{\partial y}\mathbf{i}_y + \frac{\partial \Phi}{\partial z}\mathbf{i}_z \right) \equiv \frac{1}{|dl|}dl \cdot \text{grad}\Phi$$

Here

$$\text{grad}\Phi = \frac{\partial \Phi}{\partial x}\mathbf{i}_x + \frac{\partial \Phi}{\partial y}\mathbf{i}_y + \frac{\partial \Phi}{\partial z}\mathbf{i}_z \qquad (2.2)$$

is a differential vector, which can be determined as a *differential vector operator*. To understand the meaning of this vector operator, let us present $\partial \Phi / \partial dl$ by using Definition 1.18 as follows:

$$\frac{\partial \Phi}{\partial dl} = \frac{1}{|dl|}dl \cdot \text{grad}\Phi = \frac{|dl||\text{grad}\Phi|}{|dl|}\cos(dl, \text{grad}\Phi) \qquad (2.3)$$

where now

$$|\text{grad}\Phi| = \sqrt{\left(\frac{\partial \Phi}{\partial x}\right)^2 + \left(\frac{\partial \Phi}{\partial y}\right)^2 + \left(\frac{\partial \Phi}{\partial z}\right)^2}$$

From Equation 2.3, it follows that for $\cos(dl, \text{grad}\Phi) = 1$, a derivative of scalar field Φ exceeds maximum:

$$\frac{\partial \Phi}{\partial l} = |\text{grad}\Phi| = \max \qquad (2.4)$$

According to Equation 2.4, vector dl is parallel to vector $\text{grad}\Phi$. Now, we can define $\text{grad}\Phi$ as a differential vector, which is determined by Formula 2.2 and is directed along the normal vector dl.

In the literature, instead of a vector differential operator "grad," a Hamilton operator is usually used, called the operator "nabla" or "del":

$$\nabla = \frac{\partial}{\partial x}\mathbf{i}_x + \frac{\partial}{\partial y}\mathbf{i}_y + \frac{\partial}{\partial z}\mathbf{i}_z \tag{2.5}$$

Then, in the Cartesian coordinate system, instead (2.2) we have

$$\nabla\Phi = \frac{\partial\Phi}{\partial x}\mathbf{i}_x + \frac{\partial\Phi}{\partial y}\mathbf{i}_y + \frac{\partial\Phi}{\partial z}\mathbf{i}_z \tag{2.6a}$$

In the cylindrical coordinate system, the differential vector "grad" can be presented as

$$\text{grad}\Phi \equiv \nabla\Phi = \frac{\partial\Phi}{\partial r_c}\mathbf{i}_{r_c} + \frac{1}{r_c}\frac{\partial\Phi}{\partial\phi}\mathbf{i}_\phi + \frac{\partial\Phi}{\partial z}\mathbf{i}_z \tag{2.6b}$$

In the spherical coordinate system we have, respectively,

$$\text{grad}\Phi \equiv \nabla\Phi = \frac{\partial\Phi}{\partial r_s}\mathbf{i}_{r_s} + \frac{1}{r_s}\frac{\partial\Phi}{\partial\theta}\mathbf{i}_\theta + \frac{1}{r_s\sin\theta}\frac{\partial\Phi}{\partial\phi}\mathbf{i}_\phi \tag{2.6c}$$

Let us consider the main properties of the differential vector operator:

a. For any two arbitrary scalar fields Φ and Ψ,

$$\nabla(\Phi\Psi) = \Psi\nabla\Phi + \Phi\nabla\Psi$$

$$\nabla(\Phi \pm \Psi) = \nabla\Phi \pm \nabla\Psi$$

b. For any arbitrary complicated scalar function $F(\Phi)$,

$$\nabla F(\Phi) = \frac{dF}{d\Phi}\nabla\Phi$$

c. For any arbitrary vector $\mathbf{r}$ and $\Phi = \Phi(\mathbf{r})$,

$$\nabla\Phi(\mathbf{r}) = \frac{d\Phi}{dr}\nabla\,|\,\mathbf{r}\,| = \frac{d\Phi}{dr}\frac{\mathbf{r}}{|\mathbf{r}|}$$

2.2 Divergence of the Vector Field

If there is any arbitrary vector field $A(\mathbf{r})$ (e.g., electric or magnetic fluxes in electrostatics and magnetostatics, respectively), then the *divergence* of this vector field, denoted through the Hamilton operator as "del dot" $\nabla \cdot$ (or "nabla dot"), is defined as

a. In the Cartesian coordinate system,

$$\text{div}\mathbf{A} \equiv \nabla \cdot \mathbf{A} = \frac{\partial A_x}{\partial x} + \frac{\partial A_y}{\partial y} + \frac{\partial A_z}{\partial z} \qquad (2.7a)$$

b. In the cylindrical coordinate system,

$$\text{div}\mathbf{A} \equiv \nabla \cdot \mathbf{A} = \frac{1}{r_c}\frac{\partial\left(r_c A_{r_c}\right)}{\partial r_c} + \frac{1}{r_c}\frac{\partial A_\phi}{\partial \phi} + \frac{\partial A_z}{\partial z} \qquad (2.7b)$$

c. In the spherical coordinate system,

$$\text{div}\mathbf{A} \equiv \nabla \cdot \mathbf{A} = \frac{1}{r_s^2}\frac{\partial\left(r_s^2 A_{r_s}\right)}{\partial r_s} + \frac{1}{r_s \sin\theta}\frac{\partial(A_\theta \sin\theta)}{\partial\theta} + \frac{1}{r_s \sin\theta}\frac{\partial A_\phi}{\partial\phi} \qquad (2.7c)$$

We will present now the main properties of the operator ∇.

a. For two fields, scalar $\Phi(M)$ and vector $A(\mathbf{r})$, the divergence of their product is

$$\nabla \cdot (\Phi\mathbf{A}) = \mathbf{A} \cdot \nabla\Phi + \Phi\nabla \cdot \mathbf{A} \qquad (2.8)$$

b. For any arbitrary vector $\mathbf{r}$,

$$\nabla \cdot \frac{\mathbf{r}}{|\mathbf{r}|} = \nabla \cdot \mathbf{i}_r = \frac{1}{r}\nabla \cdot \mathbf{r} + |\mathbf{r}|\nabla\left(\frac{1}{r}\right) = \frac{3}{r} - \frac{1}{r} = \frac{2}{r}$$

c. For two arbitrary vector fields $\mathbf{A}_1$ and $\mathbf{A}_1$,

$$\nabla \cdot (\mathbf{A}_1 + \mathbf{A}_2) = \nabla \cdot \mathbf{A}_1 + \nabla \cdot \mathbf{A}_2$$

and for any constant C,

$$\nabla \cdot (C\mathbf{A}) = C\nabla \cdot \mathbf{A}$$

d. If $\mathbf{A}(u)$ is the complicated scalar function of u, then

$$\nabla \cdot \mathbf{A}(u) = \frac{d\mathbf{A}}{du} \cdot \nabla u$$

2.3 Vector Operator "Curl" or "Rot"

Vector operator "curl" or "rot," which is usually denoted by "del cross" or $\nabla\times$, can be defined using the Hamilton operator ∇ as

a. In the Cartesian coordinate system,

$$\text{curl}\mathbf{A} \equiv \nabla \times \mathbf{A} = \begin{vmatrix} \mathbf{i}_x & \mathbf{i}_y & \mathbf{i}_z \\ \partial/\partial x & \partial/\partial y & \partial/\partial z \\ A_x & A_y & A_z \end{vmatrix} = \mathbf{i}_x \left(\partial A_z/\partial y - \partial A_y/\partial z \right)$$

$$+\mathbf{i}_y \left(\partial A_x/\partial z - \partial A_z/\partial x \right) + \mathbf{i}_z \left(\partial A_y/\partial x - \partial A_x/\partial y \right) \qquad (2.9a)$$

b. In the cylindrical coordinate system,

$$\text{curl}\mathbf{A} \equiv \nabla \times \mathbf{A} = \begin{vmatrix} \dfrac{\mathbf{i}_{r_c}}{r_c} & \mathbf{i}_{\phi} & \dfrac{\mathbf{i}_z}{r_c} \\[2mm] \dfrac{\partial}{\partial r_c} & \dfrac{\partial}{\partial \phi} & \dfrac{\partial}{\partial z} \\[2mm] A_{r_c} & r_c A_{\phi} & A_z \end{vmatrix} = \dfrac{\mathbf{i}_{r_c}}{r_c} \left(\dfrac{\partial A_z}{\partial \phi} - \dfrac{\partial (r_c A_{\phi})}{\partial z} \right)$$

$$+\mathbf{i}_{\phi} \left(\dfrac{\partial A_{r_c}}{\partial z} - \dfrac{\partial A_z}{\partial r_c} \right) + \dfrac{\mathbf{i}_z}{r_c} \left(\dfrac{\partial (r_c A_{\phi})}{\partial r_c} - \dfrac{\partial A_{r_c}}{\partial \phi} \right) \qquad (2.9b)$$

c. For the spherical coordinate system,

$$\text{curl}\mathbf{A} \equiv \nabla \times \mathbf{A} = \begin{vmatrix} \dfrac{\mathbf{i}_{r_s}}{r_s^2 \sin\theta} & \dfrac{\mathbf{i}_{\theta}}{r_s \sin\theta} & \dfrac{\mathbf{i}_{\varphi}}{r_s} \\[2mm] \dfrac{\partial}{\partial r_s} & \dfrac{\partial}{\partial \theta} & \dfrac{\partial}{\partial \varphi} \\[2mm] A_{r_s} & r_s A_{\theta} & r_s \sin\theta A_{\varphi} \end{vmatrix} = \dfrac{\mathbf{i}_{r_s}}{r_s^2 \sin\theta} \left(\dfrac{\partial (r_s \sin\theta A_{\varphi})}{\partial \theta} - \dfrac{\partial (r_s A_{\theta})}{\partial \varphi} \right)$$

$$+\dfrac{\mathbf{i}_{\theta}}{r_s \sin\theta} \left(\dfrac{\partial A_{r_s}}{\partial \varphi} - \dfrac{\partial (r_s \sin\theta A_{\varphi})}{\partial r_s} \right) + \dfrac{\mathbf{i}_{\varphi}}{r_s} \left(\dfrac{\partial (r_s A_{\theta})}{\partial r_s} - \dfrac{\partial A_{r_s}}{\partial \theta} \right) \qquad (2.9c)$$

We present now the main properties of the "curl" operator by using the "del cross" definition.

a. For two fields, the scalar $\Phi(M)$ and vector $A(\mathbf{r})$, the "curl" of their product is

$$\nabla \times (\Phi \mathbf{A}) = \Phi \nabla \times \mathbf{A} + \nabla \Phi \times \mathbf{A}$$

b. For two arbitrary vector fields $\mathbf{A}_1$ and $\mathbf{A}_2$,

$$\nabla \times (\mathbf{A}_1 \times \mathbf{A}_2) = (\mathbf{A}_2 \cdot \nabla)\mathbf{A}_1 - (\mathbf{A}_1 \cdot \nabla)\mathbf{A}_2$$

$$+\mathbf{A}_1 \nabla \cdot \mathbf{A}_2 - \mathbf{A}_2 \nabla \cdot \mathbf{A}_1$$

where, for example, in the Cartesian coordinate system

$$(\mathbf{A}_{1,2} \cdot \nabla) = \mathbf{A}_{x1,2} \frac{\partial}{\partial x} + \mathbf{A}_{y1,2} \frac{\partial}{\partial y} + \mathbf{A}_{z1,2} \frac{\partial}{\partial z},$$

then

$$\nabla \cdot (\mathbf{A}_1 \times \mathbf{A}_2) = \mathbf{A}_2 \cdot (\nabla \times \mathbf{A}_1) - \mathbf{A}_1 \cdot (\nabla \times \mathbf{A}_2)$$

and

$$\nabla \times (\mathbf{A}_1 \cdot \mathbf{A}_2) = \mathbf{A}_2 \times (\nabla \times \mathbf{A}_1) + (\mathbf{A}_2 \cdot \nabla)\mathbf{A}_1$$
$$+ \mathbf{A}_1 \times (\nabla \times \mathbf{A}_2) + (\mathbf{A}_1 \cdot \nabla)\mathbf{A}_2$$

2.4 Laplace Operator

Laplace's operator or *laplacian* is defined as:

a. In the Cartesian coordinate system,

$$\Delta = \frac{\partial^2}{\partial x^2} + \frac{\partial^2}{\partial y^2} + \frac{\partial^2}{\partial z^2} \tag{2.10a}$$

b. In the cylindrical coordinate system,

$$\Delta = \frac{1}{r_c} \frac{\partial}{\partial r_c} \left(r_c \frac{\partial}{\partial r_c} \right) + \frac{1}{r_c^2} \frac{\partial^2}{\partial \phi^2} + \frac{\partial^2}{\partial z^2} \tag{2.10b}$$

c. In the spherical coordinate system,

$$\Delta = \frac{1}{r_s^2} \frac{\partial}{\partial r_s} \left(r_s^2 \frac{\partial}{\partial r_s} \right) + \frac{1}{r_s^2 \sin \theta} \frac{\partial}{\partial \theta} \left(\sin \theta \frac{\partial}{\partial \theta} \right) + \frac{1}{r_s^2 \sin \theta} \frac{\partial^2}{\partial \phi^2} \tag{2.10c}$$

We can now show how to obtain such an operator for any arbitrary scalar field $\Phi(\mathbf{r})$. If we consider a double operator, a divergence of a gradient of this function, we finally have a laplacian. In fact, as follows from the properties of these operators described in Section 2.3,

$$\nabla \cdot (\nabla \Phi) = \nabla \nabla \Phi \equiv \Delta \Phi$$

it can be shown that for any arbitrary vector **A**,

$$\nabla \times \nabla \times \mathbf{A} = \nabla(\nabla \cdot \mathbf{A}) + (\nabla \nabla)\mathbf{A} = \nabla(\nabla \cdot \mathbf{A}) + \Delta \mathbf{A} \tag{2.11}$$

2.5 Integral Presentation of Differential Operators

Let us, first of all, define the line, surface, and volume integrals that allow us to determine these operators in the integral form.

2.5.1 Definitions of Line, Surface, and Volume Integrals

2.5.1.1 Line Integral

The *line integral* can be defined using scalar and vector field presentations. Let us consider, a vector electrostatic field $\mathbf{E}(\mathbf{r})$ with the potential $\Phi(\mathbf{r})$ as a scalar field. As is well known from electrostatics,

$$\mathbf{E}(\mathbf{r}) = \nabla\Phi(\mathbf{r}) \tag{2.12}$$

If any test charge q moves in the field $\mathbf{E}(\mathbf{r})$, the electric field exerts a force $\mathbf{F} = q\mathbf{E}$ on the test charge. Let us consider that the test charge moves along the AB trajectory of its path, as shown in Figure 2.2.

At each point j, a force $\mathbf{F}_j$ according to Coulomb's law will be (see Figure 2.3)

$$\mathbf{F}_j = q\mathbf{E}_j \tag{2.13}$$

The electric field produces an "elementary" work at each point j:

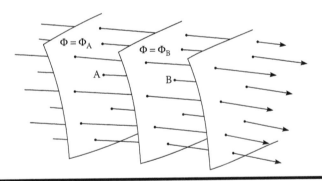

Figure 2.2   Geometrical presentation of the problem.

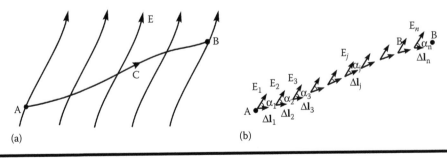

Figure 2.3   (a) Geometrical presentation of the problem; (b) geometrical explanation of Formula 2.15.

$$\Delta W_j = \mathbf{F}_j \cdot \Delta \mathbf{l}_j = q\mathbf{E}_j \cdot \Delta \mathbf{l}_j = q\,|\,\mathbf{E}_j\,\|\,\Delta \mathbf{l}_j\,|\cos\alpha_j \qquad (2.14)$$

The total work to transport a charge q from point A to point B equals

$$W_{AB} = \sum_{j=1}^{n}\Delta W_j = q\sum_{j=1}^{n}\mathbf{E}_j \cdot \Delta \mathbf{l}_j = q\sum_{j=1}^{n}|\,\mathbf{E}_j\,\|\,\Delta \mathbf{l}_j\,|\cos\alpha_j \qquad (2.15)$$

If we now consider a limit of this sum for infinitesimal $\Delta \mathbf{l}_j$ (i.e., for $\Delta \mathbf{l}_j \to 0$), we will finally define a *linear* or *line* integral:

$$W_{AB} = \lim \sum_{j=1}^{n}\Delta W_j = q\int_{A}^{B}\mathbf{E}\cdot d\mathbf{l} \equiv q\int_{C}\mathbf{E}\cdot d\mathbf{l} \qquad (2.16a)$$

Because of the relationship 2.12, we can rewrite the line integral as

$$W_{AB} = q\int_{C}\mathbf{E}\cdot d\mathbf{l} = q\int_{C}\nabla\Phi\cdot d\mathbf{l} \qquad (2.16b)$$

The integral in Equation 2.16b defines the potential difference, or *voltage*, denoted as V, at two different points, A and B:

$$V = \frac{W_{AB}}{q} = \int_{A}^{B}\nabla\Phi\cdot d\mathbf{l} = \Phi(B) - \Phi(A) \qquad (2.17)$$

The electric potential field has one important property:

The work of the electrostatic field along the closed path equals zero.

In fact (see Figure 2.4),

$$\oint_{C}\nabla\Phi\cdot d\mathbf{l} = \int_{A}^{B}\nabla\Phi\cdot d\mathbf{l} + \int_{B}^{A}\nabla\Phi\cdot d\mathbf{l} = \Phi(B) - \Phi(A) + \Phi(A) - \Phi(B) \equiv 0$$

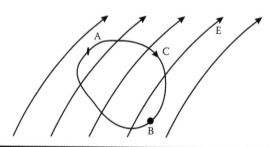

Figure 2.4 Geometrical presentation of zeros scalar product along the closed charge q path in the presence of static electrical field E.

This result also follows from Figure 2.1, because $\nabla\Phi\perp d\mathbf{l}$ in each point of the charge path, and a scalar product is equal to zero.

2.5.1.2 Surface Integral

The *surface integral* can be defined in the same manner. Let us consider a particular case of magnetic field $\mathbf{B}(\mathbf{r})$ in magnetostatics with flux oriented under the angle α to any arbitrary surface ΔS (see Figure 2.5).

Let us derive a total magnetic flux crossing this surface. For this purpose, let us divide S into n subsurfaces ΔS_j (see Figure 2.6).

The elementary flux that crosses subsurface $\Delta\mathbf{S}_j$ is a divergence of the vector $\mathbf{B}_j$ of magnetic field at the point j and the surface vector $\Delta\mathbf{S}_j$:

$$\Delta\Psi_j = \mathbf{B}_j\Delta\mathbf{S}_j \tag{2.18}$$

If so, the total magnetic flux through the surface S equals

$$\Psi = \sum_{j=1}^{n}\Delta\Psi_j = \sum_{j=1}^{n}\mathbf{B}_j\Delta\mathbf{S}_j \tag{2.19}$$

For $\Delta S_j \to 0$, the limit of the sum gives a *surface integral* definition:

$$\Psi = \lim\sum_{j=1}^{n}\Delta\Psi_j = \int_S \mathbf{B}\cdot d\mathbf{S} \tag{2.20a}$$

The integral in Equation 2.20a can be rewritten as

$$\Psi = \int_S \mathbf{B}\cdot d\mathbf{S} = \int_S \mathbf{B}\cdot\mathbf{i}_n dS \tag{2.20b}$$

where $\mathbf{i}_n$ is the normal to the surface S (see Figure 2.6).

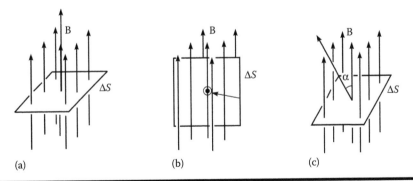

(a)   (b)   (c)

Figure 2.5 **(a–c) Geometrical presentation of three variants of orientation of the plane with area ΔS with respect to static magnetic field B.**

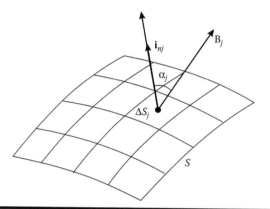

Figure 2.6   Geometrical illustration of Formula 2.18.

2.5.1.3 Volume Integral

The *volume integral* can be defined in the same manner. We consider here the electrostatic case of an electric field created by a charge Q located within a volume V. According to electrostatic law, which is called the Gauss law, the electric field flux (called *displacement flux*) from a closed surface S is equal to the charge Q contained within the volume V, which is bounded by the surface S:

$$\oint_S \mathbf{D} \cdot d\mathbf{S} = Q_V \tag{2.21}$$

where:

$\mathbf{D} = \varepsilon \mathbf{E}$ is the displacement vector (also called the induction) of electric field $\mathbf{E}$

ε is the dielectric constant

At the same time, because each elementary charge can be found using its density as $Q_j = \rho_j \Delta V_j$ (see Figure 2.7), we can introduce the volume integral:

$$Q_V = \lim \sum_{j=1}^n Q_j = \lim \sum_{j=1}^n \rho_j \Delta V_j = \int_V \rho \, dv \tag{2.22}$$

Finally, combining Equations 2.21 and 2.22, we obtain the Gauss law (also called the *Gauss theorem*) for the electrostatic potential field:

$$\oint_S \mathbf{D} \cdot d\mathbf{S} = \int_V \rho \, dv \tag{2.23}$$

where ρ is a volume charge density as an algebraic sum of all free charges contained within the volume V.

The same Gauss theorem must be defined for the magnetic field in magnetostatics. Because there are no magnetic charges, we have for the magnetic field flux $\mathbf{B}$ (also called the *induction*)

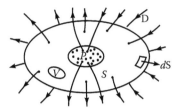

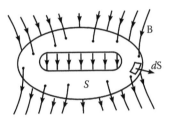

Figure 2.7 Geometrical illustration of the problem and of Formulas 2.23 and 2.24.

$$\oint_S \mathbf{B} \cdot d\mathbf{S} = 0 \tag{2.24}$$

We will use both these Gauss theorem definitions to obtain Maxwell's equation in electrodynamics. Before we start to deal with different electromagnetic laws, let us present the vector operators in their integral form by using the line, surface, and volume integral definitions presented in Section 2.5.1.

2.5.2 Integral Presentation of Vector Operators

We will give the integral form of vector operators using, examples from electrostatics and magnetostatics, as well as the Gauss theorem for such examples.

2.5.2.1 Integral Presentation of Gradient Operator

Integral presentation of the *gradient* or *del operator* can be done by introducing the electrical potential field (2.12) and the surface integral

$$\int_S \Phi(\mathbf{r})d\mathbf{S} = \int_S \Phi(\mathbf{r})\mathbf{i}_n dS \equiv \lim \sum_{j=1}^{n} \Phi_j \Delta \mathbf{S}_j \tag{2.25}$$

which describes a full displacement flux of the electric potential field in Equation 2.12 across the surface S:

$$\int_S \Phi(\mathbf{r})d\mathbf{S} = \int_V \nabla \Phi dv \tag{2.26}$$

If we now consider that $V \to 0$, we immediately obtain from Equation 2.26 that

$$\nabla\Phi = \lim_{V\to 0} \frac{\int_S \Phi(\mathbf{r})d\mathbf{S}}{V} = \lim_{V\to 0} \frac{\int_S \Phi(\mathbf{r})\mathbf{i}_n dS}{V} \tag{2.27}$$

Hence, the *integral definition of the gradient* (or "del") operator is

$$grad \equiv \nabla = \lim_{V\to 0} \frac{\int_S \mathbf{i}_n dS}{V} \equiv \frac{\partial}{\partial x}\mathbf{i}_x + \frac{\partial}{\partial y}\mathbf{i}_y + \frac{\partial}{\partial z}\mathbf{i}_z \tag{2.28}$$

2.5.2.2 Integral Presentation of Divergence Operator

The integral presentation of the *divergence operator* can be obtained in the same manner. Usually, the electric and magnetic vectors can be denoted by any vectors $\mathbf{A}$ ($\mathbf{E}$, $\mathbf{D}$ or $\mathbf{H}$, $\mathbf{B}$) as

$$J = \int_S \mathbf{A}\cdot d\mathbf{S} = \int_S \mathbf{A}\cdot\mathbf{i}_n dS = \int_S A_n dS \tag{2.29}$$

On the other hand, the Gauss theorem for electrostatics states that for close surfaces

$$\int_S \mathbf{A}\cdot d\mathbf{S} = \int_V div\mathbf{A}dv \equiv \int_V \nabla\cdot\mathbf{A}dv \tag{2.30}$$

Now, we can define the *divergence* of the vector $\mathbf{A}$ as

$$div\mathbf{A} = \frac{dJ}{dv} = \frac{\text{The flux through } dS \text{ at point } \mathbf{r}}{\text{The small volume around point } \mathbf{r}} \tag{2.31}$$

or in the *integral form* as

$$div\mathbf{A} \equiv \nabla\cdot\mathbf{A} = \lim_{V\to 0} \frac{\int_S \mathbf{A}\cdot\mathbf{i}_n dS}{V} \equiv \frac{\partial A_x}{\partial x} + \frac{\partial A_y}{\partial y} + \frac{\partial A_z}{\partial z} \tag{2.32}$$

Comparing Equations 2.24 and 2.30, one can note that for the magnetic field, $div\mathbf{B} = 0$. Such a field is called *solenoidal* in the literature.

2.5.2.3 *Integral Presentation of Curl Operator*

We can obtain the *integral presentation of curl* (or "del cross") operator by considering some cylindrical surface S with volume V, which has this surface as a boundary (see Figure 2.8). Using the Gauss theorem, we have for any vector **A**

$$\int_S \mathbf{A} \times d\mathbf{S} \equiv \int_S \mathbf{n} \times \mathbf{A} dS = \int_V curl \mathbf{A} dv \equiv \int_V \nabla \times \mathbf{A} dv \qquad (2.33)$$

We can define *curl* of any vector **A** as a limit for $V \to 0$ of ratio (see Chapter 1)

$$curl \mathbf{A} \equiv \nabla \times \mathbf{A} = \lim_{V \to 0} \frac{\int_S \mathbf{n} \times \mathbf{A} dS}{V} \qquad (2.34)$$

If so, the projection of *curl* vector at the normal **N** is equal:

$$\left[curl \mathbf{A}\right]_{\mathbf{N}} = \mathbf{N} \cdot curl \mathbf{A}$$

Now, according to Definition 2.34, the projection of the *curl* vector at the normal **N** can be presented as

$$\left[curl \mathbf{A}\right]_{\mathbf{N}} = \mathbf{N} \cdot curl \mathbf{A} = \lim_{V \to 0} \frac{\mathbf{N} \cdot \int_S \mathbf{n} \times \mathbf{A} dS}{V} =$$

$$\lim_{V \to 0} \frac{\int_S \mathbf{n} \cdot (\mathbf{A} \times \mathbf{N}) dS}{V} = \lim_{V \to 0} \frac{\int_S \mathbf{A} \cdot (\mathbf{n} \times \mathbf{N}) dS}{V} = 0$$

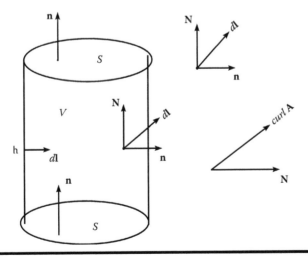

Figure 2.8   Geometrical illustration of integral presentation of curl operator.

because **n**‖**N**, and according to above definitions, we obtain **n** × N = 0. At the side surface of the cylinder,

$$\int_S \mathbf{A} \cdot (\mathbf{n} \times \mathbf{N}) dS = h \oint_C \mathbf{A} \cdot d\mathbf{l}$$

from which we immediately obtain an integral definition of vector *curl*:

$$[curl\,\mathbf{A}]_\mathbf{N} = \mathbf{N} \cdot curl\,\mathbf{A} = \lim_{V \to 0} \frac{h \oint_C \mathbf{A} \cdot d\mathbf{l}}{Sh} = \lim_{V \to 0} \frac{\oint_C \mathbf{A} \cdot d\mathbf{l}}{S} \qquad (2.35)$$

To obtain this definition, we used the mathematical presentation of a *Stoke's theorem*, which describes the relationship between the line integral of an arbitrary vector field and the surface integral of its curl (or del cross) (Figure 2.9):

$$\oint_C \mathbf{A} \cdot d\mathbf{l} = \int_S curl\,\mathbf{A} \cdot d\mathbf{S} \equiv \int_S \nabla \times \mathbf{A} \cdot d\mathbf{S} \qquad (2.36)$$

Let us show an example from electrostatics and magnetostatics. In the potential electric field, according to (2.12), $\mathbf{E}(\mathbf{r}) = \nabla\Phi(\mathbf{r})$, we get

$$\oint_C \mathbf{E} \cdot d\mathbf{l} \equiv \int_S \nabla \times \mathbf{E} \cdot d\mathbf{S} = \int_S \nabla \times \nabla\Phi(\mathbf{r}) \cdot d\mathbf{S} \equiv 0 \qquad (2.37)$$

because $\nabla \times \nabla\Phi(\mathbf{r}) = 0$.

Conversely, in the magnetic field, its lines surround any elementary current conductor. So in this case, we have $curl\,\mathbf{B} \equiv \nabla \times \mathbf{B} \neq 0$ and $\mathbf{div\,B} \equiv \nabla \cdot \mathbf{B} = 0$. Both conditions finally give us that $\oint_C \mathbf{B} \cdot d\mathbf{l} \equiv \int_S curl\,\mathbf{B} \cdot d\mathbf{S} \neq 0$, that is, the vector lines must be closed, which, in fact, is actually observed.

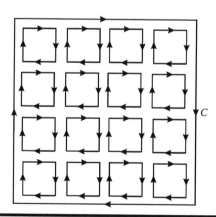

Figure 2.9   Geometrical explanation of Constraint 2.37.

PROBLEMS

Example 2.1: The trajectory of the bullet is modeled by the function $r(x,y,z) = x^2 + 2y^2 - 5$.
Find: Gradient of this function in the point (3,5,4).

Example 2.2: The potential of an electrostatic field is given by the function $\Phi(x,y,z) = x^2yz^{1/2}$.
Find: Gradient of this potential in the point (1,3,5).

Example 2.3: Given vector $\mathbf{B}(x,y,z) = xy\mathbf{i}_x + xyz\mathbf{i}_y + yz\mathbf{i}_z$.
Find: The divergence of vector $\mathbf{B}$ at the point (1,1,1).

Example 2.4: Given vector $\mathbf{A}(x,y,z) = xy^2 \cos(\pi z)\mathbf{i}_x + x^3 yz^2\mathbf{i}_y + xy \sin(\pi z)\mathbf{i}_z$.
Find: The divergence of vector $\mathbf{A}$ at the point (2,1,3).

Example 2.5: For the vector presented in Example 2.4, calculate the *curl* of this vector at the point (1,5,3).

Example 2.6: Given a vector $\mathbf{A}(\rho,\varphi,z) = \rho z\sin(\varphi)\mathbf{i}_\rho + \rho z\cos(\varphi)\mathbf{i}_\phi + \rho z^2\mathbf{i}_z$ in cylindrical coordinates.
Find: Gradient and curl of vector $\mathbf{A}$ at the point ($\rho = 4$, $\phi = 30°$, $z = 5$).

Example 2.7: Given a vector $\mathbf{A}(r,\varphi,\theta) = r \sin(\varphi)\sin(\theta)\mathbf{i}_r + r \cos(\varphi)\mathbf{i}_\phi + r \sin(\theta)\mathbf{i}_\theta$ in spherical coordinates.
Find: Gradient and curl of the vector $\mathbf{A}$ at the point ($r = 7$, $\varphi = 60°$, $z = 45°$).

References

1. Madelung, E., *Die Mathematischen Hilfsmittel des Physikers* (*Mathematical Apparatus of Physics*), Berlin: Springer, 1957.
2. Korn, G. and T. Korn, *Mathematical Handbook for Scientists and Engineers*, New York: McGraw-Hill, 1961.
3. Abramowitz, M. and I. A. Stegun, *Handbook of Mathematical Functions*, New York: Dover, 1965.
4. Dudley, D. G., *Mathematical Foundations for Electromagnetic Theory*, Piscataway, NJ: IEEE, 1994.
5. Tai, C.-T., *Generalized Vectors and Dyadic Analysis*, 2nd edn, Piscataway, NJ: IEEE, 1997.
6. Lindell, I. V., *Differential Forms in Electromagnetics*, Piscataway, NJ: IEEE, 2004.
7. Lonngren, K. E. and S. V. Savov, *Fundamentals of Electromagnetics with MATLAB*, 2nd edn, Raleigh, NC: SciTech, 2007.

INTRODUCTION TO CLASSICAL ELECTRODYNAMICS

Chapter 3

Electromagnetic Waves

3.1 Maxwell's Equations

The main laws of electromagnetism have been developed and have undergone many changes in their form and mathematical description over a long period of 150–170 years, during which many genius-level mathematicians and physicians have been involved. We cannot say exactly who was first or where the initial ideas originally came from [1,2]. Thus, it is complicated to differentiate the significant contributions of Heaviside (1885) and Lorentz (1905) to the clarification and formation of the main laws in classical electrodynamics in vector microscopic basic forms. Moreover, Heaviside, Hamilton, and Gibbs mostly contributed to the mathematical expression of these laws [1,2].

As mentioned in [1–6], Oersted, Ampere, Biot, Savart, Gauss, and Faraday assisted in the development of electromagnetic (EM) theory, which was then unified by Maxwell's unique theory. It should also be mentioned that Boltzmann, Hertz, Kirchhoff, Lorenz, and Weber all made their contemporaneous contributions to the modification of Maxwell's theory into the form that is now used in all books and articles related to classical and applied electrodynamics [3–14].

Furthermore, Faraday, Gauss, and Ampere proved their theoretical frameworks via experimental data, and revealed the basic principles of classical electrodynamics; that is, they covered the main laws of electrodynamics, magnetodynamics, electrostatics, and magnetostatics.

3.1.1 Differential Form of Maxwell's Equations

The theoretical analysis of EM wave propagation is based on Maxwell's equations. Of course, James Clerk Maxwell wrote his equations during the short period of 1861–1862 in another form (see details in [1,2]). During the long historical evolution of the basic equations, their main parameters, characteristics, functions, and operators were converted into a modern form by the so-called Maxwellians [1].

In this chapter, we will follow these modern vector- and operator-form notations. Thus, in vector notation and in the SI-unit system, their representations in the uniform macroscopic form are [3–14]

$$\nabla \times \mathbf{E}(\mathbf{r},t) = -\frac{\partial}{\partial t}\mathbf{B}(\mathbf{r},t) \qquad\qquad (3.1a)$$

$$\nabla \times \mathbf{H}(\mathbf{r},t) = \frac{\partial}{\partial t}\mathbf{D}(\mathbf{r},t) + \mathbf{j}(\mathbf{r},t) \qquad\qquad (3.1b)$$

$$\nabla \cdot \mathbf{B}(\mathbf{r},t) = 0 \qquad\qquad (3.1c)$$

$$\nabla \cdot \mathbf{D}(\mathbf{r},t) = \rho(\mathbf{r},t) \qquad\qquad (3.1d)$$

where:
$\mathbf{E}(\mathbf{r},t)$ is the electric field strength vector, in volts per meter
$\mathbf{H}(\mathbf{r},t)$ is the magnetic field strength vector, in amperes per meter
$\mathbf{D}(\mathbf{r},t)$ is the electric flux induced in the medium by the electric field, in coulombs per cubic meter (this is why, in the literature, it is sometimes called an *induction* of an electric field)
$\mathbf{B}(\mathbf{r},t)$ is the magnetic flux induced by the magnetic field, in webers per square meter (it is also called an induction of a magnetic field)
$\mathbf{j}(\mathbf{r},t)$ is the vector of electric current density, in amperes per square meter
$\rho(\mathbf{r},t)$ is the charge density, in coulombs per square meter
the curl operator, $\nabla\times$, is a measure of field rotation
the divergence operator, $\nabla\cdot$, is a measure of the total flux radiated from a point

It should be noted that for a time-varying EM wave field, Equations 3.1c and 3.1d can be derived from Equations 3.1a and 3.1b, respectively. In fact, by taking the divergence of Equation 3.1a (by use of the divergence operator $\nabla\cdot$), one can immediately obtain Equation 3.1c. Similarly, by taking the divergence of Equation 3.1b and using the well-known continuity equation [1–3]:

$$\nabla \cdot \mathbf{j}(\mathbf{r},t) + \frac{\partial \rho(\mathbf{r},t)}{\partial t} = 0 \qquad\qquad (3.2)$$

one can arrive at Equation 3.1d. Hence, only Equations 3.1a and 3.1b are independent.

In electrostatics and magnetostatics, where $\partial/\partial t = 0$, the electric and magnetic fields are decoupled. For static problems, Equation 3.1d limits to the well-known Coulomb law [1,2], which implies that the electric flux $\mathbf{D}$ is produced by a charge density ρ in the medium. The same result is obtained with Equation 3.1c, which assumes the absence of free magnetic charges in the medium. This magnetostatic law is a consequence of Gauss's law [1,2], which is a statement of the conservation of magnetic flux in the medium. Equation 3.1a is the well-known Faraday law and indicates that a time-varying magnetic flux generates an electric field with rotation; Equation 3.1b without the term $\partial\mathbf{D}/\partial t$ (displacement current term [1,2]) limits to the well-known Ampere law and indicates that a current or a time-varying electric flux (displacement current [1,2]) generates a magnetic field with rotation.

Because there are now only two independent equations, 3.1a and 3.1b, to describe the four unknown vectors $\mathbf{E}$, $\mathbf{D}$, $\mathbf{H}$, $\mathbf{B}$ two more equations relating these vectors are needed. For this purpose, we introduce relations between $\mathbf{E}$ and $\mathbf{D}$, $\mathbf{H}$ and $\mathbf{B}$, $\mathbf{j}$ and $\mathbf{E}$, which are known in electrodynamics. In fact, for isotropic media, which are usually considered in problems of land radio propagation, the electric and magnetic fluxes are related to the electric and magnetic fields, and the electric current is related to the electric field, via the constitutive relations [1–4]

$$\mathbf{B} = \mu(\mathbf{r})\mathbf{H} \tag{3.3b}$$

$$\mathbf{D} = \varepsilon(\mathbf{r})\mathbf{E} \tag{3.3a}$$

$$\mathbf{j} = \sigma(\mathbf{r})\mathbf{E} \tag{3.3c}$$

It is very important to note that the relations in Equation 3.3 are valid only for propagation processes in linear isotropic media, which are characterized by the three scalar functions of any point $\mathbf{r}$ in the medium: permittivity $\varepsilon(\mathbf{r})$, permeability $\mu(\mathbf{r})$, and conductivity $\sigma(\mathbf{r})$.

In *nonisotropic media*, such functions transform into tensors (matrixes), but this case is not important for terrestrial radio propagation, and we will not deal with it here. In Equation 3.3, we have assumed that the medium is inhomogeneous. In a homogeneous medium, the functions $\varepsilon(\mathbf{r})$, $\mu(\mathbf{r})$, and $\sigma(\mathbf{r})$ transform to the simple scalar values ε, μ, and σ. If in this case they are also functions of frequency, ω, that is,

$$\varepsilon = \varepsilon(\omega), \mu = \mu(\omega), \sigma = \sigma(\omega) \tag{3.4}$$

the medium is *frequency dispersive*. Here, we will talk about a nondispersive, isotropic, linear, and inhomogeneous medium.

In free space, these functions are simply constants: $\varepsilon = \varepsilon_0 = 8.854 \times 10^{-12}$ F/m, while $\mu = \mu_0 = 4\pi \times 10^{-7}$ H/m. The constant $c = 1/\sqrt{\varepsilon_0\mu_0}$ is the velocity of light, which has been measured very accurately and is very close to 3×10^8 m/s. In many practical cases of wireless communication environments, the value μ is close to unity, and we can assume $\mathbf{B} = \mathbf{H}$ in Equation 3.3b with great accuracy.

The system of Equation 3.1 can be further simplified if we assume that the fields are time harmonic. If the field time dependence is not harmonic, then, using the fact that the system of Equations 3.1 is linear, we may treat these fields as sums of harmonic components and consider each component separately. In this case, the time-harmonic field is a complex vector and can be expressed via its real part as [12–14]

$$\mathbf{A}(\mathbf{r},t) = \text{Re}\left[\mathbf{A}(\mathbf{r})e^{-j\omega t}\right] \tag{3.5}$$

where:
$j = \sqrt{-1}$
ω is the angular frequency in radians per second
$\omega = 2\pi f$
f is the radiated frequency in hertz
$\mathbf{A}(\mathbf{r},t)$ is the complex vector ($\mathbf{E}$, $\mathbf{D}$, $\mathbf{H}$, $\mathbf{B}$, or $\mathbf{j}$)

The time-harmonic dependence $\sim e^{-j\omega t}$ is commonly used in the literature of electrodynamics and wave propagation. If time-harmonic dependence $\sim e^{i\omega t}$ is used, then one must substitute $-j$ for j and j for $-j$ in all equivalent formulations of Maxwell's Equations 3.1a, 3.1b, and 3.2.

In Equation 3.5, the term $e^{-i\omega t}$ presents the harmonic time dependence of any complex vector $\mathbf{A}(\mathbf{r},t)$, which satisfies the relationship:

$$\frac{\partial}{\partial t}\mathbf{A}(\mathbf{r},t) = \text{Re}\left[-j\omega\mathbf{A}(\mathbf{r})e^{-j\omega t}\right] \tag{3.6}$$

Using this transformation, one can easily obtain from the system in Equation 3.1:

$$\nabla \times \mathbf{E}(\mathbf{r}) = j\omega\mathbf{B}(\mathbf{r}) \tag{3.7a}$$

$$\nabla \times \mathbf{H}(\mathbf{r}) = -j\omega\mathbf{D}(\mathbf{r}) + \mathbf{j}(\mathbf{r}) \tag{3.7b}$$

$$\nabla \cdot \mathbf{B}(\mathbf{r}) = 0 \tag{3.7c}$$

$$\nabla \cdot \mathbf{D}(\mathbf{r}) = \rho(\mathbf{r}) \tag{3.7d}$$

It can be observed that system Equation 3.7 was obtained from system Equation 3.1 by replacing $\partial/\partial t$ with $-j\omega$. Alternatively, the same transformation can be obtained by the use of the Fourier transform of system Equation 3.1 with respect to time [5]. In system Equation 3.7, all vectors and functions are actually the Fourier transforms with respect to the *time domain*, and the fields **E**, **D**, **H**, and **B** are functions of frequency as well; we call them *phasors* of time-domain vector solutions. They are also known as the *frequency domain solutions* of the EM field according to the system in Equation 3.7. Conversely, the solutions of system Equation 3.1 are the *time domain solutions* of the EM field. It is more convenient to work with system Equation 3.7 instead of system Equation 3.1, because of the absence of the time dependence and time derivatives.

3.1.2 Integral Form of Maxwell's Equations

We will now present Maxwell's equations in their integral representations. To derive the integral forms of Equation 3.1a and 3.1b, we integrate them over a cross-sectional area S and use Stokes' theorem [1–4]:

$$\int_S d\mathbf{s} \cdot \nabla \times \mathbf{E}(\mathbf{r},t) = \oint_C d\mathbf{l} \cdot \mathbf{E}(\mathbf{r},t) \tag{3.8}$$

On the right-hand side of Equation 3.8, integral C determines the contour that forms the perimeter of the area S. This expression is the statement of Faraday's law, according to which the sum of all the rotations due to field **E** over the area S is equal to the "torque" produced by these rotations on the perimeter of S with C. Here, the left-hand side is the summation over all the rotations, while the right-hand side of Equation 3.8 is the evaluation of the net "torque" on the perimeter C. The fact is that neighboring rotations within the area S cancel each other, leaving a net rotation on the perimeter.

Now, using Stokes' theorem [1–5], one can convert Equation 3.1a and 3.1b to

$$\oint_C d\mathbf{l} \cdot \mathbf{E}(\mathbf{r},t) = -\frac{\partial}{\partial t} \int_S d\mathbf{s} \cdot \mathbf{B}(\mathbf{r},t) \tag{3.9}$$

$$\oint_C d\mathbf{l} \cdot \mathbf{H}(\mathbf{r},t) = \frac{\partial}{\partial t} \int_S d\mathbf{s} \cdot \mathbf{D}(\mathbf{r},t) + \int_S d\mathbf{s} \cdot \mathbf{j}(\mathbf{r},t) \tag{3.10}$$

Equation 3.9 implies that a time-varying magnetic flux through an area S generates an electromotive force (the left-hand side in Equation 3.9) around a loop C (see Figure 3.1).

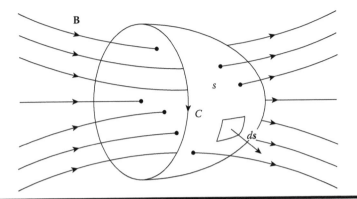

Figure 3.1 Geometrical presentation of the Faraday–Maxwell law.

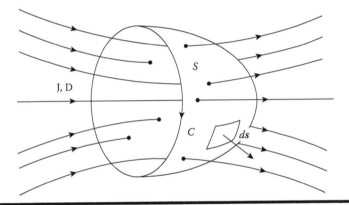

Figure 3.2 Geometrical presentation of the Ampere–Maxwell law.

In the same way, Equation 3.10 implies that a time-varying electric flux (displacement current) or a conductivity current will generate a magnetomotive force (the left-hand side in Equation 3.10) that loops around the currents (see Figure 3.2).

To convert Equation 3.1c and 3.1d into integral form, one can integrate them over a volume V and use Gauss's theorem [1–5], which states that

$$\int_V dv \nabla \cdot \mathbf{B}(\mathbf{r},t) = \int_S d\mathbf{s} \cdot \mathbf{B}(\mathbf{r},t) \tag{3.11}$$

This is a statement that the sum of all divergences of a flux **B** in a volume V is equal to the net flux that is leaving the volume V through the surface S. In other words, neighboring divergences tend to cancel each other within the volume V (see Figure 3.3).

Consequently, Equation 3.1c and 3.1d describe Gauss's laws for the magnetic (absence of magnetic charges) and the electric (existence of electric charges) fields:

$$\int_S d\mathbf{s} \cdot \mathbf{B}(\mathbf{r},t) = 0 \tag{3.12}$$

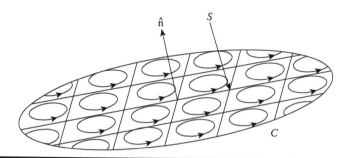

Figure 3.3 Geometrical presentation of Stock's theorem.

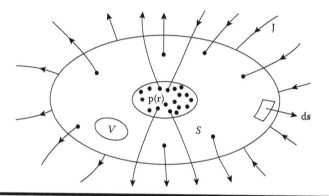

Figure 3.4 Geometrical presentation of the Gauss–Maxwell law.

$$\int_S d\mathbf{s} \cdot \mathbf{D}(\mathbf{r},t) = \int_V dv \cdot \rho(\mathbf{r},t) = Q \tag{3.13}$$

where Q is the total charge in volume V (Figure 3.4).

Equations 3.12 and 3.13 are statements of the conservation of fluxes. In fact, Equation 3.13 implies that the net flux through a surface S equals the total charge $Q = \int_S \rho(r)ds$ inside S (see Figure 3.4).

3.2 Presentation of Electromagnetic Waves

Based on basic principles and equations of Maxwell's theory, described and presented in the previous section, we can state, as have numerous authors (see, for example, [3–14]), that the EM field can be presented in the 3-D space in the form of a wave. The coupled wave components, the electric and magnetic fields, are depicted in Figure 3.5, from which it follows that the EM wave travels in a direction perpendicular to both EM-field components. In Figure 3.5, this direction is denoted as the z-axis in the Cartesian coordinate system. In their orthogonal space-planes, the magnetic and electric oscillatory components repeat their waveform after a distance of one wavelength along the y-axis and the x-axis, respectively (see Figure 3.5).

Both components of the EM wave are in phase in the time domain, but not in the space domain. Moreover, the magnetic component value of the EM field is closely related to the electric

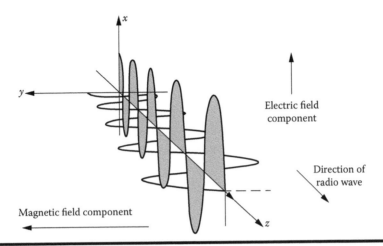

x

y

Electric field
component

Direction of
radio wave

Magnetic field component

z

Figure 3.5 Schematically presented EM wave consisting two orthogonal components, electrical and magnetic.

component value, from which one can obtain the radiated power of the EM wave propagating along the *z*-axis.

Physically, the process of EM wave propagation can be described by using two equations—one scalar and one vector. In the case of a homogeneous isotropic medium, Maxwell's Equations 3.7a through 3.7d can be replaced by two wave equations for phasors of electric and magnetic fields, respectively, based on their harmonic time-domain presentation in Equation 3.6:

$$\nabla \times \mu^{-1}(\mathbf{r})\nabla \times \mathbf{E}(\mathbf{r}) - \omega^2 \varepsilon(\mathbf{r})\mathbf{E}(\mathbf{r}) = j\omega \mathbf{J}(\mathbf{r}) - \nabla \times \mu^{-1}(\mathbf{r})\mathbf{M}(\mathbf{r})$$

$$\nabla \times \varepsilon^{-1}(\mathbf{r})\nabla \times \mathbf{H}(\mathbf{r}) - \omega^2 \mu(\mathbf{r})\mathbf{H}(\mathbf{r}) = i\omega \mathbf{M}(\mathbf{r}) - \nabla \times \varepsilon^{-1}(\mathbf{r})\mathbf{J}(\mathbf{r})$$

(3.14)

Here, $\mathbf{J}(\mathbf{r})$ and $\mathbf{M}(\mathbf{r})$ are the electric current and the magnetic momentum of the outer electric and magnetic sources, respectively.

For numerous problems of propagation in a homogeneous, isotropic, free-source ($\mathbf{J}(\mathbf{r}) = 0$ and $\mathbf{M}(\mathbf{r}) = 0$) infinite medium with constant parameters $\varepsilon(\mathbf{r}) \equiv \varepsilon$, $\mu(\mathbf{r}) \equiv \mu$, $\sigma(\mathbf{r}) \equiv \sigma$, we get [1–5]

$$\nabla \times \nabla \times \mathbf{E}(\mathbf{r}) - \omega^2 \varepsilon\mu\mathbf{E}(\mathbf{r}) = 0$$

$$\nabla \times \nabla \times \mathbf{H}(\mathbf{r}) - \omega^2 \varepsilon\mu\mathbf{H}(\mathbf{r}) = 0$$

(3.15)

Since both equations are symmetric, it is possible to use only one of them, let us say, for the vector **E**. If we now account for the well-known vector relations (from tensor algebra) $\nabla \times \nabla \times \mathbf{E} = \nabla(\nabla \cdot \mathbf{E}) - \nabla^2 \mathbf{E}$ (see [15,16]), as well as for the fact that $\nabla \cdot \mathbf{E} = 0$, we finally get

$$\nabla^2 \mathbf{E}(\mathbf{r}) + k^2 \mathbf{E}(\mathbf{r}) = 0$$

(3.16a)

where $k^2 = \omega^2 \varepsilon\mu$. In the Cartesian coordinate system, the 3-D vector Equation 3.16a can be presented in the form of three 1-D scalar equations as

$$\nabla^2 \Psi(\mathbf{r}) + k^2 \Psi(\mathbf{r}) = 0$$

(3.16b)

where $\Psi(\mathbf{r})$ can be either E_x, E_y, or E_z.

3.3 Green's Function

We consider now an arbitrary source of the EM wave $S(\mathbf{r})$ in free space (see Figure 3.6). The corresponding equation will be the same as Equation 3.16b, but with the source on its right-hand side:

$$\nabla^2 \Psi(\mathbf{r}) + k^2 \Psi(\mathbf{r}) = S(\mathbf{r}) \tag{3.17}$$

Usually, in such cases, the same equation can be introduced for the point source on its right-hand side, describing a function of the source or the Green's function

$$\nabla^2 G(\mathbf{r},\mathbf{r}') + k^2 G(\mathbf{r},\mathbf{r}') = -\delta(\mathbf{r}-\mathbf{r}') \tag{3.18}$$

given that functions $G(\mathbf{r}, \mathbf{r}')$ and $\Psi(\mathbf{r})$ can be easily computed based on the principle of linear superposition, because $G(\mathbf{r}, \mathbf{r}')$ is a solution of Equation 3.18 with a point source on the right-hand side. In fact, introducing an arbitrary source $S(\mathbf{r})$ as

$$S(\mathbf{r}) = \int d\mathbf{r}' S(\mathbf{r}') \delta(\mathbf{r}-\mathbf{r}') \tag{3.19}$$

we get a self-consistent solution of Equation 3.17:

$$\Psi(\mathbf{r}) = -\int_V d\mathbf{r}' G(\mathbf{r},\mathbf{r}') S(\mathbf{r}') \tag{3.20}$$

which is a linear superposition of Equation 3.17.

To find the Green's function in free space, or, more precisely, in an unbounded homogeneous medium consisting of a source of radiation, we introduce a spherical coordinate system with the origin determined by the vector $\mathbf{r}'$, accounting for the spherical symmetry of the Green's function $G(\mathbf{r})$. In this case, Equation 3.18 can be presented as

$$\nabla^2 G(\mathbf{r}) + k^2 G(\mathbf{r}) = -\delta(\mathbf{r}) \tag{3.21}$$

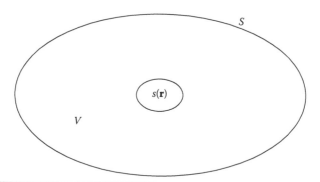

Figure 3.6 Geometry of the problem with an arbitrary outer source S(r).

Then, for an arbitrary point defined by the vector $\mathbf{r} \neq 0$, a regular symmetric solution of Equation 3.21, after some straightforward derivations, can be presented in the form, which depends only on the range between the point of observation and the point of the source location $|\mathbf{r} - \mathbf{r}'|$,

$$G(\mathbf{r}, \mathbf{r}') = G(\mathbf{r} - \mathbf{r}') = \frac{\exp\{jk|\mathbf{r} - \mathbf{r}'|\}}{|\mathbf{r} - \mathbf{r}'|} \tag{3.22}$$

If this is the case, a self-consistent general solution of Equation 3.17 can be presented in its final form as

$$\Psi(\mathbf{r}) = -\int_V d\mathbf{r}' \frac{\exp\{jk|\mathbf{r} - \mathbf{r}'|\}}{|\mathbf{r} - \mathbf{r}'|} S(\mathbf{r}') \tag{3.23}$$

This form of presentation of the Green's function is known in the literature as its scalar presentation. We will not discuss its vector presentation, both due to its complicated tensor form and because we will not use the vector form of Green's function in this chapter. The reader can refer to the well-known sources listed at the end of this chapter, such as [5–14].

3.4 Poynting Theorem

This theorem is the simple law of EM wave energy conservation. It is known from electrostatics and magnetostatics that the work of the electric field to move a single charge q is equal to $q \cdot \mathbf{v} \cdot E$, where $\mathbf{v}$ is the vector of the charge velocity. The same work of the magnetic field for this charge is equal to zero, because the magnetic field direction is perpendicular to the velocity vector [1–4]. For a continuous distribution of charges and currents in a medium, the total work of the EM field in the volume V in unit time equals [1–4,8–10]

$$\int_V \mathbf{j} \cdot \mathbf{E} dv \tag{3.24}$$

This expression determines the velocity of the decrease in the field energy within the volume V.

Let us now obtain the law of energy conservation using Maxwell's Equation 3.1. We shall substitute the current density $\mathbf{j}$ in Equation 3.1a using Equation 3.1b:

$$\int_V \mathbf{j} \cdot \mathbf{E} dv = \int_V \left[\mathbf{E} \cdot \nabla \times \mathbf{H} - \mathbf{E} \cdot \frac{\partial \mathbf{D}}{\partial t} \right] dv \tag{3.25}$$

Taking into account the vector equality (see Chapter 1)

$$\nabla \cdot (\mathbf{E} \times \mathbf{H}) = \mathbf{H} \cdot \nabla \times \mathbf{E} - \mathbf{E} \cdot \nabla \times \mathbf{H}$$

one can easily rewrite Equation 3.25 as

$$\int_V \mathbf{j} \cdot \mathbf{E} dv = -\int_V \left[\nabla \cdot (\mathbf{E} \times \mathbf{H}) + \mathbf{E} \cdot \frac{\partial \mathbf{D}}{\partial t} + \mathbf{H} \cdot \frac{\partial \mathbf{B}}{\partial t} \right] dv \tag{3.26}$$

If we now present the density of total-field energy according to [1–4,8–10] as

$$W = (\mathbf{E} \cdot \mathbf{D} + \mathbf{B} \cdot \mathbf{H}) \tag{3.27}$$

then Equation 3.26 will be rewritten as

$$-\int_V \mathbf{j} \cdot \mathbf{E} dv = \int_V \left[\frac{\partial W}{\partial t} + \nabla \cdot (\mathbf{E} \times \mathbf{H}) \right] dv \tag{3.28}$$

Because Equation 3.28 is written for any arbitrary volume *V*, it can be presented in differential form:

$$\frac{\partial W}{\partial t} + \nabla \cdot \mathbf{S} = -\mathbf{j} \cdot \mathbf{E} \tag{3.29}$$

Equation 3.29 is the equation of EM field energy conservation, or the equation of continuity. It can be easily shown that the vector $\mathbf{S} = \mathbf{E} \times \mathbf{H}$ in brackets on the right-hand side of Equation 3.29 has dimensions of watts per square meter, which are those of power density. From Equation 3.29, it is clear that it may be associated with the direction of power flow.

The vector that determines the power flow of an EM field is called the *Poynting vector*. Equation 3.28 is the *integral Poynting theorem*, and Equation 3.29 is its *vector (or differential form) presentation*.

Using the time-harmonic presentation of Maxwell's equations, one can convert Equation 3.28 to the time-harmonic form. In fact, if we now introduce instead of the derivation $\partial/\partial t$ the term $i\omega$, and present the operation of averaging $\langle \mathbf{E} \times \mathbf{H} \rangle$ as $1/2$ Re$\{\mathbf{E} \times \mathbf{H}^*\}$ according to [15,16], taking into account also Gauss's theorem (see Section 3.1) for the term $\nabla \cdot (\mathbf{E} \times \mathbf{H}^*)$, we finally obtain from Equation 3.28 the Poynting theorem presented in time-harmonic form:

$$\int_S d\mathbf{s} \cdot (\mathbf{E} \times \mathbf{H}^*) = \int_V dv (\mathbf{H}^* \cdot \mathbf{B} - \mathbf{E} \cdot \mathbf{D}^*) - \int_V dv \mathbf{E} \cdot \mathbf{j} \tag{3.30}$$

or, accounting for Equation 3.27, we can present the total energy of the EM field as

$$W_{\text{total}} = W_E + W_H = \frac{\varepsilon E^2}{2} + \frac{\mu H^2}{2} \tag{3.31}$$

Equation 3.30, together with Equation 3.31, gives a full explanation of the Poynting theorem that describes the total energy of EM field conservation.

PROBLEMS

Example 3.1: Given the electrical component of the EM wave $\mathbf{E}(z,t) = e^{-az}\cos(\omega t - kz)\mathbf{u}_x$, propagating in free space along the z-axis. Find the component of the magnetic field $\mathbf{H}_y$ and prove that these two components satisfy simultaneously Faraday's law and Ampere's law (for $\mathbf{j} = 0$).

Example 3.2: Prove that two components of the EM wave, the electric, $\mathbf{E}_y = E_0\cos(x)\cos(\omega t)\mathbf{u}_y$, and the magnetic, $\mathbf{H}_z = (E_0/\mu_0)\sin(x)\sin(\omega t)\mathbf{u}_z$, satisfy simultaneously Maxwell's Equations 3.1 and 3.2 (the last for $\mathbf{j} = 0$).

Example 3.3: The charge Q is distributed uniformly within a sphere with radius a (see Figure 3.7).

Find: The variations of the electric field inside and outside a uniformly distributed sphere.

Example 3.4: A current I passes through a cylindrical conductor and creates a magnetic field whose density is $\mathbf{B}$ (see Figure 3.8).

Find: The magnetic flux density for all values of the radius ρ inside and outside the cylinder.

Example 3.5: The current density $\mathbf{j} = e^{-x^2}\mathbf{u}_x$.

Find: (1) the time rate of increase of the charge density at $x = 1$
(2) the charge density after $t = 10$ s.

Example 3.6: The current density $\mathbf{J} = J_0\,e^{-t/\tau}/r\,\mathbf{u}_r$ in spherical coordinates.

Find: (1) the total current that leaves a spherical surface whose radius is a at the time $t = \tau$;
(2) the expression of the charge density $\rho(r,t)$.

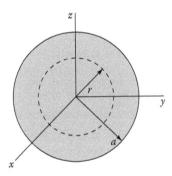

Figure 3.7 Geometrical presentation of a sphere.

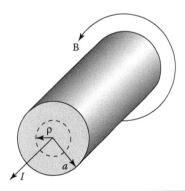

Figure 3.8 Geometrical presentation of a cylinder.

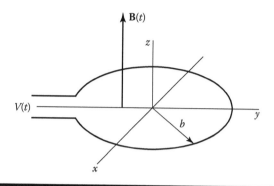

Figure 3.9   Geometry of a stationary loop of wire in the plane (*x, y*).

Example 3.7: A stationary loop of wire lies in the plane (*x, y*), as shown in Figure 3.9, crossing by the homogeneous time-varied magnetic field

$$\mathbf{B}(\rho,t) = B_0 \cos\left(\frac{\pi\rho}{2b}\right)\cos\omega t \cdot \mathbf{u}_z$$

where:
the amplitude of the magnetic flux density is $B_0 = 2\ T$(Tesla)
the radius of the loop is $b = 0.05$ m
the angular frequency is $\omega = 2\pi f = 314\ \mathrm{s}^{-1}$

Find: The voltage *V(t)* detected between the two separated terminals, as shown in Figure 3.9.

Example 3.8: Given harmonic presentation of the electrical and magnetic field components in the time and 1-D space domains, $\mathbf{E} = 150\pi \cos(9 \times 10^8\ t - 20\pi z)\mathbf{u}_x$ (V/m) and $\mathbf{H} = 150/\eta_0$ $\pi\cos(9 \times 10^8 t - 20\pi z)\mathbf{u}_y$ (A/m), in free space.
Find: Presentation of the fields in phasor notations.

Example 3.9: Given presentation of the electrical and magnetic field components in free space in phasor notations, $\mathbf{E} = 5e^{-j\beta_0 z}\mathbf{u}_x$ and $\mathbf{H} = 5/\eta_0\ e^{-j(\beta_0 z + (\pi/4))}\mathbf{u}_x$. The wave frequency is 2×10^9 Hz.
Find: Wave parameters β_0 and η_0 in free space, and present the EM-field components in the harmonic form (e.g., in the time domain).

Example 3.10: The field vectors in free space are given by the expressions $\mathbf{E} = 10\cos(\omega t + 4/3\pi z)\mathbf{u}_x$ (V/m) and $\mathbf{H} = \mathbf{u}_z \times \mathbf{E}/Z_0$ (A/m). Frequency $f = 500$ MHz; $Z_0 = 120\pi$ (Ω).
Find: The Poynting vector presented in the complex form using phasor notations.

Example 3.11: In Figure 3.10, a capacitor of radius *a* and of width *b*, which is connected with the source of voltage *V(t)* via the corresponding electrical circuit, is given.
Find: The power flowing via the area of the radial edge of a capacitor using the Poynting theorem, if the density of the total magnetic field equals zero. Show that this power equals the rate of total energy changes.

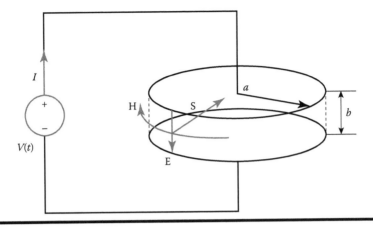

Figure 3.10 **Scheme of the problem.**

References

1. Hunt, B. J., *The Maxwellians*, Ithaca, NY: Cornell University Press, 1994.
2. Arthur, J. W., The evolution of Maxwell's equations from 1862 to the present day. *IEEE Antennas and Propagation Magazine* 55(3), 61–81, 2013.
3. Stratton, J. A., *Electromagnetic Theory*, New York: McGraw-Hill, 1953.
4. Jackson, J. D., *Classical Electrodynamics*, New York: Wiley, 1962.
5. Morse, P. M. and H. Feshbach, *Methods of Theoretical Physics*, New York: McGraw-Hill, 1953.
6. Kong, J. A., *Theory of Electromagnetic Waves*, New York: Wiley, 1986.
7. Alpert, Ya. L., V. L. Ginsburg, and E. L. Feinberg, *Radiowave Propagation,* Moscow: State Hall of Publications of Technical and Theoretical Literature, 1953 (in Russian).
8. Felsen, L. and N. Marcuvitz, *Radiation and Scattering of Waves*, Englewood Cliffs, NJ: Prentice Hall, 1973.
9. Dudley, D. G., *Mathematical Foundations for Electromagnetic Theory*, New York: IEEE, 1994.
10. Chew, W. Ch., *Waves Propagation in Inhomogeneous Media*, Englewood Cliffs, NJ: IEEE, 1995.
11. Rajeev, B., ed. *Handbook: Engineering Electromagnetic Applications*, Boca Raton, FL: CRC Taylor & Francis, 2006.
12. Blaunstein, N. and C. G. Christodoulou, *Radio Propagation and Adaptive Antennas for Wireless Communication Links*: *Terrestrial, Atmospheric and Ionospheric*, Englewood Cliffs, NJ: Wiley Interscience, 2007.
13. Pozar, D. M., *Microwave Engineering*, 4th edn, New York: Wiley, 2012.
14. Iskander, M. F., *Electromagnetic Fields and Waves*, 2nd edn, Long Grove, IL: Waveland, 2013.
15. Korn, G. and T. Korn, *Mathematical Handbook for Scientists and Engineers*, New York: McGraw-Hill, 1961.
16. Abramowitz, M. and I. A. Stegun, *Handbook of Mathematical Functions*, New York: Dover, 1965.

Chapter 4

Electromagnetic Waves Propagation in Various Media

4.1 Electromagnetic Waves in Free Space

For numerous tasks and problems of wave propagation, it can be supposed that the medium is homogeneous, isotropic, infinite, free-charge, and free-source, with the constant parameters $\varepsilon(r) \equiv \varepsilon$, $\mu(r) \equiv \mu$, and $\sigma(r) \equiv \sigma$ [1–11], that is,

$$\nabla \times \nabla \times \mathbf{E}(\mathbf{r}) - \omega^2 \varepsilon \mu \mathbf{E}(\mathbf{r}) = 0$$

$$\nabla \times \nabla \times \mathbf{H}(\mathbf{r}) - \omega^2 \varepsilon \mu \mathbf{H}(\mathbf{r}) = 0$$

(4.1)

Since both equations are symmetric, only one of them can be used, let us say, for a vector $\mathbf{E}$, and a well-known relation can be introduced (see Chapter 1):

$$\nabla \times \nabla \times \mathbf{E} = \nabla (\nabla \cdot \mathbf{E}) - \nabla^2 \mathbf{E}$$

accounting for the fact that $\nabla \cdot \mathbf{E} = \mathbf{0}$. This yields, according to Equation 4.1,

$$\nabla^2 \mathbf{E}(\mathbf{r}) + k^2 \mathbf{E}(\mathbf{r}) = 0$$

(4.2)

where $k^2 = \omega^2 \varepsilon \mu$. It can be shown that all other vector components of the electromagnetic field satisfy the same wave equation (Equation 4.1).

4.1.1 Plane Waves

In the Cartesian coordinate system, a 3-D vector equation can be presented in the form of three 1D scalar equations, accounting for the following expansion of the vector on three components along each coordinate axis:

$$\mathbf{E}(\mathbf{r}) = E_x\mathbf{x}_0 + E_y\mathbf{y}_0 + E_z\mathbf{z}_0,$$

where $\mathbf{x}_0$, $\mathbf{y}_0$, and $\mathbf{z}_0$ are the orts of the projection of the vector $\mathbf{E}$ at the coordinate axes along axes ox, oy, and oz, respectively. Consequently, Equation 4.2 can be transformed into three scalar equations of the form

$$\nabla^2\Psi(\mathbf{r}) + k^2\Psi(\mathbf{r}) = 0 \tag{4.3}$$

where $\Psi(\mathbf{r})$ can be either E_x, E_y, or E_z.

Equation 4.3 describes the propagation of a plane wave in free space in a Cartesian coordinate system, where $\Psi(\mathbf{r})$ corresponds to the components of vector $\mathbf{E}(\mathbf{r})$ or vector $\mathbf{H}(\mathbf{r})$. Sometimes in the literature another presentation of Equation 4.3 is given by introducing the phase velocity $v_{ph} \equiv v = \omega/k = c/\sqrt{\mu\varepsilon}$, instead of the wave number k. In this case, Equation 4.3 can be rewritten in the following form:

$$\nabla^2\Psi(\mathbf{r}) + \frac{\omega^2}{v^2}\Psi(\mathbf{r}) = 0 \tag{4.4}$$

The wave equations (Equations 4.3 and 4.4) have the following solution:

$$\Psi(\mathbf{r}) = \exp(j\mathbf{k}\cdot\mathbf{r}) \tag{4.5}$$

In the literature, waves that satisfy Equations 4.3 or 4.4 and are determined by Equation 4.5 are called *plane waves*. The wave vector $\mathbf{k}$ determines the direction of wave propagation in free space (see Figure 3.5). If we suppose that a plane wave propagates, let us say, along the x-axis, we will obtain a general solution of Equation 4.3 in the form of

$$\Psi(x) = A\exp(jkx) + B\exp(-jkx) \tag{4.6}$$

This solution describes plane waves propagating along the positive direction of the x-axis (with sign "−" in exponent) and along the negative direction of the x-axis (with sign "+" in exponent) with phase velocity $v_{ph} = c/\sqrt{\mu\varepsilon}$, which in free space converts to the velocity of light c

It should be noted that the wave equations in cylindrical and spherical coordinate systems have a more complicated form compared with those following from Equations 4.3 and 4.4, and their solution differs from Equation 4.6. We give a brief presentation, referring the reader to the fundamental works [1–11].

4.1.2 Cylindrical Waves

In the *cylindrical* coordinate system $\{\rho,\phi,z\}$, the scalar wave equation, which describes propagation of *cylindrical waves* in free space, can be written as [1–3,8–11]

$$\left(\frac{1}{\rho}\frac{\partial}{\partial\rho}\rho\frac{\partial}{\partial\rho} + \frac{1}{\rho^2}\frac{\partial}{\partial\phi^2} + \frac{\partial^2}{\partial z^2} + k^2\right)\psi(\mathbf{r}) = 0 \tag{4.7}$$

This equation has an approximate solution, which can be presented in the following exponential form [1–3,8]:

$$\psi(\mathbf{r}) \sim \sqrt{\frac{2}{\pi k_r \rho}} \exp\left\{-j\frac{n\pi}{2} - i\frac{\pi}{4}\right\} \exp\left\{j\left(\frac{n}{\rho}(\rho\phi) + jk_z z + jk_r \rho\right)\right\} \tag{4.8}$$

Here, $\rho\phi$ is the arc length in the ϕ direction, $k_\rho = \sqrt{k^2 - k_z^2}$ and n/ρ can be considered as the component of vector $\mathbf{k}$ if one compares the cylindrical wave presentation as in Equation 4.8 with that for a *plane wave* in Equation 4.6.

Consequently, Equation 4.8 looks like a plane wave mainly in the direction $k' = k_z z + k_\rho \rho$, when $\rho \rightarrow \infty$. This means that *in a zone distant from the source, the cylindrical wave can be considered as a plane wave.*

4.1.3 Spherical Waves

In the *spherical* coordinate system $\{r, \theta, \phi\}$, the scalar wave equation, which describes propagation of *spherical waves* in free space, can be written as [1–3,8]

$$\left(\frac{1}{r^2}\frac{\partial}{\partial r}r^2\frac{\partial}{\partial r} + \frac{1}{r^2 \sin\theta}\frac{\partial}{\partial\theta}\sin\theta\frac{\partial}{\partial\theta} + \frac{1}{r^2 \sin^2\theta}\frac{\partial^2}{\partial\phi^2} + k^2\right)\psi(\mathbf{r}) = 0 \tag{4.9}$$

As was shown in [1–3,8], the spherical wave can be approximated by $\exp\{ikr\}/r$. Thus, one can represent the spherical wave as a plane wave when $r \rightarrow \infty$. This means that *in a zone distant from the source, the spherical wave can be considered as a plane wave.*

4.2 Polarization of Electromagnetic Waves

The alignment of the electric field vector $\mathbf{E}$ of a plane wave relative to the direction of propagation $\mathbf{k}$ defines the *polarization* of the wave. If $\mathbf{E}$ is transverse to the direction of wave propagation $\mathbf{k}$, then the wave is said to be a *transverse electric (TE) wave* or *vertically* polarized. Conversely, when $\mathbf{H}$ is transverse to $\mathbf{k}$, the wave is said to be a *transverse magnetic (TM) wave* or *horizontally* polarized. Both these waves are *linearly polarized*, as the electric field vector $\mathbf{E}$ has a single direction along the entire propagation axis (vector $\mathbf{k}$).

If two plane linearly polarized waves of equal amplitude and orthogonal polarization (vertical and horizontal) are combined with a 90° phase difference, the resulting wave will be a *circularly polarized* (CP) wave, in which the motion of the electric field vector will describe a circle around the propagation vector.

The field vector will rotate by 360° for every wavelength traveled. CP waves are most commonly used in land cellular and satellite communications, as they can be generated and received using antennas, which can be oriented in any direction around their axis without loss of power [3,5–8]. They may be generated as either right-handed CP or left-handed CP, depending on the direction of vector $\mathbf{E}$ rotation (see Figure 4.1).

In the most general case, the components of two waves could be of unequal amplitude, or their phase difference could be other than 90°. The combination results in an elliptically polarized wave, where vector $\mathbf{E}$ still rotates at the same rate as for a CP wave, but varies in amplitude with

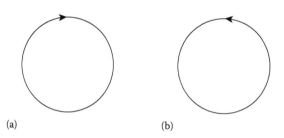

(a)   (b)

Figure 4.1   Two kinds of rotation of circularly polarized wave: (a) right-handed and (b) left-handed.

time. In the case of elliptical polarization, the axial ratio, E_{max}/E_{min}, is usually introduced. It is defined to be positive for left-handed polarization and negative for right-handed polarization (see Figure 4.2). The axial ratio usually is defined via the parameter $(1 - q)/(1 + q)$, where $q = E_-/E_+$.

Here, E_+ and E_- are the complex amplitude of two waves with CP with opposite direction of rotation, "−" in the left-hand and "+" in the right-hand direction. In the case of waves with elliptical polarization, as a general case of polarization, the total field can be presented via E_+ and E_- as follows:

$$\mathbf{E}(\mathbf{r}) = \{\mathbf{e}_+ E_+ \pm \mathbf{e}_- E_-\} \exp(j\mathbf{k} \cdot \mathbf{r}) \tag{4.10}$$

where "−" corresponds to left-handed rotation and "+" corresponds to right-handed rotation, as seen in Figure 4.2. Now, if the complex amplitudes E_+ and E_- have different phases, we can present their ratio as

$$\frac{E_-}{E_+} = q \cdot \exp(j\alpha) \tag{4.11}$$

and the ellipse axes rotate at the angle $\alpha/2$ (see Figure 4.2). In the case of $q = \pm1$, we again return to a wave with linear polarization.

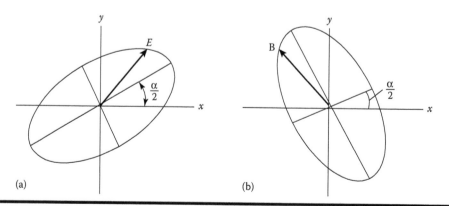

(a)   (b)

Figure 4.2   Elliptical polarized wave with two directions of rotation: (a) left-handed and (b) right-handed.

We should note that the knowledge obtained in this chapter will be basic for understanding the propagation of electromagnetic waves in a material medium in guiding structures, antennas, and radar.

4.3 Propagation of Electromagnetic Waves in Material Media

4.3.1 Main Characteristics of Plane Waves in Material Media

We base this chapter on knowledge obtained in previous chapters, according to which we use equations describing the propagation of plane waves at distances far from any source in an unbounded, homogeneous, isotropic, nondispersive material medium, for which the characteristics of medium are simply constant, that is, ε, σ, and μ do not depend on the spatial coordinates. As was shown in Chapter 3, the relations between the components of an electromagnetic wave field are [1–11]

$$\mathbf{J} = \sigma\mathbf{E},\ \mathbf{D} = \varepsilon\mathbf{E},\ \mathbf{B} = \mu\mathbf{H} \tag{4.12}$$

The first and second Maxwell's equations in that case can be written in the following form:

$$\nabla \times \mathbf{E} = -\mu\frac{\partial \mathbf{H}}{\partial t};\quad \nabla \times \mathbf{H} = \mathbf{J} + \varepsilon\frac{\partial \mathbf{E}}{\partial t} \tag{4.13}$$

Without any loss of generality, let us consider the one-dimensional case, when the wave propagates along the z-axis:

$$\mathbf{E} = \mathbf{E}_x(z,t)\mathbf{i}_x$$
$$\mathbf{H} = \mathbf{H}_y(z,t)\mathbf{i}_y \tag{4.14}$$

For this case, the corresponding 1-D first and second Maxwell's wave equations in the Cartesian coordinate system are

$$\frac{\partial E_x}{\partial z} = -\mu\frac{\partial H_y}{\partial t}$$
$$\frac{\partial H_y}{\partial z} = -\sigma E_x - \varepsilon\frac{\partial E_x}{\partial t} \tag{4.15}$$

For time dependence $e^{j\omega t}$, by introducing so-called phasors (see Chapter 3),

$$E_x(z,t) = \mathrm{Re}\left[\tilde{E}_x(z)e^{j\omega t}\right]$$
$$H_y(z,t) = \mathrm{Re}\left[\tilde{H}_y(z)e^{j\omega t}\right] \tag{4.16}$$

One can obtain from Equation 4.15 the corresponding phasor equations:

$$\frac{\partial \tilde{E}_x}{\partial z} = -j\omega\mu\tilde{H}_y;\quad \frac{\partial \tilde{H}_y}{\partial z} = -\sigma\tilde{E}_x - j\omega\varepsilon\tilde{E}_x \tag{4.17}$$

By differentiation of the first equation from the system in Equation 4.17 on z and by using the second equation from the system in Equation 4.17, we get

$$\frac{\partial^2 \tilde{E}_x}{\partial z^2} = -j\omega\mu \frac{\partial \tilde{H}_y}{\partial z} = j\omega\mu \left(\sigma + j\omega\varepsilon\right) \tilde{E}_x \equiv \gamma^2 \tilde{E}_x \tag{4.18}$$

where

$$\gamma = \sqrt{j\omega\mu\left(\sigma + j\omega\varepsilon\right)} \tag{4.19}$$

is the propagation parameter describing the propagation properties of an EM wave in arbitrary medium, with *losses* of wave energy and the wave *dispersion*, that is, a dependence of the parameters of the electromagnetic wave on frequency.

The solution of Equation 4.18 is follows:

$$\tilde{E}_x = Ae^{-\gamma z} + Be^{+\gamma z} \tag{4.20}$$

where A and B are constants that can be obtained from the corresponding boundary conditions described in Chapter 5. The propagation parameter is complex and can be written as

$$\gamma = \alpha + j\beta \tag{4.21}$$

Here, α describes the attenuation of the EM wave in the medium, that is, the wave energy losses measured in *Neper per meter* (Np/m), and β describes the phase changes of the plane wave in the material media measured in *radians per meter* (rad/m).

As an example, we show in Figure 4.3 the attenuation of the wave for two kinds of β (e.g., for two time instants, t_1 and t_2). A full description of their properties will be given later. Now, we can present the magnetic field phasor component in the same manner, as the phasor of the electric field, by using Equations 4.17 and 4.20:

$$\tilde{H}_y = -\frac{1}{j\omega\mu} \frac{\partial \tilde{E}_x}{\partial z} = \frac{\gamma}{j\omega\mu} (Ae^{-\gamma z} - Be^{+\gamma z})$$

$$\sqrt{\frac{(\sigma + j\omega\varepsilon)}{j\omega\mu}} (Ae^{-\gamma z} - Be^{+\gamma z}) \equiv \frac{1}{\eta} (Ae^{-\gamma z} - Be^{+\gamma z}) \tag{4.22}$$

where

$$\eta = \sqrt{\frac{j\omega\mu}{(\sigma + j\omega\varepsilon)}} \tag{4.23}$$

is the intrinsic impedance of the medium, which is also complex.

If we now introduce the function of the wave transition in the medium, $\tau = \exp(-\alpha z)$, via the distance z, where the wave amplitude decreases in $e \approx 2.7$ times, we can use instead of parameter α

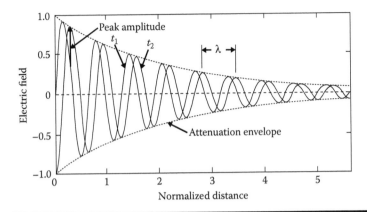

Figure 4.3 **Decay of the wave for two values of the times t_1 and t_2 vs. the normalized distance r/λ.**

another parameter of attenuation, L, measured in dB/m, where the relation between these parameters is $L = (1/z)10\log$.

As was shown in Chapter 3, in free space, the material parameters are constants, that is, the permittivity, $\varepsilon = \varepsilon_0 = (36\pi)^{-1}10^{-9}$ (F/m), the permeability, $\mu = \mu_0 = 4\pi \cdot 10^{-7}$ (H/m), the conductivity, $\sigma = 0$, and the intrinsic impedance, $\eta = \eta_0 = 120\pi$ (Ω) $= 377\ \Omega$. Then, the wave velocity in free space $c = 1/\sqrt{\varepsilon_0\mu_0}$, is also constant and equal to ~3 × 10⁸ m/s. Usually in the literature, the relative permittivity, $\varepsilon_r = \varepsilon/\varepsilon_0$, and permeability, $\mu_r = \mu/\mu_0$, are introduced into consideration of the problem of wave propagation in material media.

The solutions of Equations 4.20 and 4.22 can be detailed by use of the corresponding boundary conditions. But this is not the goal of our future analysis. We show the reader how the properties of the material medium change propagation conditions within an unbounded homogeneous material medium. For this purpose, we will analyze the propagation parameters described by Equations 4.19, 4.21, and 4.23 and associate them with a plane wave determined by Equations 4.20 and 4.22. As it follows from Equations 4.19 and 4.21,

$$\gamma^2 = (\alpha + j\beta)^2 = j\omega\mu(\sigma + j\omega\varepsilon)$$

from which

$$\alpha^2 - \beta^2 = -\omega^2\mu\varepsilon \tag{4.24}$$

$$2\alpha\beta = \omega\mu\sigma$$

Now, squaring the first and second equations in Equation 4.24, adding them and taking the square root, we finally have

$$\alpha^2 + \beta^2 = \omega^2\mu\varepsilon\sqrt{1 + \left(\frac{\sigma}{\omega\varepsilon}\right)^2} \tag{4.25}$$

Now, using Equations 4.24 and 4.25, we get

$$2\alpha^2 = -\omega^2\mu\varepsilon + \omega^2\mu\varepsilon\sqrt{1+\left(\frac{\sigma}{\omega\varepsilon}\right)^2}$$

or

$$\alpha = \frac{\omega\sqrt{2\mu\varepsilon}}{2}\left[\sqrt{1+\left(\frac{\sigma}{\omega\varepsilon}\right)^2}-1\right]^{1/2} \tag{4.26}$$

In the same manner, from Equations 4.24 and 4.25, by taking the difference between these two expressions, we get

$$2\beta^2 = \omega^2\mu\varepsilon + \omega^2\mu\varepsilon\sqrt{1+\left(\frac{\sigma}{\omega\varepsilon}\right)^2}$$

or

$$\beta = \frac{\omega\sqrt{2\mu\varepsilon}}{2}\left[\sqrt{1+\left(\frac{\sigma}{\omega\varepsilon}\right)^2}+1\right]^{1/2} \tag{4.27}$$

In Equations 4.26 and 4.27, the parameter $\sigma/(\omega\varepsilon)$ is defined as the loss tangent, $\tan\delta = \sigma/(\omega\varepsilon)$, which determines the ratio of the magnitude of the conduction current density, $|\mathbf{j}_c| \sim \sigma\tilde{E}_x$, to the magnitude of the displacement current density, $|\mathbf{j}_d| \sim \omega\varepsilon\tilde{E}_x$, in an arbitrary material medium. Clearly, this parameter is not a simple function of ω, because in dispersion material media, σ and ε also depend on frequency, ω.

The phase velocity is described by the propagation parameter β along the direction of propagation, which is defined:

$$v_{ph} = \frac{\omega}{\beta} = \frac{\sqrt{2}}{\sqrt{\mu\varepsilon}}\left[\sqrt{1+\left(\frac{\sigma}{\omega\varepsilon}\right)^2}+1\right]^{-1/2} \tag{4.28}$$

The dispersion properties follow from dependence on the frequency of the wave phase velocity $v_{ph} = v_{ph}(\omega)$. Thus, waves with different frequencies $\omega = 2\pi f$ travel with different phase velocities. In the same manner, the wavelength in the medium is dependent on the frequency of the wave:

$$\lambda = \frac{2\pi}{\beta} = \frac{\sqrt{2}}{f\sqrt{\mu\varepsilon}}\left[\sqrt{1+\left(\frac{\sigma}{\omega\varepsilon}\right)^2}+1\right]^{-1/2} \tag{4.29}$$

As for the wave attenuation with distance, field variations with distances are not purely sinusoidal, as in free space (as is seen from Figure 4.3). In other words, the wavelength is not exactly equal to the distance between two consecutive positive (or negative) extrema. It is equal to the distance between two alternative zero crossings.

The group velocity can be found from Equation 4.27 by introducing this formula into the following expression:

$$v_{gr} = \frac{d\omega}{d\beta} \equiv \left(\frac{d\beta}{d\omega} \right)^{-1} \tag{4.30}$$

The intrinsic impedance, as follows from Equations 4.20 and 4.22, is the ratio of the amplitude of the electric field phasor to the amplitude of the magnetic field phasor, that is,

$$\frac{\tilde{E}_x}{\tilde{H}_y} = \begin{cases} \eta, & \text{for the } (+) \text{ wave} \\ -\eta, & \text{for the } (-) \text{ wave} \end{cases} \tag{4.31}$$

From Equations 4.19 and 4.23, it follows that

$$\gamma\eta = j\mu\varepsilon$$

$$\frac{\gamma}{\eta} = \sigma + j\omega\varepsilon \tag{4.32a}$$

and

$$\sigma = \mathrm{Re}\left(\frac{\gamma}{\eta} \right)$$

$$\varepsilon = \frac{1}{\omega}\mathrm{Im}\left(\frac{\gamma}{\eta} \right) \tag{4.32b}$$

$$\mu = \frac{1}{j\omega}\gamma\eta$$

We can now present Formulas 4.26 and 4.27 using a general presentation of ε in the complex form, that is, $\varepsilon = \varepsilon' - j\varepsilon''$, where $\varepsilon' \equiv \varepsilon_{\mathrm{Re}}$ is the real part of the permittivity, $\varepsilon' = \varepsilon_r \varepsilon_0$, and $\varepsilon'' = \varepsilon_r' \varepsilon_0$ is the imaginary part of the permittivity, $\varepsilon'' \equiv \varepsilon_{\mathrm{Im}}$, and determines the wave losses in media. If so,

$$\gamma^2 = (\alpha + j\beta)^2 = j\omega\mu(\sigma + j\omega\varepsilon'') - \omega^2\mu\varepsilon'$$

where now

$$\alpha = \frac{\omega\sqrt{2\mu\varepsilon'}}{2} \left[\sqrt{1 + \left(\frac{\sigma + d\omega\varepsilon''}{\omega\varepsilon'} \right)^2} - 1 \right]^{1/2} \tag{4.33a}$$

and

$$\beta = \frac{\omega\sqrt{2\mu\varepsilon'}}{2}\left[\sqrt{1+\left(\frac{\sigma+d\omega\varepsilon''}{\omega\varepsilon'}\right)^2}+1\right]^{1/2}$$ (4.33b)

On the other hand, by introducing the loss tangent, $\tan\delta = \varepsilon''/\varepsilon'$ [6], one can easily rewrite Equation 4.33a and b, respectively, as

$$\alpha = \frac{\omega\sqrt{2\mu\varepsilon'}}{2}\left[\sqrt{1+\left(2\tan\delta\right)^2}-1\right]^{1/2}$$ (4.34a)

and

$$\beta = \frac{\omega\sqrt{2\mu\varepsilon'}}{2}\left[\sqrt{1+\left(2\tan\delta\right)^2}+1\right]^{1/2}$$ (4.34b)

From general Formulas 4.19, 4.26, and 4.27 follow several special cases for different kinds of material media. We will also use a general complex presentation of the dielectric permittivity and the corresponding formulas, Equations 4.33 and 4.34. Let us consider them.

4.3.2 Propagation of Plane Wave in Ideal Dielectric Medium

Perfect dielectrics are characterized by the constraint $\sigma = 0$ ($\tan\delta = 0$). Then, from Equation 4.19 we get

$$\gamma = \alpha + j\beta = \sqrt{j\omega\mu j\omega\varepsilon} = j\omega\sqrt{\mu\varepsilon}$$ (4.35)

that is, the propagation parameter is purely imaginary. If so, we finally have

$$\alpha = 0, \quad \beta = \omega\sqrt{\mu\varepsilon}$$ (4.36a)

$$v_{ph} = \frac{\omega}{\beta} = \frac{1}{\sqrt{\mu\varepsilon}}$$ (4.36b)

and

$$\lambda = \frac{2\pi}{\beta} = \frac{1}{f\sqrt{\mu\varepsilon}}$$ (4.36c)

Further,

$$\eta = \sqrt{\frac{j\omega\mu}{j\omega\varepsilon}} = \sqrt{\frac{\mu}{\varepsilon}}$$ (4.36d)

Thus, the wave in the perfect dielectric medium propagates without attenuation ($\alpha = 0$) and with **E** and **H** in phase, as in free space, but with ε_0 replaced by ε and μ_0 replaced by μ. In terms of the relative permittivity $\varepsilon_r = \varepsilon/\varepsilon_0$ and the relative permeability $\mu_r = \mu/\mu_0$ of the perfect dielectric medium, the propagation parameters are

$$\beta = \beta_0 \sqrt{\mu_r \varepsilon_r} = \frac{2\pi}{\lambda_0} \sqrt{\mu_r \varepsilon_r} \tag{4.37a}$$

$$v_{ph} = \frac{c}{\sqrt{\mu_r \varepsilon_r}} \tag{4.37b}$$

$$\lambda = \frac{\lambda_0}{\sqrt{\mu_r \varepsilon_r}} \tag{4.37c}$$

$$\eta = \eta_0 \sqrt{\frac{\mu_r}{\varepsilon_r}} \tag{4.37d}$$

where $\eta_0 = 277\ \Omega$ is the impedance of free space; all other parameters denoted by subscript "0" for free space have been introduced above.

4.3.3 Propagation of Plane Wave in Nonideal Dielectric Medium

This medium is characterized by $\sigma \neq 0$, but $\sigma/\omega\varepsilon \ll 1$ ($\tan \delta \ll 1$, $\varepsilon'' \ll \varepsilon'$); that is, the magnitude of the conduction current density, $|\mathbf{j}_c| \sim \sigma \tilde{E}_x$, is small compared with the magnitude of the displacement current density, $|\mathbf{j}_d| \sim \omega\varepsilon \tilde{E}_x$. Using the following expansion [12]

$$(1 + x)^n = 1 + nx + \frac{n(n-1)}{2!} x^2 + \cdots$$

we can rewrite Equation 4.19 as

$$\gamma = \sqrt{j\omega\mu(\sigma + j\omega\varepsilon)} = j\omega\sqrt{\mu\varepsilon} \sqrt{1 - j\frac{\sigma}{\omega\varepsilon}}$$

$$\approx \frac{\sigma}{2} \sqrt{\frac{\mu}{\varepsilon}} \left(1 - \frac{\sigma^2}{8\omega^2\varepsilon^2}\right) + j\omega\sqrt{\mu\varepsilon} \left(1 + \frac{\sigma^2}{8\omega^2\varepsilon^2}\right) \tag{4.38}$$

so that

$$\alpha \approx \frac{\sigma}{2} \sqrt{\frac{\mu}{\varepsilon}} \left(1 - \frac{\sigma^2}{8\omega^2\varepsilon^2}\right) \tag{4.39a}$$

$$\beta \approx \omega\sqrt{\mu\varepsilon} \left(1 + \frac{\sigma^2}{8\omega^2\varepsilon^2}\right) \tag{4.39b}$$

In the same manner,

$$\eta = \sqrt{\frac{j\omega\mu}{(\sigma + j\omega\varepsilon)}} = \sqrt{\frac{j\omega\mu}{j\omega\varepsilon}}\left(1 - j\frac{\sigma}{\omega\varepsilon}\right)^{-1/2}$$

$$\approx \sqrt{\frac{\mu}{\varepsilon}}\left[\left(1 - \frac{3\sigma^2}{8\omega^2\varepsilon^2}\right) + j\frac{\sigma}{2\omega\varepsilon}\right]$$

(4.39c)

$$v_{ph} = \frac{\omega}{\beta} \approx \frac{1}{\sqrt{\mu\varepsilon}}\left(1 - \frac{\sigma^2}{8\omega^2\varepsilon^2}\right)$$

(4.39d)

$$\lambda = \frac{2\pi}{\beta} \approx \frac{1}{f\sqrt{\mu\varepsilon}}\left(1 - \frac{\sigma^2}{8\omega^2\varepsilon^2}\right)$$

(4.39e)

In all expressions, all terms with power higher than two have been neglected, since $\sigma/\omega\varepsilon \ll 1$. As follows from Equations 2.39a through 2.39e, for all practical applications, the ratio $\sigma/\omega\varepsilon$ is not higher than 0.1; the only significant feature different from the perfect dielectric case is the *attenuation*, α.

We perform the same procedure, but taking into account the complexity of the dielectric permittivity, based on Equations 4.33a and b. Finally, we get

$$\alpha \approx \sqrt{\frac{\mu}{\varepsilon'}}\frac{\omega\varepsilon''}{2} = \frac{\omega}{2}\sqrt{\mu\varepsilon'}\tan\delta$$

(4.40a)

$$\beta \approx \omega\sqrt{\mu\varepsilon'}\left(1 + \frac{\varepsilon''^2}{8\varepsilon'^2}\right) = \omega\sqrt{\mu\varepsilon'}\left(1 + \frac{\tan^2\delta}{8}\right)$$

(4.40b)

4.3.4 Propagation of Plane Wave in Good Conductive Medium

Good conductors are characterized by $\sigma/\omega\varepsilon \gg 1$ ($\tan\delta \gg 1$, $\varepsilon'' \gg \varepsilon'$); it is the opposite to the imperfect dielectric case. In this case, that is, $|\mathbf{j}_c| \sim \sigma\tilde{E}_x \gg |\mathbf{j}_d| \sim \omega\varepsilon\tilde{E}_x$. For such a medium, we get

$$\gamma = \sqrt{j\omega\mu(\sigma + j\omega\varepsilon)} \approx \sqrt{j\omega\mu\sigma}$$

$$= \sqrt{\omega\mu\sigma}e^{j\frac{\pi}{4}} = \sqrt{\pi f\mu\sigma}(1 + j)$$

(4.41)

which yields

$$\alpha \approx \sqrt{\pi f\mu\sigma}$$

$$\beta \approx \sqrt{\pi f\mu\sigma}$$

(4.42a)

In the same manner, we get

$$\eta = \sqrt{\frac{j\omega\mu}{(\sigma + j\omega\varepsilon)}} \approx \sqrt{\frac{j\omega\mu}{\sigma}} = \sqrt{\frac{\omega\mu}{\sigma}} e^{j\frac{\pi}{4}} = \sqrt{\frac{\pi f \mu}{\sigma}}(1+j) \qquad (4.42b)$$

and

$$v_{ph} = \frac{\omega}{\beta} \approx \sqrt{\frac{4\pi f}{\mu\sigma}} \qquad (4.42c)$$

$$\lambda = \frac{2\pi}{\beta} \approx \sqrt{\frac{4\pi}{\mu f \sigma}} \qquad (4.42d)$$

As clearly seen from the above formulas, most parameters of propagation are proportional to $f^{1/2}$, when σ and μ are constant. This behavior is very different from the case of the imperfect dielectric.

We can also define a *skin depth* as the distance at which the field is attenuated by a factor e^{-1} or 0.368. This distance equals $1/\alpha$ and is denoted by the symbol δ:

$$\delta = \frac{1}{\alpha} = \frac{1}{\sqrt{\pi f \mu\sigma}} \qquad (4.43)$$

The phenomenon of concentration of the wave field energy near to the skin of the conductor is known as the *skin effect*.

For example, we will consider copper, as a good conductor, with conductivity of $\sigma = 5.8 \times 10^7$ S/m and permeability $\mu = \mu_0 = 4\pi \times 10^{-7}$ H/m [9]. The skin depth for copper equals

$$\delta = \frac{1}{\sqrt{\pi f\, 4\pi \times 10^{-7}\left(\frac{H}{m}\right) \times 5.8 \times 10^7 \left(\frac{S}{m}\right)}} = \frac{0.066}{\sqrt{f}}(m)$$

and the amplitude of intrinsic impedance equals

$$|\eta| = \sqrt{\frac{2\pi f \times 4\pi \times 10^{-7}}{5.8 \times 10^7}} = 3.69 \times 10^{-7}\,(\Omega)$$

As follows from these expressions, the intrinsic impedance of copper has a low magnitude, ~0.369 Ω, even at the high frequency $f = 10^{12}$ Hz (1 THz). As for the low frequency of 1 MHz, the wave field in copper attenuates by a factor e^{-1} at the distance of 0.066 mm, resulting in the concentration of the field energy near to the skin layer of the conductor.

We will now show another feature that follows from Equation 4.43. As follows from Equation 4.42b, the intrinsic impedance of a good conductor has a phase angle of 45°. Hence, the phase difference of the components **E** and **H** of the electromagnetic (EM) field in such a medium equals 45°. The amplitude of intrinsic impedance is given by

$$| \eta | = \left| \sqrt{\frac{\pi f \mu}{\sigma}} (1 + j) \right| = \sqrt{\frac{2\pi f \mu}{\sigma}} \qquad (4.44)$$

From Equations 4.35 and 4.42b, it follows that the magnitude of the intrinsic impedance of a good conductor is less than that of a good dielectric for the same ε and μ. In fact,

$$| \eta_{\text{cond}} | = \sqrt{\frac{2\pi f \mu}{\sigma}} = \sqrt{\frac{\omega \varepsilon}{\sigma}} \sqrt{\frac{\mu}{\varepsilon}} \equiv \sqrt{\frac{\omega \varepsilon}{\sigma}} | \eta_{\text{diel}} | \qquad (4.45)$$

and, because of $(\omega \varepsilon)/\sigma \ll 1$ for a good conductor, we finally have $| \eta_{\text{cond}} | \ll | \eta_{\text{diel}} |$. Hence, for the same parameters ε and μ, as well as for the constant electric field component **E**, the **H** component inside a dielectric is much less than that inside the conductor.

4.3.5 Main Results

From the results presented, as σ varies from 0 to ∞, a material medium is classified as

- Perfect dielectric for $\sigma = 0$
- Imperfect dielectric for $\sigma \neq 0$ but $\sigma/\omega \varepsilon \ll 1$
- Good conductor for $\sigma/\omega \varepsilon \gg 1$
- Perfect conductor for $\sigma \to \infty$

The same classification can be done for the "dispersive" parameter f (for $\sigma \neq 0$):

- Imperfect dielectric for $f \gg f_q \equiv \sigma/2\pi\varepsilon$
- Good conductor for $f \ll f_q \equiv \sigma/2\pi\varepsilon$

But the dispersion properties of such materials as plasma and ferromagnetic are more complicated, because ε, σ, and μ can also be functions of frequency f.

These results enable us to point out that in the case of a *perfectly conductive* medium, when $\sigma \to \infty$, as follows from Equation 4.43, $\delta \to 0$. Thus, there is no penetration of EM fields into the perfectly conductive material.

PROBLEMS

Example 4.1: Given aluminum with $\sigma = 5.8 \times 10^7$ S/m and $\mu_r = \varepsilon_r = 1$, the wave frequency propagating inside aluminum, $f = 2$ MHz.
Find: The depth of skin layer, δ, and the phase velocity, v_{ph}, of the EM wave.

Example 4.2: An EM plane wave with the magnetic component having field strength $B_0 = 10$ A/m and frequency $f = 600$ kHz propagates in the positive direction along the z-axis in copper medium with $\mu_r = 1$ and $\sigma = 5.8 \times 10^7$ S/m.
Find: The attenuation constant, α, the phase constant, β, the depth of skin layer, δ, and the component of the magnetic field, $B(z, t)$.

Example 4.3: Given a material medium with $\mu_r = 1$ and $\varepsilon_r = 5$, the wavelength in free space of the EM wave is $\lambda_0 = 0.33$ m.

Find: The conductivity of the medium, $\sigma = \omega\varepsilon$, the parameter of attenuation, α, the phase constant, β, the phase velocity, v_{ph}, and the impedance, η.

Example 4.4: Given material with parameters $\mu = \mu_0$ and $\varepsilon = 3\varepsilon_0$, the wavelength of the plane wave propagating in free space is $\lambda_0 = 0.1$ m.

Find: The wavelength of the wave in the material, the parameters of propagation α, β, and γ, and the intrinsic impedance in the material.

Example 4.5: Given a plane wave with carrier frequency equaling 900 MHz normally incident on the half-space consisting of copper with conductivity of $\sigma = 5.813 \times 10^7$ S/m and the normalized permeability $\mu_r = 1$.

Find: The skin layer depth δ, the conductivity $\sigma = \omega\varepsilon$, the intrinsic impedance η, and the propagation constants α, β, and γ.

Example 4.6: Given an electromagnetic wave propagating in the material medium with $\mu_r = 1$ and $\varepsilon_r = 2.5$, the electric component of which is given by $E_x(z,t) = 4\cos(4\pi \times 10^6 t - kz)$ (V/m).

Find: The phase velocity, the absolute value of the vector **k** in material medium, the impedance η, and the component of magnetic field $H_y(z,t)$.

Example 4.7: The plane wave with amplitude of 15 V/m and frequency of 100 MHz, having a component along vector $\mathbf{u}_y$, propagates in the direction $\mathbf{u}_z$ in material medium with the parameters $\mu_r = 1$, $\varepsilon_r = 8$, and $\sigma = 15$ S/m.

Find: The wave attenuation constant α, the phase constant β, the complex propagation constant γ, and the phase and group velocities, and present the complete expression of the electric field in the time domain.

Example 4.8: Given aluminum with $\sigma = 5.813 \times 10^7$ S/m and, $\varepsilon_r = \mu_r = 1$.

Find: The propagation parameters α, β, and γ, the intrinsic impedance η, the phase velocity v_{ph}, and the skin layer depth δ.

Example 4.9: The plane wave with electric field component $E(z,t)$ of frequency $f = 1$ GHz propagates along the x-axis in a dielectric medium with $\varepsilon = 2.5\varepsilon_0$, $\mu = \mu_0$, and $\sigma = 0$, and has a harmonic form $\mathbf{E}(z,t) = 12\cos(\omega t - \beta z)\mathbf{u}_x$.

Find: The propagation parameters α, β, and γ, the intrinsic impedance η, the phase velocity v_{ph}, the component of the magnetic field along $\mathbf{u}_x$, and the total magnetic field in its harmonic form as a function of z and t.

Example 4.10: In sea water with conductivity $\sigma = 4$ S/m and permittivity $\varepsilon = 81\varepsilon_0$, a plane wave propagates with the frequency 100 MHz.

Find: The parameter α and the attenuation L (in decibels per meter), considering that the water is a good conductor ($\sigma/\omega\varepsilon \approx 10 \gg 1$) and that the transmission of the wave is proportional to $\tau = \exp(-\alpha z)$. What will happen if the frequency increases to 100 GHz?

References

1. Al'pert, Ya. L., V. L. Ginzburg, and E. L. Fe'nberg, *Propagation of Radio Waves*, Moscow: State House of Publications, 1953.
2. Plonsey, R. and R. E. Collin, *Principles and Applications of Electromagnetic Fields*, New York: McGraw-Hill, 1961.
3. Jackson, J. D., *Classical Electrodynamics*, New York: Wiley, 1962.
4. Felsen, L. and N. Marcuvitz, *Radiation and Scattering of Waves*, Englewood Cliffs, NJ: Prentice Hall, 1973.

5. Chew, W. C., *Waves and Fields in Inhomogeneous Media*, New York: IEEE, 1995.
6. Kong, J. A., *Electromagnetic Wave Theory*, New York: Wiley, 1986.
7. Elliott, R. S., *Electromagnetics: History, Theory, and Applications*, New York: IEEE, 1993.
8. Dudley, D. G., *Mathematical Foundations for Electromagnetic Theory*, New York: IEEE, 1994.
9. Rajeev, B., Ed., *Handbook: Engineering Electromagnetic Applications*, Boca Raton, FL: CRC Taylor & Francis, 2006.
10. Pozar, D. M., *Microwave Engineering*, 4th edn, New York: Wiley, 2012.
11. Iskander, M. F., *Electromagnetic Fields and Waves*, 2nd edn, Long Grove, IL: Waveland Press, 2013.
12. Korn, G. and T. Korn, *Mathematical Handbook for Scientists and Engineers*, New York: McGraw-Hill, 1961.

Chapter 5

Reflection and Refraction of Electromagnetic Waves

5.1 Boundary Conditions

Equation 4.2 describes all propagation phenomena within an infinite inhomogeneous isotropic medium. But if we consider two inhomogeneous finite or semi-finite regions, we need to introduce *boundary conditions* at the interface between these two regions in order to solve Equation 4.1 for each of these regions. In this case, the procedure to solve the vector wave equation is as follows (see also some well-known books [1–10]).

As a first step, this equation is solved separately for each region. Then, in the second step, by patching the solution together via boundary conditions, we obtain the solution for two neighboring regions. It can be easily shown that the boundary conditions follow from Equation 4.2 for one of the two vector waves. To do so, we can, following [3,6], integrate Equation 4.2 for the first region within a small area in the interface of the two inhomogeneous semi-finite or finite regions, as presented in Figure 5.1.

Using now the Stokes' theorem for the surface integral of a *curl*, and using the same integration over surface S for Equation 4.1 in both cases, after straightforward derivations and taking the limit $\delta \to 0$ (see Figure 5.1) respectively, we finally obtain for the magnetic field component

$$\mathbf{n} \times \mathbf{H}_1 - \mathbf{n} \times \mathbf{H}_2 = \mathbf{j}_S \tag{5.1}$$

and for the electric field component

$$\mathbf{n} \times \mathbf{E}_1 - \mathbf{n} \times \mathbf{E}_2 = -\mathbf{M}_S \tag{5.2}$$

where:

$\mathbf{M}_S$ is a magnetic current sheet at the interface
$\mathbf{j}_S$ is an electric current sheet at the interface

Equation 5.1 states that the discontinuity in the tangential component of the magnetic field is proportional to the electric current sheet $\mathbf{j}_S$. This is the *first boundary condition* for solving any one

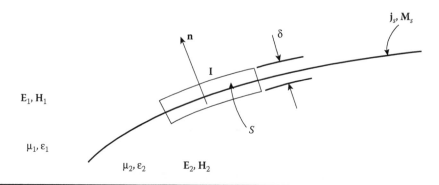

Figure 5.1 A sketch of the boundary between two media with their own parameters ε_1, μ_1 and ε_2, μ_2, distributed inside each medium and with sources, j_s, M_s, at the elementary area S and the normal n to the boundary.

vector electromagnetic equation from Equation 4.1. Equation 5.2 states that the discontinuity in the tangential component of the electric field is proportional to the magnetic current sheet M_S. This is the *second boundary condition* for Equation 4.2.

Both boundary conditions in Equations 5.1 and 5.2 can be simplified for the case of wave propagation above a flat intersection. In the case considered, the first boundary condition in Equation 5.1 for an isotropic nonmagnetized ($\mu = 1$) source-free ($M_S = 0$, $j_S = 0$) subsoil medium reduces to

$$H_{1n} = H_{2n} \quad \text{and} \quad H_{1\tau} = H_{2\tau} \tag{5.3}$$

Both conditions are valid in the case of finite conductivity of each medium, which is satisfied within the surface between two media. The first condition in Equation 5.3 states that the normal components of the magnetic field of the wave are continuous at the intersection surface of two media. The second condition in Equation 5.3 states that the tangential component of the magnetic field is also continuous at the interface of the intersection surface.

As for the second boundary condition in Equation 5.2, it also can be simplified for the interface of the air–conductor intersection as

$$\mathbf{n} \times \mathbf{E}_1 = \mathbf{n} \times \mathbf{E}_2 \quad \text{or} \quad E_{1\tau} = E_{2\tau} \tag{5.4}$$

The condition in Equation 5.4 states that the tangential components of the electric field of any electromagnetic (EM) wave are continuous at the interface of the two-media intersection surface. One may notice that conditions in Equations 5.1 and 5.2 are more general than those described by Equations 5.3 and 5.4, and satisfy various kinds of isotropic inhomogeneous media that consist of both electric and magnetic sources.

The simplest case of wave propagation over the intersection between two media is that in which the intersection surface can be assumed as a flat perfectly conductive surface. If so, for a perfectly conductive flat surface, the total electric field vector is equal to zero, that is, $\mathbf{E} = 0$. In this case, the tangential component of the electric field vanishes at the perfectly conductive flat intersection surface:

$$E_\tau = 0 \tag{5.5}$$

Consequently, as follows from Maxwell's equation $\nabla \times E(r) = i\omega B(r)$ (see Chapter 3 for the case of $\mu_r = 1$ and $\mathbf{B} \equiv \mathbf{H}$), at such a flat perfectly conductive intersection surface, the normal component of the magnetic field also vanishes:

$$H_n = 0 \tag{5.6}$$

As also follows from Maxwell's equations (Equation 3.14), the tangential component of the magnetic field does not vanish because of its compensation by the surface electric current. At the same time, the normal component of the electric field is also compensated by pulsing electrical charge at the intersection surface of two media.

Hence, by introducing the Cartesian coordinate system (see Figure 5.1), one can present the boundary conditions in Equations 5.5 and 5.6 at the flat perfectly conductive surface between two media as

$$E_x(x, y, z = 0) = E_y(x, y, z = 0) = H_z(x, y, z = 0) = 0 \tag{5.7}$$

5.2 Reflection and Refraction Coefficients at the Boundary of Two Media

Because all kinds of waves can be represented by means of the concept of plane waves, let us obtain the main reflection and refraction formulas for a plane wave incident on a flat surface between two media, as shown in Figure 5.2. The media have different dielectric properties, which are described above and below the boundary plane $z = 0$ by the permittivity and permeability ε_1, μ_1 and ε_2, μ_2, respectively, for each medium.

Without reducing the general problem, let us consider a plane wave with wave vector $\mathbf{k}_0$ and frequency $\omega = 2\pi f$ incident from a medium described by parameters ε_1 and μ_1. The reflected and refracted waves are described by wave vectors $\mathbf{k}_1$ and $\mathbf{k}_2$, respectively. Vector $\mathbf{n}$ is a unit normal vector directed from medium (ε_2, μ_2) into medium (ε_1, μ_1).

According to relations between electrical and magnetic components, which follow from Maxwell's equations, the incident wave can be represented as follows:

$$\mathbf{E} = \mathbf{E}_0 \exp\{j(\mathbf{k}_0 \cdot \mathbf{x} - \omega \cdot t)\}, \mathbf{H} = \sqrt{\varepsilon_1 / \mu_1} \cdot \frac{\mathbf{k}_0 \times \mathbf{E}}{|\mathbf{k}_0|} \tag{5.8}$$

The same can be done for the reflected wave

$$\mathbf{E}_1 = \mathbf{E}_{01} \exp\{j(\mathbf{k}_1 \cdot \mathbf{x} - \omega \cdot t)\}, \mathbf{H} = \sqrt{\varepsilon_1 / \mu_1} \cdot \frac{\mathbf{k}_1 \times \mathbf{E}_1}{|\mathbf{k}_1|} \tag{5.9}$$

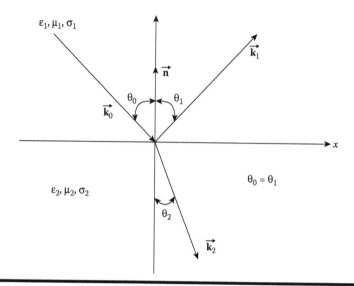

Figure 5.2   Geometry of a ray reflection and refraction from the boundary of two media.

and for the refracted wave

$$\mathbf{E}_2 = \mathbf{E}_{02} \exp\left\{ j\left(\mathbf{k}_2 \cdot \mathbf{x} - \omega \cdot t\right)\right\}, \mathbf{H} = \sqrt{\varepsilon_2 / \mu_2} \cdot \frac{\mathbf{k}_2 \times \mathbf{E}_2}{|\mathbf{k}_2|} \tag{5.10}$$

The values of the wave vectors are related by the following expressions:

$$|\mathbf{k}_0| = |\mathbf{k}_1| \equiv k = \frac{\omega}{c}\sqrt{\varepsilon_1\mu_1}, |\mathbf{k}_2| \equiv k_2 = \frac{\omega}{c}\sqrt{\varepsilon_2\mu_2} \tag{5.11}$$

From the boundary conditions that were described by Equations 5.5 and 5.6, one can easily obtain the condition of the equality of phase for each wave at the plane $z = 0$:

$$(\mathbf{k}_0 \cdot \mathbf{x})_{z=0} = (\mathbf{k}_1 \cdot \mathbf{x})_{z=0} = (\mathbf{k}_2 \cdot \mathbf{x})_{z=0} \tag{5.12},$$

which is independent of the nature of the boundary condition. Equation 5.12 describes the condition that all three wave vectors must lie in the same plane. From this equation, it also follows that

$$k_0 \sin\theta_0 = k_1 \sin\theta_1 = k_2 \sin\theta_2 \tag{5.13}$$

which is the analogue of Snell's law:

$$\varepsilon_1\mu_1 \sin\theta_0 = \varepsilon_2\mu_2 \sin\theta_2 \tag{5.14}$$

Moreover, because $|\mathbf{k}_0| = |\mathbf{k}_1|$, we find $\theta_0 = \theta_1$, obtaining the first Snell's law; this states that *The angle of incidence equals the angle of reflection.*

It also follows from the boundary conditions that the normal components of vectors **D** and **B** are continuous. In terms of the field presentation in Equations 5.8 through 5.10, these boundary conditions at the plane $z = 0$ can be written as

$$\left[\varepsilon_1\left(\mathbf{E}_0 + \mathbf{E}_1\right) - \varepsilon_2 \mathbf{E}_2\right] \cdot \mathbf{n} = 0$$

$$\left[\mathbf{k}_0 \times \mathbf{E}_0 + \mathbf{k}_1 \times \mathbf{E}_1 - \mathbf{k}_2 \times \mathbf{E}_2\right] \cdot \mathbf{n} = 0$$

$$\left[\mathbf{E}_0 + \mathbf{E}_1 - \mathbf{E}_2\right] \times \mathbf{n} = 0$$

$$\left[\frac{1}{\mu_1}\left(\mathbf{k}_0 \times \mathbf{E}_0 + \mathbf{k}_1 \times \mathbf{E}_1\right) - \frac{1}{\mu_2}\left(\mathbf{k}_2 \times \mathbf{E}_2\right)\right] \times \mathbf{n} = 0 \qquad (5.15)$$

Usually, in applying these boundary conditions for estimating the influence of the flat ground surface on wave propagation over terrain, it is convenient to consider two separate situations.

The *first* is when the vector of the wave's electric field component **E** is perpendicular to the plane of incidence (the plane defined by vectors **k** and **n**), but the vector of the wave's magnetic field component **H** lies in this plane.

The *second* is when the vector of the wave's electric field component **E** is parallel to the plane of incidence, but the vector of the wave's magnetic field component **H** is perpendicular to this plane.

In the literature that describes wave-propagation aspects, these are usually called the transverse electric (*TE*) wave and the transverse magnetic (*TM*) wave), or waves with *vertical* and *horizontal* polarization, respectively. We will present the reflection and refraction coefficients for the case of an incident plane wave with linear polarization.

For the real situation of wave propagation, it is usually permitted to put $\mu_1/\mu_2 = 1$. Introducing also the relative permittivity $\varepsilon_r = \varepsilon_2/\varepsilon_1$, we will obtain, by the expressions for the complex coefficients of reflection (R) and refraction (T) for waves with vertical (denoted by index V) and horizontal (denoted by index H) polarization, respectively,

For *vertical* polarization:

$$R_V = |R_V| e^{j\phi_V} = \frac{\varepsilon_r \cos\theta_0 - \sqrt{\varepsilon_r - \sin^2\theta_0}}{\varepsilon_r \cos\theta_0 + \sqrt{\varepsilon_r - \sin^2\theta_0}}$$

$$T_V = |T_V| e^{j\phi_V'} = \frac{2\sqrt{\varepsilon_r}\cos\theta_0}{\varepsilon_r \cos\theta_0 + \sqrt{\varepsilon_r - \sin^2\theta_0}} \qquad (5.16)$$

For *horizontal* polarization:

$$R_H = |R_H| e^{j\phi_H} = \frac{\cos\theta_0 - \sqrt{\varepsilon_r - \sin^2\theta_0}}{\cos\theta_0 + \sqrt{\varepsilon_r - \sin^2\theta_0}}$$

$$T_H = |T_H| e^{j\phi_H'} = \frac{2\cos\theta_0}{\cos\theta_0 + \sqrt{\varepsilon_r - \sin^2\theta_0}} \qquad (5.17)$$

where $|R_V|$, $|R_H|$, $|T_V|$, $|T_H|$ and $\phi_V, \phi_H, \phi'_V, \phi'_H$ are the modulus and phase of the coefficients of reflection and refraction for vertical and horizontal polarization, respectively.

It is very important to note that for normal incidence of a radio wave on a flat ground surface, there is no difference between vertical and horizontal wave polarization. In fact, for $\theta_0 = 0$, $\cos\theta_0 = 1$, $\sin\theta_0 = 0$, all these formulas reduce to

$$|\mathbf{E}_1| = |\mathbf{E}_0| \frac{\sqrt{\varepsilon_r} - 1}{\sqrt{\varepsilon_r} + 1}$$

$$|\mathbf{E}_2| = |\mathbf{E}_0| \frac{2}{\sqrt{\varepsilon_r} + 1} \tag{5.18}$$

$$R_V = R_H = \frac{\sqrt{\varepsilon_r} - 1}{\sqrt{\varepsilon_r} + 1}$$

$$T_V = T_H = \frac{2}{\sqrt{\varepsilon_r} + 1} \tag{5.19}$$

It should be noted that the results presented by Equations 5.16 through 5.19 are correct only for $\mu_{r1} = \mu_{r2} = 1$ [6]. Moreover, for the reflected wave $\mathbf{E}_1$, the sign convention is that for vertical polarization, Equation 5.19. This means that if $\varepsilon_2 > \varepsilon_1$, there is a phase reversal of the reflected wave. In the case of vertical polarization, there is a special angle of incidence, called the *Brewster angle*, for which there is no reflected wave. For simplicity, we will assume that the condition $\mu_1 = \mu_2$ is valid. Then, from Equation 5.16, it follows that the reflected wave $\mathbf{E}_1$ limits to zero when the angle of incidence is equal to Brewster's angle:

$$\theta_0 \equiv \theta_{Br} = \tan^{-1}\left(\frac{\varepsilon_2}{\varepsilon_1}\right) \tag{5.20}$$

Another interesting phenomenon that follows from the presented formulas is called *total reflection*. This takes place when the condition of $\varepsilon_2 \gg \varepsilon_1$ (or $n_2 \gg n_1$) is valid. In this case, from the second Snell's law (Equation 5.14), it follows that if $\varepsilon_2 \gg \varepsilon_1$, then $\theta_1 \gg \theta_0$. Consequently, when $\theta_0 \gg \theta_{kr}$, the reflection angle $\theta_1 = \pi/2$ where

$$\theta_{kr} = \sin^{-1}\left(\frac{\varepsilon_2}{\varepsilon_1}\right) \tag{5.21}$$

For waves incident at the surface (this case is realistic for ferroconcrete building wall surfaces) under the critical angle $\theta = \theta_{kr}$, there is no refracted wave within the second medium; the refracted wave is propagated along the boundary between the first and second media, and there is no energy flow across the boundary of these two media.

Before analyzing the reflection and refraction coefficients, we will show another form of their presentation, not only through the incident angle θ_0 but also through the angle of refraction

θ_2 (see Figure 5.2). These formulas are currently arranged and useful for many applied aspects of microwave engineering and electrodynamics (see [11,12] and the bibliography therein). Thus, following the presented approach and using our definitions, presented in Figure 5.2, we can rearrange Formulas 5.16 and 5.17 in the following form:

For *vertical* polarization:

$$R_V = |R_V| e^{j\phi_V} = \frac{\cos\theta_0 - \sqrt{\varepsilon_r}\,\cos\theta_2}{\cos\theta_0 + \sqrt{\varepsilon_r}\,\cos\theta_2}$$

$$T_V = |T_V| e^{j\phi_V'} = \frac{2\cos\theta_0}{\cos\theta_0 + \sqrt{\varepsilon_r}\,\cos\theta_2} \qquad (5.22)$$

For *horizontal* polarization:

$$R_H = |R_H| e^{j\phi_H} = \frac{\cos\theta_2 - \sqrt{\varepsilon_r}\,\cos\theta_0}{\cos\theta_2 + \sqrt{\varepsilon_r}\,\cos\theta_0}$$

$$T_H = |T_H| e^{j\phi_H'} = \frac{2\cos\theta_0}{\cos\theta_2 + \sqrt{\varepsilon_r}\,\cos\theta_0} \qquad (5.23)$$

Here, $\varepsilon_r = \varepsilon_2/\varepsilon_1$, and both angles are related via the second Snell's law (Equation 5.14). Again, all these formulas are valid for media where $\mu_r = 1$.

5.3 Properties of Reflection Coefficients for Waves with Arbitrary Polarization

The knowledge of reflection coefficient amplitude and phase variations is a very important factor in the prediction of propagation characteristics for different media. As follows from Equations 5.16 and 5.17, the amplitude and phase variations of the reflected wave from a flat surface depend on the reflection coefficient's amplitude and phase changes at the point of reflection, that is, on the intersection properties, and on the initial polarization of the incident wave. In practice, for wave propagation over flat terrain, the ground properties are determined by the conductivity and the absolute dielectric permittivity (dielectric constant) of the subsoil medium, $\varepsilon = \varepsilon_0\varepsilon_r$, where ε_0 is the dielectric constant of vacuum and ε_r is the relative permittivity of the ground surface [5]: $\varepsilon_r = \varepsilon_{Re} - j\varepsilon_{Im} = \varepsilon_{Re} - j60\omega\sigma$. Here, ε_{Re} and ε_{Im} are the real and imaginary parts of the relative permittivity of the subsoil medium, respectively. In practice, instead of the incident angle θ_0, the grazing angle $\alpha = (\pi/2) - \theta_0$ is used. Then, introducing α in Formulas 5.16 and 5.17 instead of θ_0 and accounting for the first Snell's law ($\theta_0 = \theta_0$ and $\alpha_0 = \alpha_1$) yields:

For horizontal polarization:

$$R_H = |R_H| e^{-j\phi_H} = \frac{\sin\alpha_1 - (\varepsilon_r - \cos^2\alpha_1)^{1/2}}{\sin\alpha_1 + (\varepsilon_r - \cos^2\alpha_1)^{1/2}} \qquad (5.24)$$

For vertical polarization:

$$R_V = |R_V| e^{-j\phi_V} = \frac{\varepsilon_r \sin\alpha_1 - (\varepsilon_r - \cos^2\alpha_1)^{1/2}}{\varepsilon_r \sin\alpha_1 + (\varepsilon_r - \cos^2\alpha_1)^{1/2}} \qquad (5.25)$$

Because both the coefficients presented by Equations 5.24 and 5.25 are the complex values, the reflected wave will differ in both magnitude and phase from the incident wave. Moreover, the coefficients differ from each other. In fact, for horizontal polarization, for $\varepsilon_c \rightarrow \infty, \sigma \rightarrow \infty$ (i.e., for a very conductive ground surface), the relative phase of the incident and reflected waves is nearly 180° for all angles of incidence. On the other hand, for very small grazing angles, as follows from Equation 5.24, the reflected and incident waves are equal in magnitude but differ by 180° in phase for all ground permittivities and conductivities. In other words, $R_V = -1, (\alpha \ll (\pi/2))$.

Moreover, with increasing angle α, the magnitude and phase of the reflected wave change, but only by a relatively small amount. With a decrease in conductivity of the ground surface and with an increase of frequency $f = c/\lambda$ of wave radiation, the changes of R_H and ϕ_H become greater. In the case of a real conductive ground surface ($\varepsilon_c \rightarrow \infty, \sigma \rightarrow \infty$) for small grazing angles ($\alpha \approx 0°$), the reflection coefficient for a wave with vertical polarization does not change its properties with respect to that for horizontal polarization, as follows from Equation 5.25: that is, for $\alpha \approx 0 \ll (\pi/2)$, $R_V = -1, (\alpha \ll (\pi/2))$. At the same time, for $\varepsilon_c \rightarrow \infty, \sigma \rightarrow \infty$ and for $0 < \alpha < 180°$, $R_V = 1$.

However, with increasing angle α, substantial differences appear: a rapid decrease in both magnitude and phase of the reflected wave takes place. For $\alpha \rightarrow 90°(\theta_{Br} \rightarrow 0)$, where θ_{Br} is the Brewster angle (defined by Equation 5.20), the magnitude $|R_V|$ becomes a minimum, and the phase ϕ_V reaches −90°. At values of α greater than the Brewster angle, $|R_V|$ increases again, and the phase ϕ_V tends toward zero, that is, $R_V \rightarrow 1$. In Table 5.1, typical values of ground permittivity and conductivity are presented that explain the reflection of a plane wave from the ground surface, which is very relevant for ground subsurface radar systems (see Chapter 14).

It can be seen that the conductivity of flat, perfectly conductive ground is higher than that of higher-impedance ground, found in hilly terrain, while the relative permittivity can range from 4 to 30, with a typical average value of 15.

Table 5.1 Conductivity and Permittivity of Some Practically Important Media

Surface	Conductivity, σ (Siemens)	Relative Permittivity, ε_r
Dry ground	10^{-3}	4–7
Average ground	5×10^{-3}	15
Wet ground	2×10^{-2}	25–30
Sea water	5	81
Fresh water	10^{-3}	81

PROBLEMS

Example 5.1: Accounting for the case when in each medium separated by a boundary, the corresponding permeability does not equal unity, that is, $\mu_{r1} \neq \mu_{r2} \neq 1$, and the corresponding permittivity also does not equal unity, that is, $\varepsilon_{r1} \neq \varepsilon_{r2} \neq 1$, present Equations 5.16 and 5.17 in a more general case.

Example 5.2: A plane wave incidents normally at the boundary of two materials with the relative parameters $\varepsilon_{r1} = 1, \varepsilon_{r2} = 5$ and $\mu_{r1} = \mu_{r2} = 1$. The amplitude of the electric component of the incident wave field is $E_1 = 5 \ (V/m)$.

Find: The reflected and refracted coefficients and the amplitudes of the corresponding reflected and transmitted wave.

Example 5.3: A plane wave incidents normally at the boundary of two materials with the relative parameters $\varepsilon_{r1} = 1, \varepsilon_{r2} = 3$ and $\mu_{r1} = \mu_{r2} = 1$. The amplitude of the electric component of the incident wave field is $E_1 = 3 (V/m)$.

Find: The reflected and refracted coefficients, the amplitudes of the corresponding reflected and transmitted wave, and the reflected and transmitted powers.

Example 5.4: An electromagnetic wave with an amplitude of 1 V/m normally incidents from a dielectric having parameters $\varepsilon_1 = 4\varepsilon_0$ and $\mu_1 = \mu_0$ into air with parameters $\varepsilon_1 = \varepsilon_0$ and $\mu_1 = \mu_0$.

Find: The amplitude of the reflected and the transmitted fields and the incident, reflected, and transmitted power.

Example 5.5: An EM wave with vertical polarization incidents under the angle of $\theta_0 = 60°$ at the boundary separating two media (air and the dielectric) with parameters $\varepsilon_{r1} = 1, \mu_{r1} = 1$, and $\varepsilon_{r2} = 8, \mu_{r2} = 1$, respectively.

Find: The Brewster angle of full refraction of the wave and the critical angle of full reflection from the boundary. Find these angles if, conversely, the wave penetrates into the air from the dielectric material at the same angle of incidence, $\theta_0 = 60°$.

Example 5.6: Given two media, air with the parameters $\varepsilon_1 = \varepsilon_0, \mu_1 = \mu_0, \eta_1 = \eta_0$ and glass with the parameters $\varepsilon_2 = 5\varepsilon_0, \mu_2 = \mu_0, \eta_2 = 150\Omega$. For both media, conductivities $\sigma_1 = \sigma_2 = 0$. A plane one-dimensional (1-D) wave with horizontal polarization, having the form $\mathbf{E}_{0x} = 10\exp\{j(10^8 \pi \cdot t - \beta_0 \cdot z)\}\mathbf{u}_x$ V/m, normally incidents at the boundary of two media.

Find: The parameter of wave propagation in the second medium β, the coefficients of reflection and refraction, and the amplitude of the reflected and the transmitted field from air to glass.

Example 5.7: Given the same parameters and conditions as in Example 5.7.

Find: The electric and magnetic components of the reflected and transmitted waves in time-harmonic form in the time domain.

Example 5.8: A vertical polarized plane wave with the amplitude $|\mathbf{E}_0| = 50$ V/m and the zeros initial phase incidents normally to the boundary of two media: air $(\varepsilon_1 = \varepsilon_0, \mu_1 = \mu_0, \eta_1 = \eta_0)$ and water $(\varepsilon_2 = 81\varepsilon_0, \mu_2 = \mu_0, \eta_2 \approx 42\Omega)$.

Find: The electric and magnetic components of the reflected and transmitted waves via the corresponding coefficients of reflection and refraction, respectively.

Example 5.9: A plane wave with horizontal polarization incidents normally at the boundary between air $(\varepsilon_1 = \varepsilon_0, \mu_1 = \mu_0, \sigma_1 = 0)$ and the dielectric $(\varepsilon_2 = 81\varepsilon_0, \mu_2 = \mu_0, \sigma_2 = 0)$. The field is given by the expression $\mathbf{E}_0(x, z) = [4\mathbf{u}_x - 3\mathbf{u}_z]\exp\{-j(6x + 8z)\}$ V/m.

Find: The frequency and the wavelength of this wave in the dielectric; the coefficient of reflection and the corresponding expression of the reflected field; the coefficient of refraction and the corresponding expression of the transmitted field.

Example 5.10: A plane wave with vertical polarization incidents under angle θ_0 at the boundary between air $(\varepsilon_1 = \varepsilon_0, \mu_1 = \mu_0)$ and the dielectric $(\varepsilon_2 = 6\varepsilon_0, \mu_2 = \mu_0)$. The wave is presented in the form $\mathbf{E}_0(x,z) = 5[\cos\theta_0 \mathbf{u}_x - \sin\theta_0 \mathbf{u}_y]$ V/m. The wavelength in air $\lambda_1 = 3$ cm.
Find: The angle of Brewster and the critical angle; the field expression after reflection, accounting for the incident angle that equals the Brewster angle; the field expression for the transmitted wave, accounting for the incident angle that equals the Brewster angle.

Example 5.11: A plane wave with the electric field component presented in the form $\mathbf{E}_0(x,z,t) = |\mathbf{E}_0| [(\sqrt{3}/2)\mathbf{u}_x - (1/2)\mathbf{u}_y]\cos(6\pi \cdot 10^9 t - 10\pi(x + \sqrt{3}z))$ V/m incidents at the boundary separating air $(\varepsilon_1 = \varepsilon_1, \mu_1 = \mu_0)$ and the dielectric $(\varepsilon_2 = 5\varepsilon_0, \mu_2 = \mu_0)$.
Find: The frequency and the wavelength in air and in the dielectric; the intrinsic impedance of the dielectric; the angles of incidence and refraction; the reflected and the transmitted waves, where the corresponding coefficients of reflection and refraction are shown in Equations 5.22 and 5.23 via the angle of refraction.

References

1. Stratton, J. A., *Electromagnetic Theory*, New York: McGraw-Hill, 1953.
2. Morse, P. M. and H. Feshbach, *Methods of Theoretical Physics*, New York: McGraw-Hill, 1953.
3. Alpert, Ya. L., V. L. Ginzburg, and E. L. Feinberg, *Radiowave Propagation,* Moscow: State House of Publication of Technical and Scientific Literature, 1953 (in Russian).
4. Plonsey, R. and R. E. Collin, *Principles and Applications of Electromagnetic Fields*, New York: McGraw-Hill, 1961.
5. Jackson, J. D., *Classical Electrodynamics*, New York: Wiley, 1962.
6. Stakgold, I., *Boundary Value Problems of Mathematical Physics*, vol. 1, London: Macmillan, 1967.
7. Felsen, L. and N. Marcuvitz, *Radiation and Scattering of Waves*, Upper Saddle River, NJ: Prentice Hall, 1973.
8. Kong, J. A., *Theory of Electromagnetic Waves*, New York: Wiley, 1986.
9. Chew, W. C., *Waves Propagation in Inhomogeneous Media*, Englewood Cliffs, NJ: IEEE, 1995.
10. Rajeev, B., Ed., *Handbook: Engineering Electromagnetic Applications*, Boca Raton, FL: CRC Taylor & Francis, 2006.
11. Pozar, D. M., *Microwave Engineering*, 4th edn, New York: Wiley, 2012.
12. Iskander, M. F., *Electromagnetic Fields and Waves*, 2nd edn, Long Grove, IL: Waveland, 2013.

GUIDING STRUCTURES AND GUIDING WAVES

Chapter 6

Types of Guiding Structures and Guiding Waves

6.1 Types of Guiding Structures

In this chapter, we consider only frequently used guiding structures (Figure 6.1a–d):

1. Two-wire lines and coaxial cables with the same guiding properties
2. Rectangular waveguides
3. Circular waveguides

All these structures are used to guide electromagnetic waves. Despite the fact that these structures are physically different, they share a common property, which simplifies analysis of their behavior (see Chapters 7 through 9). For each structure, every transverse cross section is the same.

Coaxial cable contains an inner wire conductor and an outer conductor. In most types of coaxial cables, the region between the two conductors is completely filled with a solid, but flexible, dielectric. Rectangular and circular waveguides, as well as optical fibers, do not contain dielectric.

All kinds of guiding structures have a common feature: they transfer power from one place to another without radiation. We consider the relationship between these main guiding structures, focusing on the description of electromagnetic phenomena, as well as on dielectric and ohmic losses inside them during electromagnetic wave propagation.

6.2 Types of Guiding Waves Propagating in Guiding Structures

As was shown in Chapter 4, each electromagnetic field component that propagates along a guiding structure can be expressed formally as

$$f(x, y, z) = f(x, y) \exp\{j(\omega t \mp \gamma z)\} \qquad (6.1)$$

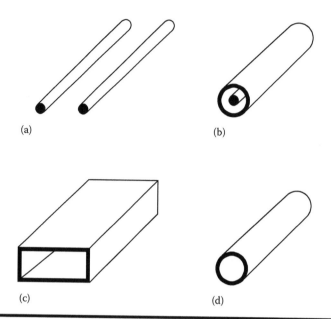

Figure 6.1   Types of guiding structures: (a) open two-wire line; (b) coaxial cable; (c) rectangular waveguide; (d) circular waveguide.

where:

x and y are the transverse coordinates

z, the coordinate along the guiding structure, is the propagation parameter along the z-axis

γ is the propagation parameter which, as was shown in Chapter 4, is complex and equals

$$\gamma = \alpha + j\beta \tag{6.2}$$

Its real part α accounts for attenuation due to ohmic and/or dielectric losses; its imaginary part β accounts for the phase velocity, since

$$\exp\left\{ j\left(\omega t \mp \gamma z\right)\right\}$$

and it describes an equivalent phase function when

$$\omega t \mp \gamma z = \text{const} \tag{6.3}$$

from which we get

$$v_{ph} = \frac{dz}{dt} = \mp \frac{\omega}{\beta} \tag{6.4}$$

Here, the minus sign denotes that propagation is in the positive z-direction; the plus sign corresponds to propagation in the negative z-direction. In Chapter 4, we presented wave equations in dielectric and conductive materials. Now, let us summarize these equations for guiding structures using the field phasor presentation in the frequency domain (see Chapter 3).

For propagation in the positive z-axis direction along unit vector $\mathbf{z}$ [1–4],

$$\mathbf{E}(x,y,z) = \left[\mathbf{E}_\perp(x,y) + \mathbf{E}_z(x,y)\right]e^{-\gamma z}$$

$$\mathbf{H}(x,y,z) = \left[\mathbf{H}_\perp(x,y) + \mathbf{H}_z(x,y)\right]e^{-\gamma z} \qquad (6.5a)$$

$$\nabla_\perp \times \mathbf{E}_\perp = -j\omega\mu\mathbf{H}_z$$

$$\nabla_\perp \times \mathbf{H}_\perp = j\omega\varepsilon\mathbf{E}_z \qquad (6.5b)$$

$$\nabla_\perp \cdot \mathbf{E}_\perp = \gamma\mathbf{E}_z$$

$$\nabla_\perp \cdot \mathbf{H}_\perp = \gamma\mathbf{H}_z \qquad (6.5c)$$

$$\mathbf{z} \times \left[\nabla_\perp \times \mathbf{E}_z + \gamma\mathbf{E}_\perp\right] = j\omega\mu\mathbf{H}_\perp$$

$$\mathbf{z} \times \left[\nabla_\perp \times \mathbf{H}_z + \gamma\mathbf{H}_\perp\right] = -j\omega\varepsilon\mathbf{E}_\perp \qquad (6.5d)$$

For propagation in the negative z-axis direction along unit vector $\mathbf{z}$,

$$\mathbf{E}(x,y,z) = \left[\mathbf{E}_\perp(x,y) + \mathbf{E}_z(x,y)\right]e^{\gamma z}$$

$$\mathbf{H}(x,y,z) = \left[\mathbf{H}_\perp(x,y) + \mathbf{H}_z(x,y)\right]e^{\gamma z} \qquad (6.6a)$$

$$\nabla_\perp \times \mathbf{E}_\perp = -j\omega\mu\mathbf{H}_z$$

$$\nabla_\perp \times \mathbf{H}_\perp = j\omega\varepsilon\mathbf{E}_z \qquad (6.6b)$$

$$\nabla_\perp \cdot \mathbf{E}_\perp = -\gamma\mathbf{E}_z$$

$$\nabla_\perp \cdot \mathbf{H}_\perp = -\gamma\mathbf{H}_z \qquad (6.6c)$$

$$\mathbf{z} \times \left[\nabla_\perp \times \mathbf{E}_z - \gamma\mathbf{E}_\perp\right] = j\omega\mu\mathbf{H}_\perp$$

$$\mathbf{z} \times \left[\nabla_\perp \times \mathbf{H}_z - \gamma\mathbf{H}_\perp\right] = -j\omega\varepsilon\mathbf{E}_\perp \qquad (6.6d)$$

Here, $\nabla_\perp$ is the transverse *del* in plane (x,y); the same is true for the field components denoted by the $\perp$ sign.

6.2.1 Transverse Electromagnetic (TEM) Waves in Guiding Structures

All guiding structures have a common feature: they guide only transverse waves inside the air or dielectric region between the conductor walls, that is, waves for which the components along the z-axis equal zero, $\mathbf{E}_z = \mathbf{H}_z \equiv 0$. In this case, Maxwell's Equations 6.5 and 6.6 reduce to [1–4]

$$\nabla_\perp \times \mathbf{E}_\perp = 0, \nabla_\perp \cdot \mathbf{E}_\perp = 0$$

$$\nabla_\perp \times \mathbf{H}_\perp = 0, \nabla_\perp \cdot \mathbf{H}_\perp = 0 \qquad (6.7a)$$

$$\gamma \mathbf{z} \times \mathbf{E}_\perp = \pm j\omega\mu\mathbf{H}_\perp; \quad \gamma \mathbf{z} \times \mathbf{H}_\perp = \pm j\omega\mu\mathbf{E}_\perp \qquad (6.7b)$$

Such waves are defined in literature (see [1–5]) as TEM waves. Since $\nabla_\perp \times \mathbf{E}_\perp(x,y) = 0$, we have an electrostatic problem and can introduce the electrostatic potential (see Chapter 1) $\Phi(x,y)$ as

$$\mathbf{E}_\perp(x,y) = -\nabla_\perp\Phi(x,y) \qquad (6.8)$$

Finally, from Equation 6.8 (if we consider this case of propagation along the positive z-axis), we have

$$\mathbf{E}_\perp(x,y,z) = \mathbf{E}_\perp(x,y)e^{-\gamma z} = -\nabla_\perp\Phi(x,y)e^{-\gamma z} \qquad (6.9)$$

Then, it satisfies Laplace's equation:

$$\nabla_\perp \cdot \mathbf{E}_\perp(x,y) = \nabla_\perp^2\Phi(x,y) = 0 \qquad (6.10)$$

If so, the well-known wave equation (see Chapter 4)

$$\nabla_\perp^2\mathbf{E}_\perp + (k^2 + \gamma^2)\mathbf{E}_\perp = 0 \qquad (6.11)$$

can be rewritten as

$$(\nabla_\perp^2 + k^2 + \gamma^2)\nabla_\perp\Phi e^{-\gamma z} = 0 \qquad (6.12)$$

We can suppress the factor $e^{-\gamma z}$, because it cannot be equal to zero. Moreover, because of Equation 6.10, we finally have

$$(k^2 + \gamma^2)\nabla_\perp\Phi = 0 \qquad (6.13)$$

Since $\nabla_\perp\Phi = -\mathbf{E}_\perp$ is not zero, this means that

$$\gamma = jk \qquad (6.14)$$

But, for lossless dielectric, k is pure real and can be given by ($\mu \equiv \mu_0$)

$$k = \omega\sqrt{\mu_0\varepsilon} = \omega\sqrt{\mu_0\varepsilon_0}\sqrt{\varepsilon_r} \equiv \sqrt{\varepsilon_r}\frac{\omega}{c} \qquad (6.15)$$

So, for the case of TEM waves propagating inside a lossless guiding structure, it follows that

$$\alpha = 0, \beta \equiv k = \sqrt{\varepsilon_r}\frac{\omega}{c} = \sqrt{\varepsilon_r}\frac{2\pi f}{c} = \sqrt{\varepsilon_r}\frac{2\pi}{\lambda_0} = \sqrt{\varepsilon_r}k_0 \qquad (6.16a)$$

and

$$v_{\text{ph}} = \pm \frac{\omega}{\beta} = \pm \frac{c}{\sqrt{\varepsilon_r}} \tag{6.16b}$$

$$\lambda = \frac{2\pi}{\beta} = \frac{2\pi\lambda_0}{2\pi\sqrt{\varepsilon_r}} = \frac{\lambda_0}{\sqrt{\varepsilon_r}} \tag{6.16c}$$

We now define the impedance of the guiding structure by introducing the symbol Z_{TEM}:

$$Z_{\text{TEM}} = \frac{\omega\mu}{k} = \frac{\omega\mu_0}{\omega\sqrt{\mu_0\varepsilon}} = \sqrt{\frac{\mu_0}{\varepsilon}} = \frac{\sqrt{\mu_0/\varepsilon_0}}{\sqrt{\varepsilon/\varepsilon_0}} \equiv \frac{\eta_0}{\sqrt{\varepsilon_r}} \tag{6.17}$$

where $\eta_0 = \sqrt{\mu_0/\varepsilon_0} = 377\ \Omega$ is the impedance of free space.

Because, as follows from Equation 6.8 and Maxwell's equations

$$\mathbf{E}_{\perp}(x,y,z,t) = -\nabla_{\perp}\Phi(x,y)\exp\left\{j(\omega t \mp kz)\right\}$$

$$\mathbf{H}_{\perp}(x,y,z,t) = \mathbf{H}_z(x,y)\exp\left\{j(\omega t \mp kz)\right\}$$

$$= \pm\frac{k}{\omega\mu}\mathbf{z}\times\mathbf{E}_{\perp}(x,y)\exp\left\{j(\omega t \mp kz)\right\} \tag{6.18}$$

we have that

$$\frac{E_x}{H_y} = -\frac{E_y}{H_x} \equiv Z_{\text{TEM}} \tag{6.19a}$$

In the same manner, one can obtain the impedance for wave propagation in the negative direction along the z-axis:

$$-\frac{E_x}{H_y} = \frac{E_y}{H_x} \equiv Z_{\text{TEM}} \tag{6.19b}$$

Then,

$$\mathbf{H}_{\perp} = \pm\frac{\mathbf{z}\times\mathbf{E}_{\perp}}{Z_{\text{TEM}}} \tag{6.20}$$

Now, we will return to transverse electric (TE) (vertical polarization) and transverse magnetic (TM) (horizontal polarization) waves, introduced in Chapter 4.

6.2.2 TE and TM Waves in Guiding Structures

Lossless guiding structures can support both TE waves (i.e., when $\mathbf{E}$ is transverse to the plane of wave propagation, but $\mathbf{H}$ lies in this plane, that is, $\mathbf{E}_z = 0$, but $\mathbf{H}_z \neq 0$) and TM waves (when, conversely, $\mathbf{E}_z \neq 0$, but $\mathbf{H}_z = 0$, that is, transverse to the plane of wave propagation).

A. Let us consider TE-wave propagation in the positive direction along the z-axis. In this case, Equations 6.5 reduce to [1–4]

$$\mathbf{E}(x,y,z) = \mathbf{E}_\perp(x,y)e^{-\gamma z}$$

$$\mathbf{H}(x,y,z) = \left[\mathbf{H}_\perp(x,y) + \mathbf{H}_z(x,y)\right]e^{-\gamma z} \tag{6.21a}$$

$$\nabla_\perp \times \mathbf{E}_\perp = -j\omega\mu\mathbf{H}_z$$

$$\nabla_\perp \times \mathbf{H}_\perp = 0 \tag{6.21b}$$

$$\nabla_\perp \cdot \mathbf{E}_\perp = 0$$

$$\nabla_\perp \cdot \mathbf{H}_\perp = \gamma\mathbf{H}_z \tag{6.21c}$$

$$\mathbf{z} \times \gamma\mathbf{E}_\perp = j\omega\mu\mathbf{H}_\perp$$

$$\mathbf{z} \times \left[\nabla_\perp \times \mathbf{H}_z + \gamma\mathbf{H}_\perp\right] = -j\omega\varepsilon\mathbf{E}_\perp \tag{6.21d}$$

In this case, we deal with the magnetic field and find

$$(\nabla_\perp^2 + \gamma^2 + k^2)[\mathbf{H}_\perp(x,y) + \mathbf{H}_z(x,y)]e^{-\gamma z} = 0 \tag{6.22}$$

Because

$$\nabla_\perp^2\mathbf{H}_\perp(x,y,z) = 0 \tag{6.23}$$

we have

$$(\nabla_\perp^2 + \kappa^2)\mathbf{H}_z(x,y) = 0 \tag{6.24}$$

where

$$\kappa^2 = \gamma^2 + k^2 \tag{6.25}$$

is the propagation parameter in the (x,y)-plane. Now, combining Equations 6.22 and 6.5c, we finally have

$$\nabla_\perp(\gamma\mathbf{H}_z) + \kappa^2\mathbf{H}_\perp = 0 \tag{6.26}$$

from which

$$\mathbf{H}_\perp(x,y) = -\frac{\gamma}{\kappa^2}\nabla_\perp\mathbf{H}_z \tag{6.27}$$

If so, from Equations 6.21d and 6.27, it follows that

$$\mathbf{E}_\perp(x,y) = -\frac{j\omega\mu}{\gamma}\mathbf{z}\times\mathbf{H}_\perp(x,y) = \frac{j\omega\mu}{\kappa^2}\mathbf{z}\times\nabla_\perp\mathbf{H}_z(x,y) \tag{6.28}$$

Then, from Equations 6.27 and 6.28, we can find the TE-field characteristic impedance:

$$Z_{TE} = \frac{|\mathbf{E}_\perp|}{|\mathbf{H}_\perp|} = \frac{j\omega\mu}{\gamma} \tag{6.29}$$

So,

$$\mathbf{H}_\perp(x,y) = \frac{\mathbf{z}\times\mathbf{E}_\perp(x,y)}{Z_{TE}} \tag{6.30}$$

So, for propagation in the positive z-direction,

$$-\frac{E_y}{H_x} = Z_{TE}, \frac{E_x}{H_y} = Z_{TE} \tag{6.31a}$$

In the same manner, for propagation in the negative z-direction, we get

$$\frac{E_y}{H_x} = Z_{TE}, -\frac{E_x}{H_y} = Z_{TE} \tag{6.31b}$$

B. For TM-wave propagation along the z-axis, $\mathbf{E}_z \neq 0$, but $\mathbf{H}_z = 0$, we have Equation 6.5 for the positive z-direction correspondingly [1–4]:

$$\mathbf{E}(x,y,z) = \left[\mathbf{E}_\perp(x,y) + \mathbf{E}_z(x,y)\right]e^{-\gamma z}$$
$$\mathbf{H}(x,y,z) = \mathbf{H}_\perp(x,y)e^{-\gamma z} \tag{6.32a}$$

$$\nabla_\perp \times \mathbf{E}_\perp = 0$$
$$\nabla_\perp \times \mathbf{H}_\perp = j\omega\varepsilon\mathbf{E}_z \tag{6.32b}$$

$$\nabla_\perp \cdot \mathbf{E}_\perp = \gamma\mathbf{E}_z$$
$$\nabla_\perp \cdot \mathbf{H}_\perp = 0 \tag{6.32c}$$

$$\mathbf{z}\times\left[\nabla_\perp \times \mathbf{E}_z + \gamma\mathbf{E}_\perp\right] = j\omega\mu\mathbf{H}_\perp$$
$$\mathbf{z}\times\gamma\mathbf{H}_\perp = -j\omega\varepsilon\mathbf{E}_\perp \tag{6.32d}$$

In this case, we deal with the electric field and find

$$(\nabla_\perp^2 + \gamma^2 + k^2)[\mathbf{E}_\perp(x,y) + \mathbf{E}_z(x,y)]e^{-\gamma z} = 0 \tag{6.33}$$

for which the longitudinal component is described by the equation

$$(\nabla_\perp^2 + \kappa^2)\mathbf{E}_z(x,y) = 0 \tag{6.34}$$

where, as above,

$$\kappa^2 = \gamma^2 + k^2 \tag{6.35}$$

is the propagation parameter in the (x,y)-plane. Using Equation 6.32b and the well-known relation (see Chapter 1)

$$\nabla_\perp \times \nabla_\perp \times \mathbf{E}_\perp = \nabla_\perp(\nabla_\perp \cdot \mathbf{E}_\perp) - \nabla_\perp^2 \mathbf{E}_\perp$$

we can write

$$\nabla_\perp(\gamma \mathbf{E}_z) + \kappa^2 \mathbf{E}_\perp = 0 \tag{6.36}$$

from which

$$\mathbf{E}_\perp(x,y) = -\frac{\gamma}{\kappa^2}\nabla_\perp \mathbf{E}_z \tag{6.37}$$

If so, from Equations 6.32d and 6.37, it follows that

$$\mathbf{H}_\perp(x,y) = \frac{j\omega\varepsilon}{\gamma}\mathbf{z} \times \mathbf{E}_\perp(x,y) = -\frac{j\omega\varepsilon}{\kappa^2}\mathbf{z} \times \nabla_\perp \mathbf{E}_z(x,y) \tag{6.38}$$

Then, from Equations 6.37 and 6.38, we can find the TM-field characteristic impedance:

$$Z_{TM} = \frac{|\mathbf{E}_\perp|}{|\mathbf{H}_\perp|} = \frac{\gamma}{j\omega\varepsilon} \tag{6.39}$$

So,

$$\mathbf{E}_\perp(x,y) = -Z_{TM}[\mathbf{z} \times \mathbf{H}_\perp(x,y)] \tag{6.40}$$

For propagation in the positive z-direction,

$$\frac{E_y}{H_x} = -Z_{TM}, \quad \frac{E_x}{H_y} = Z_{TM} \tag{6.41a}$$

In the same manner, for propagation in the negative z-direction, we get

$$\frac{E_y}{H_x} = Z_{TM}, \frac{E_x}{H_y} = -Z_{TM} \tag{6.41b}$$

We must note that for low-loss conditions, we need only to multiply the formulas obtained for lossless conditions by $\exp(-2\alpha z)$.

References

1. Jackson, J. D., *Classical Electrodynamics*, New York: Wiley, 1962.
2. Chew, W. C., *Waves and Fields in Inhomogeneous Media*, New York: IEEE, 1995.
3. Elliott, R. S., *Electromagnetics: History, Theory, and Applications*, New York: IEEE, 1993.
4. Kong, J. A., *Electromagnetic Wave Theory*, New York: Wiley, 1986.
5. Dudley, D. G., *Mathematical Foundations for Electromagnetic Theory*, New York: IEEE, 1994.

Chapter 7

Transmission Lines

Transmission lines exhibit different characteristics for different sources and wavelengths. This means that if the dimensions of an electric circuit are much smaller than the wavelength the circuit is called a distributed electromagnetic circuit and not a lumped element or a collection of lumped elements. Transmission lines, coaxial cables and waveguides are distributed electromagnetic circuits [1–9].

7.1 Infinite-Length Transmission Line

Generally, a transmission line is schematically represented as a two-wire line, since a transmission line always has at least two conductors, as shown in Figure 7.1. The view of a two-wire transmission line (see Figure 7.1) as a two-conductor line and its electrical schemes (Figure 7.2a and b) are presented in this section by giving an account of the normalized inductance $\hat{L}$ and the normalized capacitance $\hat{C}$ in an electrical circuit, ranged by a limit segment of Δz.

A radio antenna, transmitting or receiving, is an independent compound structure of radio systems, both for communication and for radar, which converts the current or voltage generated by a wire-based circuit, such as a transmission line, a waveguide, or coaxial cable, into electromagnetic field energy propagating through space.

We use here Kirchhoff's laws for the distributed transmission line and its equivalent electrical circuit (see Figure 7.2). The normalized inductance $\hat{L} = L/\Delta z$ (in henrys per meter) and capacitance $\hat{C} = C/\Delta z$ (in farads per meter) are presented in Figure 7.3.

From Kirchhoff's current law,

$$I(z,t) = \hat{C}\Delta z \frac{\partial V(z,t)}{\partial t} + I(z+\Delta z,t)$$

or

$$\frac{I(z+\Delta z,t) - I(z,t)}{\Delta z} = -\hat{C}\frac{\partial V(z,t)}{\partial t}$$

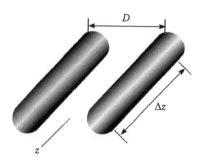

Figure 7.1 View of two-wire transmission line.

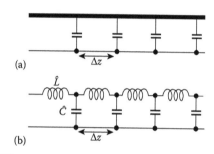

Figure 7.2 Electrical circuits showing (a) normalized capacitances $\hat{C}$ and (b) normalized inductances $\hat{L}$.

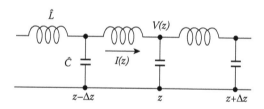

Figure 7.3 Electric circuit of the segment showing normalized inductances and capacitances.

For $\Delta z \to 0$, we obtain

$$\frac{\partial I(z,t)}{\partial z} = -\hat{C}\frac{\partial V(z,t)}{\partial t}$$

(7.1)

From Kirchhoff's voltage law,

$$V(z-\Delta z,t) = \hat{L}\Delta z\frac{\partial I(z,t)}{\partial t} + V(z,t)$$

or

$$\frac{V(z,t)-V(z-\Delta z,t)}{\Delta z} = -\hat{L}\frac{\partial I(z,t)}{\partial t}$$

For $\Delta z \to 0$, we get

$$\frac{\partial V(z,t)}{\partial z} = -\hat{L}\frac{\partial I(z,t)}{\partial t} \tag{7.2}$$

If we now differentiate Equation 7.1 on t, and account for Equation 7.2, we obtain

$$\frac{\partial^2 V(z,t)}{\partial z^2} - \hat{L}\hat{C}\frac{\partial^2 V(z,t)}{\partial t^2} = 0 \tag{7.3}$$

If we now differentiate Equation 7.2 on t, and account for Equation 7.1, we obtain

$$\frac{\partial^2 I(z,t)}{\partial z^2} - \hat{L}\hat{C}\frac{\partial^2 I(z,t)}{\partial t^2} = 0 \tag{7.4}$$

We found that in the transmission line, the current and the voltage can be presented by the well-known wave equations describing propagation with the velocity:

$$v = \frac{1}{\sqrt{\hat{L}\hat{C}}} \tag{7.5}$$

Such waves can be presented via their phasors, $I(z)$ and $V(z)$, as

$$V(z,t) = \mathrm{Re}\{V(z)e^{j\omega t}\}$$

$$I(z,t) = \mathrm{Re}\{I(z)e^{j\omega t}\}$$

If so, Equations 7.3 and 7.4 can be rewritten for the phasors:

$$\frac{\partial^2 V(z)}{\partial z^2} + \omega^2 \hat{L}\hat{C} \cdot V(z) = 0 \tag{7.6a}$$

$$\frac{\partial^2 I(z)}{\partial z^2} + \omega^2 \hat{L}\hat{C} \cdot I(z) = 0 \tag{7.6b}$$

Comparing these two equations with the classical equations described in Chapter 3, that is, with

$$\frac{\partial^2 V(z)}{\partial z^2} + k^2 V(z) = 0 \tag{7.7a}$$

$$\frac{\partial^2 I(z)}{\partial z^2} + k^2 I(z) = 0 \tag{7.7b}$$

we obtain that $k = 2\pi f \sqrt{\hat{L}\hat{C}} = 2\pi/\lambda = \omega/v$, which also proves the relation (Equation 7.5) between the wave velocity and electrical parameters of the transmission line.

Now, solutions of Equation 7.7a can be written as

$$V(z,t) = A_1 \cos kz + B_1 \sin kz$$

or as

$$V(z,t) = A_1 e^{-jkz} + B_1 e^{jkz}$$

Similar equations can be obtained also for the phasor for the current $I(z)$.

Following [10–19], we can find the inductance and capacitance of an infinite transmission line:

$$\hat{L} = \frac{\mu_r \mu_0}{\pi} \cosh^{-1}\left(\frac{D}{2a}\right) \tag{7.8a}$$

$$\hat{C} = \frac{\pi \varepsilon_r \varepsilon_0}{\cosh^{-1}\left(\dfrac{D}{2a}\right)} \tag{7.8b}$$

and the characteristic impedance of the transmission line:

$$Z_c = \frac{V(z)}{I(z)} \tag{7.9}$$

If we now take $V(z) = V_0 e^{-jkz}$, then

$$\frac{dV(z)}{dz} = -jkV(z) = -j\omega\hat{L}I(z)$$

and

$$I(z) = \frac{k}{\omega\hat{L}}V(z)$$

If so, from Equation 7.9, we get

$$Z_c = \frac{\omega\hat{L}}{k} = \frac{\omega\hat{L}}{\omega/v} = v\hat{L} = \frac{\hat{L}}{\sqrt{\hat{L}\hat{C}}} = \sqrt{\frac{\hat{L}}{\hat{C}}} \; (\Omega) \tag{7.10}$$

Introducing Equations 7.8a and 7.8b in Equation 7.10, we get

$$Z_c = \sqrt{\frac{\dfrac{\mu_r\mu_0}{\pi}\cosh^{-1}\left(\dfrac{D}{2a}\right)}{\dfrac{\pi\varepsilon_r\varepsilon_0}{\cosh^{-1}\left(\dfrac{D}{2a}\right)}}} = \sqrt{\frac{\mu_r\mu_0}{\varepsilon_r\varepsilon_0}}\frac{\cosh^{-1}\left(\dfrac{D}{2a}\right)}{\pi} \qquad (7.11)$$

7.2 Finite-Length Transmission Line

The phazor voltage and the current for any point on the finite line can be presented in the following form [1–9]:

$$V(z) = A_2 e^{-jkz} + B_2 e^{jkz} \qquad (7.12a)$$

$$I(z) = \frac{1}{Z_c}\left(A_2 e^{-jkz} - B_2 e^{jkz}\right) \qquad (7.12b)$$

If loading resistance is at the point $z = 0$, then its impedance is (see Figure 7.4)

$$Z_L = \frac{V(z=0)}{I(z=0)} = Z_c\frac{A_2 + B_2}{A_2 - B_2}$$

The reflection coefficient is

$$R = \frac{B_2}{A_2} = \frac{Z_L - Z_c}{Z_L + Z_c} \qquad (7.13a)$$

Sometimes, instead of a reflection coefficient, the transmission coefficient is introduced, which is related to the reflection coefficient through the law of conservation of energy of the propagating wave along the transmission line; that is, the incident power minus the reflected power should be equal to the power transmitted to the load:

$$1 - R^2 = \frac{Z_c}{Z_L}T^2 \qquad (7.14)$$

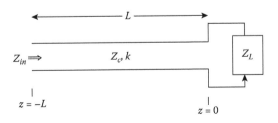

Figure 7.4 Transmission line loaded by the resistance Z_L.

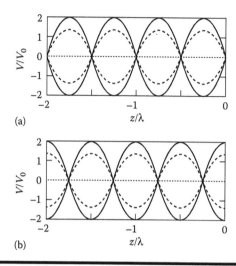

Figure 7.5 **(a,b) Standing waves in the transmission line.**

From this, accounting for Equation 7.13a, one can easily obtain the expression for the transmission coefficient:

$$T = \frac{2Z_L}{Z_L + Z_c} \tag{7.13b}$$

Now, for $A_2 = V_0$, $B_2 = R \cdot V_0$, we get from Equation 7.12

$$V(z) = V_0 \left[e^{-jkz} + \mathrm{Re}^{jkz} \right] \tag{7.15a}$$

$$I(z) = \frac{V_0}{Z_c} \left[e^{-jkz} - \mathrm{Re}^{jkz} \right] \tag{7.15b}$$

When $R = \pm 1$, we have the phenomenon called *standing voltage waves* (see Figure 7.5).

Then, the *voltage standing wave ratio* (VSWR), denoted by ρ, can be introduced by the formula [10–19]

$$\mathrm{VSWR} \equiv \rho = \frac{V_{\max}}{V_{\min}} = \frac{1 + |R|}{1 - |R|} \tag{7.16}$$

7.3 Impedance and Matching of Transmission Line

Since the impedance is not constant and changes from point to point, we should present its more general form. Thus, from Equation 7.15, we obtain

$$Z(z) = \frac{V(z)}{I(z)} = \frac{V_0 \left[e^{-jkz} + \mathrm{Re}^{jkz} \right]}{\dfrac{V_0}{Z_c} \left[e^{-jkz} - \mathrm{Re}^{jkz} \right]} = Z_c \frac{\left[e^{-jkz} + \mathrm{Re}^{jkz} \right]}{\left[e^{-jkz} - \mathrm{Re}^{jkz} \right]} \tag{7.17}$$

Accounting for Equation 7.13a, we obtain

$$Z(z) = Z_c \frac{\left[e^{-jkz} + \dfrac{Z_L - Z_c}{Z_L + Z_c} e^{jkz} \right]}{\left[e^{-jkz} - \dfrac{Z_L - Z_c}{Z_L + Z_c} e^{jkz} \right]} = Z_c \frac{Z_L - jZ_c \tan kz}{Z_c - jZ_L \tan kz} \tag{7.18}$$

From Figure 7.4, one can compute the input impedance of the loaded transmission-line segment:

$$Z_{in}(L) = Z(z = -L) = Z_c \frac{Z_L + jZ_c \tan kL}{Z_c + jZ_L \tan kL} \tag{7.19}$$

For $L = \lambda/4$, $kL = (2\pi/\lambda)L = (2\pi/\lambda)(\lambda/4) = \pi/2$, and $\tan(\pi/2) \to \infty$. Then,

$$Z_{in}(z = -\lambda/4) = Z_c \frac{Z_L + jZ_c \cdot \infty}{Z_c + jZ_L \cdot \infty} = \frac{(Z_c)^2}{Z_L} \tag{7.20}$$

7.5 Transmission Line with Losses

Additional losses that exist in real transmission lines can be modeled by introducing the inner normalized resistance $\hat{R} = R/\Delta z$ and the normalized conductivity $\hat{G} = G/\Delta z$ (see Figure 7.6).

If so, instead of Equations 7.1 and 7.2, we get

$$\frac{\partial I(z,t)}{\partial z} = -\hat{C} \frac{\partial V(z,t)}{\partial t} - \hat{G}V(z,t) \tag{7.21a}$$

$$\frac{\partial V(z,t)}{\partial z} = -\hat{L} \frac{\partial I(z,t)}{\partial t} - \hat{R}I(z,t) \tag{7.21b}$$

Introducing now the harmonic presentations of the voltage and the current waves, and the corresponding admittance $\hat{Y} = \hat{G} + j\omega\hat{C}$ and impedance $\hat{Z} = \hat{R} + j\omega\hat{L}$, we finally get for the phasors

$$\frac{dI(z)}{dz} = -\hat{Y}V(z) \tag{7.22a}$$

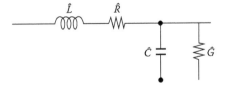

Figure 7.6 Scheme of modeling losses occurring in the transmission line.

$$\frac{dV(z)}{dz} = -\hat{Z}I(z) \tag{7.22b}$$

or, the following expression,

$$\frac{d^2 I(z)}{dz^2} = \hat{Z}\hat{Y}I(z) \tag{7.23a}$$

$$\frac{d^2 V(z)}{dz^2} = \hat{Z}\hat{Y}V(z) \tag{7.23b}$$

Their solutions are, respectively,

$$V(z) = V_1 e^{-\gamma z} + V_2 e^{\gamma z} \tag{7.24a}$$

$$I(z) = I_1 e^{-\gamma z} + I_2 e^{\gamma z} \tag{7.24b}$$

The complex propagation constant

$$\gamma = \alpha + j\beta = \sqrt{\hat{Z}\hat{Y}} = \sqrt{(\hat{R} + j\omega\hat{L})(\hat{G} + j\omega\hat{C})} \tag{7.25}$$

For the case of $\hat{R}/\hat{L} = \hat{G}/\hat{C}$,

$$\gamma = (\hat{R} + j\omega\hat{L})\sqrt{\frac{\hat{C}}{\hat{L}}}, \alpha = \hat{R}\sqrt{\frac{\hat{C}}{\hat{L}}}, \beta = \omega\hat{L}\sqrt{\frac{\hat{C}}{\hat{L}}} \tag{7.26}$$

and the characteristic impedance of the line equals

$$Z_c = \sqrt{\frac{\hat{Z}}{\hat{Y}}} = \sqrt{\frac{(\hat{R} + j\omega\hat{L})}{(\hat{G} + j\omega\hat{C})}} = \sqrt{\frac{\hat{L}}{\hat{C}}} \tag{7.27}$$

Now, using information on the propagation parameters, we can describe the full time- dependent presentations of the voltage and current waves in the following manner:

$$V(z,t) = V_1 e^{-\alpha z} \cos(\omega t - \beta z) + V_2 e^{\alpha z} \cos(\omega t + \beta z) \tag{7.28a}$$

$$I(z,t) = I_1 e^{-\alpha z} \cos(\omega t - \beta z) + I_2 e^{\alpha z} \cos(\omega t + \beta z) \tag{7.28b}$$

The plot of time-harmonic voltages of the signals for $\alpha = -1/2$ and $\beta = \pi$ is shown in Figure 7.7. For $\alpha \ll \beta$ (small losses),

$$\gamma \approx j\omega\sqrt{\hat{L}\hat{C}}\left[1 - j\left(\frac{\hat{R}}{2\omega\hat{L}} + \frac{\hat{G}}{2\omega\hat{C}}\right)\right] \tag{7.29a}$$

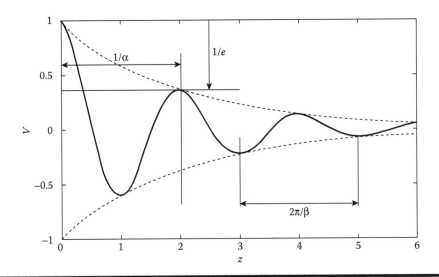

Figure 7.7 Time-harmonic voltage signals for α = −1/2 and β = 1/4. (Modified from Edwards, T. C., *Foundations for Microstrip Circuit Design*, Wiley, New York, 1987; Liao, S. Y., *Engineering Applications of Electromagnetic Theory*, West, St Paul, MN, 1988.)

$$\alpha \approx \frac{1}{2}\sqrt{\hat{L}\hat{C}}\left(\frac{\hat{R}}{\hat{L}} + \frac{\hat{G}}{\hat{C}}\right) \tag{7.29b}$$

$$\beta \approx \omega\sqrt{\hat{L}\hat{C}} \tag{7.29c}$$

In this case, the phase velocity is

$$v_{ph} = \frac{\omega}{\beta} \approx \frac{1}{\sqrt{\hat{L}\hat{C}}} \tag{7.30}$$

PROBLEMS

Example 7.1: Given transverse electromagnetic mode propagating in the two-conductor transmission line that can be described by the voltage and current scalar Equations 7.7a and 7.7b.
Find: The expressions for a characteristic impedance and the propagation constant and show that these parameters are independent of frequency.

Example 7.2: Given $f = 0.5$ Hz, $v = 4$ m/s, $V(z = 0, t = 0) = V_0$.
Find: Expression of the wave voltage.

Example 7.3: Given the transmission line with the characteristic impedance and load $Z_c = 75 + j0.05\,\Omega$, $Z_L = 70 + j50\,\Omega$.
Find: R and T; verify relation Equation 7.14 and show from it a new relation between the reflection coefficient R and the transmitted coefficient T.

Example 7.4: Given the transmission line with the characteristic parameters $Z_c = 50$ Ω, $Z_L = 40 + j30$ Ω.
Find: The reflection coefficient R and parameter VSWR from Equation 7.16.

Example 7.5: Given $\alpha = 0.01$ dB/m, $\hat{C} = 0.1 \times 10^{-9}$ F/m, $Z_c = 50$ Ω.
Find: Parameters of the transmitted line, $\hat{L}$, $\hat{R}$, $\hat{G}$, and the phase velocity v_{ph}.

Example 7.6: Given $\hat{R} = 2$ Ω/m, $\hat{C} = 0.23 \times 10^{-12}$ F/m, $\hat{G} = 0.5$mS/m, $\hat{L} = 8$nH/m, $f = 1$ GHz.
Find: The characteristic impedance Z_c and the propagation constant γ.

Example 7.7: Given a load impedance $Z_L = 25$ Ω, which is connected to a transmission line with the characteristic impedance $Z_c = 50$ Ω. Using Equation 7.19, find and plot the impedance for a distance from the load of $2\lambda = 0.1, 0.5, 1.0, 1, 5, 2.0$ m.

References

1. Jonson, W. C., *Transmission Lines and Networks*, New York: McGraw-Hill, 1950.
2. Javid, V. and E. Brenner, *Analysis, Transmission, and Filtering of Signals*, New York: McGraw-Hill, 1963.
3. Ramo, S., J. R. Winnery, and T. Van Duzer, *Fields and Waves in Communication Electronics*, New York: Wiley, 1965.
4. Adam, S. F., *Microwave Theory and Applications*, Englewood Cliffs, NJ: Prentice-Hall, 1969.
5. Brown, R. G., et al., *Lines, Waves, and Antennas*, 2nd edn, New York: Wiley, 1970.
6. Gupta, K. C., R. Garg, and I. J. Bahl, *Microstrip Lines and Slotlines*, Dedham, MA: Artech House, 1979.
7. Dworscky, L. N., *Modern Transmission Line Theory and Applications*, New York: Wiley, 1979.
8. Sinnema, W., *Electronic Transmission Technology: Lines, Waves, and Applications*, Englewood Cliffs, NJ: Prentice-Hall, 1979.
9. Hoffmann, R. K., *Handbook of Microwave Integrated Circuits*, Norwood, MA: Artech House, 1987.
10. Edwards, T. C., *Foundations for Microstrip Circuit Design*, New York: Wiley, 1987.
11. Liao, S. Y., *Engineering Applications of Electromagnetic Theory*, St Paul, MN: West, 1988.
12. Pozar, D. V., *Microwave Engineering*, Reading, MA: Addison-Wesley, 1988.
13. Seeger, J. A., *Microwave Theory, Components, and Devices*, Englewood Cliffs, NJ: Prentice-Hall, 1989.
14. Liao, S. Y., *Microwave Devices and Circuits*, 3rd edn, Englewood Cliffs, NJ: Prentice-Hall, 1990.
15. Wadell, B. C., *Transmission Line Design Handbook*, Norwood, MA: Artech House, 1991.
16. Weisshaar, A., Transmission lines, Chapter 6 in *Handbook: Engineering Electromagnetics*, ed. by R. Bansal, New York: Marcel Dekker, 2004, pp. 185–226.
17. Freeman, J. C., *Fundamentals of Microwave Transmission Lines*, New York: Wiley, 1996.
18. Pozar, D., *Microwave Engineering*, New York: Wiley, 1998.
19. Magnusson, P. C., G. C. Alexander, V. K. Tripathi, and A. Weisshaar, *Transmission Lines and Wave Propagation*, Boca Raton, FL: CRC, 2001.

Chapter 8

Coaxial Cables

Since all the characteristics and parameters, as well as the basic formulas, presented in Chapter 7 regarding the description of two-wire electric transmission lines can be exactly adapted to the description of coaxial cables, in this chapter, we will briefly describe the process of propagation in such guiding structures via the main characteristics described in the previous chapter, accounting for some peculiarities of wave propagation in cable structures via some specific examples.

8.1 Main Characteristics of Coaxial Cable

As a common transmission line, the coaxial cable is presented as a system, consisting of two conductors, the inner with radius a and the outer with radius b, separated by a dielectric (see Figure 8.1).

We also consider a cross-section of a 1 m section of a uniform coaxial cable with fields $\mathbf{E}$ and $\mathbf{H}$, as shown in Figure 8.2, where S is the cross-sectional area of the cable. The voltage and the current of the electric field component propagate along the cable (axis z) with the general laws $\sim V_0 e^{\pm \gamma z}$ and $\sim I_0 e^{\pm \gamma z}$, respectively. Here, V_0 and I_0 are the initial voltage and current from the source at cable input, while $\gamma = \alpha \pm j\beta$ is a general presentation of the propagation characteristics of electromagnetic waves, defined in Chapters 4 and 6.

If so, the main parameters and characteristics that should be taken into account for description of the processes of electromagnetic wave propagation in such a guiding coaxial cable structure are as follows [1–5].

The normalized resistance per unit cable length, $\hat{R}$, for both conductors, inner and outer, measured in ohms per meter (Ω/m), can be defined as [1–5]

$$\hat{R} = \frac{R_S}{|I_0|^2} \int_{C_1 + C_2} (\mathbf{H} \cdot \mathbf{H}^*) dl \qquad (8.1)$$

where:
$R_S = (\sigma \delta_s)^{-1}$ is the surface resistance of the inner and outer conductors
σ is the conductivity of the material
δ_S is the skin layer (see definitions in Chapter 4)

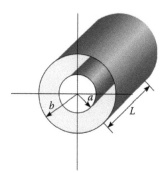

Figure 8.1   View of the coaxial cable.

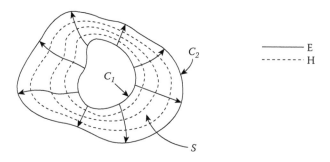

Figure 8.2   Distribution of electric and magnetic field inside the coaxial cable.

$C_1 + C_2$ represent integration paths over the conductor boundaries, as shown in Figure 8.2.

The capacitance per unit length, $\hat{C}$, measured in farads per meter (F/m), can be defined as [1–5]

$$\hat{C} = \frac{\varepsilon}{|V_0|^2} \int_S (\mathbf{E} \cdot \mathbf{E}^*) ds \tag{8.2}$$

where $\varepsilon = \varepsilon_r \varepsilon_0$ is the permittivity of the material (see notations and definitions in Chapter 4). The normalized inductance per unit length, $\hat{L}$, measured in henrys per meter (H/m), is defined as [1–5]

$$\hat{L} = \frac{\mu}{|I_0|^2} \int_S (\mathbf{H} \cdot \mathbf{H}^*) ds \tag{8.3}$$

where $\mu = \mu_r \mu_0$ is the permeability of the material (see notations and definition in Chapters 3 and 4).

The normalized conductance per unit length, $\hat{G}$, measured in siemens per meter (S/m), is defined as [1–5]

$$\hat{G} = \frac{\omega \varepsilon''}{|V_0|^2} \int_S (\mathbf{E} \cdot \mathbf{E}^*) ds \tag{8.4}$$

where ε'' is the imaginary part of the complex permittivity $\varepsilon = \varepsilon' + j\varepsilon''$.

8.2 Propagation of a Transverse Electromagnetic (TEM) Wave along the Coaxial Cable

As was shown in Chapter 6, there are several modes that can propagate in guiding structures, such as TEM, transverse electric (TE), and transverse magnetic (TM). We will consider in this section the TEM mode of propagation in the context of the general framework that has already been discussed in the corresponding literature [1–5]. The geometry of the problem is shown in Figure 8.1, where the inner conductor has a potential of V_0 volts and the outer conductor has zero volts. As was shown in [1–5], the electric field component can be obtained from a scalar potential function, $\Phi(\rho, \varphi)$. The latter is a solution of Laplace's equation, which can be presented in the cylindrical coordinate system $\{\rho, \varphi, z\}$ (see Figure 8.3a) as

$$\frac{1}{\rho}\frac{\partial}{\partial\rho}\left(\rho\frac{\partial\Phi(\rho,\varphi)}{\partial\rho}\right)+\frac{1}{\rho^2}\frac{\partial^2\Phi(\rho,\varphi)}{\partial\varphi^2}=0 \tag{8.5}$$

Using for Equation 8.5 the method of separation of nonrelated variables

$$\Phi(\rho,\varphi)=\Phi_1(\rho)\cdot\Phi_2(\varphi) \tag{8.6}$$

and following the corresponding boundary conditions (see Figure 8.3b), for $\rho = a$:

$$\Phi(a,\varphi)=V_0 \tag{8.7a}$$

for $\rho = b$:

$$\Phi(b,\varphi)=0 \tag{8.7b}$$

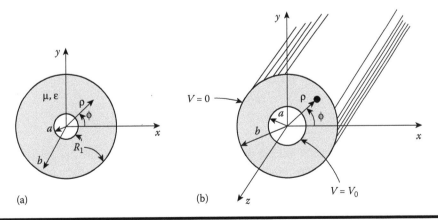

(a)   (b)

Figure 8.3 (a) The cylindrical coordinate system $\{\rho, \varphi, z\}$ presentation inside the coaxial cable. (b) View on distribution of voltage at the inner and outer surfaces of the coaxial cable.

If so, we can, following [3–5], easily obtain the final solution for $\Phi(\rho,\varphi)$:

$$\Phi(\rho,\varphi) = \frac{V_0 \ln\left(\dfrac{b}{\rho}\right)}{\ln\left(\dfrac{b}{a}\right)} \tag{8.8}$$

Correspondingly, the total electric field inside the coaxial cable structure, accounting for the propagation factor $\sim e^{-\gamma z}$ along the z-axis (in its positive direction), is

$$\mathbf{E}(\rho,\varphi,z) = \frac{V_0 e^{-\gamma z}}{\rho \ln\left(\dfrac{b}{a}\right)}\hat{\rho} \tag{8.9}$$

Now, taking into account the relations between electric and magnetic field components (see Chapters 3 and 4), it is easy to derive the total magnetic field inside the coaxial cable, including the propagation factor $\sim e^{-\gamma z}$ along the positive direction of the z-axis. Finally, we get

$$\mathbf{H}(\rho,\varphi,z) = \frac{V_0 e^{-\gamma z}}{\eta \cdot \rho \ln\left(\dfrac{b}{a}\right)}\hat{\varphi} \tag{8.10}$$

where, as in Chapter 4, $\eta = (\mu/\varepsilon)^{1/2}$ is the intrinsic impedance of the material filling the cable.

Now, to obtain the important "engineering" formulas for designers of guiding systems, we will present the potential difference between the two conductors, inner and outer, as

$$V_{ab} = V_0 e^{-\gamma z} \tag{8.11}$$

the total current on the inner conductor as (see Chapter 7)

$$I_a = \frac{2\pi V_0 e^{-\gamma z}}{\eta \cdot \rho \ln\left(\dfrac{b}{a}\right)} \tag{8.12}$$

and the total current on the outer conductor as (see Chapter 7)

$$I_b = -\frac{2\pi V_0 e^{-\gamma z}}{\eta \cdot \rho \ln\left(\dfrac{b}{a}\right)} \tag{8.13}$$

From Equations 8.12 and 8.13, it follows that $I_b = -I_a$, that is, currents are in opposite directions in the inner and outer conductors. Finally, we can show that the characteristic impedance of the coaxial cable, considered in Chapter 7, can be presented as

$$Z_c \equiv \frac{V_0}{I_0} = \frac{\eta \ln\left(b/a\right)}{2\pi} = \sqrt{\frac{\mu_r \mu_0}{\varepsilon_r \varepsilon_0}}\left(\frac{\ln(b/a)}{2\pi}\right) \tag{8.14}$$

8.3 Propagation of TE and TM Waves along the Coaxial Cable

The coaxial cable, as a transmission line, can also support other modes, such as TE and TM wave-guide modes, in addition to the TEM mode. In practical coaxial cable applications, these modes are usually cutoff, that is, evanescent, and so they have only a reactive effect near discontinuities or sources, where they are excited. At the same time, it is important in practice to be aware of the cutoff frequency of the lower-order guiding-type modes, to avoid the propagation of these modes. Avoiding the propagation of higher-order modes sets an upper limit on the size of a coaxial cable, leading to limitations in the power-handling capacity of a coaxial cable. As was shown in the literature [3–5], the TE_{11} mode is the dominant mode of the coaxial cable, and therefore it is of primary importance. For this mode, as was shown in Chapter 6, $E_z = 0$. We will not repeat all the components of the TE mode and its solutions, but we should mention that its critical (cutoff) wavenumber k_c fully depends on the inner and outer dimensions of the cable.

Thus, for the main TE mode (for its number $n = 1$), the numerical results of $k_c \cdot a$ versus various b/a ratios, obtained in [3], are presented in Figure 8.4. The approximate solution, which is often used in practical coaxial cable design, is

$$k_c = \frac{2}{a+b} \tag{8.20}$$

Once k_c is known, the propagation constant or cutoff frequency can be determined by use of the following formula [3]:

$$f_c = \frac{c \cdot k_c}{2\pi\sqrt{\varepsilon_r}} \tag{8.21}$$

We notice that the field solution for TM mode gives the same values of k_c and f_c.

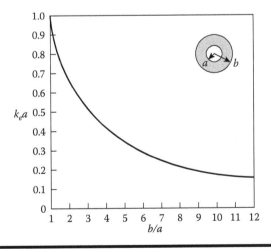

Figure 8.4 Dependence of $k_c a$ vs. the ratio b/a, where b and a are the outer and inner radius of the coaxial cable (insert). (Adapted from Pozar, D.V., *Microwave Engineering*, Addison-Wesley, Reading, MA, 1988; Weisshaar, A., in R. Bansal (ed.), *Handbook: Engineering Electromagnetics*, Marcel Dekker, New York, 2004.)

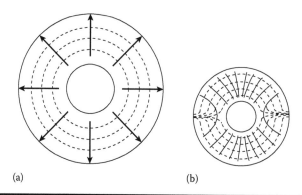

Figure 8.5 **H-field (dashed circuits) and E-field (solid lines) distribution (a) for the TEM mode and (b) for the TE$_{11}$ mode.**

Finally, we present in Figure 8.5a and b, following results obtained in [3], the field lines (solid for the E-field and dashed for the H-field) for the TEM and TE$_{11}$ modes, respectively.

It is clearly seen that the field components of the TEM mode are more symmetrically distributed inside the coaxial cable with respect to the TE$_{11}$ mode, and, therefore, this mode has the priority to propagate without any additional losses inside it at long ranges.

8.4 Leaky Coaxial Cable (LCC) Hidden in Semi-Space Dielectric Medium

Let us now consider a new kind of the standard cable called in the literature [6–12] a *perfectly shielded leaky coaxial cable*, which is usually used for radio communication and for guiding radar system applications (see Chapter 13). We will not focus on the well-known equations describing time-harmonic wave propagation inside guiding structures (see Chapter 6), but will assume that the propagation process inside the LCC is characterized by a complex propagation constant $\gamma_i = \alpha_i + j\beta_i$ and by a characteristic impedance $Z_i = R_i + jX_i$. In our model, we use the concept of a simple transmission line presented in Chapter 7, because, as mentioned at the beginning of this chapter, both the cable and the transmission line are characterized by similar processes and, therefore, are described using the same parameters.

Figure 8.6 presents the geometry of the LCC, which now additionally contains periodically shielded slots along its length (inside the outer conductor). If we now neglect the energy dissipation inside the line (since we consider a perfect leaky cable), then

$$\gamma_i \approx j\beta_i = j\omega\sqrt{\varepsilon_0\varepsilon_r\mu_0\mu_r} = \frac{j\omega\sqrt{\varepsilon_r\mu_r}}{c} \tag{8.22}$$

$$Z_i \approx j\beta_i = \sqrt{\frac{\mu_0}{\varepsilon_0}}\ln\left(\frac{b}{a}\right) = Z_0\ln\left(\frac{b}{a}\right) \tag{8.23}$$

where all parameters were defined in Chapters 6 and 7.

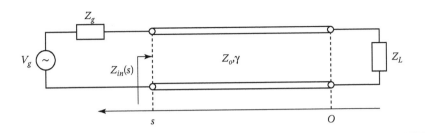

Figure 8.6 **The structure of the LCC-to-generator assembly.**

8.4.1 The Simple Coaxial Cable Model

Let us now assume that the coaxial cable is terminated in loading impedance Z_L and driven by a generator developing voltage V_g with inner impedance Z_g, as shown in Figure 8.6. This cable model is based on the transmission-line presentation described in Chapter 7. We will present this transmission-line model from another point of view.

The length of the cable is equal to s, and we use a distance variable x when increases, as we go from the load toward the generator (see Figure 8.6). Evidently, the input current drawn from the voltage generator can be obtained as

$$I_{in}(s) = \frac{V_g}{Z_g + Z_{in}(s)} \tag{8.24}$$

where the input impedance of the line is given by (see also Chapter 7)

$$Z_{in}(s) = Z_i \frac{Z_L + Z_i \tanh(\gamma_i s)}{Z_i + Z_L \tanh(\gamma_i s)} = Z_i \frac{\zeta_L + \tanh(\gamma_i s)}{1 + \zeta_L \tanh(\gamma_i s)} \tag{8.25}$$

where $\zeta_L = Z_L/Z_i$ is the normalized load impedance. The voltage at the input end of the coaxial cable (as a line) is given by

$$V_{in}(s) = Z_{in}(s) \cdot I_{in}(s) = \frac{V_g \cdot Z_{in}(s)}{Z_g + Z_{in}(s)} \tag{8.26}$$

In this case, the reflection coefficient at the load end is determined as

$$\rho_L = \frac{Z_L - Z_i}{Z_L + Z_i} = \frac{\zeta_L - 1}{\zeta_L + 1} \tag{8.27}$$

and at any distance x from the load as

$$\rho(x) = \rho_L \exp\{-2\gamma_i x\} \tag{8.28}$$

The general solutions for the phasor (see definition in Chapter 3) line voltage and current are given by the following formulas [12]:

$$V(x) = V^+ \exp\{\gamma_i x\} + V^- \exp\{-\gamma_i x\} = V^+ \exp\{\gamma_i x\}[1 + \rho(x)] \tag{8.29a}$$

$$I(x) = Y_0 \left(V^+ \exp\{\gamma_i x\} - V^- \exp\{-\gamma_i x\} \right) = Y_0 V^+ \exp\{\gamma_i x\}[1 - \rho(x)] \qquad (8.29b)$$

where $Y_0 = 1/Z_0 = G_0 + jB_0$ is the characteristic complex admittance of the line, subscripts + and − correspond to wave propagation toward the load and the generator, respectively.

As a result, we obtain for the incident wave

$$V^+ = \frac{V_{in}(s) \exp\{-\gamma_i s\}}{[1 + \rho_{in}(s)]} \qquad (8.30)$$

The voltage and current line amplitudes in the typical lossy leaky cable are given by [12]

$$|V(x)| = |V^+| \exp\{\alpha_i x\} \cdot |1 + \rho_L \exp\{-2\gamma_i x\}| \qquad (8.31)$$

$$|I(x)| = |Y_0| \cdot |V^+| \exp\{\alpha_i x\} \cdot |1 - \rho_L \exp\{-2\gamma_i x\}| \qquad (8.32)$$

Finally, we consider the standing-wave ratio (SWR), extending its standard definition to the general case of cable with loss, as a function of the distance along the cable [12]:

$$SWR(x) = \frac{1 + |\rho_L| \exp\{-2\alpha_i x\}}{1 - |\rho_L| \exp\{-2\alpha_i x\}} \qquad (8.33)$$

As follows from Equation 8.33, $1 \leq SWR(x) < \infty$.

It is important to notice that the extinction suppresses the voltage and current oscillations along the cable.

8.4.2 Insulated Cable Hidden in Semi-Space Dielectric Medium

Now, we will discuss how the characteristics of such a leaky guiding cable change when it is hidden in a homogeneous semi-space dielectric medium.

In Section 8.4.1, we introduced a simple model of LCC as a transmission line. Now, we will consider an external waveguide using the concept of an insulated hidden single-wire cable in a semi-space dielectric medium, and then go on to consider the coupling between two modes through the outer guiding system based on the layered dielectric waveguide model.

As was shown in Equations 8.34 through 8.36, there are two main characteristics that affect the performance of LCC: the *attenuation*, which limits its length, and the *coupling*, which determines the overall sensitivity of such a system. We next introduce the normalized parameters, such as the series impedance z_i per unit length of LCC and the shunt admittance y_i per unit length. Then, the main characteristics introduced above will have the form $\gamma_i = \sqrt{z_i \cdot y_i}$ and $Z_i = \sqrt{z_i / y_i}$. Based on the geometry shown in Figure 8.1, we can now present z_i, following Equations 8.34 and 8.35, as

$$z_i = \frac{1 + j}{2\pi} \sqrt{\frac{\omega \mu_0 \mu_r}{2}} \left(\frac{1}{a\sqrt{\sigma_a}} + \frac{1}{b\sqrt{\sigma_b}} \right) + j\omega l_i \qquad (8.34)$$

where σ_a and σ_b are the conductivities of the inner and outer conductors, respectively: $y_i = \sigma_i + jc_i\omega$. The other line-related parameters have the well-known form [12]

$$c_i = \frac{2\pi\varepsilon_{d1}}{\ln(b/a)}, \; \sigma_i = \frac{2\pi\sigma_{d1}}{\ln(b/a)}, \; l_i = \frac{\mu_0\mu_r}{2\pi}\ln(b/a) \tag{8.35}$$

where:

$\varepsilon_{d1} = \varepsilon_0\varepsilon_r$ is the permittivity in the coaxial cable
σ_{d1} is the conductivity in the coaxial cable

The propagation of the external mode can be considered as in the case of an insulated single-wire cable hidden at some depth in a homogeneous lossy dielectric medium. Simple estimates carried out in [12] showed that the propagation constant introduced in Section 8.4.1 is found near the wavenumber if the insulated dielectric layer where LCC was embedded is perturbed by losses in the dielectric layer and by the presence of the interface, and that this constant does not vary greatly with the depth of LCC location. The main property of this external mode is the very large value of the attenuation constant [12], where it was additionally shown that the internal and external modes interact with each other. It is important to emphasize that the internal mode, excited in the cable by the generator (see Figure 8.6), is the source of the external mode. The leakage effect can be modeled by a transfer impedance, denoted in [12] as z_t. This parameter relates the axial electric field on the shield surface E_x and the shield current I_y carried by the latter, by the equation

$$E_x = z_t I_y \tag{8.36}$$

Following [12], we suppose that

$$z_t \approx j\omega m_t \tag{8.37}$$

where the transfer inductance m_t does not depend on the frequency or on the mode propagation constant. As was shown in [12], in more strict analysis, z_t may have a resistive part and may be spatially dispersive, that is, dependent on the attenuation parameter α.

8.4.3 Coupling Effect between External and Internal Modes of LCC

As in [12], we use in further consideration the so-called coupled-line theory, where the exterior and the interior of the cable can be modeled as two transmission lines, whose currents flow along the dielectric layer and the inner conductor, respectively, and whose common return is considered to be the cable shield. We assume that the shield is electrically thin, that is, the axial field E_x is continuous across the shield. In such an assumption, the voltage V_e and the current I_e of the external transmission line satisfy the following transmission-line equations:

$$\frac{dV_e}{dx} = \pm z'_e I_e + E_x \tag{8.38}$$

and

$$\frac{dI_e}{dx} = \pm y_e V_e \tag{8.39}$$

where E_x is now defined as the axial electric field at the external surface of the cable, and $z'_e = z_e + z_t$. The sign convention used in Equations 8.38 and 8.39 considers the current as positive when it flows along the dielectric layer (where LCC is hidden) and returns along the conductor.

The voltage and current inside the coaxial cable, denoted by V_i and I_i, satisfy similar equations. Since $I_s = -(I_i + I_e)$, we can combine Equations 8.38 and 8.39 into

$$\frac{dV_e}{dx} = -z_e I_e - z_t I_i \tag{8.40}$$

and

$$\frac{dI_e}{dx} = \pm\, y_e V_e \tag{8.41}$$

Similarly, we have

$$\frac{dV_i}{dx} = -z_i I_i - z_t I_i \tag{8.42}$$

and

$$\frac{dI_i}{dx} = \pm\, y_i V_i \tag{8.43}$$

where $z_i = z'_i - z_t$.

As in [12], we will assume a weak-coupling scenario in which the approximate formula for the coupling coefficient equals

$$\varsigma_c = \frac{m_t}{2\sqrt{l_e l_i}} \frac{\sqrt{\kappa}}{\kappa - 1} \tag{8.44}$$

where:

$$\kappa = \beta_i / \beta_e$$

l_i (Equation 8.35) is related to the coaxial cable
l_e (Equation 8.35) also includes a part related to the dielectric layer

In the weak-coupling approximation, the propagation constants of the intrinsic eigenmode

$$\gamma_1 = \alpha_1 + j\beta_1,\ \alpha_1 = \alpha_i + \varsigma_c^2 \alpha_e,\ \beta_1 \approx \beta_i \tag{8.45}$$

and of the external eigenmode

$$\gamma_2 = \alpha_2 + j\beta_2,\ \alpha_2 \approx \alpha_e,\ \beta_2 \approx \beta_e \tag{8.46}$$

The coaxial eigenmode has the main part of its power propagating inside the cable. Some power is, however, also carried by the leakage fields outside the cable. This power is approximately given by [12]

$$P_m \approx \varsigma_c^2 P_c \tag{8.47}$$

and it thus appears that ς_c^2 is the relative power of the leakage fields. This explains also in a very simple way the increase of specific attenuation for the coaxial eigenmode given by Equation 8.46.

We should note that the scenario of a leaky coaxial cable considered in this chapter will be very important for understanding how the operational characteristics of a guided radar system (discussed in Chapter 13) will be changed when it is buried in an actual inhomogeneous subsoil medium with many inhomogeneous structures surrounding the leaky coaxial cable.

EXAMPLES

Example 8.1: Using definitions for the field components of TEM mode propagating inside the coaxial cable, calculate the main parameters of the coaxial cable.

Example 8.2: Given $f = 100$ MHz, $Z_c = 100$ Ω, $L = 100$ m, $v = 2 \times 10^8$ m/s, and $Z_L = 50$ Ω. *Find*: impedance at the length of $z = 50$ m along the cable.

Example 8.3: Given a coaxial cable with the length L (see Figure 8.7). In the inner conductor, the linear charge density is ρ_l. The dielectric is filled by material with permittivity ε_r. *Find*: The capacity along the length L.

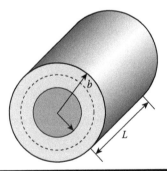

Figure 8.7 Geometry of the problem.

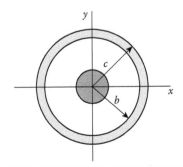

Figure 8.8 Geometry of the problem.

Example 8.4: Given a coaxial cable with a current I_0 in the inner conductor in the direction **z**. This current returns in the outer conductor.

Find: the magnetic induction B_φ in each separate area of the cable (see Figure 8.8).

Example 8.5: Given TE_{11} mode propagates inside the cable with the ratio $b/a = 3/2$ (see Figure 8.4). The permittivity of the dielectric material filling inside the cable is $\varepsilon_r = 2.2$.

Find: with what frequencies this mode can propagate inside the cable.

Example 8.6: Given a coaxial cable with inner and outer conductor diameters of 0.05 and 0.02 m, and with a dielectric filling this cable of permittivity $\varepsilon = 2.2\varepsilon_0$.

Find: Using Figure 8.4, find the cutoff frequency of the mode TE_{11}.

References

1. Dworscky, L. N., *Modern Transmission Line Theory and Applications*, New York: Wiley, 1979.
2. Sinnema, W., *Electronic Transmission Technology: Lines, Waves, and Applications*, Englewood Cliffs, NJ: Prentice-Hall, 1979.
3. Pozar, D. V., *Microwave Engineering*, Reading, MA: Addison-Wesley, 1988.
4. Liao, S. Y., *Microwave Devices and Circuits*, 3rd edn, Englewood Cliffs, NJ: Prentice-Hall, 1990.
5. Weisshaar, A., Transmission lines, in R. Bansal (Ed.), *Handbook: Engineering Electromagnetics*, chapter 6, New York: Marcel Dekker, pp. 185–226, 2004.
6. Delogne, P., *Leaky Feeders and Subsurface Radio Communications*, London: Peter Peregrinus, 1982.
7. Wait, J. R. and K. P. Spies, Surface electromagnetic fields of a line source on a conducting half-space, *Radio Sci* 6, 781–786, 1971.
8. Richmond, J. H., N. N. Wang, and H. B. Tran, Propagation of surface waves on a buried coaxial cable with periodic slots, *IEEE Trans Electromagn Compat* 23, 139–146, 1981.
9. Richmond, J. H., Propagation on a ported coaxial cable buried in flat earth, *IEEE Trans Electromagn Compat* 27, 70–71, 1985.
10. Delogne, P. and L. Deryck, Underground use of a coaxial cable with leaky sections, *IEEE Trans Antennas Propagat* 28, 875–882, 1980.
11. Gale, D. I. and J. C. Beal, Comparative testing of leaky coaxial cable for communication and guided radar, *IEEE Trans Microwave Theory Tech* 28, 1006–1013, 1980.
12. N. Blaunstein, Z. Dank, and M. Zilbershtein, Prediction of radiation pattern of a buried leaky coaxial cable, *Int J Subsurf Sens Technol App* 1(1), 1–12, 2000.

Chapter 9

Waveguides

9.1 Two-Dimensional (2-D) Plane Guiding Structure

In Figure 9.1, we present the parallel-plate guiding structure (slab), which models a simple strip line as two infinite plates along the z-axis filled by dielectric with width w along the x-axis and height b along the y-axis. The intrinsic dielectric has a permittivity ε $\mu = \mu_0$.

9.1.1 Propagation of Transverse Electromagnetic (TEM) Waves

Let us, first, consider TEM-wave propagation for which (see above) $\mathbf{E}_z = 0$ and $\mathbf{H}_z = 0$. In this case, we can, as in Chapter 6 present the field inside the slab by the Laplace equation [1–4]

$$\nabla_\perp^2 \Phi(x, y) = 0 \tag{9.1}$$

In this case, $\Phi(x,y)$ can be reduced to $\Phi(y)$ and Equation 9.1 to

$$\nabla_\perp^2 \Phi(x, y) \equiv \frac{\partial^2 \Phi}{\partial y^2} = 0 \tag{9.2}$$

which has the simple solution

$$\Phi(y) = C_1 y + C_2 \tag{9.3}$$

The constants of integration, C_1 and C_2, can be obtained from boundary conditions

$$\Phi(y = 0) = 0 \quad \text{and} \quad \Phi(y = b) = V_0 \tag{9.4}$$

where V_0 is an electrostatic potential difference of V_0 volts between plates. From Equation 9.4, we get

$$C_1 = \frac{V_0}{b}, \; C_2 = 0 \tag{9.5}$$

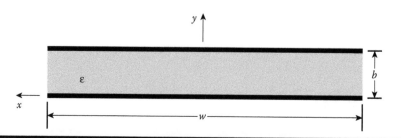

Figure 9.1 Plane 2-D guided structure filled by dielectric material.

and, finally,

$$\Phi(y) = \frac{V_0}{b} y \tag{9.6}$$

Now, using the relation between the electric field and the potential (see Chapter 6), we can obtain for propagation in the positive z-direction

$$\mathbf{E}_\perp(y,z) = -\nabla_\perp \Phi(y) \exp\{j(\omega t - kz)\}$$

$$= -y \frac{V_0}{b} \exp\{j(\omega t - kz)\} \tag{9.7a}$$

and between the magnetic and electric fields, we get

$$\mathbf{H}_\perp(y,z) = -\mathbf{z} \times \frac{\mathbf{E}_\perp}{Z_{TEM}} = \mathbf{x} \frac{V_0 \sqrt{\varepsilon_r}}{\eta_0 b} \exp\{j(\omega t - kz)\} \tag{9.7b}$$

where all parameters are defined in Chapter 6. For any arbitrary time, one can obtain a frozen picture of electric and magnetic field distribution.

In the case of a frozen field state (see Figure 9.3), the flux parameters repeat whenever kz increases by $2\pi(\lambda = \lambda_0)$. For time unfrozen, the field distributions maintain their shape but move in the $+z$-direction at the speed that light would have in an unbounded medium of permittivity ε, that is, $v_{ph} = c / \sqrt{\varepsilon_r} \equiv \omega / k$. A time-varying voltage between plates in the 1-D case, which is called the *TEM-mode voltage*, can now be obtained following [1–5]

$$V(z,t) = V_0 \exp\{j(\omega t - kz)\} \tag{9.8}$$

In the same manner, we obtain the *TEM-mode current* between plates:

$$I(z,t) = \frac{V_0 \sqrt{\varepsilon_r}}{\eta_0} \frac{w}{b} \exp\{j(\omega t - kz)\} \tag{9.9}$$

Then, the TEM impedance for a slab, expressed in ohms, is

$$Z_{TEM} = \frac{V(z,t)}{I(z,t)} = \frac{b}{w} \frac{\eta_0}{\sqrt{\varepsilon_r}} \tag{9.10}$$

The average power flow for TEM waves traveling in the +z-direction between dielectric-filled parallel plates can be determined by use of the well-known relation [1–5]

$$P = \frac{1}{2}\mathrm{Re}\left[VI^*\right] = \frac{1}{2}\mathrm{Re}\left[\lambda_0 \frac{VV^*}{Z_{TEM}}\right] = \frac{1}{2}|V_0|^2 \frac{w/b}{\eta_0/\sqrt{\varepsilon_r}} \tag{9.11}$$

We must note that for propagation in the −z-direction, we must change the exponential factor (−kz) to (+kz) and the signs in Equation 9.9 for $I(z,t)$ and Equation 9.7b for $H_\perp$.

In the general case of propagation of TEM waves in both directions, we must put general solutions in the following form:

$$V(z,t) = Ae^{j(\omega t - kz)} + Be^{j(\omega t + kz)} \tag{9.12a}$$

$$I(z,t) = \frac{A}{Z_{TEM}}e^{j(\omega t - kz)} - \frac{B}{Z_{TEM}}e^{j(\omega t + kz)} \tag{9.12b}$$

where the constants A and B can be obtained once more from the corresponding boundary conditions, and the TEM-mode impedance is expressed by Equation 9.10.

For TEM-mode propagation, we have assumed for simplicity that the guiding structure is lossless and the propagation parameter $\gamma = jk$, indicating that TEM waves are guided between the parallel plates at a speed less than that for light, taking into account the dielectric properties of the structure, that is, $v_{ph} = c/\sqrt{\varepsilon_r}$. Now, we will show that other solutions than TEM modes are possible for the slab geometry, namely, the transverse magnetic (TM) and transverse electric (TE) modes. We start with TM-mode propagation.

9.1.2 Propagation of TM Waves

TM waves, imply that $H_z = 0$. In this case, the E_z component can be found from the corresponding equations of TM waves from Section 6.2, which for $w \gg b$ can be reduced to [1–5]

$$\frac{d^2 E_z(y)}{dy^2} + \kappa^2 E_z(y) = 0 \tag{9.13}$$

Here, we consider a 1-D problem, assuming that E_z is uniformly distributed along the x-axis (see Figure 9.1). The solution of Equation 9.13 is

$$E_z(y) = A\sin \kappa y + B\cos \kappa y \tag{9.14}$$

The constants of integration, A and B, are easy to obtain from boundary conditions. We consider lossless structure, for which $E_z(0) = E_z(b) = 0$. Then, $B = 0$ and $A\sin \kappa b = 0$, from which we have

$$\kappa b = \pi n, \quad n = 1, 2, 3 \dots \tag{9.15}$$

Finally,

$$E_z(y) = A \sin \frac{\pi n y}{b} \quad (9.16a)$$

Using the corresponding equations for TEM waves from Section 6.2, we obtain for the positive (+z) propagation along the z-axis [1–5]

$$H_x(y) = \frac{j\omega\varepsilon}{\kappa^2} \frac{dE_z}{dy} = A \frac{j\omega\varepsilon b}{\pi n} \cos\frac{\pi n y}{b} \quad (9.16b)$$

$$E_y(y) = -Z_{TM} H_x = -A Z_{TM} \frac{j\omega\varepsilon b}{\pi n} \cos\frac{\pi n y}{b} \quad (9.16c)$$

$$E_x = 0, \quad H_y = 0 \quad (9.16d)$$

where, as in Section 6.2, $Z_{TM} = \gamma/j\omega\varepsilon$. Since $n > 0$ integer, from Equation 9.16, it follows that an infinite number of TM modes propagate along the guiding slab, each of which has a different field distribution. Hence, Equation 9.16 describes TM-mode propagation in a parallel-plate filling structure such as a slab. From Equation 9.15, it follows that $\kappa = \pi n/b$, so the propagation constant along the z-axis for each TM mode with number n is

$$\gamma_n = \sqrt{\left(\frac{\pi n}{b}\right)^2 - k^2} = k\sqrt{\left(\frac{n\lambda}{2b}\right)^2 - 1} \quad (9.17)$$

where $\lambda = \lambda_0/\sqrt{\varepsilon_r}$, γ_n can be pure real or imaginary depending on when $n\lambda/2b$ is greater or less than unity. The critical wavelength, called the *cutoff wavelength*, defines the transition between these two situations. We can define it from the equation

$$\frac{n\lambda}{2b} = 1 \quad \text{or} \quad \lambda_{cn} = \frac{2b}{n} \quad \text{and} \quad f_{cn} = \frac{cn}{2b} \quad (9.18)$$

In the same manner, by combining Equations 9.17 and 9.18, we can introduce the *cutoff frequency* of the TM_n modes:

$$\gamma_n \equiv j\beta_n = jk\sqrt{1 - \left(\frac{\lambda}{\lambda_{cn}}\right)^2} = jk\sqrt{1 - \left(\frac{f_{cn}}{f}\right)^2} \quad (9.19)$$

The physical meaning of the cutoff frequency definition follows from Equation 9.19. In fact, if $f > f_{cn}$, the square root is pure real, and the γ_n is pure imaginary. This means that the TM_n modes propagate without any attenuation, whereas the γ_n is pure real for $f < f_{cn}$ and the TM_n modes attenuate without phase progression. These effects are clearly seen from Figure 9.2.

This diagram is called the *dispersion diagram* because of the dependence of the propagation constant $\gamma_n = \alpha_n + j\beta_n$ on frequency. β_n is close to k for $f > f_{cn}$, whereas α_n tends to $\kappa_n = n\pi/b$ with decrease of wave frequency below f_{cn}, that is, when $f < f_{cn}$.

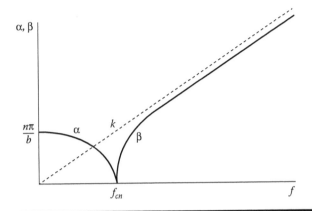

Figure 9.2 Dispersion diagram of propagation parameters vs. wave frequency.

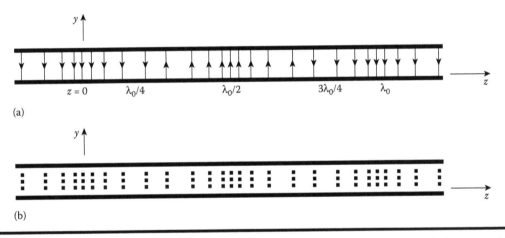

(a)

(b)

Figure 9.3 Distribution of (a) electric component in the *z,y*-plane (arrows) and (b) magnetic component in the *z,y*-plane (dots). (According to Demarest, K. R., Waveguides and Resonators, in *Handbook: Engineering Electromagnetics*, ed. by R. Bansal, Marcel Dekker, New York, pp. 227–254, 2004; Marcuvitz, N., *Waveguide Handbook*, 2nd edn, Peter Peregrinus, London, 1986.)

The TM-field characteristic impedance $Z_{TM}=\gamma/j\omega\varepsilon$ can now be written as

$$Z_{TM_n} = \frac{\eta_0}{\sqrt{\varepsilon_r}}\sqrt{1-\left(\frac{f_{cn}}{f}\right)^2} \tag{9.20}$$

Once more, if $f>f_{cn}$, Z_{TM_n} is pure real, indicating that E_y and H_x are in phase, and the TM mode with number n propagates along the +z-axis. If $f<f_{cn}$, Z_{TM_n} is pure imaginary, and there is no propagation along the z-axis, only attenuation.

Plots of a propagating mode, its E and H field lines in the xy-plane, and its electric field lines in the yz-plane are shown in Figure 9.3a and b. For a fixed time, the E-field pattern in the yz-plane is also depicted in Figure 9.3a. This pattern, as a function of time, moves in the +z-direction at the phase velocity

$$v_{ph} = \frac{\omega}{\beta_n} = \frac{c / \sqrt{\varepsilon_r}}{\sqrt{1 - \left(\dfrac{f_{cn}}{f}\right)^2}}$$

(9.21)

The same feature can be seen from analysis of the so-called *group velocity*, which is usually examined in all guiding structures. This parameter characterizes a power flow velocity inside the guiding structure and is defined as

$$v_{gr} = \frac{d\omega}{d\beta}$$

Then, for the parallel-plate lossless structure, we can obtain from Equation 9.19 that

$$\frac{d\beta_n}{d\omega} = \frac{d}{d\omega}\left(k\sqrt{1 - \left(\frac{f_{cn}}{f}\right)^2}\right) = \frac{d}{d\omega}\left(\omega\sqrt{\varepsilon\mu_0}\sqrt{1 - \left(\frac{\omega_{cn}}{\omega}\right)^2}\right) = \frac{\sqrt{\varepsilon\mu_0}}{\sqrt{1 - \left(\frac{f_{cn}}{f}\right)^2}}$$

So, we finally obtain

$$v_{gr} = \frac{1}{\sqrt{\varepsilon\mu_0}}\sqrt{1 - \left(\frac{f_{cn}}{f}\right)^2}$$

(9.22)

It is clear that both the phase v_{ph} and the group v_{gr} velocities are functions of the cutoff frequency $f_{cn} = n/2b$ or the cutoff wavelength $\lambda_{cn} = 2b/n$, according to Equations 9.18, 9.21, and 9.22. For very high frequencies ($f \gg f_{cn}$, or $\lambda \ll \lambda_{cn}$), the modes with number n, which corresponds to inequality $n \ll (2b / \lambda)$, simply slide between the plates, as shown in Figures 9.4a and b. As f decreases or λ increases, the term $n\lambda/2b$ also increases with $n = const$, and waves propagate more and more obliquely, as shown in Figure 9.4c through e, until $\lambda = \lambda_{cn} = 2b/m$, or $f = f_{cn} = cm/2b$, $m = 0, 1, 2, \ldots, n$, and the waves simply bounce back and forth normally to the plate (as shown in Figure 9.4e) without any propagation along the plate.

The illustrations in Figure 9.4 show the effect of cutoff, where there is a continuous wave propagation and wave attenuation inside the guiding parallel-plate structure. This effect also exists for other guiding structures.

9.1.3 Propagation of TE Waves

The TE waves imply that $E_z = 0$. In this case, the H_z component can be found from the corresponding equations of TE waves presented in Section 6.2, which for $w \gg b$ can be reduced to [1–5]

$$\frac{d^2 H_z(y)}{dy^2} + \kappa^2 H_z(y) = 0$$

(9.23)

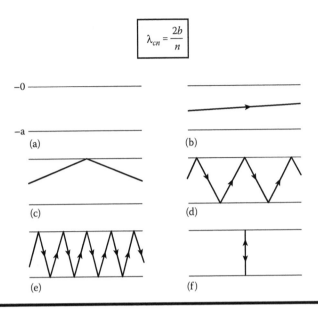

Figure 9.4 (a) View on strip line, (b–e) propagation of modes, from $m=0$ to $m=n$, along the plate, and (f) formation of standing wave in critical case of $m=n$.

Here, we once more consider a 1-D problem, assuming that H_z is uniformly distributed along the x-axis (see Figure 9.1). As above, $\kappa^2 = \gamma^2 + k^2$. The solution of Equation 9.23 is presented by Equation 9.14, in which the constants of integration, A and B, are easy to obtain from boundary conditions. Here, we consider a lossless structure, for which $H_z(0) = H_z(b) = 0$. Then, $A = 0$, $B \cos \kappa b = 0$, and according to Equation 9.15,

$$H_z(y) = B \cos \frac{\pi n y}{b} \qquad (9.24a)$$

Using Equation 6.32, we obtain for the positive $(+z)$ propagation along the z-axis

$$E_x(y) = B \frac{j\omega\mu_0 b}{\pi n} \sin \frac{\pi n y}{b} \qquad (9.24b)$$

$$H_y(y) = \frac{E_x}{Z_{TE}} = \frac{B}{Z_{TE}} \frac{j\omega\mu_0 b}{\pi n} \sin \frac{\pi n y}{b} \qquad (9.24c)$$

$$E_y = 0, \quad H_x = 0 \qquad (9.24d)$$

where, as above, $Z_{TE} = j\omega\mu_0 / \gamma$. The system of equations in Equation 9.24 describes TE mode propagation with number $n > 0$ inside a parallel-plate filling structure such as a slab. From Equation 9.19, it follows that the propagation constant along the z-axis for each TE mode with number n is described by the same expression, which we will rewrite for convenience when describing further material:

$$\gamma_n = jk\sqrt{1 - \left(\frac{\lambda}{\lambda_{cn}}\right)^2} = jk\sqrt{1 - \left(\frac{f_{cn}}{f}\right)^2} \tag{9.25a}$$

Hence, once more, if now $f > f_{cn}$, the square root is pure real and the γ_n is pure imaginary. This means that the TE_n modes propagate without any attenuation, whereas the γ_n is pure real for $f < f_{cn}$ and the TE_n modes attenuate without phase progression. These effects are clearly seen from Figure 9.4.

Figure 9.2 depicts the parameters α_n and β_n for TE_n modes and TM_n modes. Using Equations 9.24b and c, one can express the characteristic impedance of TE_n modes as

$$Z_{TE} = \frac{\eta_0 / \sqrt{\varepsilon_r}}{\sqrt{1 - \left(\frac{f_{cn}}{f}\right)^2}} \tag{9.25b}$$

For $f > f_{cn}$, Z_{TE_n} is pure real, indicating that E_x and H_y are in phase, and TE_n mode with number n propagates along the $+z$-axis. If $f < f_{cn}$, Z_{TE_n} is pure imaginary, E_x and H_y are in phase quadrature, and there is no power flow along the $+z$-axis, only attenuation. Plots of electric and magnetic field lines in an xy-plane and the magnetic lines in an xz-plane are shown for TE_1 mode in Figure 9.4b. From equations

$$\lambda = \lambda_{cn} = \frac{2b}{n} \text{ or } f = f_{cn} = \frac{An}{2b} \tag{9.26}$$

it is evident for both TM and TE modes that for the smallest number $n = 1$, the longest cutoff wavelength and lowest cutoff frequency occur for TE_1 mode and TM_1 mode. For operating wavelength $\lambda = \lambda_0 / \sqrt{\varepsilon_r}$, if $b < \lambda/2$, all TE_n and TM_n modes will attenuate without phase progression on an air-filled parallel-plate structure. Only the TEM mode will propagate in these conditions.

9.2 Rectangular Waveguides

We now start to examine wave propagation in guiding structures where TEM modes cannot be supported [1–4], first, in a rectangular waveguide (see Figure 9.5) with perfectly conducting walls at $x = 0$, a and $y = 0$, b and with a homogeneous isotropic dielectric inside it with permittivity (in practice, the waveguide interior is more likely to be air filled; see Section 6.1). Both TM and TE modes can be supported by this guiding structure [1–5].

9.2.1 Propagation of TM Modes in Rectangular Waveguide

Using the corresponding equations for TM modes described in Section 6.2, we can obtain $E_z(x,y)$ by solving the equation

$$\left(\nabla_{\perp}^2 + \gamma^2 + k^2\right)E_z(x,y) = 0 \tag{9.27}$$

The boundary conditions for this structure are: fields E_z vanish at each of four waveguide walls. To solve this equation, we will use a well-known procedure of variable separation, considering that

$$E_z(x,y) = F_1(x)F_2(y)$$

In this case, Equation 9.27 can be rewritten as

$$F_2(y)\frac{d^2F_1(x)}{dx^2} + F_1(x)\frac{d^2F_2(y)}{dy^2} + \kappa^2 F_1(x)F_2(y) = 0 \tag{9.28a}$$

in which, as before, $\kappa^2 = \gamma^2 + k^2$. Equation 9.28a can be presented as

$$-\frac{1}{F_1(x)}\frac{d^2F_1(x)}{dx^2} - \frac{1}{F_2(y)}\frac{d^2F_2(y)}{dy^2} = \kappa^2 \tag{9.28b}$$

If y is fixed and x is varied, only the first term in Equation 9.28b has the possibility to change. However, it cannot change, since κ^2 is a constant and the second term in Equation 9.28b is also constant for y=const. Thus,

$$-\frac{1}{F_1(x)}\frac{d^2F_1(x)}{dx^2} = k_x^2 = \text{const} \tag{9.29a}$$

Similarly, for x=const, but y is varied,

$$-\frac{1}{F_2(y)}\frac{d^2F_2(y)}{dy^2} = k_y^2 = \text{const} \tag{9.29b}$$

with

$$k_x^2 + k_y^2 = \kappa^2 \tag{9.30}$$

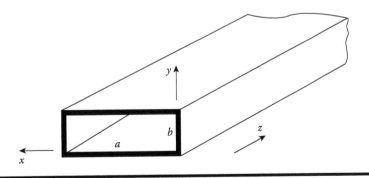

Figure 9.5 Rectangular waveguide geometry.

Because the solutions of Equation 9.29a and b are spatially harmonic, we have the common solution

$$E_z(x, y) = F_1(x)F_2(y)$$
$$= (A_1 \sin k_x x + B_1 \cos k_x x)(A_2 \sin k_y y + B_2 \cos k_y y) \tag{9.31}$$

The boundary conditions at $x=0$ and $y=0$, $E_z(0, y) = E_z(x,0) = 0$, reduce Equation 9.31 to

$$E_z(x, y) = A \sin k_x x \cos k_y y \tag{9.32}$$

where $A = A_1 A_2$. The boundary conditions at $x=a$ and $y=b$, $E_z(a, y) = E_z(x,b) = 0$, lead to conditions

$$k_x a = m\pi, \quad m = 1, 2, 3, \ldots.$$
$$k_y b = n\pi, \quad n = 1, 2, 3, \ldots. \tag{9.33}$$

and therefore Equation 9.32 can be rewritten as

$$E_z(x, y) = A \sin \frac{m\pi x}{a} \sin \frac{n\pi y}{b} \tag{9.34}$$

Now, using Equation 9.34 and setting $A = \text{const}$ to equal $\pm j$ (without any loss of generality), we get [1–5]

$$E_z(x, y) = \pm j \sin \frac{m\pi x}{a} \sin \frac{n\pi y}{b} \tag{9.35a}$$

$$E_x(x, y) = \mp \frac{j\gamma_{mn}(m\pi / a)}{\gamma_{mn}^2 + k^2} \cos \frac{m\pi x}{a} \sin \frac{n\pi y}{b} \tag{9.35b}$$

$$E_y(x, y) = \mp \frac{j\gamma_{mn}(n\pi / b)}{\gamma_{mn}^2 + k^2} \sin \frac{m\pi x}{a} \cos \frac{n\pi y}{b} \tag{9.35c}$$

$$H_z = \mp \frac{E_y}{Z_{TM}^{mn}}, \; H_y = \pm \frac{E_x}{Z_{TM}^{mn}} \tag{9.35d}$$

with

$$Z_{TM}^{mn} = \frac{\gamma_{mn}}{j\omega\varepsilon} = \frac{\gamma_{mn}\eta_0}{jk_0\varepsilon_r} \tag{9.36a}$$

$$\gamma_{mn} = \sqrt{\kappa_{mn}^2 - k^2} = \sqrt{\left(\frac{m\pi}{a}\right)^2 + \left(\frac{n\pi}{b}\right)^2 - k^2} \tag{9.36b}$$

that is,

$$\kappa_{mn}^2 = \left(\frac{m\pi}{a}\right)^2 + \left(\frac{n\pi}{b}\right)^2 \tag{9.36c}$$

To put $A = \pm j$ actually has a logical meaning. In fact, if $A = \pm j$, we have that γ_{mn} is imaginary and then Z_{TM}^{mn} is real: modes propagate inside the waveguide. In this case, E and H are both real and in phase; the Poynting theorem gives power flow inside the waveguide. In contrast, if the TM modes are cutoff, γ_{mn} is real, Z_{TM}^{mn} is imaginary, E and H are in phase quadrature with each other, and there is no power flow inside the waveguide. This effect also follows from Equation 9.36b.

In fact, if $(m\pi/a)^2 + (n\pi/b)^2 > k^2$, then γ_{mn} is real; conversely, we find that γ_{mn} is imaginary. Since $k^2 = (2\pi/\lambda)^2 = \omega^2 \mu_0 \varepsilon$, there exist a cutoff wavelength and cutoff frequency, given by

$$\kappa_{c,mn}^2 = k^2 \tag{9.37a}$$

or

$$\left(\frac{2\pi}{\lambda_{c,mn}}\right)^2 = \left(2\pi f_{c,mn}\right)^2 \mu_0 \varepsilon = \left(\frac{m\pi}{a}\right)^2 + \left(\frac{n\pi}{b}\right)^2 \tag{9.37b}$$

These parameters mark the transition from *the attenuation without phase progression* region to *the propagation without attenuation* region in the frequency domain for TM_{mn} modes inside a rectangular waveguide. From Equations 9.36b and 9.37b, we have

$$\gamma_{mn} = jk\sqrt{1 - \frac{\lambda^2}{\lambda_{c,mn}^2}} \equiv jk\sqrt{1 - \frac{f_{c,mn}^2}{f^2}} \tag{9.38},$$

which is written in the same form as for TM_n and TE_n modes propagating between two parallel plates (see Equation 9.19). Hence, the results presented in Figure 9.2 are fully applicable for TM_{mn} modes in a rectangular waveguide, if $f_{c,n}$ is instead $f_{c,mn}$. We can also present the characteristic impedance in a rectangular waveguide through this cutoff frequency as

$$Z_{TM}^{mn} = \sqrt{\frac{\mu_0}{\varepsilon}}\sqrt{1 - \frac{f_{c,mn}^2}{f^2}} \tag{9.39}$$

When $f > f_{c,mn}$, Z_{TM}^{mn} is pure real, and the TM_{mn} waves propagate inside the rectangular waveguide with phase velocity

$$v_{ph} = \frac{\omega}{\beta_{mn}} = \frac{1}{\sqrt{\mu_0 \varepsilon}}\frac{1}{\sqrt{1 - \frac{f_{c,mn}^2}{f^2}}} = \frac{c}{\sqrt{\varepsilon_r}}\frac{1}{\sqrt{1 - \frac{f_{c,mn}^2}{f^2}}} \tag{9.40}$$

where $k = \omega\sqrt{\mu_0\varepsilon}$ has been used, and $v = c/\sqrt{\varepsilon_r}$ is the velocity of light in an unbounded dielectric medium with permittivity.

9.2.2 Propagation of TE Modes in Rectangular Waveguide

The same procedure with $E_z(x,y) = 0$ and by using equations from Section 6.2 for TE waves gives [1–5]

$$\left(\nabla_\perp^2 + \gamma^2 + k^2\right)H_z(x,y) = 0 \tag{9.41}$$

With boundary conditions $H_z(0,y) = H_z(x,0) = 0$ and $H_z(a,y) = H_z(x,b) = 0$ and the variable separation method, we finally have the same solution as Equation 9.41:

$$H_z(x,y) = G_1(x)G_2(y)$$
$$= (A_1' \sin k_x x + B_1' \cos k_x x)(A_2' \sin k_y y + B_2' \cos k_y y) \tag{9.42}$$

From boundary conditions, it follows that $A_1' = A_2' = 0$ and that $B = B_1'B_2'$. If so, we reduce Equation 9.42 to with $B=j$:

$$H_z(x,y) = j\cos k_x x \cos k_y y \tag{9.43}$$

It also follows from boundary conditions that

$$k_x a = m\pi, \quad m = 0,1,2,.....$$
$$k_y b = n\pi, \quad n = 0,1,2,..... \tag{9.44}$$

The difference between TM and TE modes is that now m and n are indexed from zero (for TE modes this was from unity). But, m and n cannot be simultaneously zero, because if they are both zero, $H_z \equiv B_z = const$ and $\nabla_\perp H_z = 0$, which means that the mode TE_{00} has no transverse field components and thus no possibility of power flow. So, TM modes start from TM_{11}, but TE modes start from TE_{10} and TE_{01}.

Using the corresponding formulas for TE modes described in Section 6.2, we find that

$$E_x(x,y) = -\frac{\omega\mu_0(n\pi/b)}{\gamma_{mn}^2 + k^2}\cos\frac{m\pi x}{a}\sin\frac{n\pi y}{b} \tag{9.45b}$$

$$E_y(x,y) = +\frac{\omega\mu_0(m\pi/a)}{\gamma_{mn}^2 + k^2}\sin\frac{m\pi x}{a}\cos\frac{n\pi y}{b} \tag{9.45c}$$

$$H_z = m\frac{E_y}{Z_{TE}^{mn}}, \quad H_y = \pm\frac{E_x}{Z_{TE}^{mn}} \tag{9.45d}$$

with

$$Z_{EM}^{mn} = \frac{j\omega\mu_0}{\gamma_{mn}} = \frac{jk_0\eta_0}{\gamma_{mn}} \tag{9.46}$$

and γ_{mn} is defined by Equation 9.38. Since m and n can be arbitrary positive integer, including zero (separately), there is a two-dimensionally infinite set of modes TE_{mn} inside a rectangular waveguide, each with its own field distribution. As for TM_{mn} modes, the TE_{mn} modes propagate along the waveguide if γ_{mn} is imaginary and Z_{EM}^{mn} is pure real. Here, E and H are both real and in phase. Conversely, when γ_{mn} is pure real, Z_{EM}^{mn} is imaginary, and E and H are in phase quadrature; there is no propagation, only strong attenuation without progressive phase. This effect also follows from the formula of the characteristic impedance through the cutoff frequency:

$$Z_{TM}^{mn} = \sqrt{\frac{\mu_0}{\varepsilon}} \frac{1}{\sqrt{1 - \frac{f_{c,mn}^2}{f^2}}} \qquad (9.47)$$

As follows from Equation 9.47, and according to dispersion curves shown in Figure 9.2, $f > f_{c,mn}$ describes the propagation range in the frequency domain, where Z_{TM}^{mn} is pure real, and there is power flow; $f < f_{c,mn}$ describes the attenuation range, where Z_{TM}^{mn} is imaginary, and there is no power flow. The phase velocity dispersion properties are described once more by Equation 9.40.

Let us consider these effects for the main TM_{mn} and TE_{mn} modes, for which the cutoff frequencies and wavelengths can be presented as

$$\lambda_{c,mn} = \frac{2\pi}{\sqrt{\left(\frac{m\pi}{a}\right)^2 + \left(\frac{n\pi}{b}\right)^2}} = \frac{1}{\sqrt{\left(\frac{m}{2a}\right)^2 + \left(\frac{n}{2b}\right)^2}} \qquad (9.48a)$$

$$f_{c,mn} = \frac{v}{\lambda_{c,mn}} = \frac{1}{\sqrt{\mu_0\varepsilon}}\sqrt{\left(\frac{m}{2a}\right)^2 + \left(\frac{n}{2b}\right)^2} \qquad (9.48b)$$

Then, for $a = b$ for the main mode TM_{11}, we have, respectively,

$$\lambda_{c,11} = \frac{2ab}{\sqrt{a^2 + b^2}} = \sqrt{2}a \qquad (9.49a)$$

$$f_{c,11} = \frac{1}{\sqrt{\mu_0\varepsilon}} \frac{1}{\sqrt{2}a} \qquad (9.49b)$$

This mode has the longest cutoff wavelength and the lowest cutoff frequency compared with other TM_{mn} modes. As for TE_{mn} modes, TE_{10} and TE_{01} have the longest cutoff wavelength and the lowest cutoff frequency. For $a = b$,

$$\lambda_{c,10} = \lambda_{c,01} = 2a \,. \qquad (9.50a)$$

$$f_{c,10} = f_{c,01} = \frac{1}{\sqrt{\mu_0\varepsilon}} \frac{1}{2a} \qquad (9.50b)$$

Usually, $a > b$; then, TE_{10} has the longest cutoff wavelength and the lowest cutoff frequency with respect to all TM_{mn} and TE_{mn} modes, including TM_{11} and TE_{01}.

Analysis of Equation 9.48 shows that, if $\lambda/2 < a < \lambda$ and $0 < b < \lambda/2$, only the TE_{10} mode exists in a rectangular waveguide; all other modes attenuate without phase progressing. In this case, the cutoff wavelength and frequency are determined by Equation 9.37. The wavelength for the TE_{10} mode equals

$$\lambda_{10} = \frac{\lambda}{\sqrt{1 - \left(\dfrac{\lambda}{2a}\right)^2}} \tag{9.51a}$$

The corresponding propagation constant is

$$\beta_{10} = k\sqrt{1 - \left(\frac{\lambda}{2a}\right)^2} \tag{9.51b}$$

The phase velocity is

$$v_{ph} = \frac{\omega}{\beta_{10}} = \frac{1}{\sqrt{\mu_0 \varepsilon}} \frac{1}{\sqrt{1 - \left(\dfrac{\lambda}{2a}\right)^2}} \tag{9.51c}$$

and finally, the group velocity is

$$v_{gr} = \frac{1}{\sqrt{\mu_0 \varepsilon}} \sqrt{1 - \left(\frac{\lambda}{2a}\right)^2} \tag{9.51d}$$

The distribution of **E** and **H** fields for the TE_{10} mode inside the rectangular waveguide are shown in Figure 9.6 for +z-propagation at $t = 0$.

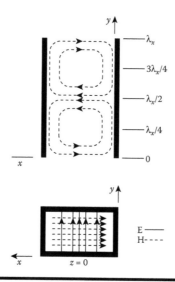

Figure 9.6 Distribution of E-field (continuous lines) and H-field (dotted lines) of electromagnetic mode TE_{10}. (Adapted from Demarest, K. R., Waveguides and Resonators, in *Handbook: Engineering Electromagnetics*, ed. by R. Bansal, Marcel Dekker, New York, pp. 227–254, 2004; Marcuvitz, N., *Waveguide Handbook*, 2nd edn, Peter Peregrinus, London, 1986.)

9.3 Cylindrical Waveguides

In this section, we give an electromagnetic interpretation of wave propagation using characteristics of the guiding modes (see Chapter 6). We should note again that as in a rectangular waveguide, the TEM modes cannot propagate inside such a structure; only TM and TE modes can do so [1–5].

As depicted in Figure 9.7, the circular waveguide has an inner radius a with unspecified wall thickness, because of the assumption of perfect conductivity. Its interior may be filled with a homogeneous isotropic lossless dielectric (with $\mu = \mu_0, \varepsilon$).

9.3.1 Propagation of TM Modes in Cylindrical Waveguide

The same procedure as for the rectangular waveguide gives the basic equation

$$\left(\nabla_\perp^2 + \gamma^2 + k^2\right) E_z(r,\phi) = 0 \tag{9.52}$$

where now in a cylindrical coordinate system

$$\nabla_\perp^2 = \frac{1}{r}\frac{\partial}{\partial r}\left(r\frac{\partial}{\partial r}\right) + \frac{1}{r^2}\frac{\partial^2}{\partial\phi^2}$$

Using, as before, the method of variable separation

$$E_z(r,\phi) = F_1(r)F_2(\phi),$$

we finally have

$$F_2\left[\frac{1}{r}\frac{d}{dr}\left(r\frac{dF_1}{dr}\right)\right] + F_1\left[\frac{1}{r^2}\frac{d^2F_2}{d\phi^2}\right] + \kappa^2 F_1 F_2 = 0 \tag{9.53a}$$

or

$$\left[\frac{r}{F_1}\frac{d}{dr}\left(r\frac{dF_1}{dr}\right)\right] + \left[\frac{1}{F_2}\frac{d^2F_2}{d\phi^2}\right] + \kappa^2 r^2 = 0 \tag{9.53b}$$

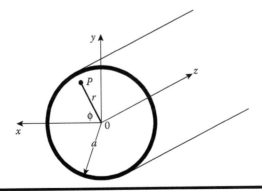

Figure 9.7 Cylindrical waveguide geometry.

If now r is fixed and ϕ is varied, no change can occur in the last term of Equation 9.53b. Thus,

$$\frac{1}{F_2}\frac{d^2F_2}{d\phi^2} = -n^2 = const \tag{9.54}$$

The parameter n must be determined. The general solution of Equation 9.54 can be presented as

$$F_2(\phi) = \left(K_1\cos n\phi + K_2\cos n\phi\right) \tag{9.55}$$

where K_1 and K_2 are constant. From Equation 9.55, it follows that whenever ϕ is increased by 2π, $F_2(\phi)$ will repeat its earlier value. This n must be integer, that is, $n = 0,1,2,\ldots$ The sum of the other two terms in Equation 9.53b must also equal $n^2 = const$. If so, after multiplication by F_1/r^2, we get

$$\frac{1}{r}\frac{d}{dr}\left(r\frac{dF_1}{dr}\right) + \left(\kappa^2 - \frac{n^2}{r^2}\right)F_1 = 0 \tag{9.56}$$

Now, using the variable

$$v = \kappa r$$

we have from Equation 9.56

$$\frac{d^2F_1}{dv^2} + \frac{1}{v}\frac{dF_1}{dv} + \left(1 - \frac{n^2}{v^2}\right)F_1 = 0 \tag{9.57}$$

This equation is usually called a Bessel's differential equation, despite the fact that its solutions can be other spherical functions, such as Hankel and Neumann, but the latter can be easily presented via a Bessel function using specific relations between them [6].

Without entering into detail and loss of generality, let us assume that the solution of Equation 9.57 is

$$F_1(v) = J_n(v) \tag{9.58}$$

where $J_n(v)$ is a Bessel function of the first kind [6]

$$J_n(v) = \sum_{m=0}^{\infty}\frac{(-1)^m(v/2)^{n+2m}}{m!(n+m)!}$$

Combining Equations 9.55 and 9.58, we finally have the solution of the general equation Equation 9.52:

$$E_z(\kappa r,\phi) = J_n(\kappa r)\left(K_1\cos n\phi + K_2\sin n\phi\right) \tag{9.59}$$

From boundary conditions $E_z(\kappa a,\phi) = 0$, we have $J_n(\kappa r) = 0$. Function $J_n(v)$ is shown in Figure 9.8, according to [6].

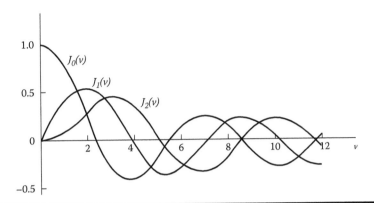

Figure 9.8 Bessel functions $J_n(\nu)$ of the first kind versus $\nu=r$; $\kappa_{c,nm}=\nu_{nm}\cdot r$ are the roots of the Bessel function. (According to Abramowitz, M. and I. A. Stegun, *Handbook of Mathematical Functions*, Dover, New York, 1965.)

It has a sequence of roots. Let ν_{nm} be the mth root of $J_n(\nu)$, defined by

$$J_n(\nu_{nm})=0 \tag{9.60}$$

This field solution must satisfy the boundary condition at $r=a$ if

$$\kappa_{c,nm}=\frac{\nu_{nm}}{a} \tag{9.61}$$

This gives, instead of Equation 9.59, the solution

$$E_z(\nu_{nm},\phi)=J_n(\nu_{nm}r/a)\left(K_{1,nm}\cos n\phi+K_{2,nm}\sin n\phi\right) \tag{9.62}$$

This is the solution for the longitudinal field (along the z-axis) for the TM_{nm} modes inside the circular waveguide. According to index of roots, for $J_0(\nu)$, we have $n=1,2,3,\dots$, and for $J_n(\nu)$ with $n\geq 1$ using $m=0,1,2,3,\dots$ with $\nu_{n0}=0$. So, $E_z\equiv 0$ for $m=0$, for arbitrary $n\geq 1$. Hence, we have $n=0,1,2,3,\dots$, $m=1,2,3,\dots$.

Here, once more, $\kappa_{c,nm}$ from Equation 7.61 allows us to distinguish between *propagation* and *attenuation without phase progression*; that is, it determines the cutoff wave number for TM_{nm} modes. From Equations 9.60 and 9.61, one can obtain the cutoff wavelength and the cutoff frequency, respectively:

$$\lambda_{c,nm}=\frac{2\pi a}{\nu_{nm}},\ f_{c,nm}=\frac{c}{\sqrt{\varepsilon_r}}\frac{\nu_{nm}}{2\pi a} \tag{9.63}$$

Further,

$$\gamma_{nm}^2=-\left(k^2-\kappa_{c,nm}^2\right)=-k^2\left[1-\left(\frac{\kappa_{c,nm}}{k}\right)^2\right] \tag{9.64}$$

or

$$\gamma_{mn} = jk\sqrt{1 - \frac{\lambda^2}{\lambda_{c,nm}^2}} \equiv jk\sqrt{1 - \frac{f_{c,nm}^2}{f^2}} \qquad (9.65)$$

Other components can be obtained by using Equation 9.55 and the relation [5]

$$\nabla_\perp F = \mathbf{i}_r \frac{\partial F}{\partial r} + \mathbf{i}_\phi \frac{1}{r} \frac{\partial F}{\partial \phi}$$

Finally, we get

$$E_z = \pm j J_n(\nu_{nm} r / a) \begin{cases} \cos n\phi \\ \sin n\phi \end{cases} \qquad (9.66a)$$

$$E_r = -\frac{j\gamma_{nm}}{\kappa_{c,nm}^2} J_n'(\nu_{nm} r/a) \begin{cases} \cos n\phi \\ \sin n\phi \end{cases} \qquad (9.66b)$$

$$E_\phi = \frac{j\gamma_{nm}}{\kappa_{c,nm}^2} \frac{n}{r} J_n(\nu_{nm} r/a) \begin{cases} \sin n\phi \\ -\cos n\phi \end{cases} \qquad (9.66c)$$

$$H_r = \mp \frac{E_\phi}{Z_{TM}}, \ H_\phi = \pm \frac{E_r}{Z_{TM}} \qquad (9.66d)$$

where $Z_{TM} = \gamma_{nm}/j\omega\varepsilon$ and $J'(\nu_{nm}r/a)$ is the derivative of the Bessel's function $J(\nu_{nm}r/a)$ over r [6]. The upper set of solutions in the system of Equations 9.66a through 9.66d arises from selecting $K_{1,nm} = \pm j$, $K_{2,nm} = 0$, and the lower set is from choosing $K_{1,nm} = 0$, $K_{2,nm} = \pm j$. Additionally, we get

$$Z_{TM} = \sqrt{\frac{\mu_0}{\varepsilon}} \sqrt{1 - \left(\frac{f_{c,nm}}{f}\right)^2} \qquad (9.67)$$

which is the same as for TM_{nm} modes in the rectangular waveguide. Equation 9.66 describes the distribution of the 2-D-infinite set of TM_{nm} modes in a transverse plane inside a circular waveguide in the range $0 < r \le a$, $0 < \phi \le 2\pi$; each of the modes has a different field distribution. By multiplying Equation 9.66 by $\exp\{j\omega t \mp \gamma_{nm}z\}$, the simple solutions for E(r,φ,z,t) and H(r,φ,z,t) can be obtained.

For arbitrary complex constant $K_{1,nm}$ and $K_{2,nm}$ we can obtain more general TM_{nm} solutions. From Equation 9.67, it follows, once more, that if $f > f_{c,nm}$, Z_{TM} is pure real, and the TM_{nmn} waves propagate inside rectangular waveguide with phase velocity

$$v_{ph} = \frac{\omega}{\beta_{mn}} = \frac{c}{\sqrt{\varepsilon_r}} \frac{1}{\sqrt{1 - \frac{f_{c,mn}^2}{f^2}}} \tag{9.68}$$

which is identical to that for the rectangular waveguide. In this case, the power flux flow is described by group velocity

$$v_{gr} = \left(\frac{d\beta_{mn}}{d\omega} \right)^{-1} = \frac{c}{\sqrt{\varepsilon}} \sqrt{1 - \frac{f_{c,mn}^2}{f^2}} \tag{9.69}$$

If, conversely, $f < f_{c,nm}$, Z_{TM} is pure imaginary, and the TM_{nmn} waves attenuate without phase progression, there is no propagation of the TM_{nmn} modes inside the circular waveguide.

9.3.2 Propagation of TE Modes in Cylindrical Waveguide

For $E_z = 0$, using the same procedure as for TM modes, we have for TE modes [5]

$$H_z(\kappa r, \phi) = J_n(\kappa r) \left(K_1' \cos n\phi + K_2' \sin n\phi \right) \tag{9.70}$$

Then, from Section 4.2 regarding TE waves, it follows that

$$E_\phi(\kappa r, \phi) = \frac{j\omega\mu_0}{\kappa^2} \frac{\partial H_z}{\partial r} \tag{9.71}$$

From boundary conditions $E_\phi(\kappa a, \phi) = 0$, we have $J_n'(\kappa a) = 0$. Let, $\tilde{v}_{nm}$ be the nth root of $J_n'(\tilde{v}_{nm})$, then

$$\kappa_{c,nm} = \frac{\tilde{v}_{nm}}{a} \tag{9.72}$$

This gives from Equation 9.72

$$H_z(\tilde{v}_{nm}, \phi) = J_n(\tilde{v}_{nm}r/a) \left(K_{1,nm}' \cos n\phi + K_{2,nm}' \sin n\phi \right) \tag{9.73a}$$

This is the solution for the longitudinal field (along the z-axis) for the TE_{nm} modes inside the circular waveguide. Here, $n = 0,1,2,3,\ldots$, $m = 1,2,3,\ldots$

Other components of TE_{nm} modes can be obtained from the corresponding equations for TE waves presented in Section 6.2 in the same manner as for TM_{nm} modes:

$$H_z = jJ_n(\tilde{v}_{nm}r/a) \begin{cases} \cos n\phi \\ \sin n\phi \end{cases} \tag{9.73b}$$

$$E_r = \frac{\omega\mu_0}{\kappa_{c,nm}^2}\frac{n}{r}J_n(\tilde{v}_{nm}r/a)\begin{cases}-\sin n\phi\\\cos n\phi\end{cases}\qquad(9.73c)$$

$$E_\phi = -\frac{\omega\mu_0}{\kappa_{c,nm}^2}J_n'(\tilde{v}_{nm}r/a)\begin{cases}\cos n\phi\\\sin n\phi\end{cases}\qquad(9.73d)$$

$$H_r = \mp\frac{E_\phi}{Z_{TE}},\quad H_\phi = \pm\frac{E_r}{Z_{TE}}\qquad(9.73e)$$

where

$$Z_{TE} = \sqrt{\frac{\mu_0}{\varepsilon}}\frac{1}{\sqrt{1-\left(\frac{f_{c,nm}}{f}\right)^2}}\qquad(9.74)$$

which is the same as for TE_{nm} modes in the rectangular waveguide. All the features we have examined are the same for the TE_{nm} modes in the circular waveguide, and Equations 9.70 and 9.71 are also common to the two types of modes.

Additional analysis of the roots of $J_n(\tilde{v}_{nm}r/a)$ and $J_n(v_{nm}r/a)$ has shown that the TE_{11} mode has the longest cutoff wavelength and the lowest cutoff frequency of all the TE or TM modes that can propagate in a circular waveguide. The next lowest is the TM_{10} mode.

Thus, when the carried frequency is f and the operating wavelength is λ, if the normalized guide radius a/λ is chosen to lie in the range $(\tilde{v}_{11}/2\pi) < (a/\lambda) < (v_{10}/2\pi)$, that is, if $0.3\lambda < a < 0.4\lambda$, then only the TE_{11} mode can propagate in a circular waveguide. The E and H field distribution for the TE_{11} mode in a circular waveguide is shown in Figure 9.9 for the upper solution of Equation 9.73.

Rotation of this picture by 90° would give the flux map for the lower solution set in the system of Equation 9.73.

Based on these formulas, similar derivations and distribution of the electrical and magnetic fields can be found for various modes propagating along rectangular and circular waveguides.

PROBLEMS

Example 9.1: Determine cutoff (critical) frequencies of the modes TE_m ($m=1,2,3$), the plane 2-D waveguide (see Figure 9.1), and the corresponding parameters: the waveguide wavelength λ_g, the phase velocity v_{ph} and the group velocity v_{gr}, and the impedance Z_{TE}.

Example 9.2: Given a rectangular waveguide (shown in Figure 9.5) with the width $a=0.04$ m and height $b=0.02$ m, filled by air (with $\varepsilon_r=1$, $\mu_r=1$), the carrier frequency is 25% higher than the cutoff frequency of the TM_{11} mode.

Example 9.3: Determine the critical frequencies of the lowest TE_{mn} and TM_{mn} modes ($m=0,1$; $n=0,1$; $m\neq n$) in the rectangular waveguide with a) $b/a=1$ and b) $b/a=0.5$.

Example 9.4: Given a rectangular waveguide (shown in Figure 9.5) with the width $a=0.0225$ m and height $b=0.01$ m. Parameters of medium inside the waveguide are $\varepsilon_r=25$, $\mu_r=1$, and the carrier frequency is $f=0.9$ GHz.

a. *Find*: Critical frequencies f_{cTE01} and f_{cTE10}.

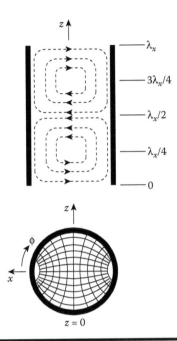

Figure 9.9 The E- and H-field distribution of the TE_{11} mode in a circular waveguide plotted with continuous and dashed curves, respectively. (According to Demarest, K. R., Waveguides and Resonators, in *Handbook: Engineering Electromagnetics*, ed. by R. Bansal, Marcel Dekker, New York, pp. 227–254, 2004; Marcuvitz, N., *Waveguide Handbook,* 2nd edn, Peter Peregrinus, London, 1986.)

   b.   For these two critical velocities, calculate the waveguide wavelength λ_g, the phase velocity v_{ph} and the group velocity v_{gr}, and the impedance Z_{TE}.

Example 9.5: Given a cylindrical waveguide, as shown in Figure 9.7, with radius $r = a = 0.01\ m$. Parameters of dielectric within the waveguide are $\varepsilon_r = 50$, $\mu_r = 1$, and the carrier frequency is $f = 10$ GHz.

   a.   *Find*: Critical frequencies $f_{cTE_{11}}$ ($\tilde{v}_{11} = 2.933$) and $f_{cTE_{01}}$ ($\tilde{v}_{01} = 2.405$).

   b.   For these two critical velocities, calculate the waveguide wavelength λ_g, phase velocity v_{ph}, group velocity v_{gr}, and impedance Z_{TE}.

References

1. Elliott, R. S., *Electromagnetics: History, Theory, and Applications*, New York: IEEE, 1993.
2. Kong, J. A., *Electromagnetic Wave Theory*, New York: Wiley, 1986.
3. Chew, W. C., *Waves and Fields in Inhomogeneous Media*, New York: IEEE, 1995.
4. Demarest, K. R., Waveguides and Resonators, in *Handbook: Engineering Electromagnetics,* ed. by R. Bansal, New York: Marcel Dekker, 2004, pp. 227–254.
5. Marcuvitz, N., *Waveguide Handbook*, 2nd edn, London: Peter Peregrinus, 1986.
6. Abramowitz, M. and I. A. Stegun, *Handbook of Mathematical Functions*, New York: Dover, 1965.

ANTENNA FUNDAMENTALS

Chapter 10

Basic Characteristics and Types of Antennas

A radio antenna is a structure of a radio system which converts the current/voltage generated by a wire based circuit, such as a transmission line, waveguide, or coaxial cable, into electromagnetic (EM) field energy propagating through space. [1–15].

10.1 Basic Characteristics of Antennas

The principal characteristics used to describe an antenna acting either as a transmitter or as a receiver are *radiation pattern*, *directivity*, *gain*, *efficiency*, *polarization*, and antenna *impedance*. We will characterize all of them briefly without entering deeply into mathematics. The reader can find all the details in excellent books and chapters in the corresponding handbooks [1–15].

10.1.1 Antenna Radiation Regions

When the antenna is determined as a radiator of EM energy, this should be differentiated into

1. A reactive near-field region
2. A radiating near-field region
3. A far-field region

As shown in Figure 10.1, the reactive near-field region exists close to the antenna aperture. The near-field region, also called the *Fresnel region*, is defined by a radius R, beyond which lies the far-field region, or the *Fraunhofer region* [10–15].

$$R = \frac{2L^2}{\lambda} \tag{10.1}$$

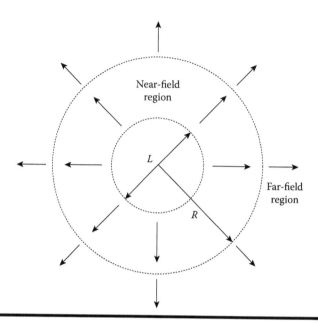

Figure 10.1   Close and far zones of the point antenna.

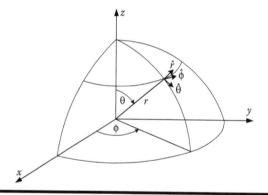

Figure 10.2   Spherical coordinate system.

where:

   L   (in meters) is the diameter of the antenna, or the area of the smallest sphere where the antenna is embedded

   λ   (in meters) is the wavelength

Mathematically, the radiation intensity can be presented as the product of the time-averaged magnitude of the Poynting vector $\boldsymbol{S}$ [1–7, 10–15] (see also Chapter 1) and the square of the distance from the antenna r:

$$I = r^2 S = r^2 E_\theta H_\varphi \tag{10.2}$$

where E_θ and H_ϕ are the components of the electrical and magnetic fields of the antenna radiation pattern in the spherical coordinate system shown in Figure 10.2.

However, as was shown in [1–6], Equations 10.1 and 10.2 are not exact, since they do not account for the reactive near-field region. In the reactive-field range of the antenna, the most important component of the EM radiated wave is H_ϕ, which varies (for a small distance r) as r^{-2}, while E_θ and E_r vary as r^{-3} [10–12].

So, all computations relating to antenna radiation should take into account both the reactive and the close-in Fresnel regions. Moreover, researchers have shown that it is important to account for the effect of the environment or material (e.g., various natural and man-made obstructions in the terrestrial links, ionospheric plasma or atmospheric pollution, turbulence in land–satellite communications, subsoil media for ground-penetrating radar, and so on; see Chapter 11) in close proximity to the antenna.

At the same time, in most practical applications, Equations 10.1 and 10.2 are correct enough to describe the antenna-radiated pattern in various kinds of media, accounting for the effects of each lossy dielectric medium as an additional reactive resistivity loading the antenna.

10.1.2 Basic Characteristics of Antennas

The radiation pattern of an arbitrary antenna is usually defined as the relative distribution of EM energy or power in space. It is called the *power pattern*. Intensity I is measured in watts or joules per unit solid angle. The measure of a solid angle is a *steradian*, which is defined as the solid angle with its vortex at the center of the sphere of radius r that is subtended by a spherical surface area equal to that of a square with each side of length r (see Figure 10.3 arranged according to [1–7]).

This spherical surface area is determined by

$$dA = r^2 \sin\theta\, d\theta\, d\phi \tag{10.3}$$

where r, θ, and ϕ are basic parameters of the spherical coordinate system. The element of solid angle $d\Omega$ that covers this spherical surface area is shown in Figure 10.3.

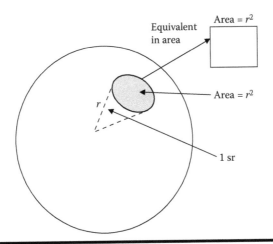

Figure 10.3 Presentation of an area on a sphere of radius r as an analog of quadrat area of size r; the solid 3-D angle is measured in steradians (sr).

The shape of the radiation pattern defines the type of the antenna: *isotropic, directional,* or *omnidirectional.* An *isotropic antenna* refers to a hypothetical antenna radiating equally in all directions without any loss, that is, its *power pattern* uniformly distributed in all directions.

$$S = \frac{P}{(\text{area of a sphere})} = \frac{P}{4\pi r^2} \tag{10.4}$$

Then, according to Equation 10.2, the total radiation intensity of the isotropic antenna equals

$$I = \frac{P}{4\pi} \tag{10.5}$$

A *directional antenna* transmits (or receives) waves more efficiently in certain directions than in others. A radiation pattern plot for a directional antenna is shown in Figure 10.4, illustrating the *main lobe,* which includes the direction of maximum radiation intensity, a *back lobe* with radiation in the opposite direction to the main lobe, and several *side lobes* separated by nulls where no radiation occurs.

For this kind of antenna, some unified parameters are usually used:

■ The *half-power beamwidth* (HPBW) (see Figure 10.4), or simply the *beamwidth,* is the solid angle that bounds the area of the main lobe where the half-power points are located.
■ The *front–back ratio* is the ratio between the peak amplitudes of the main and back lobes, usually expressed in decibels (see Figure 10.4).
■ The *side-lobe level* is the amplitude of the biggest side lobe, usually expressed in decibels relative to the peak of the main lobe (see Figure 10.4).

The parameter *directivity* (D) is used to describe nonisotropic antennas and the variation of their signal intensity in all directions. It can be generally defined as the ratio of the power of the transmitting radiation in the specific direction determined by spherical coordinates (ϕ,θ), according to Figure 10.2, to that of the equivalent isotropic antenna:

$$D(\phi,\theta) = \frac{P(\phi,\theta)}{P_{isotropy}} \tag{10.6}$$

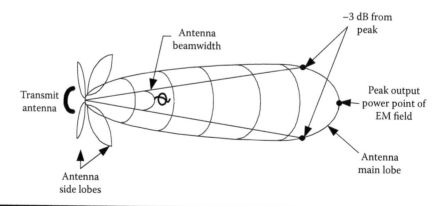

Figure 10.4   Schematic presentation of antenna beam parameters.

The use of an isotropic antenna as a reference in Equation 10.6 allows us to determine the directivity in decibels relative to an isotropic antenna (*dBi*): $D[dBi] = 10 \log D_{isotropy}$.

If we now introduce the beam solid angle Ω_A as the solid angle through which all the power of the antenna will flow, we can present directivity as

$$D = \frac{4\pi}{\Omega_A} \approx \frac{4\pi}{\Theta_{1r}\Theta_{2r}} \tag{10.7a}$$

where Θ_{1r} and Θ_{2r} are the HPBW, measured in radians, in one plane and in a plane at the right angle to the other, respectively, as defined in Figure 10.4.

The same expression can be determined if the beamwidsth is measured in degrees:

$$D = \frac{4\pi}{\Omega_A} \approx \frac{4\pi(180/\pi)^2}{\Theta_{1d}\Theta_{2d}} \approx \frac{4.12 \times 10^4}{\Theta_{1d}\Theta_{2d}} \tag{10.7b}$$

where Θ_{1d} and Θ_{1d} are the half-power beamwidth in one plane and in a plane at the right angle to the other, respectively, measured in degrees.

The *power gain* (*G*), or *antenna gain*, expressed in decibels, is defined as 4π times the ratio of the radiation intensity in a given direction to the total power accepted by the antenna. The gain is related to the radiation efficiency η and the directivity D by

$$G(\phi, \theta) = \eta D(\phi, \theta) \tag{10.8}$$

Usually, in practical antenna design, the terms *directivity* and *gain* imply the maximum value of $D(\phi, \theta) = D_{max}$, denoted simply by D, and $G(\phi, \theta) = G_{max}$, denoted simply by G. If so, we can rewrite Equation 10.8 as a simple relation:

$$G = \eta D \tag{10.9}$$

In practical applications, an approximate expression for the gain, corresponding to Equation 10.7 for the directivity, is also used:

$$G = \approx \frac{3.0 \cdot 10^4}{\Theta_{1d}\Theta_{2d}} \tag{10.10}$$

Using these notations, we can now rewrite Equation 10.4 for radiated power density of the transmitting directive antenna as

$$S = \frac{P}{4\pi r^2} \cdot G = \frac{P}{4\pi r^2} \cdot \eta D \tag{10.11}$$

Concerning the *receiving* antenna, a parameter such as *effective area* or *aperture* (also called *antenna cross section*) is usually used, and is denoted by A_e. The *effective aperture* of the receiving antenna is defined as the ratio of the power that is produced at the input of the receiver, P_R, to the power density, S, of the EM radiation of the transmitting antenna, according to Equation 10.4, that arrives at the receiving antenna:

$$A_e = \frac{P_R}{S} \tag{10.12}$$

The maximum antenna gain G is also related to the effective antenna aperture as follows [13–16]:

$$G = \frac{4\pi}{\lambda^2} A_e \tag{10.13}$$

10.1.3 Polarization of Antennas

Although EM wave field polarization was introduced in Chapter 4, we will briefly discuss this subject in more detail for the description of antenna radiation fields. Thus, as was mentioned in Chapter 4, there are two types of wave polarizations, defined by the orientation of the electric field vector **E** of a plane wave relative to the direction of propagation **k**: one normal to **k** is called a *vertically polarized* or transverse electric (TE) wave, and one in the same plane as **k** is said to be a transverse magnetic (TM) wave or *horizontally polarized*.

Both these waves are *linearly polarized*, as the electric field vector **E** has a single direction along the entire propagation vector **k** elongated along axis x (see Figure 10.5a). If two plane linearly polarized waves of equal amplitude and orthogonal polarization (vertical and horizontal) are combined with a 90° phase difference, the resulting wave will be a *circularly polarized* (CP) wave, in which the motion of the electric field vector will describe a circle around the propagation vector.

The field vector will rotate by 360° for every wavelength traveled. CP waves are most commonly used in land cellular and satellite communications, as they can be generated and received using antennas that are oriented in any direction around their axis without loss of power [10–15]. They may be generated as either right-hand CP or left-hand CP, depending on the direction of vector **E** rotation (see Figure 10.5b). In the most general case, the components of two waves could be of unequal amplitude, or their phase difference could be other than 90°. The combined result is an *elliptically polarized* wave, where vector **E** still rotates at the same rate as for a CP wave, but varies in amplitude with time. In the case of elliptical polarization, the axial ratio, $AR = E_{maj} / E_{min}$,

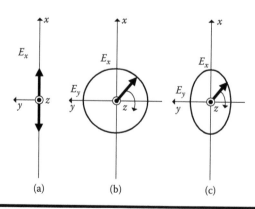

Figure 10.5 Types of wave polarizations: (a) linear, (b) circular, and (c) elliptical.

is usually introduced (see Figure 10.5c). *AR* is defined to be positive for left-hand polarization and negative for right-hand polarization.

Next, we turn our attention to the wave field polarization in the case of a free-space propagation channel. Thus, for both vectors of the EM wave, $\mathbf{E}(\mathbf{r})$ and/or $\mathbf{H}(\mathbf{r})$, one can find the following form of their presentation:

$$\mathbf{E}(\mathbf{r}) = \mathbf{e}_E E_0 \exp(i\mathbf{k} \cdot \mathbf{r}) \tag{10.14a}$$

$$\mathbf{H}(\mathbf{r}) = \mathbf{e}_H H_0 \exp(i\mathbf{k} \cdot \mathbf{r}) \tag{10.14b}$$

where $\mathbf{e}_E$ and $\mathbf{e}_H$ are the constant unit vectors, that is, $|\mathbf{e}_E| = |\mathbf{e}_H| = 1$; E_0 and H_0 are the complex amplitudes, which are constant in space and time. From conditions that satisfy free-space propagation without any sources inside, it follows that

$$\mathbf{e}_E \cdot \mathbf{k} = 0, \mathbf{e}_H \cdot \mathbf{k} = 0, \text{ and } \mathbf{e}_H = \frac{\mathbf{k} \times \mathbf{e}_E}{|\mathbf{k}|} \tag{10.15}$$

Relations 10.15 denotes that the vectors $\mathbf{E}$ and $\mathbf{H}$ are perpendicular to the direction of wave propagation $\mathbf{k}$, and that vectors $\mathbf{e}_E$, $\mathbf{e}_H$, and $\mathbf{k}$ form a system of orthogonal vectors, in which vectors $\mathbf{E}$ and $\mathbf{H}$ oscillate in phase and their ratio is constant.

At the same time, the vector $\mathbf{E}$, described by Equation 10.14a, represents a simple case of a linearly polarized plane wave. To obtain a more general case of wave polarization, we should introduce an additional linearly polarized wave independent of the first one. It can be easily shown that two linearly polarized independent solutions for the electrical component of the EM wave in free space can be presented in the following form:

$$\mathbf{E}_1(\mathbf{r}) = \mathbf{e}_1 E_{01} \exp(i\mathbf{k} \cdot \mathbf{r}) \tag{10.16}$$

$$\mathbf{E}_2(\mathbf{r}) = \mathbf{e}_2 E_{02} \exp(i\mathbf{k} \cdot \mathbf{r}) \tag{10.17}$$

Consequently, the magnetic field components of the EM wave satisfy, according to Equation 10.14b in free space (for $\mu_r = 1$), the following relations:

$$\mathbf{B}_i = \sqrt{\varepsilon_r} \frac{\mathbf{k} \times \mathbf{E}_i}{|\mathbf{k}|}, \quad \mathbf{B}_i \equiv \mathbf{H}_i \ i = 1,2 \tag{10.18}$$

Here, the amplitudes E_{01}, E_{02} and H_{01}, H_{02} are the complex values, which enable us to introduce the phase difference between the two components, electric and magnetic, of the EM wave. The electric field component fully describes all kinds of EM wave polarization. Then, the common solution for a plane EM wave propagating along vector $\mathbf{k}$ can be presented as a linear combination of E_1 and E_2:

$$\mathbf{E}(\mathbf{r}) = \{\mathbf{e}_1 E_{01} + \mathbf{e}_2 E_{02}\} \exp(i\mathbf{k} \cdot \mathbf{r}) \tag{10.19}$$

If E_1 and E_2 have the same phase, Equation 10.19 describes the linearly polarized wave with polarization vector directed to the $\mathbf{e}_1$ axis at angle

$$\theta = \tan^{-1}\left(\frac{E_{02}}{E_{01}}\right) \tag{10.20}$$

and with amplitude

$$E = \left(E_{01}^2 + E_{02}^2\right)^{1/2} \tag{10.21}$$

Next, if $\mathbf{E}_1$ and $\mathbf{E}_2$ have different phases, then the EM wave (Equation 10.19) is elliptically polarized (see Figure 10.5c). If $\mathbf{E}_1 = \mathbf{E}_2$ and phase difference equals 90°, then the elliptically polarized wave becomes a circularly polarized wave. In this case, Equation 10.18 becomes

$$\mathbf{E}(\mathbf{r}) = \{\mathbf{e}_1 \pm \mathbf{e}_2\}\exp(i\mathbf{k}\cdot\mathbf{r}) \tag{10.22}$$

The sign + corresponds to anticlockwise rotation, called the wave with *left-hand* circular polarization. The sign − corresponds to the wave with right-hand polarization (that is, with clockwise rotation), as shown in Figure 10.5.

Polarization loss factor (PLF) is used as a figure of merit to measure the degree of polarization mismatch [15]. It is defined as the square power of the cosine angle between the polarization states of the antenna in its transmitting mode and the incoming wave (see Figure 10.6).

$$\text{PLF} = |\cos\gamma|^2 \tag{10.23}$$

Generally, an antenna is designed for a desired polarization. The component of the electric field in the direction of the desired polarization is called the *co-polar component*, whereas the undesired polarization, usually taken in the orthogonal direction to the desired one, is known as *cross-polar component*. The latter can be due to a change of polarization characteristics during the propagation or scattering of waves, known as *polarization rotation*.

An actual antenna does not completely discriminate against a cross-polarized wave due to structural abnormalities of the antenna.

The directivity pattern obtained over the entire direction on a representative plane for cross-polarization with respect to the maximum directivity for the desired (co-polar) polarization is

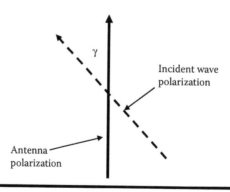

Figure 10.6 Definition of PLF.

called *antenna cross-polarization discrimination* and plays an important factor in determining the antenna performance.

10.2 Antennas in Free Space

The equations obtained in Section 10.1 allow us to obtain the relation between power at the transmitter and the receiver antenna located in free space. This relation is called the *Friis transmission formula*.

According to Equations 10.11 through 10.13, for two antennas separated by a distance, r, great enough to take into account only the far-field regions of both antennas, we get

$$P_R = S \cdot A_{eR} = \frac{P_T}{4\pi r^2} \cdot G_T \cdot A_{eR} \tag{10.24}$$

Taking into account that the effective aperture of the receiver antenna equals (see Equation 10.13) $A_{eR} = \lambda^2 G_R / 4\pi$, we finally get

$$P_R = S \cdot A_{eR} = P_T \cdot \left(\frac{\lambda}{4\pi r} \right)^2 \cdot G_T \cdot G_R \tag{10.25}$$

or, introducing a new parameter, the path gain (PG), for antennas in free space, we get

$$PG = \frac{P_R}{P_T} = \left(\frac{\lambda}{4\pi r} \right)^2 \cdot G_T \cdot G_R \tag{10.26}$$

Here, G_T and G_R are the maximum gain of the transmitter and receiver antenna, respectively.

Equation 10.26 is the *Friis transmission formula*, which describes the relation between two antennas, the transmitter and the receiver, as essential parts of a wireless communication system, as well as the range in radio propagation channel in free-space conditions.

10.3 Types of Antenna

There is a wide spectrum of available antenna systems used in different branches of wireless communications, such as *dipole, loop, helical,* and *linear,* the *aperture* antennas, mostly used as *horn* antennas, the *array* antennas, the *reflector* antennas, and the adaptive or "smart" antennas.

10.3.1 Dipole Antennas

10.3.1.1 Infinitesimal Dipole Antennas

The dimension of this antenna corresponds to the condition $d \ll L \ll \lambda$ (see Figure 10.7). The current of this dipole antenna is [14]

$$I = \frac{dQ}{dt} = j\omega Q(\mathbf{r}) \tag{10.27}$$

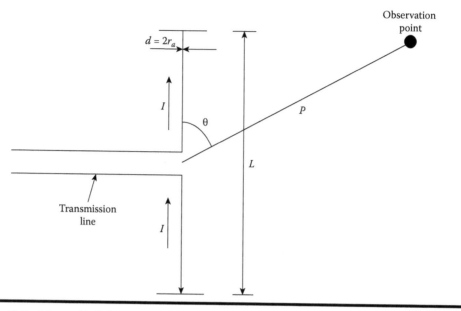

Figure 10.7 View of infinitesimal dipole.

The magnetic field component in the far region is

$$H_r = 0$$

$$H_\phi \approx \frac{j\omega IL}{4\pi} \frac{e^{-jkr}}{r} \sin\theta$$

$$H_\theta = 0 \tag{10.28a}$$

The electric field component in the far region is

$$E_r = 0$$

$$E_\theta \approx \frac{jZ_0 kIL}{4\pi} \frac{e^{-jkr}}{r} \sin\theta$$

$$E_\phi = 0 \tag{10.28b}$$

The electrical field pattern of such a dipole, described by Equation 10.28b, is presented in Figure 10.8 for the two-dimensional (2-D) case, which clearly shows symmetrical two-sided EM-field distribution.

10.3.1.2 Finite-Length Dipole Antennas

The typical picture of such a dipole is shown in Figure 10.9.

There are two possible distributions of current on an antenna: triangular and actual ($L = \lambda/2$). Both types of current distributions are shown in Figure 10.10.

For the far-field approximation, the electric field pattern can be presented as

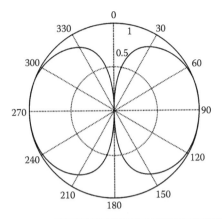

Figure 10.8   Electric field pattern of the infinitesimal dipole.

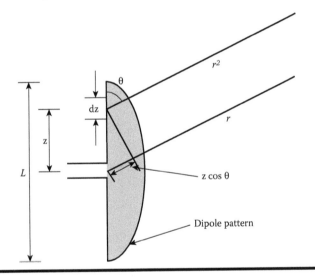

Figure 10.9   View of finite-length dipole antenna.

$$E_\theta = j60I_m \frac{e^{-jkr}}{r} F(\theta) \tag{10.29}$$

where

$$F(\theta) = \frac{\cos\left(\dfrac{kL}{2}\cos\theta\right) - \cos\left(\dfrac{kL}{2}\right)}{\sin\theta}$$

The radiation power of the infinitesimal and the finite-length dipole antenna can be described by a similar formula:

$$P_{rad} = \frac{Z_0(kL)^2 I_{av}^2}{12\pi} \tag{10.30}$$

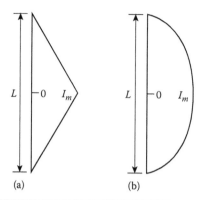

Figure 10.10 Distribution of current in (a) triangular and (b) finite-length dipole antennas.

The same is true for their resistance:

$$R_{rad} = \frac{2P_{rad}}{I_0^2} = \frac{Z_0(kL)^2 I_{av}^2}{6\pi I_0^2}$$ (10.31)

Then, for the infinitesimal dipole antenna, we get from Equation 10.31

$$R_{rad} = \frac{Z_0(2\pi L/\lambda)^2 I_{av}^2}{6\pi I_0^2} = 80\pi^2 \left(\frac{L}{\lambda}\right)^2 \left(\frac{I_{av}}{I_0}\right)^2 = 80\pi^2 \left(\frac{L}{\lambda}\right)^2$$ (10.32)

For the finite-length dipole antenna, we get correspondingly

$$R_{rad} = 80\pi^2 \left(\frac{L}{\lambda}\right)^2 \left(\frac{I_{av}}{2I_0}\right)^2 = 20\pi^2 \left(\frac{L}{\lambda}\right)^2$$ (10.33)

The distributions of the radiation pattern of the finite-length dipole antenna for different lengths L ($L = \lambda/2$, λ, $3\lambda/2$, 2λ) are presented in Figure 10.11a–d, respectively.

Finally, we can compare the path gain for the isotropic and $\lambda/2$–dipole antennas, using the Friis Equation 10.26. This yields

$$\frac{(PG)_{isotropic}}{(PG)_{\lambda/2-dipole}} = \frac{0.57 \times 10^{-9}}{1.53 \times 10^{-9}} = 0.37$$ (10.34)

that is, the path gain of the $\lambda/2$–dipole antenna is approximately three times greater than that of the isotropic antenna.

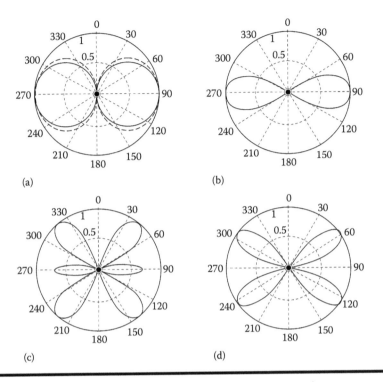

Figure 10.11 **(a–d) Radiation pattern of finite-length dipole antenna for $L = \lambda/2$, λ, $3\lambda/2$, 2λ.**

10.3.2 Loop Antennas

The loop antenna is shown schematically in Figure 10.12. The magnetic and electric fields in the spherical coordinate system using the amplitude of a magnetic dipole moment, $\mathbf{m} = I \cdot \pi a^2 \mathbf{u}_z$, are

$$H_\phi \approx -\frac{\omega\mu_0 mk}{4\pi Z_0}\frac{e^{-jkr}}{r}\sin\theta$$

$$E_\phi = -Z_0 H_\theta \approx \frac{\omega\mu_0 mk}{4\pi}\frac{e^{-jkr}}{r}\sin\theta$$

The radiated power for the loop antenna equals

$$P_{rad} = \frac{R_{rad}}{2}I^2(\phi) \tag{10.35}$$

The radiation resistance of the loop antenna is

$$R_{rad} = 20\pi^2(ka)^4 \tag{10.36}$$

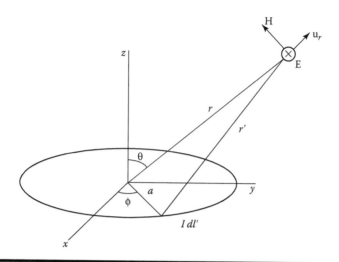

Figure 10.12   Loop antenna.

10.3.3 Antenna Arrays

The two-element antenna array is shown in Figure 10.13. The individual element of the antenna array is characterized by its own pattern $F_0(\theta,\phi)$.

At point P, the total far-zone electric field component of the two individual elements equals

$$E(\mathbf{r}) = E_1(\mathbf{r})e^{j\psi/2} + E_2(\mathbf{r})e^{-j\psi/2} \qquad (10.37)$$

At the middle point (0) of the segment d, since the phase difference between two point sources is $\psi = kd\cos\theta + \delta$, δ is the phase excitation, and there is symmetry around point (0) $[E_1(\mathbf{r}) = E_2(\mathbf{r})]$, we get

$$E(\mathbf{r}) = 2E_1(\mathbf{r})\cos\left(\frac{\psi}{2}\right) \qquad (10.38)$$

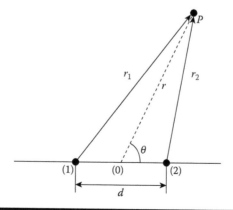

Figure 10.13   Two-element antenna array.

The total-field pattern $F(\theta,\phi)$ in such a situation equals

$$F(\theta,\phi) = F_0(\theta,\phi)F_a(\theta,\phi) \qquad (10.39)$$

where:

$$F_a(\theta,\phi) = \cos\left(\frac{kd\cos\theta + \delta}{2}\right) \qquad (10.40)$$

is the array factor and δ is the phase difference between two antennas.

10.4 Multibeam Antennas

There are several types of multibeam phased-array antennas that are successfully used for stable recording of signals, for division and differentiation of subscribers of existing wireless networks, for tracking any object (in radio location), and for rejection of obstructions and noises in the channels of radio communication. These array antennas can be in linear, circular, or plane formation, as shown in Figure 10.14.

Without loss of generality, let us consider a linear antenna array (see Figure 10.14a). The array contains N *identical* elements, as shown in Figure 10.15. Then, the total field is

$$E(\mathbf{r}) = E_0(\mathbf{r})\left[1 + e^{j\psi} + e^{j2\psi} + e^{j3\psi} + \cdots + e^{j(N-1)\psi}\right] \qquad (10.41)$$

It is known from mathematics that, if we denote $q = e^{j\psi}$, then

$$\sum_{n=0}^{N-1} q^n = \frac{1-q^n}{1-q}$$

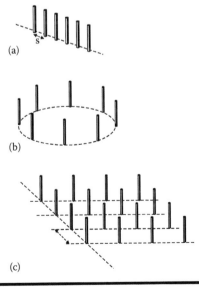

(a)

(b)

(c)

Figure 10.14 Types of multibeam phased-array antennas: (a) linear, (b) circular, and (c) planar.

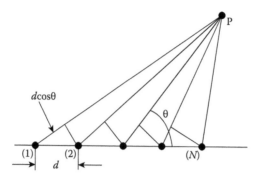

Figure 10.15 An array of *N*-element antennas separated by a range *d*.

If so, we get

$$E(\mathbf{r}) = E_0(\mathbf{r})\left[\frac{1-e^{jN\psi}}{1-e^{j\psi}}\right] \tag{10.42}$$

Accounting for relationships

$$\left|1-e^{jN\psi}\right| = \left|2\,je^{jN\psi/2}\sin\frac{N\psi}{2}\right| = 2\sin\frac{N\psi}{2}$$

and

$$\left|1-e^{j\psi}\right| = \left|2\,je^{j\psi/2}\sin\frac{\psi}{2}\right| = 2\sin\frac{\psi}{2}$$

we finally get

$$E(\theta) = E_0\left[\frac{\sin\left(\frac{N\psi(\theta)}{2}\right)}{\sin\left(\frac{\psi(\theta)}{2}\right)}\right] \tag{10.43}$$

where, as for the two-element antenna array, $\psi(\theta) = kd\cos\theta + \delta$. For $\psi(\theta) \to 0$,

$$E_{\max} = N \cdot E_0 \tag{10.44}$$

If so, the normalized total field, or the array-normalized array factor of such an antenna, equals

$$F_a(\theta) = \left[\frac{\sin\left(\frac{N\psi}{2}\right)}{N\sin\left(\frac{\psi}{2}\right)}\right] \tag{10.45}$$

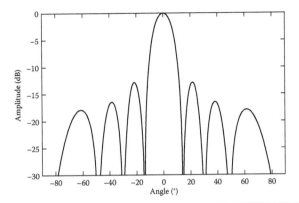

Figure 10.16 **Normalized radiation pattern of the antenna array according to Equation 10.47.**

For $N\psi = 0$,

$$e^{jN\psi} = 1 \tag{10.46}$$

and the zeroes in the numerator give nulls the main beam if

$$\psi = \pm \frac{n2\pi}{N} \tag{10.47}$$

Zeros in the denominator will yield maxima in the pattern, as follows from Figure 10.16.

Finally, we should note that the ability to arrange beam-forming antennas in an array are valuable for many applications, including communication and radar applications. A general solution for antenna arrays related to the specific problem of wideband beam patterns from sparse arrays was resolved in [15]. According to this framework, the sequences of pulses were controlled in the time domain by means of a differential time delay between each element, which allows each beam position to be steered. Beam steering by means of time control can be achieved despite the fact that the inter-element time delay is limited to the maximum equivalent to the distance between elements.

An alternative beam-forming technique by means of an array was proposed in [11–14]. In this technique, the main goal was to create directivity in the azimuth plane, which was achieved by means of a beam-forming network using wideband hybrid elements. Thus, a 10×10 element array antenna with peak side-lobe amplitude of −26 dB (compared with the main lobe) achieves beam steering of up to 50° [13,14].

PROBLEMS

Example 10.1: Given the dipole antenna dimensions are $L = 1$ cm and $d = 1$ mm, the radiated frequency $f = 1$ GHz, and the maximum current $I_{max} = 10\mu A$.
Find: The maximum electric field at $r = 20$ cm from the antenna.

Example 10.2: Determine the radiated intensity I_r and the current that is required to radiate 10 W from a loop with $L = 2\pi a = \lambda / 5$.

Example 10.3: Plot the radiation pattern $F(\theta,\phi)$ of two parallel half-wave dipoles (see Figure 10.13) that are separated by a distance $d=\lambda/4$ and excited by currents that have a phase difference $\delta=90°$.

Example 10.4: There are three two-element antenna arrays (see Figure 10.15) that differ only in separation distance d between antennas: $d=5$, 10, and 20 cm. $f=1.5$ GHz. All elements are isotropic radiators ($F_0(\theta,\phi)=1$).

Find: The radiation pattern $F(\theta,\phi)$ and plot it graphically for the three cases.

Example 10.5: A four-element antenna array ($N=4$) with physical separation of isotropic elements $d=\lambda/2$ (see Figure 10.14) is given, and $\delta\in[-3\pi/4;3\pi/4]$ with the step $\Delta\delta=\pi/4$.

Find: The radiation pattern $F_a(\theta)$ and plot it for each δ.

Example 10.6: Determine the input impedance for an array of two half-wave parallel dipoles, separated by a distance of $d=\lambda/2$ (see Figure 10.13). Calculate the input impedance for the two currents: (a) $I_2=-I_1$ and (b) $I_2=+I_1$.

Example 10.7: Calculate the input impedance for an array of two half-wave parallel dipoles, separated by distances $d=0.25\lambda$, $d=0.5\lambda$, $d=1.0\lambda$, and $d=1.25\lambda$.

References

1. Schelkunoff, S. K. and H. T. Friis, *Antennas: Theory and Practice*, New York: Wiley, 1952.
2. Blake, L. V., *Antennas*, New York: Wiley, 1966.
3. Weeks, W. L., *Antenna Engineering*, New York: McGraw-Hill, 1968.
4. Collin, R. E. and F. J. Zucker, eds, *Antenna Theory*, Part 1, Part 2, New York: McGraw-Hill, 1969.
5. Hollis, J. S., T. J. Lyon, and L. Clayton Jr., eds, *Microwave Antenna Measurements*, San Jose, CA: Scientific-Atlanta, 1970.
6. Elliott, R. S., *Antenna Theory and Design*, Englewood Cliffs, NJ: Prentice-Hall, 1981.
7. Johnson, R. C. and H. Jasik, eds., *Antenna Engineering Handbook*, 2nd edn, New York: McGraw-Hill, 1984.
8. Collin, R. E., *Antennas and Radio Propagation*, New York: McGraw-Hill, 1985.
9. Krauss, J. D., *Antennas*, New York: McGraw-Hill, 1988.
10. Balanis, C. A., *Advanced Engineering Electromagnetics*, New York: Wiley, 1989.
11. Siwiak, R., *Radiowave Propagation and Antennas for Personal Communications*, 2nd edn, Boston: Artech House, 1998.
12. Balanis, C. A., *Antenna Theory: Analysis and Design*, 2nd edn, New York: Wiley, 1997.
13. Thiel, D., *Antennas Fundamentals*, in *Handbook: Engineering Electromagnetics*, ed. by R. Bansal, New York: Marcel Dekker, 2004, pp. 255–276.
14. Jackson, D. R., J. T. Williams, and D. R. Wilton, *Antennas Representative Types*, in *Handbook: Engineering Electromagnetics*, ed. by R. Bansal, New York: Marcel Dekker, 2004, pp. 277–346.
15. Blaunstein, N. and Ch. Christodoulou, *Radio Propagation and Adaptive Antennas for Radio Communication Networks: Terrestrial, Atmospheric and Ionospheric*, 2nd edn, New York: Wiley, 2014.

RADAR
FUNDAMENTALS

Chapter 11

Radars

First of all, we will introduce the reader to the main definitions, which are important for a detailed explanation of the subject.

11.1 Basic Definitions and Characteristics of Radar

Radar is a device that transmits and receives electromagnetic signals for a variety of applications, including detection, tracking, classification, identification, surveillance, imaging, and guiding targets. The acronym "RADAR" stands for "Radio Detection And Ranging" system, which includes the most prevalent applications of microwave and millimeter-wave technology [1–17].

Target is the object of interest, which is embedded in noise and clutter together with interfering signals.

Noise is a floor signal, which limits the smallest signal that can be measured by the receiver.

Clutter is a radar (or background) echo or group of echoes from ground, sea, rain, birds, and so on that is operationally unwanted in the situation being considered for detecting, tracking, and identification of the desired target.

However, we note that these definitions are relative and depend on the situation of application. What is clutter for some purposes may be a target for others. For example, an echo from rain is clutter for airport surveillance radar, but it is the target for weather radar.

Surveillance is the systematic observation of a region (aerospace, surface, or subsurface areas) by different numbers of various sensors for detecting, tracking, classifying, and identifying targets and activities of interest [2,4,6–13]: air-to-air (A-A), air-to-ground (A-G), air-to-surface (A-S), surface to air (S-A), surface-to-surface (S-S), and so on.

Frequency (or *wavelength*) is a basic radar parameter that determines not only the design and construction of radar, but also its application and performance.

Table 11.1 presents most specific radar frequency bands. Ground-based penetrating radars are usually in the L, S, and C frequency band regions, whereas airborne radars are usually in the X-band region. Millimeter-wave (MMW) radars operate at frequencies exceeding 30 GHz; V-band (40–75 GHz), and W-band (75–110 GHz) are also used in MMW radars [11].

Table 11.1 Radar Frequency Bands

Band	Frequency Range (GHz)	Wavelength (cm)
VHF	0.03–0.3	1000–100
UHF	0.3–1.0	100–30
L	1.0–2.0	30–15
S	2.0–4.0	15–7.5
C	4.0–8.0	7.5–3.75
X	8.0–12.5	3.75–2.40
Ku	12.5–18.0	2.40–1.67
K	18.0–26.5	1.67–1.13
Ka	26.5–40.0	1.13–0.75
MMW	40.0–100	0.75–0.3

Resolution is the radar's ability to distinguish two targets in close proximity to each other in three-dimensional (3-D) space: (a) range (in the space domain); (b) velocity (in the Doppler domain).

Accuracy is the ability of the radar to measure the true value (true range, velocity, direction, etc.).

In its basic operation, a radar transmitter sends out a radio signal, continuous or pulsed, which is partly reflected by a desired target and then detected by a sensitive radar receiver. If the radar uses a narrow-beam antenna, the target's direction can be accurately given with respect to the position of the radar antenna. But, the accuracy of detecting the target's dimensions and form strongly depends on antenna size as well as antenna beamwidth, that is, on the angular resolution of the radar. This angular resolution of the radar (e.g., the radar antenna bandwidth) depends on the wavelength λ of the radio signal and on the antenna aperture dimension D; that is, the antenna bandwidth θ_{BW} measured in radians equals [13–17]

$$\theta_{BW} = \frac{\lambda}{D} \tag{11.1}$$

The example of a radar antenna with diameter $D = 3.22$ m, operated at frequency of 9 GHz ($\lambda = 3.33$ cm), is presented in Figure 11.1.

According to the geometry illustrated in Figure 11.1, for a range between the radar and the target of 10 km, $\lambda = 3.33$ cm, and a beamwidth of a 1 foot antenna of 6.3°, the beam dispersion will exceed 1 km; that is, we have a problem with accuracy to detect the desired target.

At the same time, by knowledge of the antenna beamwidth, one can easily evaluate its gain G (see definitions in Chapter 10):

$$G = \frac{4\pi}{\theta_{BW}^2} \tag{11.2}$$

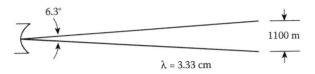

Figure 11.1   Beam dispersion of 1.1 km at the range of 10 km for a radar operating at $f=9$ GHz and with the antenna creating beamwidth of 6.3°.

where 4π is the area of a sphere of unit radius in steradians. Thus, for the case illustrated in Figure 11.1, the antenna gain will be

$$G = \frac{4 \cdot 3.14}{(6.3/57.3)^2} = 1038$$

or in decibels,

$$G = 30.09 \text{ dB}$$

where 57.3 is the conversion from degrees, that is, $180° / \pi \equiv 180° / 3.14 = 57.3°$.

Therefore, with knowledge of the antenna beamwidth and the pulse duration τ, one can easily estimate the angular resolution spread (or *ambiguity* in target detection) of the radar and the accuracy of target range estimations, as is clearly shown in Figure 11.2.

There are two kinds of radar system, *monostatic* and *bistatic*, as shown in Figure 11.3. It is clearly seen from Figure 11.3a that in the monostatic radar, the same antenna is used for both transmitting and receiving signal, while the bistatic radar uses two separate antennas, one as the transmitter and the second as the receiver (see Figure 11.3b) [11–14,17].

Here, P_t is the transmit signal power and G is the antenna gain (Equation 11.2).

We should note that most radar systems are of the monostatic type, but in some applications (see Figure 11.3), the target is illuminated by separate transmit/receive antennas. Separate antennas are sometimes used to achieve the necessary isolation between the transmitter and the receiver.

As will be shown below, the distance to the desired target can be determined by the time required for the signal to propagate to the target and back. The radial frequency of the target (if it is not stationary, but moving) is related to the Doppler shift of the return signal.

We have discussed *active* radar systems, which use their own energy source for target illumination. In contrast, *passive* radars do not illuminate a target. They depend on natural environmental or the target's own conditions (such a temperature contrast) for detection. A common example

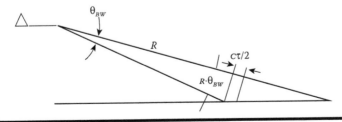

Figure 11.2   View of angular resolution spread $w = R \cdot \theta_{BW}$ and width $d = c\tau/2$ in the target range R estimated by the radar.

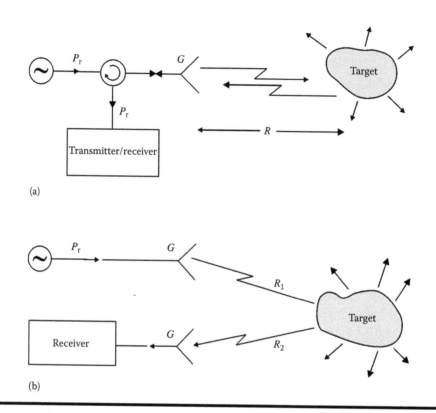

Figure 11.3 **Schematically sketched basic radar systems: (a) monostatic radar and (b) bistatic radar.**

is the MMW radiometer. It uses radiated heat energy from the natural background and human-made objects as its source of detection energy or contrast between the temperature of the background and the object under detection.

11.2 Classification of Radars according to Their Application

Radars can be classified according to purpose, application, type, installation, operation frequency, transmit waveform, receiver processing technique, and so on (see Table 11.2).

Table 11.3 presents the most useful frequencies for different applications of radar systems, described in Table 11.2.

11.3 Classification of Radars Associated with Types of Radiated Signals

According to the type of signal of operation, radars can be differentiated as continuous-wave (CW), or narrowband, and *pulsed*, or wideband, radars.

Pulsed radar uses pulses to detect and track targets based on two principles: calculating differences between the transmitted and the received pulse for range definition, and using the frequency shift between these pulses for definition of the range rate. Pulsed radar, which is based on the

Table 11.2 Some Applications of Radars

Civilian Applications	*Military Applications*
Airport surveillance	Air and marine navigation
Air traffic control and flight management	Detection and tracking of targets
Aircraft landing and precision approach	Missile defense and guidance
Weather radar and ocean monitoring	Airborne early warning
Vessel traffic management (harbors, waterways, straits)	Classification and identification ballistic missiles and rockets
Speed measurements (police radar)	Fire control
Burglar alarms	Mortar and artillery location
Ground surveillance and intruder alarms	Ground probing and subsurface
Ground probing and subsurface imaging	Subsurface mine detection
Multifunctional radars	Multifunctional radars

Source: Skolnik, M. I., *Radar Handbook,* McGraw-Hill, New York, 1990; Nathanson, F. E., *Radar Design Principles,* McGraw-Hill, New York, 1991; Kingsley, S. and Quegan, S., *Understanding Radar Systems,* McGraw-Hill, London, 1992; Pozar, D., *Microwave Engineering,* Wiley, New York, 1998; Ince, N., Topuz, E., Panayirci, E., and Isik, C., *Principles of Integrated Maritime Surveillance Systems,* Kluwer Academic, Boston, MA, 2000; Sullivan, R. J., *Microwave Radar: Imaging and Advanced Concepts,* Artech House, Norwood, MA, 2001.

timing principle to find the range to the target, transmits a pulse and measures the returned pulse from the target. The time τ between the transmitted signal and the signal returned from the target equals (see Figure 11.4)

$$\tau = \frac{2R}{c} \tag{11.3}$$

and the range from the radar to the desired target equals

$$R = \frac{c \cdot \tau}{2} \tag{11.4}$$

where c is the speed of light in free space.

The maximum range measured by the radar is [11–17]

$$R_{max} = \frac{c \cdot T}{2} \tag{11.5}$$

where T is the pulse time period (see Figure 11.4).

A new characteristic of pulsed radar is generally used, called *pulse repetition*

Table 11.3 Frequency Ranges Assigned to Usual Radar Applications

Frequency Range (GHz)	Types of Radars and Applications
1.35–1.4	Military radar
1.435–1.535	L-band telemetry
2.45–2.69	Commercial radar systems
2.9–3.7	Miscellaneous radar
4.2–4.4	Radar altimeter
5.25–5.925	Miscellaneous radar
8.5–10.55	Miscellaneous radar
9.3–9.5	Weather and navigation radar
13.25–14	Satellite radars
15.7–17.7	Miscellaneous radars
24.25–25.25	Navigation radar
33.4–36.0	Miscellaneous radars

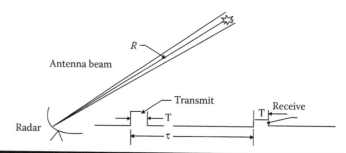

Figure 11.4   Range detection principle in pulsed radar. (Modified from Eaves, J. L. and Reedy, E. K., *Principles of Modern Radars*, Van Nostrand Reinhold, New York, 1987; Sevgi, L., Radar, in Bansal, R. (ed.), *Handbook: Engineering Electromagnetics*, Marcel Dekker, New York, 2004, pp. 377–416.)

frequency (PRF) [7,11–17]:

$$\text{PRF} = \frac{1}{T} \tag{11.6}$$

where c is the speed of light in free space.

It is known that shorter pulses give better target range resolution, while longer pulses result in a better signal-to-noise ratio (SNR). The range for PRFs is from 100 to 100 KHz, because higher PRFs give more returned pulses per unit time, yielding better performance of the pulse radar, whereas lower PRFs avoid the range ambiguity that can occur when $R = c \cdot T / 2$ (this follows from Equations 11.5 and 11.6).

CW Doppler radar uses frequency shift for determination of the range rate and the target velocity and direction based on the Doppler effect. If the target has a radial velocity component (with respect to the radar) v, the Doppler effect states that the returned signal will be shifted in frequency relative to the transmitted frequency. This Doppler shift can be easily evaluated via knowledge of radiated frequency f_0 and radial velocity of the moving target v [7,11,13,17]:

$$f_D = \frac{2vf_0}{c} \tag{11.7}$$

The received frequency is then $f_0 \pm f_D$, where the plus sign corresponds to a target approaching the radar, and the minus sign corresponds to a target receding from the radar.

Since the return of a pulsed radar from a moving target will contain a Doppler shift, it is possible to determine the range, velocity, and position of a target (in the last case, if a narrow-beam antenna is used) with a single radar. This kind of radar is known as a *pulsed Doppler radar*, which offers several advantages over pulsed or Doppler radar. Let us briefly describe these advantages.

Pulsed Doppler radar uses the Doppler frequency shift between the transmit (Tx) and the receive (Rx) pulses for definition of the range rate [7,11,13,17]:

$$f_D = -\frac{2\dot{R}}{\lambda} \tag{11.8}$$

Therefore, for the range rate (called the range derivative) $\dot{R} < 0$, the radiated frequency increases, and for $\dot{R} > 0$, the radiated frequency decreases. This means that if the target moves in the opposite direction to the direction in which the radar signal is traveling, $f_D > 0$ and $f_1 > f_0$, where f_0 is the transmitted signal frequency and f_1 is the received signal frequency. Conversely, if the target moves in the direction in which the radar signal is traveling, $f_D < 0$ and $f_1 < f_0$.

Now we will briefly explain the difference between pulsed radar (Figure 11.5a) and pulsed Doppler radar (Figure 11.5b).

If the PRF is about 300 Hz for pulsed radar, for pulsed Doppler radar it equals roughly 200 kHz. What does this mean? It means that the time between the transmitted and received pulses for pulsed radar is large enough in the time domain to differentiate both kinds of pulses and, finally, to determine the target range from the radar more accurately, if the time difference between the two pulses, received and transmitted, is too short, their possible overlapping leads to ambiguity of the target range and estimation of its velocity.

11.4 Pulse Repeated Frequency and Maximum Range

Let us return to the target range evaluation, based on Figure 11.5. This figure shows an ideal transmitted and received time series of pulsed radar (without carrier signal), in which each transmitted

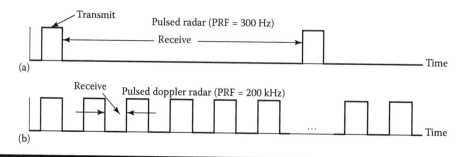

Figure 11.5 **(a) Pulsed radar and (b) pulsed Doppler radar PRF difference.**

and received pulse is vividly illuminated. Each transmitted pulse has width τ and is sent when the receiver is off. This is repeated every T s, which we call the *pulse repetition interval* (PRI). The PRF was introduced in Equation 11.6. Then, τ/T is a *duty factor*. During the time interval $(T-\tau)$, the transmitter is off and the receiver is on to receive any possible target echoes. The range, R, of the target is measured from the time delay τ_d between the transmitted and received signals as (covering the range R twice—forward and back propagation):

$$R = \frac{c \cdot \tau_d}{2}\, [\text{m}] \tag{11.9}$$

The maximum useful range can be rewritten via PRF or PRI as [7,11,13,17]

$$R_{\text{max}} = \frac{c \cdot T}{2} = \frac{c}{2 \cdot \text{PRF}}\, [\text{m}] \tag{11.10}$$

The radar receiver samples the received time echo signal every τ s, and each sample represents a distance ΔR, called a *range bin* or *range gate* [7,17]:

$$\Delta R = \frac{c\tau}{2}\, [\text{m}] \tag{11.11}$$

This measure is called a *range resolution*. Then, the number of range bins N is equal to

$$N = \frac{R_{\text{max}}}{\Delta R} \tag{11.12}$$

The narrower the pulse width τ, the better the range resolution and the higher the number of the range bins N, but the bandwidth becomes wider, since $B_\omega \sim 1/\tau$. For a pulse width τ, the range accuracy is given as [7,17]

$$\delta R \cong \frac{c \cdot \tau}{2\sqrt{2 \cdot SNR}} = \frac{c}{2B_\omega \sqrt{2 \cdot SNR}} \ [\text{m}] \tag{11.13}$$

11.5 Doppler Effect and Doppler Shift Frequency

A radial movement of the target causes a slight increase or decrease of the carrier frequency of the radar, proportional to the radial speed, called the *Doppler effect*. Radars that use the Doppler effect are called pulse Doppler or moving-target-indicator (MTI) radars. For a finite-duration (f_D) time series with Δt sampling interval, one can obtain the f_D response via discrete Fourier transform (DFT) or fast Fourier transform (FFT), with a maximum frequency f_{max} and a minimum frequency resolution [7,17]

$$f_{max} = \frac{1}{2\Delta t} \ [\text{Hz}] \tag{11.14}$$

$$\Delta f = \frac{1}{T_{obs}} \ [\text{Hz}] \tag{11.15}$$

where T_{obs} is the time of the finite time series or observation time. The corresponding Doppler shift of a target depends on the radial velocity v_r and the carrier signal wavelength λ_0:

$$f_d = \frac{2v_r}{\lambda_0} \ [\text{Hz}] \tag{11.16}$$

The velocity estimation accuracy of a desired target equals [7,17]

$$\delta v_r \cong \frac{\Delta f_d}{\sqrt{2 \cdot SNR}} \approx \frac{\lambda}{2T_{int}\sqrt{2 \cdot SNR}} \ [\text{m/s}] \tag{11.17}$$

11.6 Path-Loss Prediction in Propagation Environment

There are many factors that determine the character of the radar signal propagation, depending on the channel response.

11.6.1 Free-Space Propagation

For A-A and S-A radars (see definitions in Section 11.1), free-space propagation is possible with the path loss [18,19]

$$L_{FS} = 32.44 + 20\log d_{[\text{km}]} \,|\, 20\log f_{[\text{MHz}]} \tag{11.18}$$

For A-G, A-S, and S-S radars (see definitions in Section 11.1), the loss exceeds L_{FS} and should include additional losses, such as:

- Absorption loss (due to atmospheric and ionospheric gases)
- Curvature of the earth
- Reflection and scattering from ground roughness
- Refractivity of the atmosphere and ionosphere
- Depolarization (troposphere scattering, vegetation, trees)

For S-S millimeter wave (MW) radars, effective work is only possible in line-of-sight (LOS) conditions. For this purpose, radars located at a height h (in meters) are usually used, for which losses can be evaluated as

$$\text{LOS} = 4.12\sqrt{h} \quad (\text{km}) \tag{11.19}$$

11.6.2 Effects of the Earth

The effect of the earth's curvature is shown in Figure 11.6, from which it follows that this effect can be obtained by additional loss due to diffraction. To account for this diffraction effect, one should use the following Fock's model [19,20].

To take into account terrain curvature and diffraction from the curved terrain, Fock introduced special scales: the *range scale*, $L = \left(\lambda R_e^2 / \pi\right)^{1/3}$, and the *height scale*, $H = 0.5 \cdot \left(\lambda^2 R_e / \pi^2\right)^{1/3}$, respectively, where $R_e \approx 6375\,\text{km}$ is the radius of the earth. These parameters were determined for the range of radio path, R, and the heights of both terminal antennas, h_T and h_R, using the dimensionless parameters $x = R/L, y_1 = h_T/H, y_2 = h_R/H$ [20]. The attenuation factor with respect to flat terrain has the form [20]

$$F = 2\sqrt{\pi x} \left| \sum_{k=1}^{\infty} \frac{\exp\left(ixt_k\right)}{\left(t_k + p^2\right)} \frac{A(t_k + y_1)}{A(t_k)} \frac{A(t_k + y_2)}{A(t_k)} \right| \tag{11.20}$$

where

$$p = i(\pi R_e / \lambda)^{1/3} / \sqrt{\varepsilon_{r0} - i60\lambda\sigma} \tag{11.21}$$

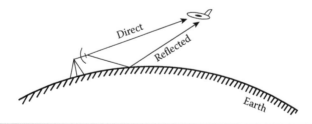

Figure 11.6   Influence of the earth's curvature on total path loss of the signal to the moving target.

A(w) denotes a special Airy function, which is related to the special Hankel function of the order 1/3 through

$$A(w) = \sqrt{\pi/3}\,\exp(-i2\pi/3)w^{1/2}H_{1/3}(2w^{3/2}/3)\qquad(11.22)$$

t_k in Equation 11.20 are the roots of the equation

$$A'(t) - pA(t) = 0\qquad(11.23)$$

It can be shown that the value of t_k for finite values of p can be estimated as follows:

$$t_k(p) \approx t_k(0) + p/t_k(0), \left|p/\sqrt{t_k}\right| < 1\qquad(11.24a)$$

and

$$t_k(p) \approx t_k(\infty) + 1/p, \left|p/\sqrt{t_k}\right| > 1\qquad(11.24b)$$

We could compute the first set of roots $f_i(0)$ and $f_i(\infty)$ of Equation 11.23, but instead of this, we will present an estimation of the signals of the ultrahigh (UHF)/X-frequency band, for which it can be assumed that $|p| \gg 1$ and $y_{1,2} \geq 1$, which allows us to obtain the attenuation factor due to diffraction from the curved surface that can give additional loss (with respect to the case of flat terrain) from 10 to 40 dB [18,19].

We should emphasize that the Fock's model can be used only for land radio paths with ranges of more than 15–20 km. At the same time, we should note that for long radio paths (more than 100 km), the real terrain profile of the path is obviously beyond the capabilities of the Fock's model. This is true for radar tracking of satellites and missiles moving in the middle and upper atmosphere and ionosphere. In this case, the tropospheric (ranging from 0.1–1 to 20–30 km) and the ionospheric (ranging from 50 to 400–450 km) effects should be taken into account. Let us briefly consider the main effects.

11.6.3 Effects of the Atmosphere

11.6.3.1 Effects of Refraction

In the atmosphere, another parameter is used, refractivity, a function of the refractive index $n = \sqrt{\varepsilon_r}$, which equals [18,19]

$$N = (n-1)\cdot 10^6 \text{ [N-units]}\qquad(11.25)$$

Refractivity is a function of the pressure P (millibars), absolute temperature (K), and the partial pressure of water vapor e (millibars) [18,19]:

$$N = 77.6\frac{P}{T} + 3.73\cdot 10^5\frac{e}{T^2} \text{ [N-units]}\qquad(11.26)$$

The variation of the refraction index is approximately exponential within the first few tens of kilometers of the earth's atmosphere, the region called the *troposphere* [18,19]:

$$N = N_S \exp\left\{-\frac{h}{H}\right\} \tag{11.27}$$

where:
    h is the height above sea level
    $N_S \approx 315$ and $H = 7.35$ km are standard reference values
    H is defined as the height scale of the standard atmosphere

Equation 11.27 is called the standard exponential model of the troposphere.

This refractive index variation with height causes the phase velocity of radio waves to be slightly slower closer to the Earth's surface, such that the ray paths are not straight, but tend to curve slightly toward the ground. In this case, the gradient of the refractivity is given by [18,19]

$$g(h) = dN/dh \tag{11.28}$$

Usually, it is assumed [18,19] that near the earth's surface, this gradient varies exponentially as

$$g_s(h) = -0.04 \exp(-0.136\,h)(\mathrm{km}^{-1}) \tag{11.29}$$

According to Equation 11.27, the gradient depends nonlinearly on height. However, as the first approximation, we can use a linear model, setting the gradient as a constant equal to its value at $h = 0$: $g = g(0)$. This is the case for small heights, when the standard atmosphere in Equation 11.29 can be approximated as linear, according to the equation [18,19]

$$N \approx N_S - \frac{N_S}{H} h \tag{11.30}$$

The refractivity thus has a nearly constant gradient of about -43 N-units per kilometer. If so, the curvature of the ray trajectory is constant (this follows in the case of $dn/dh = \mathrm{const.}$). A common way to take this factor into account is to introduce, instead of the actual radius of the earth, the effective radius of the earth:

$$R_{\mathrm{eff}} = \kappa R_e \tag{11.31}$$

where:
    R_e $= 6375$ km
    κ is the earth-radius factor

As was shown in [18], high values of the κ-factor facilitate propagation over long paths, and small values may cause obstruction fading. In order to predict such fading, the statistics of the low values of the κ-factor have to be known. However, since the instantaneous behavior of the κ-factor differs at various points along a given path, an effective κ-factor for the path, $κ_e$, should be considered. In general, $κ_e$ represents a spatial average, and the distribution of $κ_e$ shows less variability than that derived from point-to-point meteorological measurements. The variability decreases with increasing distance. The effective factor is given by [19]

$$κ_e = \frac{1}{R_e \frac{dn}{dh} + 1} \cong \frac{R_e}{1 - R_e / ρ} \tag{11.32}$$

As the variation of refractive index is mostly vertical, rays launched and received with relatively high elevation angles, usually used in radiolocations fixed to atmospheric targets (helicopters, aircraft, missiles, etc.), will be mostly unaffected. But for near-horizontal rays, where

$$ρ ≈ -10^6 / g \tag{11.33}$$

we obtain

$$R_{eff} = κ_e R_e \tag{11.34}$$

where now the effective earth-radius factor is

$$κ_e = \left(1 + 10^{-6} g R_e\right)^{-1} \tag{11.35a}$$

Another form of this relation is [18,19]

$$κ_e = \frac{0.157}{0.157 + g} \tag{11.35b}$$

For the standard atmosphere and in the limits of a linear model ($g = -3.925$ 1/km), one can immediately obtain from Equation 11.35b $κ_e = 4/3$, so the effective radius from Equation 11.34 is about 8500 km. Although the linear model leads to excessive ray bending at high altitudes, this is not so important in our calculations, because the critical part of the trajectory is located near the ground-based radar antenna.

11.6.3.2 Effects of Attenuation

Atmospheric attenuation is caused by the gaseous structure of the atmosphere, consisting mainly of molecules and atoms, rain and cloud effects, turbulent structures, and so on. We will show here only the effects of absorption by the gaseous structure of the troposphere, referring the reader to other works [18,19] where a full description of atmospheric effects is presented.

Let us consider the wave attenuation caused by atmospheric gas. In the following sections, we will consider all effects of hydrometeors, as the most important factor in determining communication system reliability. Molecular absorption is due primarily to atmospheric water vapor and oxygen. Although for frequencies around 1–20 GHz this kind of attenuation is not large, it exists as a permanent factor. The absorption in the atmosphere over a path length *r* is given by

$$A = \int_0^r dr\, \gamma(r)\,[\text{dB}]$$

(11.36)

where $\gamma(r)$ is the specific attenuation, consisting of two components:

$$\gamma(r) = \gamma_o(r) + \gamma_w(r)\,[\text{dB}/\text{km}]$$

(11.37)

where:

$\gamma_o(r)$ is the contribution of oxygen
$\gamma_w(r)$ is the contribution of water vapor

Using these formulas, one finds that the attenuation due to water vapor dominates, and for earth's typical middle-latitude summer weather conditions, the specific attenuation does not exceed 0.02 dB/km at sea level. This corresponds to the maximal attenuation of 7 dB for a horizontal path length of 350 km. Under summer conditions, the absorption due to oxygen does not exceed 8×10^{-3} dB/km, which corresponds to 2.8 dB for the maximal distance. In the winter, the oxygen contribution to the specific attenuation does not exceed 10^{-2} dB/km. The total attenuation at sea level due to atmospheric gases can be estimated as 0.025 dB/km. However, for slanting paths, the total attenuation does not exceed the value of 1 dB, but for the 99% level of probability, it may be estimated as 2 dB.

The total atmospheric attenuation L_a for a particular path is then found by integrating the total specific attenuation over the total radio path of the radar signal, r_T, in the atmosphere:

$$L_a = \int_0^{r_T} \gamma_a(l)dl = \int_0^{r_T} [\gamma_w(l) + \gamma_o(l)]dl\;(\text{dB})$$

(11.38)

The main resonance peaks of H_2O are around 22.3, 183.3, and 323.8 GHz, and those for O_2 are around 60 GHz, covering a complex set of closely spaced peaks that prevent the use of the 57–64 GHz band for practical satellite communication (see Figure 11.7).

As an example, Figure 11.7 presents possible signal attenuation at sea level (the upper curve) and at the altitude of about 10 km, that is, at tropospheric height (the lower curve). It is clearly seen that the oxygen and water molecules are the best candidates to affect radio signals operating with frequencies around the ranges of 60–65 GHz and 100–120 GHz, causing difficulties for MMW radar applications.

As for the generally used frequencies presented in Table 11.2, we can state that the troposphere is either partly or fully transparent to most microwave radars.

11.6.4 Effects of the Ionosphere

11.6.4.1 Structure of the Ionosphere

For the ionosphere, the main effects on radar signal propagation result from plasma, a gas consisting of ionized particles, electrons, and ions (plasma is quasi-neutral over sufficiently large areas, that

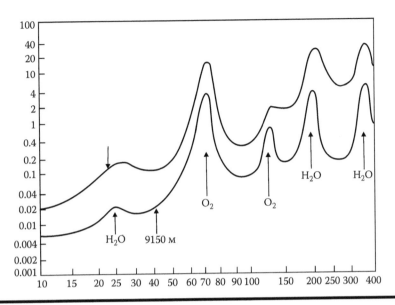

Figure 11.7 **Attenuation (in decibels per kilometer) of signal at sea level (upper curve) and at altitude of 9.15 km (lower curve) vs. the carrier frequency (in GHz) of the radar system.**

is, the concentration of electrons roughly equals the concentration of ions). We do not go into these details in depth, referring the reader to [19,21]. The ionosphere consists of several layers with their own plasma concentrations. In order of increasing plasma density, these layers are referred to as D (from 50 to 80 km), E (from 90 to 130 km), F_1 (from 150 to 200 km), and F_2 (from 250 to 270 km). Of course, these ranges vary depending on altitudinal, latitudinal, and weather conditions occurring in the ionosphere. For us, it is important to show when the ionosphere is transparent to the radar signals passing through its layers and when it is nontransparent. To understand this problem, we should first introduce the intrinsic plasma frequency (due to oscillations of electrons around ions to satisfy the condition of quasi-neutrality) and compare it with the radar signal frequency.

11.6.4.2 Main Parameters of Propagation through the Ionosphere

It has been shown both theoretically and experimentally (see [18,19,21] and bibliographies therein) that plasma is characterized by the number of electrons (or ions) per unit volume, called the density or the plasma concentration. Depending on this density and the plasma frequency, a radar wave can be reflected or absorbed, or can pass through the plasma medium as a transparent homogeneous layer. An effective permittivity of plasma can be defined for the uniformly distributed ionospheric plasma as

$$\varepsilon_{\text{eff}} = \varepsilon_0 \left(1 - \frac{\omega_p^2}{\omega^2} \right) \qquad (11.39)$$

where the plasma frequency is

$$\omega_p^2 = \frac{e^2 N_e}{m_e \varepsilon_0} \qquad (11.40)$$

where:

m_e, e, and N_e are mass, charge, and concentration of plasma electrons (or ions, since $N_e \approx N_i$ due to plasma's electrical neutrality)

ε_0 is the dielectric constant of free space introduced in Chapter 3

If the reader returns to Chapters 3 and 4, where propagation of radio waves was considered via Maxwell's equations, he or she will immediately notice from Equation 11.39 that when the carrier wave frequency is $\omega = \omega_p$ and $\varepsilon_{eff} = 0$, such a radio wave will reflect from the ionospheric layer. Moreover, when $\omega < \omega_p$, a wave cannot propagate via plasma due to a strong absorption of its energy. So, the wave propagation through the plasma is only possible for $\omega > \omega_p$ (when $\varepsilon_{eff} > 0$), and the ionosphere is transparent for such wave propagation [21].

Generally speaking, this picture is very basic, because there are ambient electrical and magnetic fields in the ionosphere [21]. Due to their effects, the plasma becomes anisotropic. The existence of wind and ionization-recombination factors causes the plasma to be inhomogeneous. In such situations, Equation 11.39 becomes more complicated; however, in principle, constraint $\omega > \omega_p$ should work for effective detection and tracking of moving vehicles at altitudes inside and above the ionosphere by radar.

11.6.4.3 Effects of Wave Refraction

The refractive index n_r of an ordinary radio wave depends on both the plasma density N (per cubic meter) and the wave frequency f (in megahertz) according to [21]

$$n_r^2 = 1 - \frac{f_c^2}{f^2} \tag{11.41}$$

where f_c is the critical frequency of plasma at the given height, defined by the expression [21]

$$f_c = 8.9788\sqrt{N} \ [\text{Hz}] \tag{11.42}$$

Apparent reflection from the ionosphere back to the earth can occur whenever the wave frequency is below this critical frequency f_c, from which it follows that the "working" frequencies for satellite communications must be above this critical frequency f_c [18,19,21]. The greatest critical frequency usually observed in the ionosphere does not exceed 12 MHz. This is the other extreme of an overall atmospheric "window," which is bounded at the high-frequency end by atmospheric absorption at hundreds of gigahertz. A number of ionospheric effects for radio waves with frequencies above 12 MHz, which are very important in land–ionosphere radiolocation, will be considered briefly according to [18,19,21].

Absorption of Radio Waves. In the absence of local inhomogeneities of the ionospheric plasma, the radio wave passing through the ionosphere as a homogeneous plasma continuum is absorbed due to pair interactions between electron and ion components of plasma. In such a situation, the intensity of the radio wave is determined as [18,19,21]

$$I = I_0 \exp\left\{-2\frac{\omega}{c}\int \kappa ds\right\} \tag{11.43}$$

where:

I_0 is the intensity of the incident radio wave

κ is the coefficient of absorption

ω is the angular frequency of the incident wave

$\omega = 2\pi f$

c is the velocity of light in free space; $c = 3 \times 10^8$ m/s

integration occurs along the wave trajectory s

For weakly magnetized plasma, when $\omega \gg \omega_{He}$ (ω_{He} is the hydro-frequency of plasma electrons), and for high radio frequencies, when $\omega \gg \omega_{pe}$ (ω_{pe} is the plasma frequency, $\omega_{pe} = (e^2 N / \varepsilon_0 m_e)^{1/2}$, e and m_e are the charge and mass of an electron, respectively, and ε_0 is the average dielectric parameter of the ambient ionospheric plasma), the coefficient of absorption can be presented as [19,21]

$$\kappa = \frac{1}{2} \frac{\omega_{pe}^2 (\nu_{em} + \nu_{ei})}{\omega[\omega^2 + (\nu_{em} + \nu_{ei})^2]} \quad (11.44)$$

where ν_{em} and ν_{ei} are the frequencies of interactions of plasma electrons with neutral molecules and atoms, and with ions, respectively, defined in [18,19].

The expected value of absorption at the ionospheric radio links can usually be estimated by using the measured radiometric absorption along radio traces at the fixed frequency and by experimental knowledge of frequency dependence of absorption determined by Equation 11.44 (see also [19,21] and bibliographies therein).

Ionospheric Scintillation. There is a wind present in the ionosphere, just as in the troposphere, which causes rapid variations in the local electron density, particularly close to sunset. These density variations cause changes in the refraction of the radio wave in the earth–ionosphere channel and hence in signal levels. Portions of the ionosphere then act like lenses, causing focusing, defocusing, and divergence of the wave, and hence lead to signal level variations, that is, signal scintillation (see definitions in [18,19,21]).

For frequencies beyond the range of 20–50 GHz, which are usually employed for earth–ionosphere radiolocation links, the effects of Faraday rotation are negligible (about a dozen degrees), the propagation delay is very small (a dozen nanoseconds), and the radio-frequency dispersion is very weak (a dozen picoseconds per megahertz), so we can omit them from our computations. As for the attenuation caused by absorption and refraction, and signal amplitude and phase scintillations (i.e., fading), these effects are strongly dependent on the nonregular features of the ionosphere, usually referred to as inhomogeneities or irregularities [18,19,21].

11.7 Radar Equations

Let take an isotropic antenna with a power P_T. In this case, the power density (PD) at the target located at a distance R (meters) is [11–17]

$$PD = \frac{P_T}{4\pi R^2} \ [W/m^2] \quad (11.45)$$

For the directive antenna (see definitions in Chapter 10),

$$PD = \frac{P_T}{4\pi R^2} \times G_T \; [\text{W/m}^2]$$

(11.46)

After reflection from a target, we should take into account its radar cross section (RCS) σ [4]. Coming back after reflection from a target, the PD arriving at the receiving antenna equals

$$PD = \frac{P_T}{4\pi R^2} \times G_T \times \sigma \times \frac{1}{4\pi R^2} \; [\text{W/m}^2]$$

(11.47)

The power received by the receiving antenna will be

$$P_R = \frac{P_T}{4\pi R^2} \times G_T \times \sigma \times \frac{1}{4\pi R^2} \times A_{eR} \; [\text{W}]$$

(11.48)

As was defined in Chapter 10, the area of the receiving antenna aperture

$$A_{eR} = \frac{G_R \lambda^2}{4\pi} \; [\text{m}^2]$$

(11.49)

Finally, the minimum power received by the radar receiver is

$$P_{\min} = P_T \times G_T \times G_R \times \sigma \times \frac{\lambda^2}{(4\pi)^3 R^4} \; [\text{W}]$$

(11.50)

Then, the maximum range can be obtained as

$$R_{\max} = \left[\frac{G_T \times G_R \times \sigma \times \lambda^2}{(4\pi)^3 \times P_{\min}} \right]^{1/4} \; [\text{m}]$$

(11.51)

We now present a free-space path loss in energetic values (joules or watts), introduced by Equation 10.18, to satisfy the formula, introduced in Chapter 10:

$$L_{FS} = \left(\frac{4\pi R}{\lambda} \right)^2 \; [\text{W}]$$

(11.52)

A total free-space path loss of one-way propagation by introducing an attenuation factor A can be presented as

$$\tilde{L}_{FS} = \left(\frac{4\pi R}{\lambda A} \right)^2 \; [\text{W}]$$

(11.53)

Using Equation 11.52 or 11.53, we finally get

$$P_{\min} = \left[\frac{P_T \times G_T \times G_R \times \sigma \times 4\pi}{\lambda^2 L_{FS}^2} \right] [\text{W}] \qquad (11.54)$$

11.8 Clutter Effects on RCS

11.8.1 Radar Cross Section

RCS, σ, can be defined as [4]

$$\sigma = \text{RCS} = \lim]_{R \to \infty} \left[\left(4\pi R^2 \right) \left| \frac{E_s}{E_i} \right|^2 \right] [\text{m}^2] \qquad (11.55)$$

For a square plate of radius a, the RCS equals for vertical or horizontal normal illumination [4]

$$\sigma = \text{RCS} = \frac{4\pi a^2}{\lambda^2} [\text{m}^2] \qquad (11.56)$$

Thus, for $f = 3$ GHz (S-band radar), a 1 m² plate yields about 1200 m² RCS (~31 dB); and at $f = 10$ GHz (X-band radar), RSC increases to 10,000 m² (~40 dB).

As was shown in [7], for different kinds of radar, a specific formula for RCS can be evaluated. To show this, let us start with ground radar and find the ground clutter RCS. Thus, at a range R from the ground surface, the antenna beam with beamwidth θ_{BW} covers a circular area of approximate radius $R \cdot \theta_{BW}$, as shown in Figure 11.8.

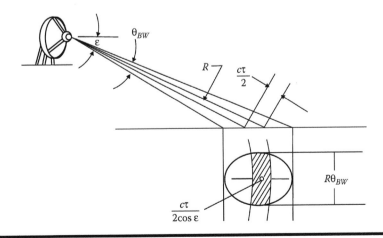

Figure 11.8   Definition of ground clutter RCS.

If the pulse duration of the signal is τ, then it covers a ground cell-section of $c\tau/2\cos\varepsilon$, where ε is the look angle of the antenna on the ground cell-section (see Figure 11.8). Using this expression and accounting for the antenna coverage, we can easily obtain the equivalent ground RCS, σ_R:

$$\text{RCS} \equiv \sigma_R = \frac{R \cdot \theta_{BW} \cdot c \cdot \tau}{2\cos\varepsilon}\sigma_0 \tag{11.57}$$

where σ_0 is the ground backscattering coefficient, which depends on transmitted frequency, type of wave polarization, type of ground terrain, and the look angle. As was shown in [7], it can be obtained experimentally.

11.9 Clutter and Target Effects on Radar Signals

11.9.1 SNR

The thermal Gaussian white (additive) noise [18,19]

$$N_0 = k_B T_0 B_\omega F \; [\text{W}] \tag{11.58}$$

where:

$k_B = 1.38 \times 10^{-23} \, (\text{W} \cdot \text{s})/K$
F is the noise factor $F = 1 + T_e / T_0$
B_ω is the noise bandwidth at the receiver

Then where $T_0 = 290K$ is *room* temperature, and T_θ is the effective noise temperature,

$$\text{SNR} \equiv P / N_0 = P_T \frac{G_T G_R \lambda^2 \sigma}{(4\pi)^3 R^4 k_B T_0 B_\omega F} \tag{11.59}$$

or via the path loss in free space

$$L_{FS} = \left(\frac{4\pi R}{\lambda}\right)^2 \tag{11.60}$$

we get

$$\text{SNR} = 4\pi \frac{P_T G_T G_R \sigma}{\lambda^2 L_{FS}^2 k_B T_0 B_\omega F} \tag{11.61}$$

Next, the free-space path loss of one-way propagation, described by Equation 11.18 and introducing attenuation factor A, yields

$$\text{SNR} = 4\pi \frac{P_T G_T G_R \sigma A^2}{\lambda^2 L_P^2 k_B T_0 B_\omega F} \qquad (11.62)$$

11.9.2 Clutter Influence

Unwanted echoes usually occur as distributed clutter. Clutter is characterized in terms of RCS density. The surface clutter, the average RCS density σ_0, that is, RCS σ_c of the clutter per unit area A_c, equals [4,7,14,17]

$$\sigma_0 = \frac{\sigma_c}{A_c} \text{ [dimensionless]} \qquad (11.63)$$

The volume clutter RCS density is given via the clutter RCS per unit volume V_c:

$$\eta_0 = \frac{\sigma_c}{V_c} \text{ [1/m]} \qquad (11.64)$$

The geometry is presented in Figure 11.8. If τ is the pulse length, R is the range, ϕ is the phase (in radians), and θ is the elevation angle, then RCS of the clutter equals [4,7]

$$\sigma_c = \sigma_0 R \phi \frac{c\tau}{2} \sec\theta \text{ [m}^2\text{]} \qquad (11.65)$$

Then, the clutter-limited detection equivalent to SNR (called the *signal-to-clutter ratio* (SCR)), can be presented via the target RCS σ_t and clutter cross section σ_c [4,7,17]:

$$\text{SCR} = \frac{\sigma_t}{\sigma_c} = \frac{\sigma_t}{\sigma_0 R \phi \dfrac{c\tau}{2} \sec\theta} \qquad (11.66)$$

Thus, for the ocean at S-band and 0.1° grazing angle, RCS is −89 dB (for vertical polarization) and increases to −45 dB at X-band and 3° grazing angle. For the HF band, RCS is −30 and −35 dB, respectively, for the same polarization.

PROBLEMS

Example 11.1: Given parameters of the radar $\tau = 320\ \mu s$, PRF = 600 pulses per second.
Find: Distances to the target: R and R_{max}.
Example 11.2: Given $\tau_d = 320\ \mu s$, $f = 1/T = 600$ pulses per second.
Find: Distances to the target: R and R_{max}.
Example 11.3: Given $P_T = 1$ kW, $G_T = G_R = 5$ dB, $f = 1$ GHz, $\sigma = 25$ m^2, and $R = 10$ km.
Find: Parameters of the radar: A_{eR}, PD, P_R, and the maximum distance R_{max}.
Example 11.4: Given $\tau = 1\ \mu s$, $\theta_{BW} = 0.5°$, $\varepsilon = 10°$, and $\sigma = 0.01$. For the range of R = 5 km,
Find: Radar cross section σ_R.

Example 11.5: Given $P_T = 25$ kW, $G_T = G_R = 7$ dB, $f = 3.5$ GHz, $\sigma = 9$ m², $R = 15$ km, $T_0 = 300°K$, and $F = 3.5$.

Find: The path loss L_{FS}^2 and SNR.

References

1. Meeks, M. L., *Radar Propagation at Low Altitudes*, Norwood, MA: Artech House, 1982.
2. Hovanessian, S. A., *Radar System Design and Analysis*, Dedham, MA: Artech House, 1984.
3. Skolnik, M. I., *Introduction to Radar Systems*, New York: McGraw-Hill, 1990.
4. Shaeffer, J. F., M. T. Tuley, and E. F. Knot, *Radar Cross Section*, Norwood, MA: Artech House, 1985.
5. Blackman, S. S., *Multiple-Target Tracking with Radar Applications*, Norwood, MA: Artech House, 1986.
6. Leonov, A. I. and K. I. Fomichev, *Monopulse Radar*, Norwood, MA: Artech House, 1986.
7. Eaves, J. L. and E. K. Reedy, *Principles of Modern Radars*, New York: Van Nostrand Reinhold, 1987.
8. Hovanessian, S. A., *Introduction to Sensor Systems*, Norwood, MA: Artech House, 1988.
9. Barton, D. K., *Modern Radar System Analysis*, Norwood, MA: Artech House, 1988.
10. Balanis, C. A., *Advanced Engineering Electromagnetics*, New York: Wiley, 1989.
11. Skolnik, M. I., *Radar Handbook*, New York: McGraw-Hill, 1990.
12. Nathanson, F. E., *Radar Design Principles*, New York: McGraw-Hill, 1991.
13. Kingsley, S. and S. Quegan, *Understanding Radar Systems*, London: McGraw-Hill, 1992.
14. Pozar, D., *Microwave Engineering*, New York: Wiley, 1998.
15. Ince, N., E. Topuz, E. Panayirci, and C. Isik, *Principles of Integrated Maritime Surveillance Systems*, Boston, MA: Kluwer Academic, 2000.
16. Sullivan, R. J., *Microwave Radar: Imaging and Advanced Concepts*, Norwood, MA: Artech House, 2001.
17. Sevgi, L., Radar, in *Handbook: Engineering Electromagnetics*, ed. by R. Bansal, New York: Marcel Dekker, 2004, pp. 377–416.
18. Blaunstein, N., and C. G. Christodoulou, *Radio Propagation and Adaptive Antennas for Wireless Communication Links: Terrestrial, Atmospheric and Ionospheric*, 1st edn, New York: Wiley InterScience, 2007.
19. Blaunstein, N. and C. G. Christodoulou, *Radio Propagation and Adaptive Antennas for Wireless Communication Networks: Terrestrial, Atmospheric and Ionospheric*, 2nd edn, New York: Wiley, 2014.
20. Fock, V. A., *Electromagnetic Diffraction and Propagation Problems*, Oxford: Pergamon, 1965.
21. Blaunstein, N. and E. Plohotniuc, *Ionosphere and Applied Aspects of Radio Communication and Radar*, New York: CRC, Taylor & Francis, 2008.

Chapter 12

Millimeter-Wave Radars

In the last few decades, microwave- and millimeter-wave radars, active and passive (the latter are usually called in the literature *radiometers*, see [1–12]) have become important technical facilities in various remote sensing applications of the earth's environment, such as ground subsoil medium, atmosphere, and ocean. Radiometers of this kind were developed from the mid-1980s to the early 1990s simultaneously in the former USSR, the United States, and Europe [12–19]. Recently, several kinds of passive millimeter-wave (MMW) radiometers have been developed and reported in [20–24]. They are capable of imaging during poor weather conditions and nocturnal time periods. Moreover, passive radar is undetectable and is not degraded by path error or speckle noise. Essentially, detecting various thermic emissions from the target under searching MMW-radar provides additional information about its peculiarities compared with that obtained by low-frequency radars or optical and infrared (IR) detectors, for more accurate estimation of the target "response."

The increasing requirements for practical applications of active or passive MMW radar dictate increased efficiency of the system design and instrumentation, as well as the corresponding signal-processing and imaging performance. Such a system should pass through any environmental clutter, such as fog, clouds, drizzle, rain, snow, smoke, vegetation, and other obstacles, where IR and visual optical sensors and cameras become inefficient. All these features and advances of the passive MMW radiometer increase interest in introducing it in more and more applications [14–23]. At the same time, we should note that, as is well known, the minimum atmospheric absorption of MMW radiation by molecules of water and oxygen (see Chapter 11) occurs at frequencies around 35 and 94 GHz (the corresponding wavelengths are around 8 and 3 mm, respectively), where higher spatial resolution of the target under investigation can also be achieved.

In this chapter, we introduce the reader to the definition of MMW radar, its main operational characteristics, and its main applications. MMW radars differ from microwave radars by the use of higher frequencies (from 40 to 200 GHz (see Table 11.1)), by their narrower bandwidth, and by the greater difficulty and cost of their production [1–10]. At the same time, accounting for the atmospheric attenuation effects described in the previous chapter, this bandwidth is divided into "windows" that are transparent to radar signal propagation in land–atmospheric links.

12.1 Main Properties of Active MMW Radar

The narrow bandwidth of this kind of radar results in good angular resolution (e.g., the antenna beamwidth) as well as the possibility of detecting non-moving targets in the presence of ground clutter, as shown in Figure 12.1.

Comparing this figure with Figure 11.1, we note that the MMW radar gives better angle resolution of the desired target and/or precise searching of the desired clutter. Thus, going from the microwave radar presented in Figure 11.1 (with f_c=9 GHz) to the MMW radar presented in Figure 12.1 (with f_c=94 GHz) will improve the angular accuracy by a factor of ~10. At the same time, MMW radars having narrower bandwidth cannot search large areas compared with microwave radar.

However, the same formula as Equation 11.1 fully describes the angle resolution or beamwidth of MMW radar, which we present here again for convenient further explanation by rewriting it through the radiated frequency f_c:

$$\theta_{BW} = \frac{\lambda}{D} = \frac{c}{f_c D} \tag{12.1}$$

where, as in Chapter 11:

    θ_{BW} is the antenna beam width measured in radians
    λ is the wavelength of the radiated signal
    D is the antenna aperture dimension (in Figure 12.1, D=1 foot)
    c is the wave velocity in free space

This example allows us to suppose that having higher frequencies (i.e., smaller beamwidth) allows MMW radars to subtend smaller ground clutter areas, in which the target is located, and finally to find and detect the desired target. Finally, this property of MMW radars yields a better target-to-clutter-signal ratio (TCSR).

Moreover, despite the higher resolution of electro-optical systems, which at the same ranges achieve the angle resolution of targets with dimensions of a few centimeters, MMW radars are less sensitive to weather effects (snow, rain, fog, smoke, and flares, briefly discussed in Chapter 11) and are therefore more effective against thermal imaging systems.

Additionally, the high Doppler shift sensitivity of MMW radars gives good resolution of slowly moving targets. In fact, in recent decades, detection of slowly moving and stationary (non-moving) targets by airborne MMW radars mounted on helicopters has received great attention from the community of radar designers [1–19].

At the same time, in practice, the detection ranges of MMW radars are not very long—tactically they are produced for shorter-range detection of targets (less than 5–10 km). Usually, MMW radars are produced at 35, 94, 140, and 240 GHz because of the low atmospheric attenuation at these frequencies (see Figure 11.21).

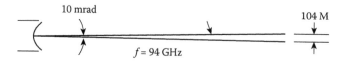

Figure 12.1 **Resolution cell of 104 m at a range of 10 km from the MMW radar operated at frequency of f_c=94 GHz with aperture angle resolution of 10 mrad.**

12.2 Effects of Environment on MMW Active Radar Operation Properties

12.2.1 Range of Target Detection

In Chapter 11, we presented the ground *clutter radar cross section* (CRCS) by Equation 11.48, defining this parameter geometrically in Figure 11.8. The same formula corresponds well to MMW radars too, and therefore, we present it for the reader's convenience:

$$(RCS)_c \equiv \sigma_c = \frac{R \cdot \theta_{BW} \cdot c \cdot \tau}{2 \cos \varepsilon} \sigma_0 \qquad (12.2a)$$

This formula is more precise than that introduced in [7]:

$$(RCS)_c \equiv \sigma_c = \frac{R \cdot \theta_{BW} \cdot c \cdot \tau}{2} \sigma_0 \qquad (12.2b)$$

where σ_0 is the ground backscattering coefficient, which depends on the MMW radar radiated frequency, the type of wave polarization, the type of ground terrain, and the look angle θ_{BW}.

The MMW radar search range equation can be written following [4,7], but using notations introduced in Chapter 11:

$$R = \left[\frac{\bar{P} \cdot A \cdot \sigma}{16 \cdot N_0 \cdot L(S/N)} \frac{t_s}{\Omega} \right]^{1/4} \qquad (12.3)$$

where:

$\bar{P}$ is the average signal power $\left(\bar{P} = P_p \cdot \tau \cdot \mathrm{PRF} \right)$
P_p is the pulse peak power
τ is the pulse duration
N_0 is the noise power, defined by Equation 11.57
L is the system losses
t_s is the radar scan time
Ω is the radar angular search coverage area
σ is the radar target cross section
A is the antenna aperture

The other parameters are defined in Chapter 11.

12.2.2 Target-to-Clutter and Target-to-Rain Signal-to-Noise Ratio (SNR) Effects

Now, using Equation 12.3, one can easily obtain the *target-signal-to-noise ratio* $(SNR)_t$:

$$(SNR)_t = \frac{\bar{P} \cdot A \cdot \sigma}{16 \cdot N_0 \cdot L \cdot R^4} \left[\frac{t_s}{\Omega} \right] \qquad (12.4)$$

We should notice that these equations were obtained without accounting for the atmospheric attenuation effects.

Now, to obtain the *clutter-signal-to-noise ratio* $(SNR)_c$, where clutter effects are caused by the rough ground surface, we will introduce Equation 12.2a into Equation 12.4 by changing σ to σ_c from Equation 12.2a, and following the geometry presented in Figure 11.8, which yields

$$\left(SNR\right)_c = \frac{\overline{P} \cdot A \cdot \theta_{BW} \cdot c \cdot \tau \cdot \sigma_0}{32 \cdot N_0 \cdot L \cdot R^3 \cos\varepsilon} \left[\frac{t_s}{\Omega}\right] \tag{12.5a}$$

or by introducing Equation 12.2b, and following [7], we rewrite Equation 12.5a in our notations as

$$\left(SNR\right)_c = \frac{\overline{P} \cdot A \cdot \theta_{BW} \cdot c \cdot \tau \cdot \sigma_0}{32 \cdot N_0 \cdot L \cdot R^3} \left[\frac{t_s}{\Omega}\right] \tag{12.5b}$$

Equations 12.5a and 12.5b represent the clutter-signal-to-noise ratio, against which the target signal of a ground target (car, truck, tank, etc.) competes for detection. We should note that the $(SNR)_c$ from these equations is inversely proportional to R^3, while the $(SNR)_t$ is inversely proportional to R^4. This fact follows from Equations 12.2a and 12.2b, where the CRCS $(RCS)_c$ is directly proportional to the range R.

For MMW radars for searching and tracking atmospheric targets (helicopters, aircraft, etc.), the corresponding SNR, accounting for rain and other hydrometeors (called the *rain-signal-to-noise ratio* $(SNR)_r$ [2,4,7]), can be easily obtained by combining the corresponding *rain radar cross section* $(RCS)_r$:

$$\left(RCS\right)_r \equiv \sigma_r = \frac{\pi \cdot \left(R \cdot \theta_{BW}\right)^2 \cdot c \cdot \tau}{8} \sigma_i \tag{12.6}$$

and introducing it into Equation 12.4. Finally, this yields

$$\left(SNR\right)_r = \frac{\pi \cdot \overline{P} \cdot A \cdot \theta_{BW}^2 \cdot c \cdot \tau \cdot \sigma_i}{128 \cdot N_0 \cdot L \cdot R^2} \left[\frac{t_s}{\Omega}\right] \tag{12.7}$$

Equation 12.7 represents the rain SNR, against which the target signal competes for detection. Now, comparing Equations 12.4 and 12.7, one notes that the SNR from rain (or snow) backscattering is inversely proportional to R^2, while the ground target signal power is inversely proportional to R^4. Comparing Equations 12.4, 12.5, and 12.7, one can emphasize that the target signal of a non-moving target can exceed the ground clutter signal.

We will now show an example of how, using specified radar, target, and clutter (ground and/or atmospheric), one can compute target, clutter, and rain backscattering SNR as a function of range given by Equations 12.4, 12.5a, 12,5b, and 12.7. Of course, for precise computation of different SNRs, we need to know the effects of ground surface, atmospheric attenuation and rain, the type of hydrometeor, and the different kinds of clutter. Such effects were described briefly in

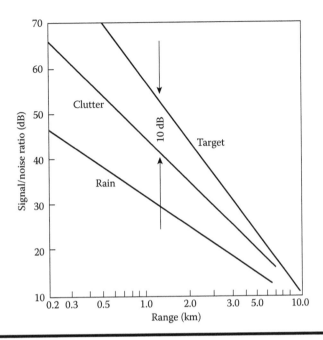

Figure 12.2   Target, clutter, and rain backscattering SNRs vs. the range to target.

Chapter 11, and we will not repeat the description here. Rather, we will present the result of one such computation that takes into account atmospheric attenuation. The result of this example is shown in Figure 12.2 according to computations made in [4,7]. As can be seen from this figure, the target detection range can be obtained for any given SNR.

In other words, the target-to-clutter signal power requirement should result in a range of 1.4 km if a difference of 10 dB is achieved. At the same time, to achieve the same range of 1.4 km during moderate rain (with a rate of 4 mm/h), the target-to-rain-signal power should not be less than 20 dB (see Figure 12.2).

Consequently, to detect a target at a range of 1.4 km, the signal power from a target must exceed that received from the ground clutter by 10 dB, as denoted in Figure 10.2 by the corresponding vertical vectors between two curves.

So, using Equations 12.4, 12.5, and 12.7, we can find the difference in SNR between these three main parameters for detection of a range under consideration. Thus, for the case of stationary ground targets, dividing SNR from Equation 12.4 by the clutter-to-noise ratio from Equations 12.5a and 12.5b, we can find the target SNR to clutter SNR, and finally, the target-to-clutter signal ratio, respectively, as

$$\frac{(SNR)_t}{(SNR)_c} \equiv \frac{S_t}{S_c} = \frac{2 \cdot \sigma \cdot \cos \varepsilon}{c \cdot \tau \cdot \theta_{BW} \cdot R_t \cdot \sigma_0} \tag{12.8a}$$

$$\frac{(SNR)_t}{(SNR)_c} \equiv \frac{S_t}{S_c} = \frac{2 \cdot \sigma}{c \cdot \tau \cdot \theta_{BW} \cdot R_t \cdot \sigma_0} \tag{12.8b}$$

We note again that these equations do not include atmospheric attenuation. Here, R_t is the target range from the MMW radar, which can be solved for a required target-to-clutter signal ratio from Equations 12.8a or 12.8b:

$$R_t = \frac{2 \cdot \sigma \cdot \cos\varepsilon}{c \cdot \tau \cdot \theta_{BW} \cdot (S_t / S_c) \cdot \sigma_0} \tag{12.9a}$$

or

$$R_t = \frac{2 \cdot \sigma}{c \cdot \tau \cdot \theta_{BW} \cdot (S_t / S_c) \cdot \sigma_0} \tag{12.9b}$$

From Equations 12.9a and 12.9b, it follows that the target detection range is inversely proportional to range gate size $\Delta R = (c \cdot \tau)/2$ (also called the *range resolution cell* [7]), the antenna beam width θ_{BW}, and the backscattering coefficient σ_0. Since, for given antenna dimensions, the 95 GHz radar will have smaller beamwidth than the 35 GHz radar, its detection range will be accordingly higher.

Similarly, dividing Equation 12.4 by 12.7, yields a target-signal-to-rain-backscattering signal:

$$\frac{(SNR)_t}{(SNR)_r} \equiv \frac{S_t}{S_r} = \frac{8 \cdot \sigma}{\pi \cdot c \cdot \tau \cdot \theta_{BW}^2 \cdot R_t^2 \cdot \sigma_i} \tag{12.10}$$

Here, R_t is the target range from the MMW radar, which can now be solved for a required target-to-clutter signal ratio from (12.10):

$$R_t^2 = \frac{8 \cdot \sigma}{c \cdot \tau \cdot \pi \cdot \theta_{BW}^2 \cdot (S_t / S_r) \cdot \sigma_i} \tag{12.11}$$

From Equation 12.11, it follows that the square of detection range of a target in rain is inversely proportional to the range gate size $\Delta R = (c \cdot \tau)/2$, the antenna beam width $\sim\pi \cdot \theta_{BW}$, and the rain backscattering coefficient σ_i.

It is important to note, as follows from Equations 12.9a, 12.9b, and 12.11, that the detection range can be estimated in clutter and/or in rain only in the case when the target, clutter, or rain signals are above the system noise level. For this reason, in computations of actual detection ranges, for the determination of the complete detection range, it is preferable to use Equations 12.4, 12.5, and 12.7.

Accounting for atmospheric attenuation values taken from [7], we get $R = 12$ km (for $f = 35$ GHz) and $R = 9$ km (for $f = 95$ GHz). Rain and fog can decrease the range of target detection to 7 km (for $f = 35$ GHz and for moderate rain) and to 3.5 km (for $f = 95$ GHz and for moderate rain).

12.3 Passive MMW Radars

Active MMW radars obtain information about a target by transmitting a signal and receiving the echo from the target. Passive MMW radars are based on the radiometry technique and are therefore called radiometers. What does this mean? Radiometry is a passive technique, which develops information about a target solely from the MMW portion of the black body radiation (noise) that it either emits directly or reflects from surrounding bodies. Therefore, the radiometer is a sensitive receiver specially designed to measure this noise power.

12.3.1 Typical Applications of MMW Radiometers

MMW radiometry, based on MMW passive radar systems—radiometers—is a relatively new area of microwave radar technology that has been developed during recent decades. It is widely interdisciplinary, drawing on results from many fields, such as electrical and radio engineering, geophysics, oceanography, atmospheric and near-the-earth sciences, and so forth.

There are many practical applications of passive MMW radiometric systems. These systems have attracted increasing interest over the past years due to their imaging capability to see through fog, clouds, drizzle, dry snow, smoke, and other obstacles, where IR and optical systems become inefficient. The minimum atmospheric absorption of MMW radiation occurs near 35 and 94–95 GHz. Therefore, these bands are used for MMW imaging. The choice of operating frequency band depends on the particular application. It was shown in [12–20] that at 35 GHz, better temperature contrast in a scene is obtained compared with 94–95 GHz, at which higher spatial resolution is achieved. The main problem consists of obtaining an image in real time in the same way as IR thermal imagers. This can be achieved by using simultaneous receiving of the radiation from the different parts of a scene. For simultaneous receiving, the creation of an array with a large number of receiving channels and a multibeam quasi-optical antenna is required. Passive MMW imaging systems have developed from a single-channel scanning imager to the fully steering array, which contains thousands of receivers or more [12–20].

In [21–24], a passive MMW imager, which occupies an intermediate position between a single-channel imager and a fully steering array, was described. The 3 mm wave passive system was designed especially for demonstration of the possibilities of the single-channel MMW radiometer for remote observation and for experimental (evaluation) purposes. At the same time, the main advantage of the scanning imager, is the possibility of obtaining a wide field of view [12]. The 32-channel 8 mm wave passive scanning system contains a linear array of radiometric sensors [12,21–23]. In Table 12.1, we will present some typical applications of MMW radiometry.

We will now present several examples of the use of MMW passive radars (radiometers) for detection and imaging of objects hidden in different kinds of clutter, based on results presented in [12,21–24]. These compared the results of imaging the desired urban scene with a visual-optic camera, as usual, and with a radiometer operated at the wavelengths of 3 and 8 mm. In Figures 12.3 and 12.4, we present this comparison for different scenarios occurring in the urban scene at the ranges of 150–200 and 500–600 m, respectively, from a MMW passive radar operated at $\lambda = 8$ mm.

Other types of MMW radiometer applications described in [20–23] show its great potential to discriminate cars and other "warm" targets (Figure 12.5), with their brightness resulting from the difference between their temperature and the background temperature, despite the fact that such objects are located in complicated terrestrial clutter conditions.

Another example is related to the use of the passive detection of concealed foreign objects under clothes on the human body. Here, designs of a single-channel 3 mm passive imaging system

Table 12.1 Typical Applications of MMW Passive Radars (Radiometers)

Civilian Applications	Measurements of soil and subsoil moisture
	Snow and ice cover mapping
	Ocean surface wind speed measurements
	Atmospheric temperature profile measurements
	Atmospheric humidity height profile measurements
Military Applications	Detection of targets buried in clutter conditions
	Recognition of targets hidden in clutter environment
	Surveillance of moving targets
	Mapping of targets and desired areas with clutter
Astronomical Applications	Planetary mapping
	Solar emission mapping
	Mapping of galactic objects
	Measurements of cosmological background radiation

(radiometer) are based on the fact that all bodies radiate, absorb, reflect, and pass on electromagnetic energy, namely, a human body "reacts" as a "black body" (see Figure 12.6 and discussions there).

At the same time, if an object is hidden in the clothes, the quantity of the energy that is radiated, absorbed, and reflected and passes through depends on the object's material. Because millimeter waves pass through clothing easily, the human body absorbs them, which is equivalent to its own thermal radiation. However, when the radiation encounters a foreign object, it is partly reflected and partly absorbed by the material [21–23].

As a result (the measurements were carried out in indoor conditions (see Figure 10.7) according to [21–23]), the radiometric sensor will show the contrast between the radiation of a body with temperature around $T_b = 309$ K and the indoor temperature, which is usually around $T_i = 279$ K. Thus, the passive formation of the images in a 3 mm wavelength band represents an effective, noninvasive method for the detection and recognition of any foreign object hidden in clothes near the human body. Of course, there will be other problems of environmental influence (clutter), signal processing, and practical realization in a real system.

As the result of imaging without the corresponding post-processing, we present in Figure 12.7 one of the numerous images of the foreign objects concealed under clothes near the human body (tests were done at a range between 5 and 10 m from the radiometer).

Figure 12.3 Built-up scene imaging obtained by (a) MMW radiometer and (b) optical camera. (Modified from Gorishnyak, V. P., et al., 8-mm passive imaging system with 32 channels, *Proceeding of EurRAD-2004*, Amsterdam, 2–14 October, p. 6, 2004.)

As is clearly seen in Figure 12.7, direct measurements of the contract using such an imaging system but without pre-processing and post-processing techniques cannot differentiate and identify the embedded objects. Only by using post-processing based on the framework of diffraction tomography [24] can one identify the metal ring, modeling a concealed mine as an explosive structure, and a plastic pistol, modeling a real weapon hidden in clothes near the human body (see Figure 12.8).

Figure 12.4 Imaging of a specific urban scene obtained by (a) MMW radiometer and (b) optical camera. (Modified from Gorishnyak, V. P., et al., 8-mm passive imaging system with 32 channels, *Proceeding of EurRAD-2004*, Amsterdam, 2–14 October, p. 6, 2004.)

Figure 12.5 **Moving and stationary cars outside and inside clutter with vegetation. (Modified from Gorishnyak, V. P., et al., 8-mm passive imaging system with 32 channels,** *Proceeding of EurRAD-2004*, **Amsterdam, 2–14 October, p. 6, 2004.)**

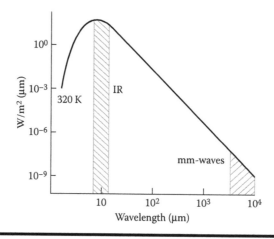

Figure 12.6 **Visualization of Planck's law for a "black body" radiation.**

The examples of MMW radiometer applications that we have presented allow us to suggest that a passive radiometric imaging system can be successfully used to provide navigation and searching in built-up ground terrain and sea-water surface at long distances (from 100 m up to 1–2 km), even if the surface radar clutter is high, as well as in indoor/outdoor applications for imaging and identification of foreign objects at short ranges (from a few meters up to 15–25 m). So, they can be used for remote sensing in space and air investigations, for all-weather surveillance, for discovery of objects, and for many other civilian and special military applications.

12.3.2 Theoretical Aspects of MMW Radiometry

The principle of use of MMW radiometers is based on the fundamental Planck's radiation law, according to which a body in thermodynamic equilibrium at a temperature, T, exceeding absolute zero radiates energy (power) [11,13–16]

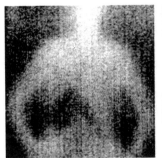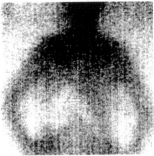

Figure 12.7 Image of foreign objects hidden in clothing by use of a 3 mm single-channel demonstration radiometer. (Rearranged from Gorishnyak, V. P., et al., 8-mm passive imaging system with 32 channels, *Proceeding of EurRAD-2004*, Amsterdam, 2–14 October, p. 6, 2004.)

Figure 12.8 Imaging after post-processing based on diffraction tomography theoretical framework. (From Blaunstein, N., Recognition of foreign objects hidden in clutter by novel method of diffraction tomography, *Proceeding of IEEE Conference on Radar Applications*, Kiev, Ukraine, p. 5, 2010.)

$$P = k_B B_\omega T \tag{12.12}$$

where:

k_B is Boltzmann's constant
B_ω is the MMW radar bandwidth (which can be easily converted into the wavelength range)

This law strictly applies only to a black body and is therefore called a *blackbody law of radiation*. Usually in the literature, a black body is defined as an ideal body that absorbs all incident energy without reflection, and also radiates energy at the same rate as it absorbs energy, thus maintaining thermal equilibrium. A density of the radiated energy per square area and the wavelength of micrometer was presented above in Figure 12.6 according to Planck's law [12,24]. It is seen that the maximum of radiation of the ideal black body is located at the wavelength surrounding $\lambda = 10\ \mu m$. At the same time, at the range between 3 and 8 mm, it is also possible to detect radiated energy from a black body arriving at the radiometric receiver.

A nonideal black body will partially reflect incident energy or, conversely, will not radiate the same power as would a black body at the same temperature. Usually, to verify this difference, a new characteristic, called *emissivity*, is introduced:

$$E = \frac{P_{nbb}}{P_{bb}} = \frac{P}{k_B B_\omega T} \tag{12.13}$$

It is seen from Equation 12.13 that emissivity is a measure of the power radiated by a nonideal black body relative to that radiated by an ideal black body at the same temperature, from which it follows that $0 \le E \le 1$, and $E = 1$ for a perfect body, the radiative properties of which are similar to those of a black body.

We should note that for radiometric purposes, a *brightness temperature* T_B is usually introduced to quantify radiated energy (in the same manner as a noise power N_0 is presented in terms of effective temperature T_{eff}:

$$T_B = E \cdot T \tag{12.14}$$

where T is the physical temperature of the real body. Equation 12.14 shows that for the radiometric receiver, a body is "cooler" with respect to a real body temperature, since $0 \le E \le 1$.

Now, we will consider how the antenna of the passive radiometer differentiates the noise power from different "sources" located in the surroundings. This process is shown in Figure 12.9.

A desired terrestrial area searched by the radiometer antenna has the apparent brightness temperature T_B. The atmosphere emits radiation in all directions isotropically, and its component directed to the ground-based radiometer is proportional to T_{AD}, whereas the power reflected from the ground to the radiometer antenna is proportional to T_{AR}.

Of course, there are other sources of radiation, such as the sun, that affect the receiver antenna. Thus, as illustrated by Equation 12.4, the total brightness temperature seen by the radiometer is a function of the desired area of observation, the observed angle, the frequency atmospheric attenuation, antenna pattern, and so on.

Now we can formulate the main objective of any MMW radiometer: to infer information about the desired area from the measured T_B and then, via signal processing, to find relations between brightness temperature and physical conditions of the tested area (the same radiometric mechanism occurs for each body or scene under consideration). For example, the power reflected from a uniform layer of snow over soil can be treated as plane wave reflection from a multilayer dielectric region, leading to the development of an algorithm that gives the thickness of the snow layer in terms of measured brightness temperature at various frequencies.

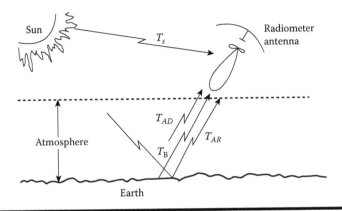

Figure 12.9 **The noise power "sources" in typical MMW radiometer applications.**

12.3.3 MMW-Radiometer Parameters Estimation

The subject of radiometry and the corresponding MMW passive radar schematic aspects are of most interest to the radio-frequency (RF) engineers dealing with the design of the radiometer itself. The basic problem here is to build a receiver that can distinguish between the desired radiometric noise, and the noise of the receiver, even though the radiometric power is usually less than the receiver noise power. We will not go into details or illustrate the difficulties involved in a radiometer design, referring the reader to the relevant literature [11,13–17,20–23], since this subject is outside the scope of this book.

At the same time, we will discuss how we can estimate the output voltage V_0 by knowledge of the antenna gain G, the brightness temperature of the area under searching, T_B, defined by Equation 12.14, the antenna noise power, $P_A = k_B T_B B_\omega$, and the power at the receiver input, $P_R = k_B T_R B_\omega$, where T_R is the overall noise temperature of the receiver. Thus, accounting for all these characteristics, we finally get

$$V_0 = G \cdot k_B \cdot (T_B + T_R) \cdot B_\omega \tag{12.15}$$

After special calibration by replacing the antenna input with two calibrated noise sources, the system constants, $G \cdot k_B \cdot B_\omega$ and $G \cdot k_B \cdot T_R \cdot B_\omega$, can be determined. Finally, the desired brightness temperature, T_B, can be directly measured with the systems.

12.3.4 Measurements of Errors in Brightness Temperature

There are two kinds of error that can occur during radiometer operational work. The first is an error, ΔT_B, in the measurement of brightness temperature due to noise fluctuations. Since noise is a random process, the measured noise power at the integrator can vary from one integration period to the next. The integrator (or low-pass filter) acts to smooth out random oscillations in V_0 with frequency components greater than τ^{-1}. It can be shown that the error due to noise fluctuations is [5,13–16]

$$\Delta T_N = \frac{T_B + T_R}{B_\omega \cdot \tau} \tag{12.16}$$

This result shows that if a longer measurement time, τ, can be tolerated, the error due to noise fluctuations can be reduced to a negligible value.

A more serious error occurs due to random variations of the radiometer antenna gain, G. Such variations generally occur in the RF amplifier, mixer, or intermediate frequency (IF) amplifier, over a period of 1 s or more. So, if the system is calibrated with a certain value ΔG, which changes by the time a measurement is made, an error can be obtained, as follows [5,13–16]:

$$\Delta T_G = \frac{(T_B + T_R)}{G}\Delta G \qquad (12.17)$$

where ΔG is the root mean square (rms) of change in the system gain G.

Finally, we will present some typical numbers following [1–7]: a 10 GHz total power radiometer having a bandwidth of 100 MHz, a receiver temperature $T_R = 500$ K, an integrator time constant $\tau = 0.01$ s, and a system gain variation of $\Delta G/G = 0.01$.

If the antenna temperature is the same as the brightness temperature and equals $T_B = 300$ K, then from Equation 12.16, one can obtain the error due to noise fluctuations as $\Delta T_N = 0.8$K. At the same time, Equation 10.17 gives the error due to gain variations as $\Delta T_G = 8$ K. These estimations, which are based on realistic data, show that gain variations are most critical factor that affects the accuracy of the MMW radiometer. We will finish this chapter by providing the reader with some examples of how to estimate the operational parameters of MMW radar systems, active and passive, which we ask him or her to solve individually.

PROBLEM

Given two radars operating at $f = 35$ GHz and $f = 95$ GHz. For both frequencies, we have the following parameters:

a. $P = 20$ W, $PRF = 10^4$ Hz, $\sigma = 30$ m^2, $A = 0.073$ m^2, $\tau = 50 \times 10^{-9}$ s, $\Omega = 60° \times 4°$, $\sigma_0 = 0.01$, SNR = 10.
b. At the same time, other parameters are different:
   $t_s = 3.6$ s (for $f = 35$ GHz) and $t_s = 4.1$ s (for $f = 95$ GHz), $T_{eff} = 1170$ K (for $f = 35$ GHz) and $T_{eff} = 1470$ K (for $f = 95$ GHz), $L = 9$ dB (for $f = 35$ GHz) and $L = 13$ dB (for $f = 95$ GHz), $\theta_{BW} = 1.6°$ (for $f = 35$ GHz) and $\theta_{BW} = 0.6°$ (for $f = 95$ GHz).
   Find: For $f = 35$ GHz and $f = 95$ GHz: (a) the range accuracy, ΔR; (b) the mean power of brightness, $\overline{P}$; (c) the target range, R.

References

1. Johnston, S. I., ed. *Millimeter Wave Radar*, Dedham, MA: Artech House, 1980.
2. Button, K. J. and Wiltse, J. C., *Infrared and Millimeter Waves*, vol. 4, New York: Academic, 1981.
3. Wiltse, J. C., Millimeter wave trends, *Journal of Millimeter Wave Technology* 337, 85–96, 1982.
4. Hovanessian, S. A., *Radar System Design and Analysis*, Dedham, MA: Artech House, 1984.
5. Hovanessian, S. A., Detection of non-moving targets by airborne MMW radars, *Microwave J* (2), 158–169, 1986.
6. Currie, H. C., ed., *Principles and Applications of Millimeter Wave Radars*, Norwood, MA: Artech House, 1988.
7. Hovanessian, S. A., *Introduction to Sensor Systems*, Norwood, MA: Artech House, 1988.

8. Goldsmith, P. F., C. T. Hsieh, G. R. Huguenin, J. Kapitzky, and E. L. Moore, Focal plane imaging systems for millimeter wavelength, *IEEE T Microw Theory* 41(10), 612–621, 1993.
9. Yujiri, I., H. Agravante, M. Biedenbender, G. S. Dow, M. Flannery, et al., Passive millimeter wave camera, *Proc SPIE* 3064, 15–22, 1996.
10. Appleby, R., R. N. Anderton, S. Price, N. A. Salmon, G. N. Sinclair, et al., Compact real-time (video rate) passive millimeter-wave imager, *Proc SPIE* 3703, 13–19, 1998.
11. Yujiri, I., H. Agravante, S. Fornaca, B. Hauss, R. Johnson, et al., Passive millimeter wave video camera, *Proc SPIE* 3378, 14–19, 1998.
12. Denisov, A. G., Possibilities of designing matrix millimeter imaging systems at the base of superconducting elements, *Proc SPIE* 3064, 144–147, 1996.
13. Ferris, D. D. and N. C. Currie, Overview of current technology in MMW radiometric sensors for law enforcement applications, *Proceedings of the SPIE Conference on Passive Millimeter-Wave Imaging Technology*, April, San Diego, CA, pp. 61–71, 2000.
14. Lang, R. J., L. F. Ward, and J. W. Cunningham, Close range high-resolution W-band radiometric imaging system for security screening applications, *Proceedings of the SPIE Conference on Passive Millimeter-Wave Imaging Technology*, April, San Diego, CA, pp. 34–39, 2000.
15. Gaiser, P. W., K. M. St. Germain, E. M. Twarog, G. A. Poe, W. Purdy et al., The WinSAT space borne polarimetric microwave radiometer sensor description and early orbit performance, *IEEE T Microw Theory* 52(11), 2347–2361, 2004.
16. Suess, H. and M. Soellner, Fully polarimetric measurements of brightness temperature distribution with a quasi-optical radiometer system at 94 GHz, *IEEE T Geosci Remote* 43(5), 473–479, 2005.
17. Luthi, T. and C. Matzler, Stereoscopic passive millimeter-wave imaging and ranging, *IEEE T Microw Theory* 53(8), 2594–2599, 2005.
18. Yujiri, I., M. Shoucri, and P. Moffa, Passive millimeter wave imaging, *IEEE T Microw Theory* 4(3), 39–50, 2003.
19. Martin, C. A., W. Manning, V. G. Kolinko, and M. Hall, Flight test of a passive millimeter-wave imaging system, *Proc SPIE* 5789, 24–34, 2005.
20. Gorishnyak, V. P., A. G. Denisov, S. E. Kuzmin, V. N. Radzikhovsky, and B. M. Shevchuk, Radiometer imaging system for the concealed weapon detection. *Proceeding of CriMiCo'2002.* Sevastopol, Ukraine, 9–13 September, pp. 187–188, 2002.
21. Radzikhovsky, V. N., V. P. Gorishnyak, S. E. Kuzmin, and B. M. Shevchuk, 16-channels millimeter-waves radiometric imaging system. *MSMW'2001 Symposium Proceedings.* Kharkov, Ukraine, 4–9 June, pp. 466–468, 2001.
22. Radzikhovsky, V. N., V. P. Gorishnyak, S. E. Kuzmin, and B. M. Shevchuk, Passive millimeter-wave imaging system. *Proceeding of CriMiCo'2001.* Sevastopol, Ukraine, 10–14 September, pp. 263–264, 2001.
23. Gorishnyak, V. P., A. G. Denisov, S. E. Kuzmin, V. N. Radzikhovsky, and B. M. Shevchuk, 8-mm passive imaging system with 32 channels. *Proceeding of EurRAD-2004*, Amsterdam, 2–14 October, p. 6, 2004.
24. Blaunstein, N., Recognition of foreign objects hidden in clutter by novel method of diffraction tomography. *Proceeding of IEEE Conferencc on Radar Applications*, Kiev, Ukraine, p. 5, 2010.

Chapter 13

Guiding GPRs Based on Leaky Coaxial Cables

13.1 Background

The leaky coaxial cable technique is successfully used both for the purpose of open and subsurface radio communication and to provide intrusion detection in security systems [1–29]. During recent decades, leaky coaxial cables (LCCs) have generated increasing interest as tool of intrusion detection in guided radar systems (GRSs) [21–25]. Many types of LCC are now available, and the surface transfer impedance has been used to characterize the mean electromagnetic properties of braided cable shields [9–15,19–23]. This description has been useful in analyzing propagation along an LCC in a guiding radar system.

Such analyses predict the existence of two dominant modes that seem to explain the basic propagation mechanisms quite successfully [30–36]. In other words, a buried LCC can support two transverse electromagnetic (TEM)-like modes (see definitions in Chapters 6 through 9). The first one (called *bifilar*) is the perturbed transmission line mode, which is referred to as the *internal mode*. The main part of its energy is confined under the cable shield, but with some leakage outside it. As long as this leakage remains weak, the power dissipated into the earth remains small, and the specific attenuation does not differ much from that of a well-shielded coaxial cable with the same characteristics.

The second mode (called *monofilar*) is the external mode, and its properties are exactly the reverse. Essentially, it uses the cable shield and the earth as conductors, but with some leakage under the cable shield.

The bifilar mode carries most of its energy inside the cable with leakage outside, while the monofilar mode carries most of its energy outside the cable with leakage to the inside of the shield. This construction enables the signals to be coupled into immediately adjacent objects, and the temporal variations of these signals can be used in guided radar as an intrusion detection system.

The radiation properties of LCCs have been investigated in [1–29], but with exception of a few of them [4,21–23,26], only the open installation of the cable was considered. However, it is known that the radiation pattern of a buried cable differs essentially from that of an open installation [30–36]. Theoretical and experimental investigations carried out in [30–36] based on theoretical models developed in [15–20,26–29] have shown that there are two main parameters affecting the performance of LCCs in guiding radar systems: attenuation, which limits the longitudinal range, and coupling, which determines the overall sensitivity.

These features can be explained by the losses in the multilayer guiding structure of this kind of radar based on LCC, which consists of the layers denoted in Figure 13.1.

Attenuation is relatively easy to measure by simple insertion loss techniques, although the accurate prediction of losses in an actual working environment is much more difficult. Coupling is the measure of the signal accessibility at a given radial distance outside the cable, and, being very dependent on the particular installation and environmental aspects, it is very difficult to assess. Some attempts have been made to predict it based on the transfer impedance concept.

During recent decades, a theoretical framework [30–36] for the outer and inner fields produced by LCCs, based on the results of [26–29], has been developed. The principal purpose of this investigation was to predict the fraction of the power radiated in the external region and the fraction converted into a surface wave supported by the dielectric jacket (see definitions in Chapter 8). To simplify the calculations, the jacket was assumed to be a lossless dielectric material. We therefore considered the effect of conduction losses in the jacket material.

The study of homogeneous and inhomogeneous boundary problems has been based both on a simple analytical model and on some special numerical techniques. Using these algorithms for the problem of buried and open LCC installations, we have predicted the effective characteristics of a radar system based on an LCC with the required parameters, including its directional properties. As has been shown experimentally, the prediction technique presented in [30–36] can give designers of such a radar system the possibility of controlling the directional features of the radiation pattern of the LCC. This is necessary both for *open* installations in clutter conditions, that is, above the ground surface in the presence of obstructions of various configurations (such as walls, guarding structures, fences, etc.) and for radar systems *buried* in subsoil media based on the LCC.

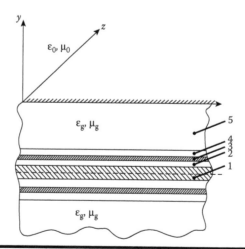

Figure 13.1 Structure of a buried LLC: 1 is the inner conducting core, 2 is the insulating jacket of the core, 3 is the conductive loading structure, 4 is the dielectric jacket of LCC, and 5 is the subsoil medium.

In this chapter, we present the analysis of a radiation pattern of the LCC as a basic element of a guided radar system. Using the unified analytical approach, proposed in [33–36], we analyze the influence of geometry of braided cable shields and the jacket material on redistribution of field pattern both across and along the LCC system. Then, based on this theoretical framework, the influence of local and external inhomogeneities on the directivity of the LCC radar system will be considered, based on simplified models that follow from the theoretical results and comparing them with some experimental measurements carried out and described in [30–36].

13.2 Theoretical Framework

In order to illustrate the physical mechanism of the interaction between the LCC cable, introduced in Chapter 8, and the environment, we start our analysis, first of all, with a general presentation of the time-harmonic Helmholtz equation in a scalar form, based on the general Maxwell's equations introduced in Chapter 3 (see also [1–3]).

13.2.1 Basic Equations

Despite the fact that the general Maxwell's equations were introduced and discussed in Chapter 3, for convenience and for better understanding the proposed framework, we present them in the time-harmonic form, that is, in the phasors' form (see Chapters 1 and 3), for a homogeneous isotropic source-free medium:

$$\nabla \times \mathbf{H} = j\omega\varepsilon\mathbf{E} \tag{13.1a}$$

$$\nabla \times \mathbf{E} = -j\omega\mu\mathbf{H} \tag{13.1b}$$

where:
  ε is the complex permittivity
  μ is the complex permeability

As was shown in Chapter 3, these parameters determine the complex wave number

$$k = \omega\sqrt{\varepsilon\mu} \tag{13.2}$$

and the intrinsic impedance of the medium

$$\eta = \sqrt{\mu/\varepsilon} \tag{13.3}$$

In a homogeneous medium (where $\varepsilon = const$ and $\mu = const$), we have also that

$$\nabla \cdot \mathbf{H} = 0 \tag{13.4}$$

and

$$\nabla \cdot \mathbf{E} = 0 \tag{13.5}$$

These equations may be obtained from Equations 13.1a and 13.1b because the divergence of a curl is zero, $\nabla \cdot (\nabla \times A) \equiv 0$ (see Chapter 2). In a homogeneous medium, the electric and magnetic Hertz vectors Π_e and Π_m are usually introduced [1–3].

Then, according to Equation 13.1a, the vector $\mathbf{H}$ satisfies the following *curl* equation through a suitable vector Π_e:

$$\nabla \times \mathbf{H} = j\omega\varepsilon\nabla \times \Pi_e \tag{13.6}$$

The curl Equation 13.1b for $\mathbf{E}$ gives the same relations with a suitable vector Π_e:

$$\nabla \times \mathbf{E} = k^2\nabla \times \Pi_e \tag{13.7}$$

Because the curl of a gradient is equal identically to zero (see Chapter 2), the integral of Equation 13.7 has the form

$$\mathbf{E} = k^2\Pi_e - \nabla\phi_e \tag{13.8}$$

where ϕ_e is an arbitrary scalar function. Substituting Equations 13.6 and 13.8 in the curl Equation 13.1 for $\mathbf{H}$ gives

$$\nabla \times \nabla \times \Pi_e = k^2\Pi_e - \nabla\phi_e \tag{13.9}$$

Now, using the identity $\nabla \times \nabla \times \mathbf{A} = \nabla(\nabla \cdot \mathbf{A}) - \nabla^2\mathbf{A}$ (see Chapter 2), which may serve as a definition for the operator $\nabla^2\mathbf{A}$ in an arbitrary curvilinear coordinate system, we get

$$\nabla(\nabla \cdot \Pi_e) - \nabla^2\Pi_e = k^2\Pi_e - \nabla\phi_e \tag{13.10}$$

Since both ϕ_e and $\nabla \cdot \Pi_e$ are still arbitrary, we make them satisfy the relation $\phi_e = -\nabla \cdot \Pi_e$, which leads to

$$\nabla^2\Pi_e + k^2\Pi_e = 0 \tag{13.11}$$

By taking the divergence of Equation 13.8 and taking into account Equation 13.5, we find that ϕ_e is a solution of the scalar equation

$$\nabla^2\phi_e + k^2\phi_e = 0 \tag{13.12}$$

The electric and magnetic fields are now given by

$$\mathbf{E} = \nabla\left(\nabla \cdot \Pi_e\right) + k^2 \Pi_e \qquad (13.13a)$$

$$\mathbf{H} = j\omega\varepsilon\nabla\Pi_e \qquad (13.13b)$$

Obviously, we do not need to determine the scalar function ϕ_e explicitly, since it is equal to $-\nabla \cdot \Pi_e$ and has been eliminated from the equation determining the electric field $\mathbf{E}$.

In the same manner, we obtain the equations for the magnetic Hertz vector Π_m. Thus, using Equation 13.5, we present the electric field as

$$\mathbf{E} = -j\omega\mu\nabla \times \Pi_m \qquad (13.14)$$

The curl Equation 13.1 for $\mathbf{H}$ gives

$$\nabla \times \mathbf{H} = k^2\nabla \times \Pi_m \qquad (13.15)$$

The curl of a gradient is equal identically to zero, then the integral of Equation 13.15 has the form

$$\mathbf{H} = k^2\Pi_m - \nabla\phi_m \qquad (13.16)$$

where ϕ_m is an arbitrary scalar function. Substituting Equations 13.14 and 13.16 in the curl Equation 13.1b for $\mathbf{E}$ gives

$$\nabla \times \nabla \times \Pi_m = k^2\Pi_m - \nabla\phi_m \qquad (13.17a)$$

or

$$\nabla\left(\nabla \cdot \Pi_m\right) - \nabla^2\Pi_m = k^2\Pi_m - \nabla\phi_m \qquad (13.17b)$$

Since both ϕ_m and $\nabla \cdot \Pi_m$ are still arbitrary, we make them satisfy the relation $\phi_m = -\nabla \cdot \Pi_m$, which leads to

$$\nabla^2\Pi_m + k^2\Pi_m = 0 \qquad (13.18)$$

By taking the divergence of Equation 13.16 and taking into account Equation 13.4, we find that ϕ_m is a solution of

$$\nabla^2\phi_m + k^2\phi_m = 0 \qquad (13.19)$$

The electric and magnetic fields are now given by

$$\mathbf{E} = -j\omega\mu\nabla \times \Pi_m \qquad (13.20a)$$

$$\mathbf{H} = \nabla(\nabla \cdot \Pi_m) + k^2 \Pi_m \tag{13.20b}$$

Obviously, we do not need to determine the scalar function ϕ_m explicitly, since it is equal to $-\nabla \cdot \Pi_m$ and has been eliminated from the equation determining the magnetic field $\mathbf{H}$.

The general solution is the sum of the two solutions obtained:

$$\mathbf{E} = \nabla(\nabla \cdot \Pi_e) + k^2 \Pi_e - j\omega\mu\nabla \times \Pi_m \tag{13.21a}$$

$$\mathbf{H} = \nabla(\nabla \cdot \Pi_m) + k^2 \Pi_m + j\omega\varepsilon\nabla \times \Pi_e \tag{13.21b}$$

It can be shown that these fields are the solutions of the Maxwell's equations.

13.2.1.1 Cylindrical Structures

Now, we consider a cylindrical structure which is transitionally invariant in the longitudinal direction, say z, and supports the propagation of a wave traveling in this direction. In this case, it is possible to solve the problem using only two scalar potentials, U and V, which are the z-components of the electric and magnetic Hertz vectors, respectively:

$$\Pi_e = (0,0,U) \tag{13.22a}$$

$$\Pi_m = (0,0,V) \tag{13.22b}$$

Then, the components of the electric and magnetic fields in the cylindrical coordinate system are given by

$$E_r = \frac{\partial^2 U}{\partial r \partial z} - \frac{j\omega\mu}{r}\frac{\partial V}{\partial \phi} \tag{13.23a}$$

$$E_\phi = \frac{1}{r}\frac{\partial^2 U}{\partial \phi \partial z} + j\omega\mu\frac{\partial V}{\partial r} \tag{13.23b}$$

$$E_z = \left(\frac{\partial^2}{\partial z^2} + k^2\right)U \tag{13.23c}$$

$$H_r = \frac{j\omega\varepsilon}{r}\frac{\partial U}{\partial \phi} + \frac{\partial^2 V}{\partial r \partial z} \tag{13.24a}$$

$$H_\phi = -j\omega\varepsilon\frac{\partial U}{\partial r} + \frac{1}{r}\frac{\partial^2 V}{\partial \phi \partial z} \tag{13.24b}$$

$$H_z = \left(\frac{\partial^2}{\partial z^2} + k^2 \right) V \tag{13.24c}$$

The solution for the field may be written as an infinite sum of cylindrical harmonics. In the thin-cable approximation, we can neglect all asymmetrical harmonics. In the case of axial symmetry ($\partial/\partial\phi = 0$), the system Equations 13.23 and 13.24 breaks into two sets: one is the transverse magnetic (TM) mode (E_z, E_r, H_ϕ) arising from the electric potential U, and another is the transverse electric (TE mode) (H_z, H_r, E_ϕ) arising from the magnetic potential V (see definitions in Chapter 6). If the boundary conditions do not lead to interaction between the TM and TE modes, then we can consider the propagation of these modes independently.

13.2.1.2 Symmetrical TM mode

Here, we assume that only an electric current is applied, and, as a result, there is only a TM wave traveling along the cable. Then, the nonzero components of the field are given by [1–3]

$$E_r = \frac{\partial^2 U}{\partial r \partial z} \tag{13.25a}$$

$$E_z = \left(\frac{\partial^2}{\partial z^2} + k^2 \right) U \tag{13.25b}$$

$$H_\phi = -j\omega\varepsilon \frac{\partial U}{\partial r} \tag{13.25c}$$

The scalar potential U satisfies the Helmholtz equation

$$\nabla^2 U + k^2 U = 0 \tag{13.26}$$

We expect that the solution has the form of a traveling wave

$$U(r,z) = u(r)\exp(-\gamma z) \tag{13.27}$$

with the complex propagation constant introduced in Chapter 4

$$\gamma = \alpha + j\beta \tag{13.28}$$

Then, the components of the field are given by

$$E_r = -\gamma \frac{\partial u}{\partial r}\exp(-\gamma z) \tag{13.29a}$$

$$E_z = -\kappa^2 u \exp(-\gamma z) \qquad (13.29b)$$

$$H_\phi = -j\omega\varepsilon \frac{\partial u}{\partial r} \exp(-\gamma z) \qquad (13.29c)$$

where the transverse wave number κ is defined as

$$\kappa^2 = -\left(k^2 + \gamma^2\right) \qquad (13.30)$$

The reduced potential u satisfies

$$\left(\nabla_t^2 - \kappa^2\right) u(r) = 0 \qquad (13.31)$$

where the transverse Laplace's operator is (see Chapter 1)

$$\nabla_t^2 = \frac{\partial^2}{\partial r^2} + \frac{1}{r}\frac{\partial}{\partial r} \qquad (13.32)$$

The general solution of Equation 13.31 has the form

$$u(r) = BI_0(\kappa r) + AK_0(\kappa r) \qquad (13.33)$$

where $I_0(z)$ and $K_0(z)$ are the modified Bessel functions. According to the properties of these functions, their derivatives are expressed as [33–36]

$$I_0'(z) = I_1(z) \qquad (13.34a)$$

$$K_0'(z) = -K_1(z) \qquad (13.34b)$$

Also, their asymptotic behavior for small values of the argument is defined by

$$I_0(z) \approx 1, |z| \ll 1 \qquad (13.35)$$

$$K_0(z) \approx \ln\left(\frac{2}{Cz}\right), C = 1.781..., |z| \ll 1 \qquad (13.36)$$

For large values of the argument, we have

$$I_0(z) \approx \frac{1}{\sqrt{2\pi z}} \exp(z), |z| \gg 1 \qquad (13.37)$$

$$K_0(z) \approx \sqrt{\frac{\pi}{2z}} \exp(-z), |z| \gg 1 \qquad (13.38)$$

Now, using the general solution Equation 13.33, we will consider separately both outer (i.e., *external*) and inner (i.e., *internal*) regions of the LCC structure.

13.2.2 External Region of LCC Irradiation

First, we consider the region that is external for the cable of radius a, that is, $r \geq a$. For $r \to \infty$, only a decreasing solution describes the real situation, and we then have

$$u(r) = AK_0(\kappa r) \qquad (13.39)$$

Consequently, the field components are

$$E_r = \gamma \kappa A K_1(\kappa r) \exp(-\gamma z) \qquad (13.40a)$$

$$E_z = -\kappa^2 A K_0(\kappa r) \exp(-\gamma z) \qquad (13.40b)$$

$$H_\phi = j\omega\varepsilon\kappa A K_1(\kappa r) \exp(-\gamma z) \qquad (13.40c)$$

In Equations 13.40a and 13.40c, $K_1(z)$ is the Bessel function that behaves asymptotically as

$$K_1(z) \sim z^{-1}, |z| \ll 1 \qquad (13.41)$$

and

$$K_1(z) \sim \sqrt{\pi/z} \exp(-z), |z| \gg 1 \qquad (13.42)$$

for small and large values of the argument, respectively. We will use the specific boundary condition at the surface of the cable ($r = a$) proposed in [1–3,12],

$$E_z(a) = Z_0(\gamma) H_\phi(a) \qquad (13.43)$$

where $Z_0(\gamma)$ (in ohms) is the external surface impedance, which is generally complex, and depends on the propagation constant γ. Then, using Equations 13.40b and 13.40c to express the components of the field in Equation 13.43 through the parameter of the solution, we get the characteristic equation

$$\kappa K_0(\kappa a) = -j\omega\varepsilon Z_0(\gamma) K_1(\kappa a) \qquad (13.44)$$

Now, we introduce the specific external impedance $\zeta_0(\gamma)$ (in ohms per meter), which is defined by

$$\zeta_0(\gamma) = \frac{Z_0(\gamma)}{2\pi a} \qquad (13.45)$$

Then, Equation 13.44 can be presented in the form

$$\zeta_0(\gamma) = j \frac{\kappa K_0(\kappa a)}{2\pi a \omega \varepsilon K_1(\kappa a)} \qquad (13.46)$$

In the thin-cable approximation, that is, when the radius of the cable a satisfies $|\kappa a| \ll 1$, we have

$$\zeta_0(\gamma) = j(2\pi \omega \varepsilon)^{-1} \kappa^2 \ln(2/C\kappa a) \qquad (13.47)$$

The external surface impedance has to be calculated by accounting for the internal cable structure.

13.2.3 Internal Cable Structures

In order to calculate the specific external impedance of the cable, we follow the analysis of [14,15,26]. Before defining the structures, we consider in cylindrical coordinates a homogeneous medium located between radii r_1 and r_2. This region is located inside a thin cable, and we can approximate the general solution

$$u(r) = BI_0(\kappa r) + AK_0(\kappa r) \qquad (13.48)$$

by

$$u = B + A\ln(C\kappa r/2) \qquad (13.49)$$

We will consider the quantity

$$\zeta(r) = \frac{E_z(r)}{2\pi r H_\phi(r)} \qquad (13.50)$$

We may write

$$\frac{2\pi j \omega \varepsilon}{\kappa^2} \zeta(r) = \frac{B}{A} + \ln(C\kappa r/2) \qquad (13.51)$$

Considering two radii r_1 and r_2 and eliminating the ratio B/A, we obtain the general relation

$$\zeta(r_2) = \zeta(r_1) + \frac{\kappa^2}{2\pi j \omega \varepsilon} \ln\left(r_2/r_1\right) \tag{13.52}$$

This relation is very useful for obtaining the specific external impedance of an arbitrary coaxial structure.

Here, we analyze the structure, which consists of dielectric (for instance, ferrite-loaded poly-vinyl chloride [PVC]) with or without conductive coating (see Figure 13.2). We assume that the cable core assembly can be modeled by a metallic wire with conductivity σ_1 and permeability μ_1. Radius of the wire is w.

This conductor is covered by a concentric layer, of outer radius a, with permittivity ε_2 and permeability μ_2. Finally, to account for the conductive coating, we have a thin outer layer of conductive material with a specific surface impedance ζ_c. The surface impedance of the cable core (metallic wire) is given by

$$\zeta_w = \frac{1}{2\pi w} \sqrt{j\omega\mu_1/\sigma_1} \tag{13.53}$$

The dielectric layer has a wave number $k_2 = \omega\sqrt{\varepsilon_2\mu_2}$, and we obtain for the impedance at the external surface of the layer

$$\zeta_a = \zeta_w + \zeta_l \tag{13.54}$$

where the layer impedance ζ_l is

$$\zeta_l = \frac{\kappa_2^2}{2\pi j \omega \varepsilon_2} \ln\left(a/w\right) \tag{13.55}$$

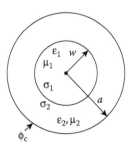

Figure 13.2   Cross section of an LCC consisting of ferrite-loaded PVC; w is the radius of the metallic wire, a is the radius of the cable.

and

$$\kappa_2^2 = -\left(k_2^2 + \gamma^2\right) \tag{11.56}$$

The value of ζ_l can also be presented as

$$\zeta_l = \frac{\kappa_2^2}{k_2^2}\zeta_i \tag{13.57}$$

where ζ_i is the γ-independent factor of the form

$$\zeta_i = \frac{k_2^2}{2\pi j\omega\varepsilon_2}\ln\left(a/w\right) \tag{13.58}$$

To calculate the contribution of the outer layer of conductive material, we use the boundary conditions at $r = a$:

$$E_z\left(a\right) = 2\pi a\zeta_c\left[H_\phi\left(a+0\right) - H_\phi\left(a-0\right)\right] \tag{13.59}$$

The z-component of the electric field may be presented either through the external surface impedance $\zeta_0(\gamma)$,

$$E_z\left(a\right) = 2\pi a\zeta_0\left(\gamma\right)H_\phi\left(a+0\right) \tag{13.60}$$

or through the value of ζ_a,

$$E_z\left(a\right) = 2\pi a\zeta_a H_\phi\left(a-0\right) \tag{13.61}$$

Then, combining Equations 13.58 through 13.60, we obtain

$$\frac{1}{\zeta_0\left(\gamma\right)} = \frac{1}{\zeta_a} + \frac{1}{\zeta_c} \tag{13.62}$$

which gives us finally

$$\zeta_0\left(\gamma\right) = \frac{\zeta_c\left(\zeta_w + \zeta_l\right)}{\zeta_c + \zeta_w + \zeta_l} \tag{13.63}$$

Equation 13.63 may be represented by the ladder network shown in Figure 13.3.

For $\zeta_c \to \infty$, that is, when the conductive coating is absent, we have $\zeta_0(\gamma) \approx \zeta_{w+}\zeta l$.

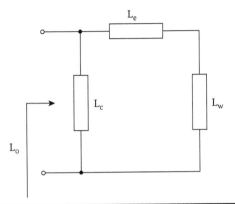

Figure 13.3 **Electrical scheme of an LCC as a ladder network according to Equation 13.63.**

13.3 Radiation Pattern in the Presence of Interface

Based on the results obtained in Section 13.2.3, we now take into consideration the presence of the interface between two different lossy media (air: ground or air: wall). In this case, we evaluate the γ-dependent external surface impedance $\zeta_0(\gamma)$ of the cable located at height h from the interface. We assume that the ground (wall) is fully described by a complex wavenumber k (permittivity ε, permeability $\mu = \mu_0$, and conductivity σ). The upper halfspace (air) is characterized by the respective free space values, so that the wavenumber is simply k_0. According to [7,9,11], the value of $\zeta_0(\gamma)$ can be calculated as

$$\zeta_0(\gamma) = \zeta(\gamma) - \gamma^2/\eta(\gamma) \tag{13.64}$$

where the dispersive impedance $\zeta(\gamma)$ and admittance $\eta(\gamma)$, respectively, are given by

$$\zeta(\gamma) = \frac{\mu_0 \omega}{2\pi j}\left[\Lambda(\gamma) + 2A(\gamma)\right] \tag{13.65}$$

$$\eta(\gamma) = -j2\pi\varepsilon_0\omega\left[\Lambda(\gamma) + 2B(\gamma)\right]^{-1} \tag{13.66}$$

The functions $\Lambda(\gamma)$, $A(\gamma)$, and $B(\gamma)$ have the form

$$\Lambda(\gamma) = K_0\left(\kappa_0 a\right) - K_0\left(\kappa_0 a\sqrt{1 + 4h^2/a^2}\right) \tag{13.67}$$

$$A(\gamma) = \int_0^\infty dx\left[u_0(x) + u(x)\right]^{-1}\cos\left(ax\right)\exp\left[-2hu_0(x)\right] \tag{13.68}$$

$$B(\gamma) = \frac{k_0^2}{k^2} \int_0^\infty dx \left[u_0(x) + \left(k_0^2/k^2\right) u(x) \right]^{-1} \cos(ax) \exp\left[-2hu_0(x)\right] \qquad (13.69)$$

where, as above, the transverse wavenumber in air is given by

$$\kappa_0^2 = -\left(k_0^2 + \gamma^2\right) \qquad (13.70)$$

and

$$u_0(x) = \sqrt{x^2 - \gamma^2 - k_0^2} \qquad (13.71)$$

$$u(x) = \sqrt{x^2 - \gamma^2 - k^2} \qquad (13.72)$$

In the case when $|\kappa_0 a| \ll 1$ and $|2\kappa_0 b| \ll 1$, the modified Bessel function in Equation 13.67 can be replaced by their small argument approximations. Then, if also $2b \gg a$, we have the quasi-static form

$$\Lambda(\gamma) = \ln\sqrt{1 + 4h^2/a^2} \cong \ln(2h/a) \qquad (13.73)$$

If, in addition the ground (wall) satisfies the condition $k_0^2/|k|^2 \ll 1$ and $k_0 h \ll 1$, we see that

$$A(\gamma) = -J_c/2 \qquad (13.74)$$

where

$$J_c = \frac{2}{k^2} \int_0^\infty dx \left[w(x) - x \right] \exp(-2hx) \qquad (13.75)$$

is the Carson integral [1,22], in which

$$w(x) = \sqrt{x^2 - k^2} \qquad (13.76)$$

Under the same conditions, the integral $B(\gamma)$ can be neglected. As a consequence, the impedance $\zeta(\gamma)$ and admittance $\eta(\gamma)$ parameters are approximated by their nondispersive forms:

$$\zeta(\gamma) \cong \zeta_c = \frac{\mu_0 \omega}{2\pi j} \left[\ln(2h/a) - J_c \right] \qquad (13.77)$$

$$\eta(\gamma) \cong \eta_c = -j2\pi\varepsilon_0 \omega \left[\ln(2h/a) \right]^{-1} \qquad (13.78)$$

Now, we approximate the Carson integral by the simple engineering formula [1,22]

$$J_c = \ln \frac{j\rho/2}{1 + j\rho/2} \tag{13.79}$$

where

$$\rho = 2kh \tag{13.80}$$

Then, the impedance and admittance acquire the final forms

$$\zeta_c = \frac{\mu_0 \omega}{2\pi j} \ln\left[(2h/a)(1 - j2/\rho) \right] \tag{13.81}$$

$$\eta_c = -j2\pi\varepsilon_0\omega\left[\ln(2h/a) \right]^{-1} \tag{13.82}$$

In the case of a perfectly conducting wire, we have the mode equation

$$\zeta(\gamma) - \gamma^2/\eta(\gamma) = 0 \tag{13.83}$$

the solution of which is

$$\gamma = \sqrt{\zeta(\gamma)\eta(\gamma)} \tag{13.84}$$

In the quasi-static limit, this becomes an explicit formula for the transmission line mode. Since it will be used as an initial value in the iterative calculation procedure, we denote it by γ_c:

$$\gamma_c = \sqrt{\zeta_c\eta_c} = jk_0\sqrt{\frac{\ln\left[(2h/a)(1-j2/\rho)\right]}{\ln(2h/a)}} \tag{13.85}$$

For a coaxial cable with finite surface impedance, the mode equation has the form

$$\zeta(\gamma) - \gamma^2/\eta(\gamma) = \zeta_0(\gamma) \tag{13.86}$$

The solution is then presented as

$$\gamma = \sqrt{\eta(\gamma)\left[\zeta(\gamma) - \zeta_0(\gamma)\right]} \tag{13.87}$$

or, in the quasi-static limit,

$$\gamma = \gamma_c \sqrt{1 - \zeta_0(\gamma)/\zeta_c} \tag{13.88}$$

Equation 13.88, with the impedance $\zeta_0(\gamma)$ given by Equation 13.63, is the nonlinear equation for the complex propagation constant $\gamma = \alpha + j\beta$. We start with the approximate values of γ, namely, γ_{init} given by Equation 13.85. We use this value to calculate the external surface impedance $\zeta_0(\gamma)$. Then, we calculate a new value of γ and repeat this procedure several times. We also calculate the transverse wavenumber

$$\kappa = j\sqrt{k_0^2 + \gamma^2} \tag{13.89}$$

13.4 Characteristics of Radiation Field for Different Types of LCC

Let us obtain numerical solutions of the mode equations for different geometry, which is described by the outer radius a, and for various values of outer jacket material, which is described by the resistivity, of LCC cable using the numerical procedure developed in [32,33]. Equation 13.47, with the external impedance given by Equation 13.63, is the nonlinear equation for the complex propagation constant $\gamma = \alpha + j\beta$. More strictly, we have a system of two nonlinear equations (one is the real part and the other is the imaginary part) for two variables: extinction coefficient α and phase constant β. As is well known, there are no good, general methods for solving systems of more than one nonlinear equation. However, in our particular case, the problem can be essentially simplified. In fact, we may present Equation 13.47 in the form

$$\kappa = \sqrt{\frac{2\pi\omega\epsilon\zeta_0(\gamma)}{j\ln(2/C\kappa a)}} \tag{13.90}$$

Having this representation, we start with some approximate values of γ. We use this value to calculate the external surface impedance $\zeta_0(\gamma)$, the transverse wavenumber

$$\kappa = j\sqrt{k^2 + \gamma^2} \tag{13.91}$$

and the logarithm. Then, according to Equation 13.90, we calculate a new value of κ and the propagation constant

$$\gamma = j\sqrt{k^2 + \kappa^2} \tag{13.92}$$

Obviously, we have to repeat this procedure several times to obtain the exact result by convergence. The problem, therefore, is reduced to the choice of the initial approximation for $\gamma = \alpha + j\beta$.

A special numerical algorithm and the corresponding numerical code that is based on the iteration procedure described in this section has been developed in [34–36]. The input data of this numerical code are the geometrical parameters of the cable structure, the material parameters of the media, and the frequency. The corresponding algorithm allows us to calculate the propagation constant $\gamma = \alpha + j\beta$ of the existing surface mode. The value of the extinction coefficient α is measured in decibels per meter (or in nepers per meter: 1 Np/m = 8.686 dB/m), and that of the phase constant β is in radians per meter, which can be presented via the normalized phase velocity

$$s = v_p/c = k_0/\beta, 0 < s < 1 \tag{13.93}$$

as

$$\beta = k_0/s \tag{13.94}$$

where K_0 is the wavenumber in free space.

Obviously, the solution for the transverse wavenumber $\kappa = \kappa_r + j\kappa_i$ is of primary interest, because the value of κ defines the field distribution of the mode in the external region. The program calculates the normalized value of κ:

$$q = q_r + jq_i = \kappa/k_0 \tag{13.95}$$

which, in general, consists of the real and imaginary parts, q_r and q_i.

First of all, we analyzed the influence of the jacket material on the characteristics of LLC radiation, such as the external field attenuation, the phase velocity, the normalized transverse wavenumber, the real part q_r and the imaginary part q_i, using the procedure described in [33–36]. Some results of the calculations for LCC installation in infinite air and subsoil lossy medium are shown in Figures 13.4 through 13.6.

All the calculations were done for the frequency $f = 40.68$ MHz. The outer jacket layer of the LCC (see Figure 13.2) has permittivity $\varepsilon_{r2} = 60 - j18$ and permeability $\mu_{r2} = 16 - j3.2$. For the data of Figures 13.4 through 13.6, we used the geometrical parameters of the cable $w = 2.50$ and $a = 3.75$ mm (see Figure 13.2).

The parameters of the environment are $\varepsilon_r = 1.00$, $\mu_r = 1$, $\sigma = 0$ (air) for the calculations presented in Figure 13.4; $\varepsilon_r = 4.00$, $\mu_r = 1$, $\sigma = 10^{-3}$ S/m (dry soil) in Figure 13.5; $\varepsilon_r = 10.00$, $\mu_r = 1$, $\sigma = 1.5 \times 10^{-2}$ S/m (wet soil) in Figure 13.6.

In these figures, we plot the dependence of the extinction coefficient α (in all figures denoted by (a)), normalized phase velocity s (denoted by (b)), real part q_r (denoted by (c)), and imaginary part q_i (denoted by (d)), as functions of a specific surface impedance ζ_c of the LCC thin outer conductive layer (see Figure 13.2). In all three cases of environment depicted in Figures 13.4 through 13.6, the attenuation of the radiated field is maximal for $\zeta_c \approx 300$–600 Ω/m. The phase velocity s is a monotonic function decreasing with the increase of ζ_c.

Consequently, the normalized transverse wavenumber monotonically increases to unity with ζ_c, which defines a stronger concentration of radiated electromagnetic energy near the cable in the direction across the cable for the higher values of ζ_c. As shown in Figures 13.5a,b and 13.6a,b, the increase of the soil conductivity for the wet soil medium with respect to dry soil medium leads to an increase of the attenuation and a decrease of the phase velocity.

As also follows from numerical computations, the radiated electromagnetic energy dependence on ζ_c is complicated, with a minimum near the range of $\zeta_c \approx 300$–600 Ω/m, where attenuation is maximal and there are no oscillations of the surface field across the cable. It is evident that the oscillatory character of the outer mode across the cable decreases monotonically with increased thickness of the jacket layer (with increase of the outer radius a) and for higher parameters of jacket resistance ζ_c.

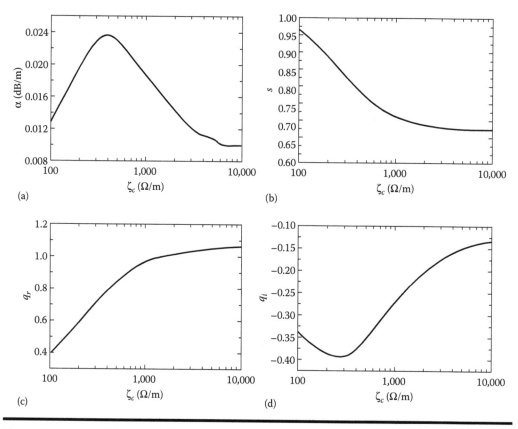

Figure 13.4 (a–d) The LCC field radiation characteristics, defined by Equations 13.90 through 13.95, versus a specific surface impedance ζ_i for a cable installed in an unbounded air environment with $\varepsilon_r = 1.0$, $\mu_r = 1$, $\sigma = 0$ (air).

In further numerical analysis, we concentrated on the influence of clutter on open installations of an LCC system. Some results of the computations are shown in Figure 13.8a–d for a wall with parameters $\varepsilon_r = 4.00$, $\mu_r = 1$, $\sigma = 10^{-3}$ and for a cable located at height h above the wall surface. In Figure 13.7a–d, we plot, the dependence of the extinction coefficient α (a), normalized phase velocity s (b), real part q_r (c), and imaginary part q_i (d) of the normalized transverse number q on the height h for a specific constant surface impedance of the LCC thin outer conductive layer $\zeta_c = 500$ Ω/m.

As for the results illustrated in Figures 13.4 through 13.7, all the calculations were performed for the frequency $f = 40.68$ MHz and the LCC lossy jacket layer permittivity $\varepsilon_{r2} = 60 - j18$ and permeability $\mu_{r2} = 16 - j3.2$; the geometrical parameters of the cable $w = 2.50$ mm and $a = 3.75$ mm (see Figure 13.2) correspond to the LCC systems used.

The dependence of the same parameters, α, q_r, q_i, as presented in Figure 13.8a–c, on the resistivity ζ_c of the conductive layer for a constant height above the wall, as the clutter, is presented in Figure 13.9a–c.

For comparison, in Figure 13.9a–c, we present the dependence of the same external radiated mode propagation parameters as are shown in Figure 13.8a–c on the outer radius a of the outer

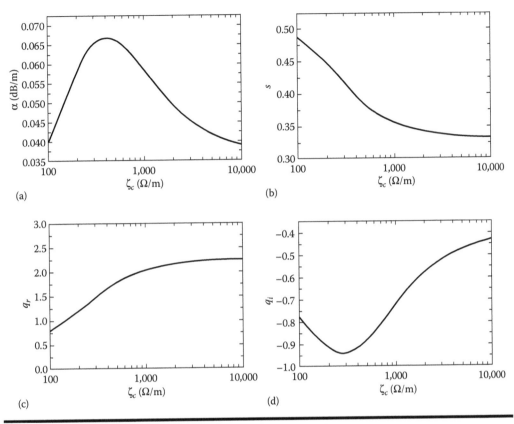

Figure 13.5 **(a–d) The LCC field radiation characteristics, defined by Equations 13.90 through 13.95, versus a specific surface impedance ζ_i for a cable installed in a bounded dry soil environment with $\varepsilon_r = 4.00$, $\mu_r = 1$, $\sigma = 10^{-3}$ S/m.**

lossy layer of LCC located at height $h = 5$ cm above the wall surface and $\zeta_c = 10^8 \,\Omega/\text{m}$ (the lossless conductive jacket).

The same trend as in Figure 13.4a–c through Figure 13.7a–c is evident, with additional small perturbation effects of clutter (due to the existence of the wall).

13.5 Effects of Inner and Outer Obstructions on the Pattern of Buried LCC

Let us now consider some realistic internal and external clutter phenomena that can actually affect the directivity and pattern distribution of the guided radar system based on a buried LCC.

13.5.1 End Discontinuity Effect

As was shown in Chapter 8, circuits connected at the end of the LCC are in general coupled to both eigenmodes, external and internal. As was specified in Chapter 8, a generator is connected to

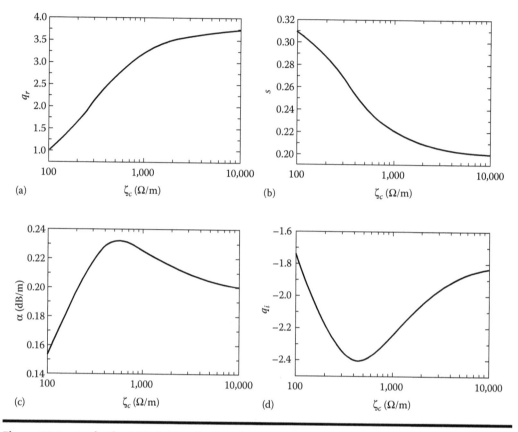

Figure 13.6 **(a–d) The LCC field radiation characteristics, defined by Equations 13.90 through 13.95, versus a specific surface impedance ζ_i for the cable installed in a bounded wet soil environment with $\varepsilon_r = 10.00$, $\mu_r = 1$, $\sigma = 1.5 \times 10^{-2}$ S/m.**

the input of the semi-infinite cable located along the positive half of the *x*-axis (see Figure 13.1). We assume that the generator has no connection to the ground at the input of the cable, and that no cable exists for $x < 0$. Thus, we have $I_e(0) = 0$, where I_e is the current of the external mode introduced in Chapter 8. Progressive waves of both eigenmodes, external and internal, are excited by the generator, and the external current is presented in the following form [34]:

$$I_e(x) = I_{e0}\left[\exp(-\gamma_1 x) - \exp(-\gamma_2 x)\right] \tag{13.96}$$

where the propagation constants of both eigenmodes, γ_1 and γ_2, were introduced in Chapter 8. The normalized external wave pattern (to that from input of the generator) is shown in Figure 13.10a,b for two values of the propagation parameters defined in Chapter 8. Here and in all further illustrations, λ_1 and λ_2 are presented relative to wavelength $\lambda_0 = 75$ m inside the conventional cable operated at a frequency of 40 MHz.

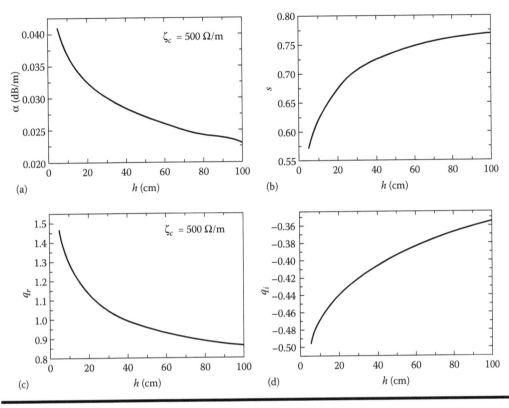

Figure 13.7 **(a–d) Influence of the wall, as the clutter, with parameters ε_r = 4.00, μ_r = 1, σ = 10^{-3} S/m on main characteristics of the LCC radar for open its installation.**

The results of computations made in [34] and presented in Figure 13.10a,b were obtained for the constraint of $\lambda_1 > \lambda_2$, where $\alpha_1 < \alpha_2$ (for $\alpha_1 = 0$, the internal mode propagates inside the inner guiding structure without attenuation). Apparent standing waves observed in both figures are due to the fact that the two terms travel with different phase velocities, according to Equation 13.90, and are respectively in phase and in antiphase. The same results follow from illustrations presented in Figure 13.11a,b for $\lambda_2 = 0.7 \cdot \lambda_0$, which is more than twice as large as in the case presented in Figure 13.10a,b.

We see a fundamental difference between the classical standing waves in a conventional cable and those plotted in Figures 13.10 and 13.11. Indeed, the classical standing waves are generated by two waves traveling with the same velocity but in opposite directions, and the standing-wave patterns for current and voltage are offset by a quarter of a wavelength. This scenario does not occur in the illustrated cases. On the contrary, the standing-wave patterns for $V_c(x)$ and $I_c(x)$ are coincident. The reason for this is that the ratio V/I is positive for progressive waves and negative for regressive waves. Consequently, Equation 13.91 is also valid for $V_c(x)$ (i.e., for the electric field along the cable, and finally also for the power flow in the earth subsoil medium). Actually, the power of the leakage fields jumps alternately in and out of the cable. Similar phenomena occur near the end of the cable when the latter is terminated, since we have to deal with one progressive and two regressive eigenmodes [34–36].

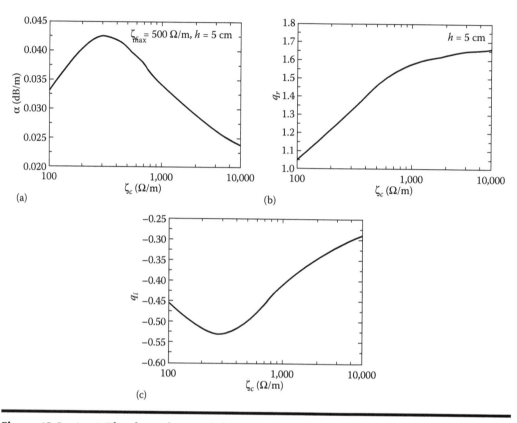

Figure 13.8 **(a–c) The dependence of the parameters, α, q_r, q_i, versus the specific surface impedance ζ_c of the conductive layer for the constant height $h = 5$ cm above the wall.**

13.5.2 Coupling Inhomogeneities Effect

Next, we consider an idealized situation, modeling the distribution of the coupling coefficient ς_c along the infinite cable by the constraint

$$
\varsigma_c(x) = \begin{cases} \varsigma_c, & -\infty < x < 0 \\ \varsigma_{cd}, & 0 \le x \le d \\ \varsigma_c, & d < x < \infty \end{cases}
$$

(13.97)

where d is the characteristic scale of the artificial (or natural) disturbance of the coupling coefficient along the LCC. In computations, following [34–36], we assume that the propagation constant does not depend on the distance, and we introduce the ratio $q = \varsigma_{cd}/\varsigma_c$. The corresponding results of computations for the external wave pattern are shown in Figure 13.12a,b for $d/\lambda_1 = 1$. In both cases, parameter q runs from 0.3 to 1.3.

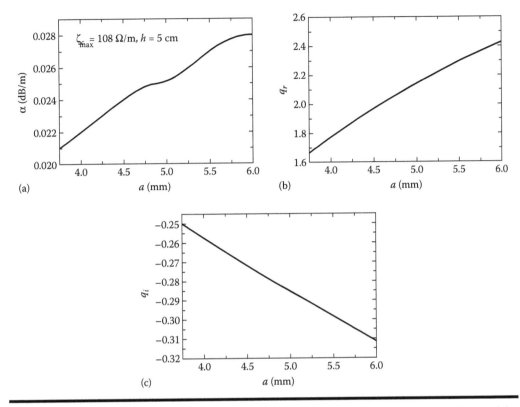

(a)

(b)

(c)

Figure 13.9 **(a–c) The dependence of the parameters, α, q_r, q_i, versus the outer radius a of the outer lossy layer of an LCC located at height $h = 5$ cm above the wall surface and for $\zeta_c = 10^8$ Ω/m.**

It is evident that the inhomogeneity in coupling coefficient distribution can cause very strong fluctuations of the signal level distribution, the effect depending on the characteristic scale d of such a disturbance with respect to λ_1.

13.5.3 Effect of Inhomogeneities on External Mode Propagation Constant

In this case we assume, following [34–36], that the coupling coefficient $\varsigma_c = const$, and model the distribution of the propagation constant γ_2 along the infinite line by the function

$$\gamma_2(x) = \begin{cases} \gamma_2, & -\infty < x < 0 \\ \gamma_d, & 0 \le x \le d \\ \gamma_2, & d < x < \infty \end{cases} \tag{13.98}$$

where:

$$\gamma_d = \alpha_d + j\beta_d$$

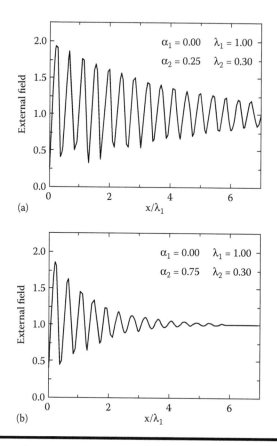

Figure 13.10 The external mode pattern along the LCC for (a) $\lambda_1 = 1.00$, $\lambda_2 = 0.30$, $\alpha_1 = 0.00$, and $\alpha_2 = 0.25$; (b) $\lambda_1 = 1.00$, $\lambda_2 = 0.30$, $\alpha_1 = 0.00$, and $\alpha_2 = 0.75$.

$$\beta_{2d} \approx \lambda_d^{-1}$$

The results of computations for the external wave pattern are shown in Figure 13.13a,b for $d/\lambda_1 = 1$ and varied α_d and β_d.

In both cases, we use the following values: for the propagation constants for the internal mode, $\alpha_1 = 0$, $\lambda_1 = 1$, and for the external mode, $\alpha_2 = 0.5$, $\lambda_2 = 0.7$. The propagation constant of the artificially induced inhomogeneity γ_d was varied to be lower and higher than those for both eigenmodes, external and internal. As can also be seen, the wave pattern of the external mode is not as sensitive to both attenuation and phase velocity inhomogeneities as in the case of coupling coefficient inhomogeneity (compare Figures 13.12a,b and 13.13a,b).

13.6 Comparison with Experimental Measurements

During experiments, a loop of the LCC was buried in such a manner that the buried depth was around 10–15 cm. The length of the LCC radar was equal to 145 m. The carrier frequency for operation was ~40 MHz. The measured characteristic impedance of the cable was 51 Ω at the operated carrier frequency.

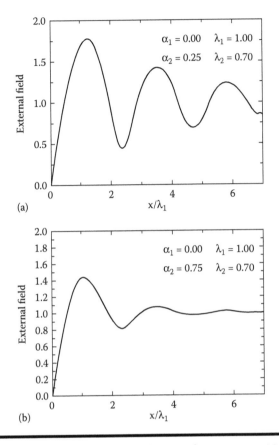

(a)

(b)

Figure 13.11 **The external mode pattern along the LCC for (a)** $\lambda_1 = 1.00$, $\lambda_2 = 0.70$, $\alpha_1 = 0.00$, **and** $\alpha_2 = 0.25$; **(b)** $\lambda_1 = 1.00$, $\lambda_2 = 0.70$, $\alpha_1 = 0.00$, $\alpha_2 = 0.75$.

In the first tests, the distribution of the external mode radiation along the cable was studied. The electric field intensity was measured every 1.5 m along the cable with the help of a field detector located at the height of ~0.8 m above the ground surface. The results of measurements of LCC radar radiation level versus the distance along the cable for dry subsoil medium are presented in Figure 13.14a for the matched load impedance $Z_L = 51$ Ω (see definitions in Chapter 8). The same data, but measured in wet subsoil medium, are presented in Figure 13.14b for the matched load impedance $Z_L = 51$ Ω.

It is evident that even for the matched load, the radiation level of the external mode exceeds some oscillations at the input of the cable. It can be suggested that the effect may be caused by coupling of the internal and external modes, which was described by Equation 13.96.

As was mentioned in Section 13.5, in the common situation where standing waves are due to two waves traveling with a different velocity in different directions, the standing-wave patterns for $I_e(x)$ and $V_e(x)$ are coincident. The reason for this is that the ratio V/I is positive for progressive waves and negative for regressive waves. Consequently, Equation 13.96 is also valid for $V_e(x)$, that is, for the electric field along the cable, and finally also for the power flow in the subsoil medium. We note a marked fading of the measured power pattern near the range of 30 m from the generator

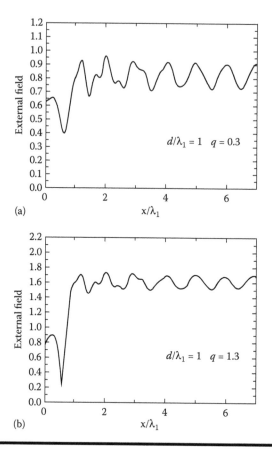

Figure 13.12 **The external mode pattern along the LCC for (a)** $d/\lambda_1 = 1$ **and** $q = 0.3$; **(b)** $d/\lambda_1 = 1$ **and** $q = 1.3$.

as the result of the influence of a water pipe, which is also buried and crosses the buried LCC-radar system.

In the second tests, the vertical distribution of radiation was studied at some reference points along the transmitting cable. The measurement of the field level was performed at the reference points located at distances of 15, 45, 75, 105, and 135 m from the input end of the cable. At each reference point, the field level was measured in the transverse direction every 0.25 m. The results of measurements for dry soil are presented in Figure 13.15a, and for wet soil in Figure 13.15b, both for the matched load impedance $Z_L = 51$ Ω.

An LCC-radar system above the ground surface was studied. We present only two examples of such measurements. In the first, the influence of screening metallic sheets located near the transmitting cable above the surface of the ground was investigated.

Six sheets of iron (1.5 × 2.0 m each) were used for the measurements.

In the next series of experiments, the influence of foreign objects buried or located near the transmitted LCC was investigated. The distance between the cable and the solid iron strip (at 90–102 m from the input) was equal to 0.2 m, and the aperture width between the right and left strips (at 90–96 m from the input) was 0.4 m. The results of the measurements are presented in Figure 13.16 for two-sided screening as described for this specific experiment.

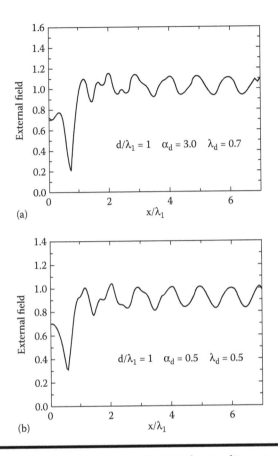

(a)

(b)

Figure 13.13 **The external mode pattern along the LCC for (a)** $d/\lambda_1 = 1$**,** $\alpha_d = 3.0$**, and** $\lambda_d = 0.7$**; (b)** $d/\lambda_1 = 1$**,** $\alpha_d = 0.5$**, and** $\lambda_d = 0.5$**.**

The experimental results presented above were motivated by a final theoretical study. In the study an idealized scenario was considered, modeling the discontinuity of the coupling coefficient along the infinite line by the function in Equation 13.97. Assuming that the propagation constant does not depend on distance, it was found that a discontinuity comparable with the wavelength can result in strong interference fading of the outer mode signal distribution along the cable (see Figures 13.14a,b). The results of simulations are similar to those obtained in the experimental investigation at a distance of ~30 m from the input of the cable (see Figures 13.11 through 13.13). A similar treatment was applied to the case when $\varsigma_c = constant$ and the distribution of the propagation constant has some discontinuity.

13.7 General Comments

A very important task of this chapter was to show the possibilities of predicting and controlling the radiation pattern of the guided radar system based on LCC by changing the cable geometry and outer jacket material. Another was to show the LCC-radar system pattern distribution both along

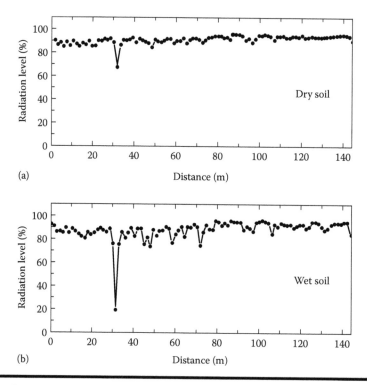

Figure 13.14   The LCC radar pattern along the cable for (a) dry and (b) wet subsoil medium.

and above the buried cable, both theoretically and experimentally. The study of these problems has required the use of a special analytical framework and numerical technique.

First, in order to explain the dependence of the field intensity on the transverse coordinate to LCC, we have used in our theoretical approach the concept of the surface wave, which is characterized by an exponentially decreasing field. The decreasing rate and the localization area of the field with or without sufficient oscillations are shown to be functions of the external mode excitation parameter α, the normalized phase velocity s, the real part q_r, and the imaginary part q_i of the transverse wavenumber, respectively. These propagation parameters of the radiated field can be controlled and regulated by changing the properties of the insulation jacket, accounting for losses in the environment (in the case investigated here, subsoil medium), as well as by change of outer jacket lossy layer thickness.

Second, the results obtained for the simple cases of the environment, the infinite subsoil medium or unbounded air, as well as for the case of the ground surface in the presence of obstructions such as walls, allow us to conclude that the principal effects are to attenuate the external surface wave and to slow down the propagation of this mode without sufficient oscillations in directions radial to the LCC, which can be regulated and controlled by the optimal parameters of the thickness of the lossy outer jacket a and the specific surface impedance of the thin outer conductive layer ζ_c. Correspondingly, we expect some change in the radiation pattern in directions close to the axis of the cable for different kinds of LCC open installations.

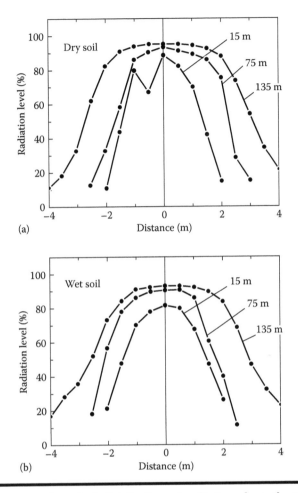

(a)

(b)

Figure 13.15 **The measured vertical distribution of radiation along the transmitting cable at reference points of 15, 45, 75, 105, and 135 m for (a) dry and (b) wet subsoil medium.**

Finally, analyzing the presented experimental data, we can conclude that the field pattern of a buried guiding radar system along the LCC has a regular structure at a range of more than 20–30 m from the generator. Near the generator, strong fading of the external mode signal was observed even for the matched load. This effect can be explained by use of the proposed theoretical framework and the corresponding models, according to which the strong oscillations of the external mode at the input of the cable are caused by two modes traveling with different phase velocities, which are respectively in phase and antiphase.

Moreover, the possibility of the creation of a very complicated picture of the radiation pattern distribution of the LCC-radar system caused by the local above- and under-the-ground inhomogeneities (or man-made foreign objects) and their influence on the radiation properties of the buried LCC system, as a guiding radar, was examined both theoretically and experimentally and briefly shown to the reader. We should notice that all the phenomena under consideration can decrease the performance and operational efficiency of a guiding radar system.

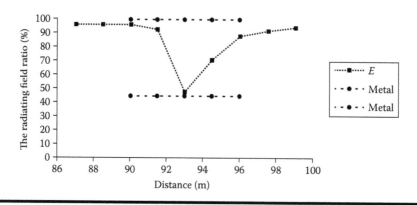

Figure 13.16 **The influence of the metallic sheets on the transmitting LCC electric field, *E*, distributed along the cable (two-side screening).**

References

1. Colin, R. E., *Field Theory of Guided Waves*, New York: McGraw-Hall, 1960.
2. Wait, J. R. and K. P. Spies, Surface electromagnetic fields of a line source on a conducting half-space, *Radio Sci* 6, 781–786, 1971.
3. Wait, J. R., Theory of wave propagation along a thin wire parallel to an interface, *Radio Sci* 7, 675–679, 1972.
4. Wait, J. R., Electromagnetic wave propagation along a buried insulated wire, *Can J Phys* 50, 2402–2409, 1972.
5. Harrison, C. W. and R. W. P. King, Excitation of a coaxial line through a transverse slot, *IEEE Trans Electromagn Compat* 14, 107–112, 1972.
6. Taylor, C. D. and C. W. Harrison, On the excitation of a coaxial line by an incident field propagating through a small aperture in the sheath, *IEEE Trans Electromagn Compat* 15, 107–112, 1973.
7. Wait, J. R., Electromagnetic theory of the loosely braided coaxial cable: Part I, *IEEE Trans Microw Theory Techn* 24, 547–593, 1976.
8. Cree, D. J. and L. J. Giles, Practical performance of radiating cables, *J I Electron Rad Eng* 45, 215–223, 1975.
9. Wait, J. R. and D. A. Hill, Electromagnetic fields of a dielectric coated coaxial cable with an interrupted shield-quasi-static approach, *IEEE Trans Antennas Propag* 23, 679–682, 1975.
10. Wait, J. R. and D. A. Hill, On the electromagnetic field of a dielectric coated coaxial cable with an interrupted shield, *IEEE Trans Antennas Propag* 23, 470–479, 1975.
11. Hill, D. A. and J. R. Wait, Effect of a lossy jacket on the external fields of a coaxial cable with an interrupted shield, *IEEE Trans Antennas Propag* 25, 726–734, 1977.
12. Lee, K. S. and C. E. Baum, Application of modal analysis to braided-shield cables, *IEEE Trans Electromagn Compat* 17, 159–169, 1975.
13. Casey, K. F., On the effective transfer impedance of thin coaxial cable shields, *IEEE Trans Electromagn Compat* 18, 110–117, 1976.
14. Casey, K. F. and E. F. Vance, EMP coupling through cable shields, *IEEE Trans Antennas Propag* 26, 100–106, 1976.
15. Wait, J. R., Electromagnetic field analysis for a coaxial cable with periodic slots, *IEEE Trans Electromagn Compat* 19, 7–13, 1977.
16. Wait, J. R., Excitation of currents on a buried insulated cable, *J Appl Phys* 49, 876–980, 1978.
17. Gale, D. J. and J. C. Beal, Comparative testing of leaky coaxial cables for communication and guided radar, *IEEE Trans Microw Theory Techn* 28, 1006–1013, 1980.
18. Hill, D. A. and J. R. Wait, Electromagnetic theory of the loosely braided coaxial cable: Part II, Numerical results. *IEEE Trans Microw Theory Techn* 28, 326–331, 1980.

19. Hill, D. A. and J. R. Wait, Propagation along a coaxial cable with a helical shield, *IEEE Trans Microw Theory Techn* 28, 84–89, 1980.
20. Delogne, P. and M. Safak, Electromagnetic theory of the leaky coaxial cable, *J I Electron Rad Eng* 45, 233–240, 1975.
21. Delogne, P. and L. Deryck, Underground use of a coaxial cable with leaky sections. *IEEE Trans Antennas Propag* 28, 875–882, 1980.
22. Delogne, P., *Leaky Feeders and Subsurface Radio Communications*, London: Peter Peregrinus, 1982.
23. Richmond, J. H., N. N. Wang, and H. B. Tran, Propagation of surface waves on a buried coaxial cable with periodic slots, *IEEE Transactions on Electromagnetic Compatibility* 23, 139–146, 1981.
24. Richmond, J. H., Propagation on a ported coaxial cable buried in flat earth. *IEEE Trans Electromagn Compat* 27, 70–71, 1985.
25. Gale, D. I. and J. C. Beal, Comparative testing of leaky coaxial cable for communication and guided radar, *IEEE Trans Microw Theory Techn* 28, 1006–1013, 1980.
26. Chang, D. C. and J. R. Wait, Extremely low frequency (ELF) propagation along a horizontal wire located above or buried in the earth, *IEEE Trans Commun* 22, 421–427, 1974.
27. Hill, D. A., Magnetic dipole excitation of an insulated conductor of finite length, *IEEE Trans Geosci Remote Sens* 28, 289–294, 1990.
28. Kuester, E. F., D. C. Chang, and R. G. Olsen, Modal theory of long horizontal wire structures above the earth, I. Excitation, *Radio Sci* 13, 605–613, 1978.
29. Hill, D. A., M. L. Crawford, M. Kanda, and D. I. Wu, Aperture coupling to a coaxial air line: Theory and experiment. *IEEE Trans Electromagn Compat* 35, 69–74, 1993.
30. Blaunstein, N., Z. Dank, and M. Zilbershtein, Wave pattern of a buried leaky coaxial cable under local inhomogeneous conditions, *Proceedings of 27th European Microwave Conference '97*, Jerusalem, Israel, 8–12 September, 153–156, 1997.
31. Blaunstein, N., Z. Dank, and M. Zilbershtein, Wave pattern of a buried leaky coaxial cable in a guiding radar system, *Proceedings of 1998 IEEE AP-S International Symposium and URSI Radio Science Meeting*, Atlanta, Georgia, 21–26 June, 1718–1722, 1998.
32. Blaunstein, N., Z. Dank, and M. Zilbershtein, Radiation directivity of a buried leaky coaxial cable in guided radar systems, *Proceedings of EMC'98*, Rome, Italy, 14–18 September, 458–463, 1998.
33. Blaunstein, N., Z. Dank, and M. Zilbershtein, Prediction of radiation pattern of a buried leaky coaxial cable, *Journal of Subsurface Sensing Technologies and Applications* 1 (1), 79–100, 2000.
34. Blaunstein, N., Z. Dank, and M. Zilbershtein, Analysis of radiation pattern of radar systems based on leaky coaxial cable. *Journal of Subsurface Sensing Technologies and Applications* 2 (1), 61–73, 2001.
35. Blaunstein, N., Z. Dank, and M. Zilbershtein, Wave pattern of a leaky coaxial cable in a guiding radar system under various clutter conditions, *Journal of Subsurface Sensing Technologies and Applications* II, 4 (12), 544–554, 2000.
36. Blaunstein, N., Z. Dank, and M. Zilbershtein, Radiation characteristics of guiding radar systems based on *H*-field leaky coaxial cable, *Journal of Subsurface Sensing Technologies and Applications* 3 (2), 321–336, 2002.

Chapter 14

Physical Fundamentals of Ground-Penetrating Radars and Remote Sensing Systems

14.1 Overview

Ground- or subsurface-penetrating radars (GPRs) and remote sensing systems (RSSs) are used to detect natural (minerals, oil, and so on) and man-made (mines, tunnels, rocks, and so on) structures below the ground surface [1–25]. GPRs are related mostly to the defense industry, while RSSs are related mostly to civilian applications. During recent decades, RSSs have been introduced in practice that are more applicable for the detection and identification of various subsoil minerals and other foreign objects hidden in the clutter environment (walls, constructions, and underground and underwater surfaces). The latter are related mostly to civilian applications, despite the fact that they can also be successfully used in military applications by variation of broad-frequency bandwidth, narrow pulses, and the corresponding theoretical frameworks and numerical techniques [26–51].

From the beginning, the corresponding technology has been adopted most enthusiastically by geophysicists to describe delineation zones in land-form structures [2,8]. Next, GPRs found general use in the detection of buried objects, such as pipes, oil drums, and man-made objects, such as mines, tunnels, and rocks [12,13]. It has been found, during the long-term evolution of GPR technology that plastic or dielectric objects are generally more difficult to detect than metallic ones. This occurs because the dielectric permittivity difference from the subsoil medium is usually too small to provide significant reflection of the radar signal penetrating into the subsoil layers.

The terms *ground-penetrating*, *subsurface*, or *surface-penetrating radars* refer to a range of electromagnetic technologies designed for the location of objects or interfaces buried beneath the ground surface or located within visually opaque structures [5–12]. Thus, the main goal of geophysical radars, using special algorithms and post-acquisition signal processing, is to extract sometimes unexpected information from an unwanted or specially desired subsoil background. Usually, the data obtained from many different subsoil structures are combined with previously obtained data to provide an overall picture of a ground structure, such as mineral-located layers or oil drums.

The requirements of GPR for civilian and military applications may be quite different. The approximate position and type of target may be known. However, the highest resolution attainable for a given target range may be required to determine the precise location and conditions of its position (depth), size, and form (or shape) definition. Also, and this is important for defense and military applications, the real-time data acquired should be of good quality, allowing an immediate decision to be made on the buried object or target (e.g., in landmine detection) [12,13].

Hence, from the beginning, it must be clear that the detection and identification of buried metallic and nonmetallic objects using GPRs operating in the electromagnetic frequency band is a pure radio-frequency (RF) engineering area of current and future importance. Recent developments in GPR technologies regarding different kinds of such radars operating in the time, frequency, and combined time-frequency domains, and using in the applications an extremely wide frequency band, from 10 MHz up to a few gigahertz, are among the possible means of achieving such a goal [10–14]. Parallel to this, different post-acquisition signal-processing methods have been investigated for identifying a wide spectrum of buried objects and structures. Among them, for example, we should mention methods based on the target dependent method, target "response" resonance (in the frequency domain), target polarization properties, the microwave holographic synthetic aperture radio (SAR) imaging method, the diffraction tomography method, and so forth [10,12].

The history of GPR technology development started at the beginning of the twentieth century, with the use of continuous-wave (CW) (also called *narrowband*) electromagnetic waves to determine the presence of remote terrestrial metallic objects due to their higher conductivity with respect to the surrounding subsoil medium (see details in [14–21]). The pulsed (e.g., *wideband*) signal technologies, developed in the middle of the twentieth century, allow us to penetrate into subsoil media to considerable depths, greater than a few meters [1–4]. The same high difference between the dielectric constant of air and the permittivity of the buried objects, as well as their dielectric impedances, allow these objects to be differentiated, detected, and identified more precisely.

Subsoil media radar is a relatively new discipline, developing worldwide as the basis for various applications. The best-known example of this type of radar is the GPR, but other types also exist. The technological difficulty is because in subground media, as opposed to the air environment in which classical radar is usually operated, the propagation of radio waves is a complicated problem and varies as a function of the medium, the main parameters of which are usually unknown. It is also not possible, as it is with other radars, to find the depth, shape, and dielectric properties of an object, as a result of possible effects from clutter (stones, pieces of clay, etc.).

Therefore, the problem of signal processing for object detection in subground media is a very important problem for practical radio engineering, due to the transition of the radio signals through different layers, scattering effects caused by clutter, diffraction from other foreign objects surrounding the investigated structure or object, and many losses due to absorption and refraction caused by the multilayered clutter. This is why only the main effects mentioned in Chapter 11 remain relevant for the detection, imaging, and identification of underground or undersurface objects that should be investigated, taking into account their spectral and time-dispersion properties occurring in the frequency, time, and time-frequency domains.

Therefore, in our further description of the matter, we will introduce the reader to the subject of GPRs and will describe briefly some important technologies and theoretical and numerical frameworks.

14.2 Problems in GPR System Design

The operational characteristics of a GPR system, its range of operation frequencies, the individual peculiarities of the receiving and transmitting signals, different electronic configurations, and the type of radar antennas, as well as the corresponding signal pre-processing and, then, post-processing—all these depend on a number of specific factors related to the subsoil background and to the individual properties of the hidden or embedded target itself. Thus, the type, material, size, and shape of the buried target or subsoil structure, and the transmission properties of the subsoil medium and its layered structure, play an important role in further detection, imaging, and identification of the target under real-time study using the corresponding GPR.

In practice, adequate and precise achievement by the GPR is influenced by all these factors, and the following operational characteristics are most important for its successful performance: signal-to-noise ratio (SNR), signal-to-clutter ratio (SCR), spatial resolution of the target, introduced and defined in Chapter 11, and, finally, depth resolution of the target—the most important and specific characteristic of all GPRs.

Among all factors, as has been shown by numerous experimental and theoretical investigations [14–25], the most important are the dielectric and conductive properties of subsoil media, their nonhomogeneous characteristics affecting, as clutter, the transmitting and receiving signals arriving from a desired target. To understand this issue, we will briefly discuss the dielectric and conductive properties of subsoil media, as well as their influence, as clutter, on the propagation of electromagnetic waves of various frequencies through subsoil or subsurface media, following [12–25].

14.2.1 Dielectric and Conductive Properties of Subsoil Media

In Chapter 4, a problem of electromagnetic wave propagation in the material medium was illuminated. Here, we will return to this problem to describe the peculiarities of electromagnetic wave propagation through the subsoil medium, accounting for its nonhomogeneous structure affecting, as clutter, the wave energy loss and the additive and multiplicative noise occurrence. For different kinds of subsoil media and their dependence on the radar operational frequencies and on clutter effects we refer the reader to the excellent books [1,10,12,16].

Generally, any GPR, using any kind of antenna, operating at any height above the ground surface and above the ground clutter, should find the desired buried target as an anomaly of the background permittivity and permeability of the subsoil medium. This is schematically sketched in a simple manner in Figure 14.1, where we show a simple geometry of incidence of the GPR's electromagnetic wave of the electrical field amplitude $\mathbf{E}^i$ at the air–soil boundary.

The subsoil medium is a frequency-dispersive environment [1,10,12,16] and, therefore, is characterized by the complex permittivity $\varepsilon = \varepsilon_0 \varepsilon_r = \varepsilon_0(\varepsilon_r' + j\varepsilon_r'')$ and the complex conductivity $\sigma = \sigma' + j\sigma''$. If so, we can introduce relations between the normalized parameters $\varepsilon_r = \varepsilon_r' + j\varepsilon_r''$ (to that in free space, ε_0), and $\sigma_r = \sigma_r' + j\sigma_r''$ (to $\sigma_0 \sim 1$ S/m related to a weakly conducting dry subsoil medium):

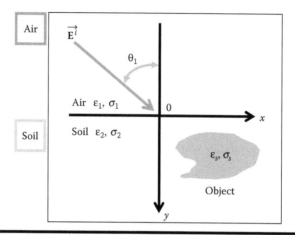

Figure 14.1 **Simple sketch of the problem, where the object is buried in a subsoil medium with the parameters ε_3 and σ_3 different from those in the air, ε_1 and σ_1.**

$$\sigma_r = j\omega\varepsilon_r \tag{14.1}$$

Moreover, in terms of wave-propagation equations, introduced in Chapter 4, we can introduce the parameters ε_r and σ_r, which can be presented in combination with their real and imaginary parts as

$$\sigma_r + j\omega\varepsilon_r = \sigma'_r + \omega\varepsilon''_r + j\omega\left(\varepsilon'_r - \frac{\sigma''_r}{\omega}\right) \tag{14.2}$$

14.2.2 Attenuation and Losses of Electromagnetic Waves in Subsoil Medium

The corresponding parameters of the attenuation α and of the phase velocity β, defined in Chapter 4 in the definition of the propagation parameter $\gamma = \alpha + j\beta$, can now be presented in the same manner as in Chapter 4 but using the parameters introduced by Equations 14.1 and 14.2:

$$\alpha = \frac{\omega}{c}\sqrt{\frac{\mu_r\varepsilon'_r}{2}\left(\sqrt{1+\left(\frac{\varepsilon''_r}{\varepsilon'_r}\right)^2}-1\right)} \tag{14.3}$$

$$\beta = \frac{\omega}{c}\sqrt{\frac{\mu_r\varepsilon'_r}{2}\left(\sqrt{1+\left(\frac{\varepsilon''_r}{\varepsilon'_r}\right)^2}+1\right)} \tag{14.4}$$

Usually, another three parameters are used for GPR applications and its operational characteristics: the material loss tangent, $\tan\delta$, the propagation velocity, **v**, and the intrinsic impedance, Z_i, of a subsoil medium. According to the results obtained in Chapter 4 and those described in

[1,10,12,16], we present these parameters using these new notations. Thus, in the loss material, such as a wet and nonhomogeneous subsoil medium, the material loss tangent equals

$$\tan \delta = \frac{\sigma_r' + \omega \varepsilon_r'}{\omega \varepsilon_r' + \sigma_r''} \tag{14.5}$$

For the case of nonconductive pure dielectric medium, when σ_r' and σ_r'' vanish, we get a commonly used expression (see also Chapter 4):

$$\tan \delta = \frac{\varepsilon_r''}{\varepsilon_r'} \tag{14.6}$$

As was shown in [1,10,12,16], the velocity of wave propagation in pure dielectric subsoil medium with losses is strongly dependent on the loss tangent. We present it using our notations as

$$|\mathbf{v}| = c\sqrt{\frac{\left(\sqrt{(1+\tan^2 \delta)^2} + 1\right)}{2\varepsilon_r'}} \tag{14.7}$$

However, $\tan \delta$ can be lower than unity for any high-loss subsoil medium under and therefore, it is reasonable to assume that for $\tan \delta < 1$, Equation 14.7 yields

$$|\mathbf{v}| = \frac{c}{\sqrt{\varepsilon_r'}}, \tag{14.8}$$

that is, presented in the same manner as was determined earlier in Chapter 4.

Next, as was shown in Chapter 4, the intrinsic impedance Z_i can be found according to the relation between electric and magnetic field components, and, finally, it can also be presented as a function of the loss tangent, $\tan \delta$ [10,12,16]:

$$Z_i = \sqrt{\frac{\mu_r}{\varepsilon_r}} \frac{Z_0}{\left(1+\tan^2 \delta\right)^{1/4}} \left[\cos \frac{\delta}{2} + j \sin \frac{\delta}{2}\right] \tag{14.9}$$

where $Z_0 = 120\pi \cong 377 \ \Omega$ is the characteristic impedance of free space introduced in Chapter 4; all other normalized parameters were also defined in Chapter 4.

If we now return to the scheme sketched in Figure 14.1, we can find the reflection coefficient via intrinsic impedances of the air (denoted by subscript "a") and subsoil medium (denoted by subscript "s"):

$$\Gamma = \frac{Z_{is} - Z_{ia}}{Z_{is} + Z_{ia}} \tag{14.10}$$

In a nonconductive (i.e., perfect dielectric; see Chapter 4) medium, where $\sigma \to 0$, and considering only a single frequency of radiation by the radar, Equation 14.10 yields

$$\Gamma = \frac{\sqrt{\varepsilon_{rs}} - \sqrt{\varepsilon_{ra}}}{\sqrt{\varepsilon_{rs}} + \sqrt{\varepsilon_{ra}}} \tag{14.11}$$

Now, using the above formulas and expressions, we can evaluate the total losses occurring in the any subsoil medium.

Let us pose the question: when will the simple Formulas 14.6, 14.8, and 14.11 be useful for description of the main characteristics of wave propagation in a subsoil environment? For this purpose, we should estimate the main parameters of the subsoil medium in real conditions. This task was fully resolved in [14–25]. Therefore, we will analyze the main parameters and propagation characteristics for those kinds of soil that are always used in GPR applications. For this purpose, we need to estimate the ratio $(\omega/c)\cdot/(\sigma_r'/\varepsilon_r')^2$ that really represents the attenuation factor α [m^{-1}]. If this term is much higher than unity, that is, the corresponding parameter $\alpha \gg 1$ [m^{-1}], the radar operates in a high-loss subsoil medium. Conversely, if this term is much less than unity, that is, $\alpha \ll 1$ [m^{-1}], the radar operates in a weak-loss subsoil medium.

$$P_r = \Gamma^2 \cdot P_{in} \tag{14.12}$$

For *simple loamy* soil, the reflection coefficient determined by Equation 14.11 gives for different moisture conditions [26] $\Gamma \in (0.3; 0.63)$. For *sandy* soil with different degrees of moisture (from 2.18% to 16.8%) [26], $\Gamma \in (0.23; 0.63)$, respectively.

It is evident that for a high-loss nonconductive soil medium, Formulas 14.6, 14.8, and 14.11 are precise enough for estimation of the propagation characteristics of the probing electromagnetic wave entering the high-loss subsoil medium. Moreover, the most important parameter, the attenuation factor described by Equation 14.3, can be also simplified in soils with high losses. Thus, for these media, the parameter of attenuation, introduced in Chapter 4, can be presented in our new notations as

$$\alpha \cong \frac{\pi \cdot \varepsilon_r''}{\lambda_0 \cdot \sqrt{\varepsilon_r'}} = \frac{\pi \cdot f_0 \cdot \varepsilon_r''}{c \cdot \sqrt{\varepsilon_r'}} \quad \text{[m}^{-1}\text{]} \tag{14.13}$$

where:
f_0 is the radiated frequency in free space
$\lambda_0 = c/f_0$ is free-space wavelength

If so, we find the wave penetration depth h as

$$h = (2\alpha)^{-1} \tag{14.14}$$

Finally, following [24,26], we present in Table 14.1 the main characteristics of the wave propagation in different high-loss subsoil media estimated for the radiated frequency of 500 MHz. We should note that at frequencies above 2.5 GHz, with the dispersion effect due to dielectric relaxation at high moisture content (i.e., in wet soils with moisture exceeding 10%), the validity of the simplified formulas becomes incorrect, and the corresponding Formulas 14.3, 14.4, 14.6, and 14.14 should be used.

Table 14.1 Soil and Propagating Wave Parameters and Characteristics

Soil Moisture (%)	Relative Dielectric ε_r'	Loss Tangent tan δ	Effective Loss Factor ε_r''	Depth h (m)	Reflection Coefficient Γ
Sandy Soil					
Dry	2.55	6.2×10^{-4}	1.581×10^{-2}	1.96	0.23
2.18	2.5	3.0×10^{-2}	7.5×10^{-2}	0.41	0.23
3.88	4.4	4.6×10^{-2}	2.024×10^{-1}	0.20	0.35
16.8	20.0	1.3×10^{-1}	2.6×100	0.03	0.63
Clay Soil					
Dry	2.27	1.5×10^{-2}	3.405×10^{-2}	0.86	0.20
20.09	11.30	2.5×10^{-1}	2.85×100	0.02	0.54

Finally, we will show how to convert the attenuation parameter α, measured in nepers per meter, to another dimension, decibels per meter, which is usually used in practice. Thus, the attenuation coefficient $\tilde{\alpha}$ written in decibels per meter can be rewritten using the attenuation coefficient α measured in nepers per meter in the following form [10–16,49]:

$$\tilde{\alpha} \ [\text{Np/m}] = 8.66 \cdot \alpha \ (\text{dB/m}) \qquad (14.15)$$

It follows from this formula that the attenuation coefficient of the material medium is, to a first order, linearly related in decibels per meter to frequency (according to Formula 14.3 or 14.13).

14.3 Theoretical Framework of Target Detection and Imaging

The research in this section, which is based on results obtained and discussed in [26–51], concerns the problem of reconstructing the unknown object on the basis of the field scattered by this object. In literature, this problem is known as *inverse scattering* or *diffraction tomography* [26–40,45–51]. In the one-dimensional (1-D) case, the problem is known to be exactly soluble by use of the Born's approximation, valid only for a "weak response" of the target on the incident electromagnetic wave [46–48]. In the multidimensional case, it has been shown that the solution is not unique. However, even the uniqueness of the solution does not help us to find it in practice. The key problem here is that even the direct problem (evaluation of the field scattered by a known scatterer) is essentially nonlinear. To obtain a reasonable analytical solution for the direct problem, it is usually confined to the first (linear) term in the whole series of expansions of the terms on first-, second-, and higher-order terms of the main scattered-field perturbations introduced by a target under detection. This leads to the Born's approximation, when the perturbation approach is applied to the field itself, or to the Rytov's approximation, when this is performed for the complex phase. These linearized approximations are valid for small (smooth) weak scatterers, but fail when strong scattering is observed. The Rytov's approximation, being nonlinear with respect to the wave field, accounts for the multiple scattering effects, and, in this sense, is more advantageous as compared with the Born approximation. However, this gain is not sufficient. To improve the Rytov's approximation it was proposed to evaluate the wave intensity of the scattered field by using an essentially nonlinear propagator [46–48]. This will allow us to reconstruct strong scatterers with better accuracy and to remove the problem of phase estimation.

Additionally, we suppose that this approach will allow us to estimate high spatial frequencies, which are related to the evanescent waves under single scattering conditions, that is, to attack the super-resolution problem. The drawback of the approach is that the result of reconstruction is not the scattering potential itself, but the static structure function of the object. However, this does not seem to be a serious problem, since in most practical cases, it is possible to transfer from the structure function to the scattered function.

14.3.1 Diffraction Tomography Method Based on Rytov's Approximation

The basic equation of diffraction tomography may be obtained as a result of the solution of a scattering inverse problem of a plane electromagnetic wave diffracted by the object under investigation with a radius of 2 k, where $k = 2\pi/\lambda$ is the wave number [45–48]. Following [45–48], we consider an object characterized by a refractive index $n(\mathbf{r}) = 1 + n\delta(\mathbf{r}) \equiv 1 + f$, where f is equal to zero outside the refracting object. The incident plane harmonic ($\exp(-i\omega t)$) wave $U_I(\mathbf{r}) = \exp[ik(\theta \cdot \mathbf{r})]$ is scattered by the object, where θ is a unit vector pointing the direction of the wave propagation; $n\delta(\mathbf{r})$ is the deviation of the refractive index; $k = \omega/c$; ω is radiation frequency; c is the velocity of light. In the case of direct scattering, the total field $U = U_1 + U_S$ (where $U_S(\mathbf{r})$ is a scattered wave) satisfies the given wave equation

$$\Delta U + k^2 (1 + f)^2 U = 0 \tag{14.16}$$

and the boundary condition in infinity, that is, conditions of radiation. Here, Δ is the Laplace's operator introduced in Chapter 1. The scattered field U_s may be found using Equation 14.16 in the first-order Born approximation. So, for the scattered field, $U_S^{(1)}(\mathbf{r})$ may be written in an integral form:

$$U_S^{(1)}(\mathbf{r}) = \int G(\mathbf{r} - \mathbf{r}')Q(\mathbf{r}')U_I(\mathbf{r}')dr' \tag{14.17}$$

where:
$G(\mathbf{r} - \mathbf{r}') = (i/4)H_0^{(1)}(k|\mathbf{r} - \mathbf{r}'|)$ is a Green function
$H_0^{(1)}$ is the Hankel function of the first type of zero order; $Q(r) = k^2(2f + f^2)$

The integral representation 14.17 of the scattered field $U_S^{(1)}(\mathbf{r})$ is permitted under the condition $U_S \ll U_I$.

In the inverse scattering problem, the function f should be found with a known scattered field U_s. The solution of such a problem using the relations in Equation 14.17 allows us to obtain the main equation of diffraction tomography [31–39,45–48]. After that, we may find the functions $Q(\mathbf{r})$ and $f(\mathbf{r})$ if we know (after calculations or experimental results) $U_S^{(1)}$ or $U_I(k\Phi_R)$. In our case, we deal with Rytov's approximation, which can describe a situation in which both $U_s \ll U_I$ and $U_s \geq U_I$; that is, it can describe both weak and strong inhomogeneities and allow the designers to obtain information about the amplitude and phase of waves scattered and diffracted from the tested objects.

14.3.2 Imaging of Buried Objects Based on the Open Waveguide Structures

As the waveguide line directs a traveling wave in a straight line, such a wave may be considered as a beam propagating in free space. It is known that in line with losses, the amplitudes of vectors **E** and **H** are decreased exponentially with wave propagation. At piece Δz, due to decreased transmitting power P, the following relation is valid:

$$\Delta P = -2\alpha P \Delta z \tag{14.18}$$

where $\alpha = const$ is the attenuation coefficient of the wave in a given transmission line, introduced in Chapter 7. If $\alpha = \alpha(z)$ is a function of coordinate z, then from Equation 14.17, the expression may be transformed into

$$P = P_0 \exp\left(-2 \int_{z_0}^{z_l} \alpha(z) dz\right) \tag{14.19}$$

where:

P_0 is transmitting power at the beginning (the coordinate z_0) of the piece of the waveguide line with length of $l = |z_l - z_0|$

P is transmitting power at the end of this line (coordinate: z_l, see Chapter 7)

Thus, after measuring the ratio P/P_0, the function $\alpha(x, y)$ may be found by means of tomography. In a more general case, for the reconstruction function

$$k_z(x, y) = \beta(x, y) + i\alpha(x, y) \tag{14.20}$$

where $\beta(x, y)$ is a phase constant, information about the changing of amplitude and phase of the waveguide wave at its interaction with an object located near the waveguide may be used.

In this section, we will briefly consider our approach to image processing in subsurface diffraction. First, we will briefly consider the approach developed in [45-48] for image processing in subsurface diffraction tomography. The scattered field $\psi(x, y_1)$ at line $y = y_1$ (1-D case; see Figure 14.2) can be represented in the form of the Fourier integral of the polarization current function $K(x', y')$, which is found by means of inverse Fourier transformation and by the function $\hat{\psi}(\nu(\alpha,\beta), y_1)$:

$$\psi(x, y_1) = \int_{-\infty}^{\infty} \hat{\psi}(\nu, y_1) \exp(2\pi i x \nu) d\nu \tag{14.21}$$

Here, $\hat{\psi}(\nu, y_1)$ is the Fourier image of $\psi(x, y_1)$, and it is defined as

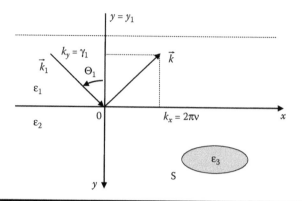

Figure 14.2 **The region under consideration in plane (x, y) and projections of a plane wave vector k from the wave spectrum of a scattered field on the axes of reference.**

$$\hat{\psi}(v, y_1) = c_1(v)c_2(v)\exp(-i\gamma_1 y_1)$$ (14.22)

where:

$$\gamma_1 = \sqrt{k^2 - (2\pi v)^2}$$

$k = (\omega/c)$ is the wavenumber of a plane wave in free space
ω is cyclic frequency
c is the velocity of light

The function $c_1(v)$ can be written as

$$c_1(v) = \frac{ik_2^2 T}{\gamma_1 + \gamma_2}$$ (14.23)

where:
   T is the Fresnel transmittance of the boundary between two media with dielectric permittivities: $\varepsilon_1 = \varepsilon_0$ (air, medium 1) and $\varepsilon_2 = \varepsilon_{r2}\varepsilon_0$ (ε_{r2} is the relative dielectric permittivity of medium 2)
   $\gamma_j^2 = k_j^2 - 4\pi^2 v^2$
   $k_j^2 = \omega^2 \varepsilon_j \mu_0 + i\omega\mu_0\sigma_j$, $j = 1, 2$ ($j = 1$ and $j = 2$ are used for medium 1 and medium 2, respectively)
   σ_j is the conductivity of the j-th medium
   k_j is the wavenumber of the j-th medium
   ε_0 is the dielectric permittivity of the vacuum
   μ_0 is the magnetic permeability of the vacuum

The function $c_2(v)$ may be written in the integral form

$$c_2(\nu) = \iint_S K(x', y') \exp\left[-2\pi i(\alpha x' + \beta y')dx'dy'\right] \tag{14.24}$$

where

$$\alpha = \nu - \omega \frac{\sin\theta_1}{2\pi c} \tag{14.25}$$

$$-2\pi\beta = \sqrt{\left[\left(\frac{\omega}{c}\right)^2 \varepsilon_{r2} - 4\pi^2\nu^2\right] + i\frac{\omega}{c}120\pi\sigma_2} + \frac{\omega}{c}\sqrt{\left(\varepsilon_{r2} - \sin^2\theta_1\right) + i\frac{c}{\omega}120\pi\sigma_2} \tag{14.26}$$

where:

θ_1 is an angle of incidence

symbol S at the bottom side of the integral in Equation 14.24 denotes that integration takes place over the cross section S of the object under investigation

function $K(x', y')$ represents the normalized polarization current

Thus, the desired function $K(x', y')$ is found by means of inverse Fourier transform in Equation 14.24 and by function $\hat{\psi}(\nu(\alpha, \beta), y_1)$. Function $K(x, y)$ is calculated for a dielectric half-space with permittivity of ε_2 in an investigated rectangle region. If the variables x, y are taken in region S, then the function $K(x, y) \cong K(x', y')$ will give the polarization current distribution of the object under investigation. We take the image function in the form of $|K(x, y)|$. Functions $K(x, y)$ depend on frequency f and can be calculated for a set of frequencies $f_1, f_2,...,f_N$ from the band of Δf. In this case, the image functions are defined as $|K(x, y)| = \left|\sum_{i=1}^{N} K f_i(x, y)\right|$.

14.3.3 Method of Diffraction Tomography Based on Feynman's Path Integrals

In this paragraph, we present a nonlinear approach of diffraction tomography based on Feynman's path integral evaluation that allows us to obtain better imaging of the shape and dimensions of any foreign object embedded in clutter conditions. To show the efficiency of such a technique, it was shown experimentally in [38,39] that by using the proposed approach of reconstruction of objects, better imaging of any object hidden in the clutter can be obtained, which finally allows the shape and dimensions of the tested object to be clearly seen. Namely, the efficiency of this method was shown by using passive millimeter-wave radiometry (see Chapter 12) and active centimeter-wave tomography.

Now, to enter more deeply into the subject, we start with the reduced Helmholtz equation describing the propagation and scattering of scalar time-harmonic waves in an inhomogeneous medium. If so, following [38,39], we can define the Green's function as

$$\nabla^2 G(\mathbf{R}|\mathbf{R}_0) + k^2\left[1 + \tilde{\varepsilon}(\mathbf{R})\right]G(\mathbf{R}|\mathbf{R}_0) = -\delta(\mathbf{R} - \mathbf{R}_0) \tag{14.27}$$

where:

$\quad$ **R** $\quad$ denotes the position vector in m-dimensional space ($m = 2$ or 3)

$\quad$ k $\quad$ is the wavenumber associated with a homogeneous medium

$\varepsilon(\mathbf{R}) = 1 + \tilde{\varepsilon}(\mathbf{R})$ is the random permittivity distribution

We suppose that while ε is a real function, k contains an infinitesimally small positive imaginary part which provides the convergence of some integrals appearing in the course of the work. Equation 14.27 is known to serve as a reasonable model for acoustic wave propagation and also for some electromagnetic problems in which the polarization effects can be neglected.

Next, we introduce, according to [38,39], an auxiliary parabolic equation

$$2ik\partial_\tau g + \nabla^2 g + k^2 \tilde{\varepsilon}(\mathbf{R}) g(\mathbf{R}, \tau \,|\, \mathbf{R}_0, \tau_0) = 0, \tau > \tau_0 \tag{14.28}$$

with the initial condition

$$g(\mathbf{R}, \tau_0 \,|\, \mathbf{R}_0, \tau_0) = \delta(\mathbf{R} - \mathbf{R}_0) \tag{14.29}$$

Then, the Green's function $G(\mathbf{R}|\mathbf{R}_0)$ is defined through the solution of Equation 14.29 as

$$G(\mathbf{R}\,|\,\mathbf{R}_0) = \frac{i}{2k} \int_{\tau_0}^{\infty} d\tau \exp\left[i\frac{k}{2}(\tau - \tau_0)\right] g(\mathbf{R}, \tau \,|\, \mathbf{R}_0, \tau_0) \tag{14.30}$$

The generalized parabolic Equation 14.28 for the Green's function $g(\mathbf{R}, \tau|\mathbf{R}_0, \tau_0)$ coincides with the nonstationary Schrodinger equation in quantum mechanics. Using this analogy, the solution of Equation 14.28 can be presented via the Feynman's path integral according to [38,39]:

$$g(\mathbf{R}, \tau \,|\, \mathbf{R}_0, \tau_0) = \int_{\mathbf{R}(\tau_0) = \mathbf{R}_0}^{\mathbf{R}(\tau) = \mathbf{R}} D\mathbf{R}(t) \exp\{iS[\mathbf{R}(t)]\} \tag{14.31}$$

where the integration $\int D\mathbf{R}(t)$ in the continuum of possible trajectories is interpreted as a sum of contributions of arbitrary paths over which a wave propagates from the point $\mathbf{R}_0$ at the moment τ_0 to the point R at the moment τ, and the functional

$$S[\mathbf{R}(t)] = \frac{k}{2} \int_{\tau_0}^{\tau} dt \left\{ [\dot{\mathbf{R}}(t)]^2 + \tilde{\varepsilon}[\mathbf{R}(t)] \right\} \tag{14.32}$$

can be related to the phase accumulated along the corresponding path. To simplify the propagator obtained, we use a self-consistent two-step procedure, as follows. First, to dispose the integral over τ, which is hard to invert, we present the Green's function in Equation 14.30 as a product of two factors, the first corresponding to free space and the second related to the effects of the scatterer. Equation 14.30 is then presented in the following form [38,39]:

$$G\left(\mathbf{R}\mid\mathbf{R}_0\right) = \frac{i}{2k}\int_{\tau_0}^{\infty}d\tau\exp\left[i\frac{k}{2}\left(\tau-\tau_0\right)\right]g_0\left(\mathbf{R},\tau\mid\mathbf{R}_0,\tau_0\right)g_\varepsilon\left(\mathbf{R},\tau\mid\mathbf{R}_0,\tau_0\right) \quad (14.33)$$

Evaluating asymptotically the latter integral allows us to obtain

$$G\left(\mathbf{R}\mid\mathbf{R}_0\right) = G_0\left(\mathbf{R}\mid\mathbf{R}_0\right)G_\varepsilon\left(\mathbf{R}\mid\mathbf{R}_0\right) \quad (14.34)$$

where the inhomogeneous factor $G_\varepsilon(\mathbf{R}|\mathbf{R}_0)$ in the three-dimensional (3-D) case is given by the series in derivatives of the generalized parabolic equation solution:

$$G_\varepsilon\left(\mathbf{R}\mid\mathbf{R}_0\right) = g_\varepsilon\left(\mathbf{R},\tau_0+L\mid\mathbf{R}_0,\tau_0\right) + i\left(L/2k\right)g_\varepsilon''\left(\mathbf{R},\tau_0+L\mid\mathbf{R}_0,\tau_0\right)$$

$$+\left(L/2k^2\right)g_\varepsilon'''\left(\mathbf{R},\tau_0+L\mid\mathbf{R}_0,\tau_0\right)+\ldots \quad (14.35)$$

Keeping only the first term in this series and neglecting all the derivatives, we obtain

$$G_\varepsilon\left(\mathbf{R}\mid\mathbf{R}_0\right) \approx g_\varepsilon\left(\mathbf{R},\tau_0+L\mid\mathbf{R}_0,\tau_0\right) \quad (14.36)$$

Though the path integral cannot be evaluated exactly, we may propose a perturbation approach, which will allow us to obtain its value with a reasonable accuracy. The propagator obtained in such a way was tested recently in the problems of wave propagation and localization in random media [32–39]. The results have been compared with those obtained in the framework of the naive Rytov approximation. In particular, it was found that the improved propagator applied in [36] to the mean (coherent) field leads to the result coinciding exactly with that given by the Bourret approximation for the Dyson equation (see Chapter 3 in [40]). At the same time, the Rytov approximation applied directly, without any embedding procedure, to the Helmholtz equation leads to a result that not only differs from that of the Bourret approximation but, being divergent with the distance from the source, contradicts the energy conservation principle [49].

14.3.4 Finite-difference time-domain (FDTD) Modeling of Buried Objects in Subsoil Media

The FDTD technique is well suited for calculating the fields scattered by buried objects when the sources are close enough to the air–ground interface that they can be incorporated into the solution space [42,52–59,62–69]. Difficulties arise, however, when the sources are far from the interface, since the total fields in the solution space are not all outgoing waves. Using well-known formulas for the fields transmitted and reflected by stratified media, and dealing only with the fields scattered by a buried object, the FDTD technique can be easily adapted to the case when the incident field is a simple plane wave.

When the sources of the incident fields are located far from the air–ground interface, the total fields at the outer boundary of the solution space consist of both incoming and outgoing waves. As was mentioned in [52], it is necessary to extract the incident field from the total field so that only the scattered field will be presented at the outer boundary.

There are two standard techniques used in the FDTD numerical framework to accomplish this [42,52–59,62–69]. The first technique is based on computation of only the scattered fields throughout the entire solution space. This technique is called the *scattered-field method*. The second technique involves partitioning of the solution space into the total-field and the scattered-field regions. This numerical scheme is called the *total-field method*, since the fields calculated in the vicinity of the scatterer are total (i.e., incident plus scattered) fields.

Both the total-field technique and the scattered-field technique require that the incident field should be known at either the scatterer (for the scattered-field method) or the total-field–scattered-field boundary (for the total-field method) for the entire time history of the transient event. The explanation of both methods is shown in Figure 14.3a and b, respectively, rearranged from [57].

In the scattered-field method, only the scattered field is calculated throughout the entire cell space. In this case, the incident field is not carried by the FDTD lattice, but rather, is impressed upon the scatterer as a boundary condition. For perfectly conducting scatterers, this boundary condition is simply the condition in which the tangential components of the scattered and transmitted E-fields are opposite.

For *buried* scatterers, the field that is incident upon the scatterer is the transmitted field, that is, the field that is coupled by the ground surface [25–29,63]. Hence, this transmitted field must be known a priori for the entire transient event for the FDTD technique to proceed. According to [25–29,63], we can show how a frequency-domain representation of the transmitted field can be used in conjunction with the FDTD technique where the incident field is a plane wave generated by a distant antenna. This formulation can be used for a ground that consists of a number of planar strata (or layers), which may be lossless (see Figure 14.4).

Following [42,52–57,59,62,67], we will present some numerical results obtained in these works that illustrate possibilities of the FDTD technique for two-dimensional (2-D) and 3-D geometries of the problem.

Figure 14.4 illustrates a transverse magnetic (TM)-polarized time-harmonic plane wave that incidents from free space on a multilayer structure of M homogeneous layers that extends below the

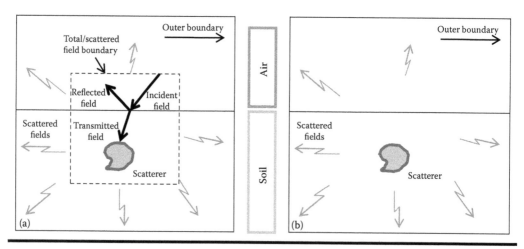

Figure 14.3 FDTD solution space: (a) for the total-field method; (b) for the scattered-field method.

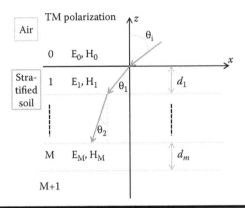

Figure 14.4   TM-polarized time-harmonic plane wave propagation in stratified subsoil medium.

plane $z = 0$. The angle of incidence is θ_i, and each layer has thickness d_m and constitutive parameters μ_m, ε_m, and σ_m (see definitions in Chapter 4). After obtaining the values of reflected and transmitted field equations for TM and transverse electric (TE) polarizations, it was shown how the FDTD solution space is typically partitioned when the scatterer is buried and the total-field method is used.

We should mention that, despite the fact that Figure 14.4 is drawn for the 2-D case, the same scheme can be used for both 2-D and 3-D geometries (see [57]). The region enclosed by the dotted line is the total-field region, and all points outside this region constitute the scattered-field region. The scatterer lies within the total-field region, and the E- and H-fields are advanced in both regions using the standard FDTD field advance equations, using the appropriate values of μ_m, ε_m, and σ_m for each cell (we do not present here the corresponding equations, due to their complexity and because they are outside the scope of this book; we refer the reader to the bibliography). It is clear that the FDTD method requires that the incident fields should be known at all points along the total-field–scattered-field boundary in the space domain and for all points in the time domain.

We will present in this section some examples of numerical computations based on both FDTD methods: *scattered-field* and *total field*.

As an example, Figure 14.5a, extracted from [57], illustrates the cross-sectional view of a 3-D buried dielectric cubic object, which is illuminated by a normally incident plane wave. Here, Figure 14.5a represents the FDTD solution space, showing the stratified ground, the scatterer, and a plane wave that normally incidents upon the interface, Figure 14.5b represents the scattered E-field 3 m above the scatterer (in the air), and Figure 14.5c represents the scattered E-field 1 m to the side of the buried scatterer. In cases (b) and (c), the solid and dotted curves were calculated using the scattered-field and total-field methods, respectively, according to [57].

In numerical computations, according to suggestions made in [57], the following parameters were taken into account. The scatterer is a solid cube with dimensions of $2 \times 2 \times 2$ m, with a relative permittivity of 5.0 and a conductivity of 0.01 S/m, and is buried so that its top face is 2 m below the ground surface. The ground consists of 45 layers, each with a thickness of 0.2 m. The relative permittivities of the strata vary linearly with depth from 2.0 to 2.5, but the conductivity of each stratum is the same: 0.001 S/m. The solution space used for numerical computations has a volume of $12 \times 12 \times 12$ m, of which $12 \times 12 \times 3$ m is in free space and $12 \times 12 \times 9$ m is below the ground surface. Each cell is 0.2 m on a side, so the entire FDTD lattice consists of a $60 \times 60 \times 60$ grid. The incident wave is a y-polarized, 20 ns Gaussian plane wave that normally incidents upon the ground interface and has a peak amplitude of 100 V/m.

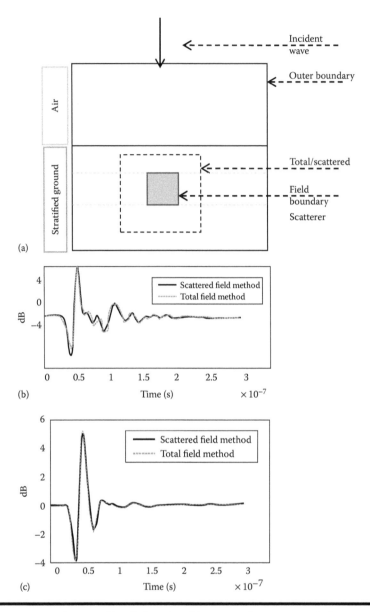

Figure 14.5   Scattering by a cubic dielectric object: (a) the FDTD solution space (Extracted from Demarest D. et al., *IEEE Trans. Antennas Propag.,* **43, 10, 617–622, 1995.); (b) the scattered E-field (in decibels) computed 3 m above the scatterer located in the air (Rearranged from Demarest D. et al.,** *IEEE Trans. Antennas Propag.,* **43, 10, 617–622, 1995.); (c) the scattered E-field (in decibels) computed 1 m from the side of the buried scatterer. (Rearranged from Demarest D. et al.,** *IEEE Trans. Antennas Propag.,* **43, 10, 617–622, 1995.)**

The waveforms in Figure 14.5b show the calculated electric field 3 m above the top face of the scatterer, which is 1 m above the air–ground interface. The solid curve was calculated using the scattered-field method, and the dotted line was calculated using the total-field method. Figure 14.5c shows a similar comparison between the proposed FDTD methods for the electric fields calculated 1 m to the side of the buried scatterer. In both cases, the total-field and scattered-field methods yield comparable results, although there are some noticeable errors in the total-field method calculations in the air (shown in Figure 14.5b) that are a result of nonphysical reflections of the incident field from the total-field–scattered-field boundary.

These results illustrate an extension of the FDTD technique that allows us to model any scatterer that is buried in stratified subsoil medium. This technique uses well-known expressions for the fields transmitted and reflected from stratified media to separate the outgoing fields caused by the scatterer from the total fields.

These examples allow us to improve the standard absorbing boundary conditions (such as discussed in [50]) by closing the FDTD lattice with minimal reflections. The numerical results presented in [52] showed that this technique can be used either for a total-field mode or for a scattered-field mode. On the other hand, the major difference is that the total-field mode demands that the transmitted field should be evaluated at the total-field–scattered-field boundary, whereas the transmitted fields are evaluated only on or within the scatterer for the scattered-field mode. The numerical results presented in [52] have shown that the noise floor for the scattered fields is roughly 35 dB down from the transmitted field at the position of the scatterer.

Now, we will discuss briefly how to use the above FDTD technique for modeling of the extremely-short-pulse (ESP) (in the time domain) ultra-wideband (UWB) (in the frequency domain) remote sensing systems and radars, the operation characteristics and the corresponding applications of which will be discussed in Chapter 15. The main problem here is also the scattering and diffraction effects resulting from artificial or natural targets buried in the subsoil media in clutter multilayered conditions.

Detection of, for example, abandoned mines or pipelines showed that ESP scattering analysis is a very helpful technique, either by itself or combined with other information recorded by additional sensors or using additional ranged receiving antennas (see the next paragraph). It is well known that the field scattered by a target illuminated by an ESP/UWB pulse contains a lot of information: high-resolution imaging (location and strength of diffracting centers), dispersive phenomena and resonances, and so forth.

The main goal is to be able to extract the supposed discriminating features from the received total signals, and that the computations should be accurate enough to highlight these features without introducing numerical artifacts. As is clear from this section, the FDTD technique looks to be an appropriate numerical method to model the electromagnetic diffraction of a buried object by a ESP/UWB pulse. Indeed, it may model the soil properties in detail (surface roughness, volume heterogeneities) as well as taking into account the arbitrary constitution and shape of the scatterer. Another advantage of FDTD is its ability to take into account large computational volumes due to its computational power. We will not discuss the disadvantages and advantages of the FDTD technique, referring the reader to the works [42,52–60] where these aspects are fully described and discussed.

14.3.5 Geometrical Optic Model

As mentioned in previous paragraphs, most of the GPRs existing today are working in a configuration where the transmitter and the receiver are at the same point. The classical GPR system, consisting of the transmitting and the receiving antennas arranged together, for detecting any buried object in the multilayered subsoil medium can be presented schematically in the following manner (see Figure 14.6).

In this section, we will consider and analyze a situation in which there are two antennas located near the transmitter: one in its proximity and the other at a range exceeding several tens of

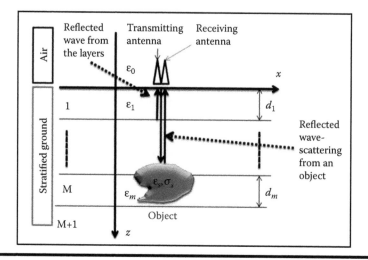

Figure 14.6 Geometry of the problem in the (x, y) plane for the classical GPR system.

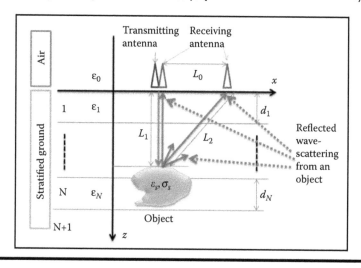

Figure 14.7 Geometry of the problem for the proposed configuration: one transmitting antenna and two receiving antennas at a distance L_0.

wavelengths, as shown in Figure 14.7 (called in the literature the *space diversity* [40]). If we separate the transmitter and the receiver, we can figure out the depth of a hidden object more accurately and get more information about the permittivity of the various layers and the buried object. We start our discussion with the simplest "virtual" model, depicted in Figure 14.7, only to show its difference with respect to a realistic model accounting for the refraction phenomena that occur in the subsoil multilayered medium.

In the case presented in Figure 14.7, the signal recorded by the receiver is a sum of the returning (reflecting) signals as a result of the transition via the different layers of the transmitted signal. During the development of the simple model, we suggested that in addition to information available for the existing radar systems, an additional antenna is arranged that records reflected signals just several wavelengths or more from the transmitter. This can be achieved by the addition of an extra receiving antenna or by separation between the receiver system and the transmitter system. In the second case, we need to perform the test twice: first, in the classical form with the transmitting and the receiving antennas placed at the same point; second, by moving the receiving antenna at least several wavelengths relative to the position of the transmitting antenna. It is clear that practically, the test can be performed several separate times for the purpose of increasing the accuracy of the system. Figure 14.7, extracted from [70], describes, in principle, the proposed system.

In this virtual case, the transmitter sends an RF pulse into the ground; the pulse passes several layers and hits the object, and the reflected signal returns from it and arrives at both receiving antennas. The distance between the receiving antennas is L_0, the object's depth is L_1, and L_2 is a distance between the underground object and the additional receiving antenna, separated from the transmitter/receiver. The depth of each layer of the number n is d_n; the permittivity of each layer of number n is ε_n; the buried object is located between the n and the $(n - 1)$ layer.

Now, we can analyze scattering of the transmitted RF signal from the buried object. Even in the "virtual" case by ignoring refraction, which can explain the more realistic model (see below), the situation here is not so simple, because the RF waves propagate and are then received by both antennas: the first (1) located near the transmitter and the second (2) ranged by a distance L_0 from the transmitter (see Figure 14.7). In the case of existence of N layers (the so-called multilayer model), the buried object should be found inside the N-layer. Figure 14.7 presents N layers of the subsoil medium, where the straight object's depth in the last layer is L_1, and the distance from the second antenna to the hidden object is L_2 (the oblique object's depth). For each layer with a number n, there is a different permittivity ε_n. Finally, we present a model assuming that the wave propagation through the layers' boundaries takes place along straight lines, without accounting for refraction. We will improve this model in continuation of the proposed framework by accounting for the refraction phenomenon to be adapted for most practical GPR systems.

In further presentation of the models, we denote the time T_1 as the reflected pulse time received by the first antenna located near the transmitter, and the time t_1 as the propagation time of the RF pulse from the transmitter to the buried object. It is clear that in this case, $t_1 = T_1/2$ (see Chapter 11). The pulse propagation time to the second antenna equals $T_2 = t_1 + t_2$, where the time T_2 is the receiving RF pulse time at the second antenna, and the time t_2 is the pulse propagation time to the second antenna from the buried object. In addition, ε_1 is the permittivity of the first layer, and ε_n is the permittivity of the n-layer. The width of the n-layer is d_{1n}, and the distance d_{2n} is the path length of the scattered pulse in the layer n from the buried objects to the second receiving antenna under angle α directed relative to a horizontal axis.

In other words, like the distance d_{1n}, the time t_{1n} is the propagation time of the pulse propagating vertically in the n-layer, and t_{2n} is the shortest wave-propagation time in the n-layer from the buried object to the second receiving antenna along the oblique radio path. It can be noted that d_{1N} is the depth of the object in layer N. From [70], and according to geometry presented in Figure 14.7, by assuming that $L_1 = \sum_{n=1}^{N} d_{1n}$ and $t_1 = \sum_{n=1}^{N} t_{1n}$, we finally get

$$L_1 = \sum_{n=1}^{N} \frac{t_{1n}\, c}{\sqrt{\varepsilon_n}} = \sum_{n=1}^{N} \frac{t_{2n}\, \sin\alpha\, c}{\sqrt{\varepsilon_n}} = \frac{t_1\, c}{\sqrt{\varepsilon}} \tag{14.37}$$

where c is the speed of light in free space.

In Formula 14.37, a new value $\bar{\varepsilon}$ was introduced as a weighted (or average) permittivity according to the relative weight of subsoil material of each layer. $\sqrt{\bar{\varepsilon}}_1 = \dfrac{t_1\, c}{L_1}$, from which we can also get the distance L_2:

$$L_2 = \sum_{n=1}^{N} d_{2n} = \sum_{n=1}^{N} \frac{t_{2n}\, c}{\sqrt{\varepsilon_n}} = \frac{t_2\, c}{\sqrt{\bar{\varepsilon}}} \tag{14.38}$$

By analyzing a "one-layer" model, presented schematically in Figure 14.1, the following formulas were obtained:

$$L_1 = L_0 \frac{t_1}{\sqrt{(t_2 + t_1)(t_2 - t_1)}} \tag{14.39a}$$

or in the times T_1 and T_2

$$L_1 = L_0 \frac{T_1}{2\sqrt{T_2(T_2 - T_1)}} \tag{14.39b}$$

Comparison between the simple multilayer model without accounting for the refraction phenomenon, described by Formulas 14.37 and 14.38, and the "one-layer" model, described by Formula 14.39, shows that the number of layers and their own relative permittivity values are not required to be included in calculations of the depth of the object.

Unlike the "virtual" case sketched in Figure 14.7, which does not account for refraction occurring in multilayer subsoil media with their own parameters of refraction and described in [70], we will discuss only the realistic case that takes into account effects of refraction, because in the realistic case, the detection of the object's depth depends on the time delay of partial waves propagating inside and from underground layers. As was mentioned above, the main problem in the calculation of depth of the buried objects or layers is to calculate the electromagnetic wave speed when the permittivity ε is unknown. We propose here a geometrical optic model accounting for the refraction occurring in the multilayer subsoil structure as it is shown in Figure 14.8. Based on the presented geometry, we can now analyze the existence of the effects of refraction in wave transition between layers. As was described in Chapter 11, refraction is the change in direction of propagation of the wave due to a change in its transmission through the medium.

The phenomenon is explained by a law of conservation of the total wave field energy and of the momentum of the wave field. Due to change of medium, the phase velocity of the wave is changed, but its frequency remains constant.

As was shown in Chapter 5, the refraction phenomenon is described by Snell's law, according to which we can describe mathematically the problem depicted in Figure 14.8, where the negative gradient of $n(z)$ is taken into account, because in a multilayered (of N layers) soil medium [12–25,61] the following constraints, $\varepsilon_N < \varepsilon_1 < \varepsilon_n$, $\varepsilon_N > \bar{\varepsilon}_2$, and $\beta > \gamma_n > \gamma_1$, are always valid for describing refraction effects. It is clearly seen that if weighted permittivity $\bar{\varepsilon}_2$ of all layers along the wave-propagation track from the object after scattering to antenna 2 is less than ε_N, then L_0 can be larger than L_0^*, and vice versa. In other words, one gets the constraint $\varepsilon_N > \bar{\varepsilon}_2$, which leads to

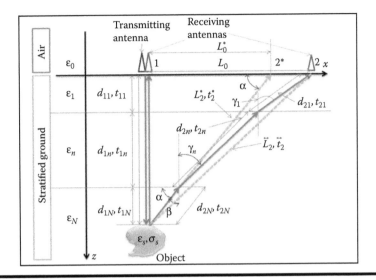

Figure 14.8 **The multilayer case accounting for the refraction phenomenon.**

$L_0 > L_0^*$. If, conversely, which may correspond to other material media, we present an inverse constraint $\varepsilon_N < \bar{\varepsilon}_2$, which leads to $L_0 < L_0^*$. Moreover, L_0 differs from L_0^*, except in the case of $\varepsilon_N = \bar{\varepsilon}_2$, which is not realistic for the proposed subsoil model.

In the realistic case related to the properties of subsoil media and schematically drawn in Figure 14.8, the RF wave changes direction according to the ratio of the refractive indexes or the layers' permittivity. Here, β and γ are the angles of the wave propagation in the corresponding environment through any two layers denoted by symbols i and j, respectively, relative to a vertical line at the point of refraction. In general, this situation can be described as a case in which there are N layers, and the RF wave, after scattering and diffraction from a buried object, propagates at an angle α relative to the horizontal axis (angle $\beta = 90 - \alpha$ relative to a vertical line; see Figure 14.8)

Now, we will show what has happened to Formulas 14.38, 14.39a and 14.39b that we developed above for the estimation of the depth L_1 and of the permittivity $\bar{\varepsilon}$ and used for the "virtual" case without accounting for the refraction L_1effect by converting them to the case of the multilayer model with the effect of refraction. We will use the same system operating with two antennas and will estimate the times t_1 and t_2 defined above. In the "virtual" case without refraction, we presented Formulas 14.37 and 14.38 for L_1 and L_2, respectively.

In Figure 14.8, the angle β was introduced as the angle of the line connecting the object scattering point and point 2* (see Figure 14.8), and defined as an angle of the reflected wave, γ_N, inside the N-layer, as the layer in which the buried object is placed; that is, $\beta \equiv \gamma_N$. The line is defined by a pair of parameters $\vec{t_2}$ and $\vec{L_2}$ as a "virtual" time and the "virtual" line that links the buried object with the receiving antenna located at point 2. The angle of this line is now $\vec{\beta}$, which is the angle of a straight line between the buried object and the line to the real receiving point. The pair of values, $\vec{t_2}$ and $\vec{L_2}$, determine the "virtual" time and the length of the "virtual" line accordingly. Now, to make a correct calculation, Expression 14.39a should be written as follows:

$$L_1 = L_0^* \frac{t_1}{\sqrt{(t_2^* + t_1)(t_2^* - t_1)}} \qquad (14.40)$$

But actually, we do not know the parameters L_0^* and t_2^*. In any case, we should estimate the error. If we calculate the depth of the buried object, as follows from (14.39a), we will take the data measurements of t_2, t_1, and L_0, and will estimate the depth $\underline{L_1}$ in the following manner:

$$\underline{L_1} = L_0 \frac{t_1}{\sqrt{(t_2 + t_1)(t_2 - t_1)}} = L_0 \frac{t_1}{\sqrt{t_2{}^2 - t_1{}^2}} \tag{14.41}$$

To obtain the correct value of L_1 in Formula 14.40 for a given L_0, it is required to take the time $\overrightarrow{t_2}$ instead of the time t_2, where the time $\overrightarrow{t_2}$ is the "virtual" time of wave propagation in a straight line, without refraction effect, between the scattering point of the buried object and the direction to the real receiving point 2. Time t_1 is the "real" time for this formula. Finally, we get

$$L_1 = L_0 \frac{t_1}{\sqrt{\overrightarrow{t_2}{}^2 - t_1{}^2}} \tag{14.42}$$

The calculation error $\Delta L_1 = L_1 - \underline{L_1}$ of L_1 is proportional to the absolute value of the corresponding time difference $\Delta t_2 = \overrightarrow{t_2} - t_2$. From Equation 14.42, we get several constraints:

1. If $\overrightarrow{t_2} > t_2$, then $L_1 < \underline{L_1}$
2. If $\overrightarrow{t_2} < t_2$, then $L_1 > \underline{L_1}$
3. If $\overrightarrow{t_2} = t_2$, then $L_1 = \underline{L_1}$

It is also clear that the difference $\Delta t_2 = \overrightarrow{t_2} = t_2$ is a function of scattering angle $\beta = \gamma_N$. As the angle β becomes closer to zero, the accuracy of estimation becomes higher. Depending on the created geometry, we can clearly see from Figure 14.8 that the signal path length $\overrightarrow{L_2}$ will always be larger than the actual signal path length L_2. A transit time of the signal t_{2n} for the actual n-layer is a function of the width of the layer and of the refractive index in this layer, $n_n = \sqrt{\varepsilon_n}$:

$$t_{2n} = \frac{d_{2n}\sqrt{\varepsilon_n}}{c} \tag{14.43}$$

from which it follows that

$$t_2 = \sum_{n=1}^{N} \frac{d_{2n}\sqrt{\varepsilon_n}}{c} \tag{14.44}$$

These two formulas indicate that the weight of the time t_{2n}, as a component of t_2, is greater for layers where ε_n is larger. And, vice versa, the weight of the time t_{2n} is smaller for layers with a smaller permittivity ε_n, although the angle γ_n is not changed from time t_{2n} to time t_{1n} in the transition between d_{2n} and d_{1n}.

As for the average permittivity, it becomes an important factor. Thus, if $\bar{\varepsilon} > \varepsilon_n$, it leads to the constraint $\gamma_n > \vec{\beta}$, and, conversely, if $\bar{\varepsilon} < \varepsilon_n$, to the constraint $t_{2n} > \vec{t}_{2n}$. It is also important to notice that $\vec{\beta}$ represents the weight (after averaging over all N layers) of permittivity $\bar{\varepsilon}$ via Snell's law:

$$\frac{\sin\vec{\beta}}{\sin\gamma_n} = \frac{\varepsilon_n}{\bar{\varepsilon}} \tag{14.45}$$

If $\bar{\varepsilon} < \varepsilon_n$, it means that for most of the layers, the angle γ_n of a propagation wave passing the layer with number n becomes bigger than angle $\vec{\beta}$, and a true path of the signal, d_{2n}, is longer than the width of the "virtual" path $\vec{d}_{2n}$ passing by the wave under the angle $\vec{\beta}$.

Similarly, we can estimate the difference between the validations of the real depth of the buried object, L_1, relative to the depth $\underline{L_1}$ calculated without refraction. Thus, according to the above-mentioned relationships, $t_{2n} = t_{1n}/\cos\gamma_n$ and $\vec{t}_{2n} = t_{1n}/\cos\vec{\beta}$, we get for a layer with number n the following differences between the real and the estimated time:

$$\vec{t}_{2n} - t_{2n} = t_{1n}\left(\frac{1}{\cos\vec{\beta}} - \frac{1}{\cos\gamma_n}\right) \tag{14.46}$$

Finally, the total error in the propagation time can be written as

$$\vec{t}_2 - t_2 = \sum_{n=1}^{N} t_{1n}\left(\frac{1}{\cos\vec{\beta}} - \frac{1}{\cos\gamma_n}\right) \tag{14.47}$$

It can be seen that the error in calculations of $\underline{L_1}$, resulting from introduction of the refraction effect, is proportional to the absolute value of Expression 14.47.

The average permittivity $\bar{\varepsilon}_2$ estimation was obtained using the expression

$$\bar{\varepsilon} = \frac{c^2 T_2(T_2 - T_1)}{L_0^2} = \frac{c^2(t_2 + t_1)(t_2 - t_1)}{L_0^2} = \frac{t_1^2 c^2}{\underline{L_1}^2} \tag{14.48}$$

The corresponding error of its estimation is proportional to the absolute value of Expression 14.47.

The relationships between the real average permittivity $\bar{\varepsilon}$ and the estimated average permittivity $\bar{\varepsilon}$ correspond to the following constraints: (a) if $\Delta t_2 = \vec{t}_2 - t_2 > 0$, then $\bar{\varepsilon}_2 < \bar{\varepsilon}$; (b) if $\vec{t}_2 - t_2 < 0$, then $\bar{\varepsilon}_2 > \bar{\varepsilon}$; (c) If $\vec{t}_2 - t_2 = 0$, then $\bar{\varepsilon}_2 = \bar{\varepsilon}$.

Hence, using the geometrical optic model, accounting for the refraction phenomenon occurring in each layer with number n, and without entering into discussion regarding the sign of the gradient of the refractive index, we can state that the depth of each layer in a multilayer subsoil structure, the depth of the buried object, and the average (weighting) permittivity of each layer and the buried object can be estimated with great accuracy.

This statement will be proved in Chapter 15 by the corresponding experimental tests.

References

1. Skolnik, M. I., *Introduction to Radar Systems*, 2nd edn, New York: McGraw-Hill, 1970.
2. Wait, J. R. (Ed.), *Electromagnetic Probing in Geophysics*, London: Golem Press, 1971.
3. Cook, J. C., Status of ground-probing radar and some recent experience, *Proceedings of Conference on Subsurface Exploration for Underground Excavation and Heavy Construction*, American Society of Civil Engineers, 175–194, 1974.
4. Morey, R. M., Continuous sub-surface profiling by impulse radar, *Proceedings of Conference on Subsurface Exploration for Underground Excavation and Heavy Construction*, American Society of Civil Engineers, 213–232, 1974.
5. Cook, J. C., Radar transparencies of mine and tunnel rocks, *Geophysics* 40, 865–885, 1975.
6. Kadava, P. K., Penetration of 1 GHz to 1.5 GHz electromagnetic waves into the earth surface for remote sensing applications, *Proceedings of IEEE SE Region 3 Conference* 48–50, 1976.
7. Daniels, D. J., D. J. Gunton, and H. F. Scott, Introduction to subsurface radar, *IEE Proceedings* 135 (4), 278–321, 1988.
8. McCann, D. M., D. J. Jackson, and P. J. Fenning, Comparison of the seismic and ground probing methods in geological surveying, *IEE Proceedings F* 135, 380–390, 1988.
9. Fisher, S. C., R. S. Steward, and M. J. Harry, Processing ground penetrating radar data, *Proceedings of 5th International Conference on Ground Penetrating Radar*, Kitchener, Canada, 1994.
10. Hamran, S., D. T. Gjessing, J. Hjelmstad, and E. Aarholt, *Ground Penetrating Synthetic Pulse Radar: Dynamic Range and Modes of Operation*, Amsterdam, Holland: Elsevier Science, 1995.
11. Murray, W., C. J. Williams, J. T. A. Pollock, P. Hatherly, and D. Hainsworth, Ground probing radar applications in the coal industry, *GPR '96 Proceedings*, Sendai, Japan, 1996.
12. Daniels, D. J., *Surface-Penetrating Radar*, London: Institute of Electrical Engineers, 1996.
13. Institute of Electrical Engineers, *IEE Proceedings on European Int. Conf. on the Detection of Abandoned Land Mines: A Humanitarian Imperative Seeking a Technical Solution*, Edinburgh, 7–9 October, 1996, Conference Publication Number 431, London.
14. Unterberger, R. R., Radar and sonar probing of salt, *Proceedings of 5th International Symposium on Salt*, Hamburg, Northern Ohio Geophysics Society, 423–437, 1978.
15. Evans, S., Radio techniques for the measurement of ice thickness, *Polar Rec* 11, 406–410, 1963.
16. Parkhomenko, E. I., *Electrical Properties of Rocks*, New York: Plenum Press, 1967.
17. Al-Attar, A., H. F. Scott, and D. J. Daniels, Wideband measurement of microwave characteristics of soils, *IEEE Electron Lett* 18, 192–198, 1982.
18. De Loor, G. P., Dielectric properties of wet materials, *IEEE Trans Geosci Remote Sens* 28, 364–369, 1983.
19. Scott, W. R. and G. S. Smith, Measured electrical constitutive parameters of soil as function of frequency and moisture content, *IEEE Trans Geosci Remote Sens* 30 (3), 621–623, 1992.
20. Wait, J. R. and K. A. Nabulsi, Performing an electromagnetic pulse in lossy medium, *IEEE Electron Lett* 26 (6), 542–543, 1992.
21. Wobschall, D., A theory of the complex dielectric permittivity of soil containing water. The semi-disperse model, *IEEE Trans Geosci Remote Sens* 15, 49–58, 1977.
22. Wang, J. R. and T. J. Schmugge, An empirical model for the complex dielectric permittivity of soil as a function of water content, *IEEE Trans Geosci Remote Sens* 18, 288–295, 1980.
23. Hoekstra, P., and A. Delaney, Dielectric properties of soils at UHF and microwave frequencies, *J Geophys Res* 79, 1699–1708, 1974.
24. Hipp, J. E., Soil electromagnetic parameters as functions of frequency, soil density and soil moisture, *Proc IEEE* 62 (1), 98–103, 1974.

25. Hallikainen, M. T., F. T. Ulaby, M. C. Dobson, M. A. Elrayes, and L. K. Wu, Microwave dielectric behavior of wet soil, Parts 1 and 2, *IEEE Trans Geosci Remote Sens* 23 (1), 25–34, 1985.
26. Ramm, A. G., *Multidimensional Inverse Scattering Problems*, London: Longman, 1992.
27. Witten, A. J., J. E. Molyneux, and J. E. Nyquist, Ground penetrating radar tomography: Algorithms and case studies. *IEEE Trans Geosci Remote Sens* 32 (2), 461–467, 1994.
28. Colton, D. and R. Kress, *Inverse Acoustic and Electromagnetic Scattering Theory*, New York: Springer, 1998.
29. Sanchez-de-la-Llave, A. Morales-Porras, M. Testorf, R. V. McGahan, and M. A. Fiddy, Nonlinear filtering of back propagated fields, *J Opt Soc Am A* 16, 1799–1807, 1999.
30. Johansen, P. M., A 2.5-D diffraction tomography inversion scheme for ground penetrating radar, *Proceedings of IEEE International Symposium on Antennas and Propagation* 3, 2132–2135, 1999.
31. Hansen, T. B., and P. M. Johansen, Inversion scheme for ground penetrating radar that takes into account the planar air-soil interface, *IEEE Trans Geosci Remote Sens* 38 (1), 496–506, 2000.
32. Jun Cui Tie and Weng Cho Chew, Novel diffraction tomographic algorithm for imaging two-dimensional targets buried under a lossy earth, *IEEE Trans Geosci Remote Sens* 38 (4), 2033–2041, 2000.
33. Jun Cui Tie and Weng Cho Chew, Diffraction tomographic algorithm for detection of three-dimensional objects in a lossy half-space, *IEEE Trans Antennas Propag* 50 (1), 42–49, 2002.
34. Lin-Ping Song, Qing Muo Liu, Fenghua Li, and Zhong Qing Zhang, Reconstruction of three-dimensional objects in layered media: Numerical experiment, *IEEE Trans Antennas Propag* 53 (4), 1556–1561, 2005.
35. Meincke, P., Efficient calculation of Born scattering for fixed-offset ground-penetrating radar surveys, *IEEE Geosci Remote Sens Lett* 4 (1), 88–92, 2007.
36. Qiuzhao Dong and C. M. Rappaport, Microwave subsurface imaging using direct finite-difference frequency-domain-based inversion, *IEEE Trans Geosci Remote Sens* 47 (11), 3664–3670, 2009.
37. Lo Monte, L., D. Erricolo, F. Soldovieri, and M. C. Wicks, Radio frequency tomography for tunnel detection, *IEEE Trans Geosci Remote Sens* 48 (3), 1128–1137, 2010.
38. Samelsohn, G. and R. Mazar, Path-integral analysis of scalar wave propagation in multiple-scattering random media, *Phys Rev Lett E* 54, 5697–5706, 1996.
39. Blaunstein, N., Recognition of foreign objects hidden in clutter by novel method of diffraction tomography, *Proceeding of IEEE Conference on Radar Applications*, Kiev, Ukraine, 2010, 5 pages.
40. Blaunstein, N., and Ch. Christodoulou, *Radio Propagation and Adaptive Antennas in Wireless Communication Links: Terrestrial, Atmospheric and Ionospheric*, Chapter 3, 1st edn, New Jersey: Wiley InterScience, 2007.
41. Cloude, S. R., A. Milne, C. Thornhill, and G. Crips, UWB SAR detection of dielectric targets, *IEE Proceedings on European Int. Conf. on the Detection of Abandoned Land Mines*, Edinburgh, 7–9 October, Conference Publication Number 431, 114–118, 1996.
42. Jaureguy, M. and P. Borderies, Modeling and processing of Ultra Wide Band scattering of buried targets, *IEE Proceedings on European Int. Conf. on the Detection of Abandoned Land Mines*, Edinburgh, 7–9 October, Conference Publication Number 431, 119–123, 1996.
43. Bezrodni', K. P., V. B. Boltintzev, and V. N. Ilyakhin, Geophysical testing of injection section of the behind-installed space by method of electromagnetic pulse ultra wide band sounding, *Journal of Civilian Construction* 5, 39–44, 2010 (in Russian).
44. Boltintzev, V. B., V. N. Ilyakhin, and K. P. Bezrodni', Method of electromagnetic ultra wide band pulse sounding of the surface medium, *Journal of Radio Electronics* 1, 39 pages, 2012 (in Russian).
45. Gavrilov, S. P., and A. A. Vertiy, Detection of the cylindrical object buried in dielectric half-space by using wave interference of the two different frequencies, *4th International Conference on Millimeter and Submillimeter Waves and Applications*, 20–23 July, San Diego, CA, 5 pages, 1998.
46. Vertiy, A. A., S. P. Gavrilov, and G. Gençay, Microwave tomography systems for investigation of the wave structure, *4th International Conference on Millimeter and Submillimeter Waves and Applications*, 20–23 July, San Diego, California, 5 pages, 1998.
47. Gavrilov, S. P. and A. A. Vertiy, Application of tomography method in millimeter wavelengths band, I. Theoretical, *IJIMW* 18 (9), 1739–1760, 1997.

48. Vertiy, A. A. and S. P. Gavrilov, Application of tomography method in millimeter wavelengths band, II. Experimental, *IJIMW* 18 (9), 1761–1781, 1997.

49. Vertiy, A. A. and S. P. Gavrilov, Modelling of microwave images of buried cylindrical objects, *IJIMW* 19 (9), 1201–1220, 1998.

50. Vertiy, A. A. and S. P. Gavrilov, Microwave imaging of cylindrical inhomogenities by using a plane wave spectrum of diffracted field, *Proceedings of International Conference on The Detection of Abandoned Land Mines*, Edinburgh, 12 October 1998.

51. Vertiy, A. A., S. P. Gavrilov, I. Yoynovskyy, A. Kudelya, V. Stepanuk, and B. Levitas, GPR and microwave tomography imaging of buried objects using the short-term (picosecond) video pulses, *Proceedings of 8th International Conference on Ground Penetrating Radar*, Gold Coast, Australia, 23–26 May, 530–534, 2000.

52. Mur, G., Absorbing boundary conditions for the finite-difference approximation of the time domain electromagnetic-field equations, *IEEE Trans Electromagn Compat* 23, 377–382, 1981.

53. Taflove A. and K. R. Pier, *Finite Element and Finite Difference Methods in Electromagnetic Scattering*, Chapter 8, London-New York, 1992.

54. Civanovic, S. S., K. S. Yee, and K. K. Mei, A subgridding method for the time-domain finite-difference method to solve Maxwell's equations, *IEEE Trans Microw Theory Techn* 39 (3), 218–226, 1991.

55. Luebbers, R., D. Steich, and K. Kuntz, FDTD calculation of scattering from frequency-dependent materials, *IEEE Trans Antennas Propag* 41 (9), 546–553, 1993.

56. Jayreguy, M. and P. Borderies, UWB remote sensing of multi-layer cylindrical scatterers, *IEEE Trans Antennas Propag* 2, 1454–1496, 1995.

57. Demarest, D., R. Plumb, and Z. Huang, FDTD modeling of scatterers in stratified media, *IEEE Trans Antennas Propag* 43 (10), 617–622, 1995.

58. Poggio, A. J., M. L. Van Blaricum, E. K. Miller, and R. Mittra, Evaluation of a processing technique for transient data, *IEEE Trans Antennas Propag* 26, 165–173, New York, 1978.

59. Cloude, S. R., P. D. Smith, A. Milne, D. Parkes, and K. Trafford, Analysis of time domain UWB radar signals, *SPIE, Pulse Engineering* January 1992, Denver, Co, 111–122, 1631.

60. Bolomey, J. Ch. and Ch. Pichot, Microwave tomography: From theory to practical imaging systems, *Int J Imag Syst Tech* 2, 144–156, 1990.

61. Dourthe, C. and G. Pichot, Microwave imaging algorithms for arbitrary space and time incident waveforms using ultra wide bandwidth GPR technique. *IEEE Proceedings on European International Conference on Detection of Abandoned Land Mines*, Edinburgh, 7–9 October, 431, 124–126, 1996.

62. Van Blaricum, M. L. and R. Mittra, A technique for extracting the poles and residues of a system directly from its transient response, *IEEE Trans Antennas Propag* 23, 777–781, 1975.

63. Moore, J. and A. Ling, Super-resolved time-frequency analysis of wideband backscattered data, *IEEE Trans Antennas Propag* 43, 623–626, 1995.

64. Ruck, G. T., D. E. Barrick, W. D. Stuart, and C. K. Krichbaum, *Radar Cross Section Handbook*, Chapter 4, New York, Plenum, 1970.

65. Iizuka, K. and A. P. Freundofer, Detection of nonmetallic buried objects by a step frequency radar, *Proc IEEE* 71, 274–279, 1983.

66. Chan, L. C., D. L. Moffat and L. Peters, Subsurface radar target imaging estimates, *Proc IEEE* 67, 991–1000, 1979.

67. Warhus, J. P., E. Jeffrey, J. E. Mast, and E. M. Johansson, Advanced ground-penetrating radar, *Proc SPIE*, Special Issue, 2275–2279, 1994.

68. Chommeloux, L., Ch. Pichot, and J. Ch. Bolomey, Electromagnetic modeling for microwave imaging of cylindrical buried inhomogeneities, *IEEE Trans Microw Theory Techn* 34 (10), 1064–1076, 1986.

69. Kalmykov, A. I., I. M. Fuks., V. N. Tsymbal, I. V. Shcherbinin, O. Ya. Matveyev, A. S. Gavrilenko, M. E. Fiks, and V. D. Freilikher, Radar observations of strong subsurface scatterers. A model of back-scattering, *Telecomm Radio Eng* 52.i5.10, 1–17, 1998.

70. Mejibovsky, M. and N. Blaunstein, Geometric-optical model of radio wave refraction in multi-layered sub-soil media and its verification via GPR experiments, *Proceedings of IEEE Workshop on Radar Methods and Systems*, Kiev, Ukraine, 6 pages, September 27–28, 2016.

Chapter 15

ESP/UWB Radar Systems Applications

15.1 ESP/UWB Radar Operation Methodology

An Extremely-short-pulse ultra-wideband (ESP/UWB) radar uses a very wide bandwidth to ensure that the scatter energy from any target buried in a host (subsoil) medium extends from low to high frequencies in the frequency domain. This provides information on the structure, material, and shape of the desired target, which can then be used for detection, identification and classification.

It is well known [1–4] that the field scattered by a target illuminated by a UWB pulse contains a lot of information about high-resolution imaging for localization and identification of diffracting centers of the target under investigation (based on the methods of diffraction tomography described in Section 14.3.3); dispersive features of the media surrounding such an object and the corresponding resonances of its "response" to radiation in the frequency domain; and polarization characteristics, which can be useful in detecting and identifying the object [5–13].

These characteristics and parameters should include those related to the medium, such as surface roughness, volume heterogeneities, and frequency dispersion, as well as those related to the measurement devices of the UWB sensing system, such as pulse duration, pulse shape, output power, and types and form of receiving and transmitting antennas. Moreover, to extract from the measured data useful information on the target or medium under testing, these data from scattered signals should be accurate enough to highlight the most important features of the tested object, before introducing the corresponding numerical methods.

As was shown in Chapter 4, an electromagnetic wave, spreading in the medium, undergoes the processes of absorption and reflection, which in turn are determined by the medium's personal properties, such as dielectric permittivity and conductivity; polarization; residence time of the self-oscillations; composition homogeneity; and the medium's porosity and humidity.

The ESP/UWB technique of electromagnetic remote sensing is based on synthesizing the image of geological sections or mineral-containing layers, or engineering reconstruction of the structure of objects under testing, according to the reflected signal during the spreading of electromagnetic pulses of a few nanoseconds in duration.

The proposed technique is a variation of the subsurface sensing radar method, based on the finite-difference time-domain (FDTD) framework as the most appropriate method to model electromagnetic scattering of a buried object by a UWB pulse (see Section 14.3.4). It uses the operating principle of the pulse radar rangefinder for measurement data gathering and subsurface structure identification technology, as a set of dynamic systems with the space variable parameters. Furthermore, it accounts for the soil properties and the constitution and shape of the buried target. Another advantage of the FDTD framework is its ability to take into account large computational data and volumes of signal pre- and post-processing due to its computational power. Indeed, EMP UWB sensing technology based on elements of the FDTD framework allows various natural and artificial objects to be surveyed to a depth of 150 m or more.

Any subsurface structure has its own specific set of similar characteristics. It is theoretically possible to identify any engineering–geological structure by measuring its absorption and reflection characteristics. If the transit time and velocity of the signal coming from the object to the receiver are also known, then it is easy to calculate the distance to the object. For these purposes, a geometrical optic model was proposed in Section 14.3.5, which allows us to estimate not only the depth and permittivity of the buried object, but also these parameters for each layer in a multilayer subsoil inhomogeneous structure with its own parameters.

However, at any sensing point, there is a complex interlacing of structure, with the subsurface horizons being unrestrictedly oriented in space, and the engineering–geological elements themselves can have different inclusions, such as bubbles and cavities. As a result, the signal received at the particular location of geophysical monitoring is a superposition of many reflections and attenuations, and the process of structure identification and measuring distance becomes extremely difficult.

15.2 Problems in ESP/UWB Radar Operation

In the ESP/UWB approach, by using the FDTD numerical technique, the dielectric and magnetic losses of material of buried objects or subsoil structures (minerals, tunnels, mines, etc.) are taken into account conventionally through real electric and magnetic constants and conductivities [1–4]. There are several problems that need to be addressed here.

The first problem is the high sampling rate in joint time and space domains [1–4], imposed by the shortest significant wavelengths included in the pulse spectrum. It is inversely proportional to the refractive index of the material (via its permittivity and permeability) and should be enough to satisfy boundary conditions at air-to-ground and soil-to-object levels. Thus, due to multipath phenomena from rays scattered from subsoil clutter in which a target is hidden, many spurious reflections are observed, as shown in Figure 15.1, according to [3,4].

It is clearly seen that the short pulse of (T_p −15–20 ns) sent to the buried object returns with a huge spread in the time domain, with strong oscillations caused by the multiscattering and multidiffraction phenomena from the layered heterogeneous structure of the subsoil and from the target itself.

The second problem is the influence of ground, or the target surface (called the *Huygens surface* in [1–4]), which clearly responds to actual situations in which the scatterer is fully surrounded by subsoil clutter, and one should take into account the scattered and diffracted waves and separate them from each other, accounting for the reflections from a flat or rough interface and the multilayered subsoil medium.

The third problem is with the absorbing boundaries, air–soil and soil–target (object), that occur in host media containing inhomogeneous structures in their vicinity. This leads to loss due to absorption by materials, a parameter that plays an important role in detection of buried targets.

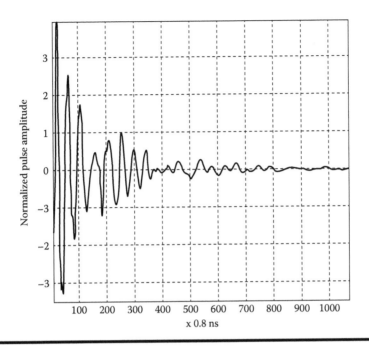

Figure 15.1   Spread and multiray effect of the ultrashort pulse in the time domain. The scale along the horizontal axis is 0.8 ns per point.

The fourth problem is the frequency dispersion in materials of buried objects. This effect is caused by dependence of complex dielectric permittivity and magnetic permeability, which vary significantly with changes of radiated frequency in most kinds of soil [5–10]. Therefore, it is necessary to account for the presence of such dispersive materials. Finally, the "response" of the tested target or object in the frequency domain will spread over the frequency range, with a masking effect on target detection and identification, as is clearly seen from Figure 15.2, according to [1,2]. At the ranges of 20–60 and 80–120 MHz, there are several maxima that may mask the object "response" observed around 30 MHz (see Figure 15.2).

To overcome the problems occurring in such conditions, a positive result can be achieved through the following key task solutions:

- Generating an electromagnetic pulse with optimum bandwidth and sufficient power
- Quality manufacturing of receiving and transmitting antennas
- Providing a wide dynamic range of the signal-receiving appliances, which actually determine the sensing depth
- Creating an efficient algorithm for processing the received signal

15.3 ESP/UWB System Operational Characteristics

The proposed ESP/UWB sensing technique combines the latest achievements in the field of high-power voltage nanosecond pulse generation, in the quality of electromagnetic radiation to subsurface structures, and in receiving wideband signals.

Small nanosecond generators, with a peak power up to hundreds of kilowatts per pulse, have been developed based on new semiconductor contact-breaking switches. Using these has

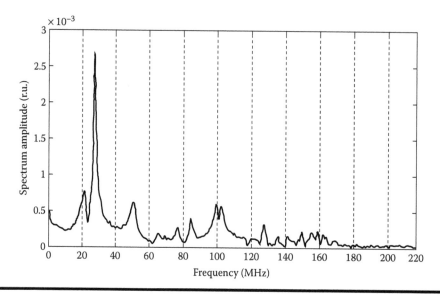

Figure 15.2   A sample of the scattered power spectrum in the frequency domain for an object buried in the subsoil medium at the depth of several meters.

allowed a series of generators to be developed, providing a frequency band from 10 MHz to 3 GHz.

The measuring complex is equipped with broadband antennas that are well matched with the transmission paths and have high sensitivity to the received signal.

The main condition for obtaining wide depth of sensing and high accuracy of identification of geotechnical differences is a special mathematical program for signal processing, combined with a large experimental database, composed according to EMP UWB research results for numerous objects.

All the information coming from different horizons is displayed and recorded "in the field" in the timeline—in nanoseconds. Determination of the horizons' actual position in the metric scale L (along the depth section) is performed according to the formula $L = c \cdot \Delta t / 2\sqrt{\varepsilon'_{ref}}$, $c = 3 \times 10^8$ m/s is the velocity of light; Δt is the sounding signal delay; and ε'_{ref} is the real part of the effective normalized dielectric permittivity. The sounding signal delay is measured by the receiver, and the ε'_{ef} values can be determined individually for every buried object separately during tests.

We will present in this section one of the examples of existing UWB remote sensing systems (RSSs) according to [1,2]. The whole complex of the UWB sensing system consists of

- A pulse generator with peak pulse amplitude of 4.77 kV, duration from 1 to 10 ns, and clock speed of pulse frequency 10 kHz
- Receiving and transmitting broadband antennas, metrologically certified over the frequency band from 10 to 1200 MHz
- Receiving and recording device (oscilloscope) with high noise immunity, providing a record of signals received in the field environment
- A microcomputer for digital information dubbing and its subsequent processing for the section constructing in the geophysical data collection point

The whole field apparatus complex can be powered by a direct current (DC) voltage of 12 V. The apparatus power consumption is no more than a few hundred watts. The set weight is up to 15 kg. The corresponding narrow-beam broadband meter and decimeter wavelength antennas allow operators to use a wide spectrum in the frequency domain and to achieve better sensitivity in the detection and identification of buried objects.

15.4 Applications of Ground-Penetrating Radars and RSSs

Extensive experiments have been conducted during recent years to estimate the imaging capabilities of objects buried in different soils by side looking real aperture radar (SLRAR) and synthetic aperture radar (SAR).

Experiments were conducted over different soil zones. Gas and water mains have been observed as major strong subsurface scatterers. Multifrequency airborne radar system (MARS) has been used as a powerful tool for these investigations [12,13]. The MARS system consists of two SLRARs with wavelength $\lambda = 0.8$ cm (vertical-to-vertical (v-v) and horizontal-to-horizontal (h-h) polarizations) and 3 cm (polarization v-v), and two SARs with $\lambda = 23$ and 180 cm (polarizations v-v, v-h, h-h, h-v). The azimuthal resolution of all radars ranges from 25 to 100 m, depending on the wavelength of operation. The most important feature of MARS for subsurface imaging is the synchronous use of $\lambda = 0.8$ cm, 3 cm, 23 cm, and 1.8 m radars at all kinds of polarization. While $\lambda = 0.8$ and 3 cm signals are reflected by vegetation and interface, waves with $\lambda = 23$ cm and 1.8 m penetrate into soil, their penetration depths being large enough (but significantly different). Simultaneous processing of images in these four bands enables us to separate reflections from interface and from buried objects and to map subsurface structures.

Some interesting features have been revealed during observations of buried pipelines:

- The azimuthal orientation of a pipe does not practically affect the contrast of its radar image.
- The horizontal polarization contrast (the electrical field vector is perpendicular to the plane of incidence) always exceeds the vertical one; the subsurface object is not observable very often on vertical polarization, especially for incidence angles $\theta > 30°$.
- The horizontal polarization contrast of the radar image increases slightly with the angle of incidence for $\theta \sim 30°–60°$.

Finally, the contrast dependence on incidence angle θ does not conform to habitual conceptions: the contrast must decrease with θ, since the reflection coefficient of a horizontally polarized electromagnetic wave from a flat interface always increases with θ, and the transmission coefficient must decrease. Again, an inverse dependence has been observed. The same main features of backscattering from buried pipelines (independence from pipe orientation and strong dependence on polarization) have been disclosed in areas with clay soils. Therefore, it seems reasonable to say that these features are typical for radar imaging of lengthy, strongly reflecting objects under a soil layer, and depend only slightly on the soil type.

Another campaign of experiments was reported in [14–20], in which special ground-penetrating radars (GPRs) were designed, and then, corresponding microwave measurements by use of RSSs were carried out for the optimization of each unit and to prove the usefulness of subsurface diffraction tomography methods in the pre-processing stage of detection and identification of buried objects or objects located in clutter. In this section, we briefly present these results.

Table 15.1 Main Parameters of the GPR

Parameter	Value	Unit	Notes
Operating frequency	1900–3700	MHz	
Microwave radiating power	≤100.0	mW	Pick value in active mode
Dynamic range	90	dB	
Data collection rate	0–2500	points/s	New frequencies per second
PC interface	Serial		RS232 or USB
Power supply (DC: 12–24 V)	≤15	W	Pick value in active mode
Weight of the unit	≤1.5	kg	
Dimensions	≤160×100×60	mm	

Thus, [16–20] reported on the use of microwave GPR for detection of people under ruins and behind walls, as well as detection and identification of mines. It was shown that the creation of a portable microwave measurement unit is an important part of the research, for several reasons. First of all, the application of subsurface tomography processing imposes specific requirements on the technical specification of the underlying data-collection hardware, which unfortunately cannot be satisfied by existing instruments, if the time taken for image reconstruction and convenience of work are a matter of concern. The corresponding requirements are

- Wide frequency range of operation, at least twice the initial frequency
- Ability to measure the transmission coefficient on thousands of frequencies per second
- High microwave frequency stability
- Built-in hardware means of compensation for huge first reflection from air/medium interface
- Wide dynamic range and linearity to be able to recover a weak useful signal from the target in the presence of huge background signals from the interface
- Minimum weight, size, and power consumption

The main technical specifications of one of the GPRs developed for the measurement are summarized in Table 15.1 according to [15–20].

15.4.1 Detection, Imaging, and Identification of Small Local Buried Objects

We will start with some useful applications of GPRs regarding detection of mines buried in subsoil medium, because this is a real problem around the world. The tomography principle of deriving images allows images to be obtained of a vertical cut, in the case of 1-D scanning, and both vertical and horizontal cuts, in the case of 2-D scanning. The experimental setup according to [15–20] is schematically presented in Figure 15.3.

Figure 15.4 shows print screen images obtained during real measurements of dielectric (antipersonnel) and metal (antitank) mines buried in subsoil media at depths varying from 11 to 18.5 cm

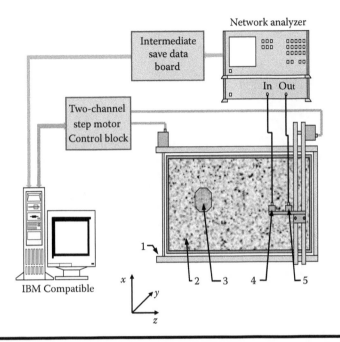

Figure 15.3 Schematic view of experimental setup: 1—XY scanner; 2—medium; 3—target; 4—receiving antenna; 5—transmitting antenna. (Rearranged from Gavrilov, S.P. and Vertiy, A.A., *IJIMW*, 18(9), 1739–1760, 1997; Vertiy, A.A. and Gavrilov, S.P., *IJIMW*, 18(9), 1761–1781, 1997; Vertiy, A.A. and Gavrilov, S.P., *IJIMW*, 19(9), 1201–1220, 1998; Vertiy, A.A. and Gavrilov, S.P., *Proceedings of the International Conference on the Detection of Abandoned Land Mines*, Edinburgh, 12 October 1998.)

(data was summarized from [16–20]). Here in the left panels, top and bottom, of Figure 15.4, an image of buried mines (denoted by white and dark) is clearly seen in the soil, with the surrounding stones as specific clutter for each slice.

The same shape of buried mines (surrounded by stones as clutter) is clearly seen from the right panels, top and bottom, in which each slice, which presents images in the vertical plane, corresponds to the specific depth from 11 to 18.5 cm.

The next series of experiments were carried out for the detection and identification of tunnels. We present only one example from many similar published in [16–19]. Thus, in Figure 15.5, the first experimental setup of GPR (a) is shown with a photo of the cross view of the real tunnel (b), while (c) presents the obtained image of a real tunnel at the depth of 8–10 m after pre-processing using elements of diffraction tomography.

The above examples, although only a few, show that the created experimental prototypes of a GPR imaging system with special pre-processing, based on elements of diffraction tomography, allow buried objects to be obtained with sufficiently high resolution and image quality, and experimental data to be processed at a rate sufficient for image reconstruction during the process of scanner movement.

It was shown in [14,15] that the maximum speed of the surface analysis does not exceed 10 cm/s and is limited by the maximum velocity of scanner movement in a transversal direction.

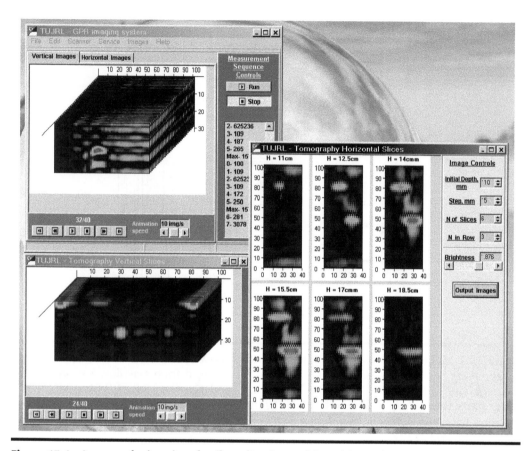

Figure 15.4 Images of mines in subsoil media (denoted by white and dark) obtained by developed tomography system: left panels (top and bottom) show slices in the vertical plane along each depth; right panels show vertical photo of each slice of the mines buried at depths from 11 to 18.5 cm. (Summarized from Gavrilov, S.P. and Vertiy, A.A., *IJIMW*, 18(9), 1739–1760, 1997; Vertiy, A.A. and Gavrilov, S.P., *IJIMW*, 18(9), 1761–1781, 1997; Vertiy, A.A. and Gavrilov, S.P., *IJIMW*, 19(9), 1201–1220, 1998; Vertiy, A.A. and Gavrilov, S.P., *Proceedings of the International Conference on the Detection of Abandoned Land Mines*, Edinburgh, 12 October 1998.)

The examples presented show the efficiency of pre-processing based on novel approaches in diffraction tomography for the detection and identification of different kinds of buried mines, from small (antipersonnel) to large (antitank), as well as the detection of tunnels at depths up to 10–15 m.

15.4.2 Detection and Identification of Minerals and Subsoil Structures

A set of experimental tests carried out in various sand and ground media using an ESP/UWB remote sensing system was described in [3,4] (see also bibliography therein), where 45 experimental measurements were carried out. During measurements, at each point of observation, an electromagnetic pulse signal was radiated to the subsurface environment, and at the same time, its response was registered by the radar complex.

During measurements, the experimentally determined relative effective dielectric permittivity of the rocks in the surveyed area was found to be $\varepsilon = 10$ (corresponding to 1 ns per 0.0475 m).

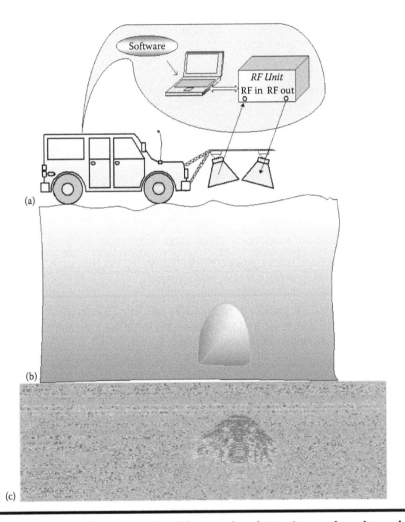

Figure 15.5 (a) GPR setup, (b) cross section of the tunnel, and (c) an image of a real tunnel after pre-processing using elements of diffraction tomography. (Rearranged from Gavrilov, S.P. and Vertiy, A.A., *4th International Conference on Millimeter and Submillimeter Waves and Applications*, San Diego, CA, 5, 20–23 July, 1998; Vertiy, A.A. et al., *4th International Conference on Millimeter and Submillimeter Waves and Applications*, San Diego, CA, 5, 20–23 July, 1998.)

For calculation of the depth scale, the complex effective dielectric permittivity value $\varepsilon'_{ef} = 10$, obtained during the experiment carried out in the tested area, was used. This means that the timeline of 400 ns should be understood as a depth interval, equal to 19.0 m. On the basis of the above calculations, the maximum depth of the surveyed geologic formation was determined to be equal to 133 m. The results of one of the tested underground areas (according to [3,4]) are shown in Figure 15.6.

As a method for analyzing the signal spectral characteristics and presenting the information, the following evaluation criteria of frequency spectra were chosen.

■ The frequency interval from 20 to 40 MHz, from 70 to 80 MHz, and from 120 to 170 MHz, which correspond to testing points PS-56 to PS-40, respectively in Figure 15.6, in the

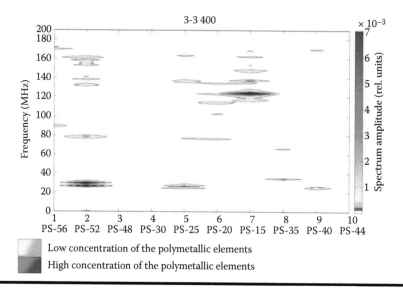

Figure 15.6   The distribution pattern of frequencies with the characteristic values of the spectral density of the signal spectrum and its relationship with the concentration of polymetallic elements in the points along one of the tested areas.

reflected electromagnetic signals indicates the presence of minerals (polymetallic elements) in the area sections.

■ In the frequency interval from 20 to 55 MHz (points PS-56, PS-52, and PS-25) and from 120 to 140 MHz (for points PS-20, PS-15, PS-35), polymetallic elements with high values of permittivity, permeability, and conductivity were found, accompanied by high density of metal components.

■ In the frequency interval 20-40 MHz (points PS-35 to PS-40 in Fig. 15.6), 80-90 MHz (points PS-56 to PS-48), and 120-170 MHz (PS-25 to PS-15), in the affected polymetallic elements with low values of permittivity, permeability, and conductivity were found, accompanied by low density of metal components.

The value of the signal spectral power depends on the concentration of objects buried in the subsoil medium, and therefore, it can be easily differentiated and assigned as having a high or low concentration of polymetallic elements. In this way, two types of polymetallic element concentration in the tested area were distinguished: high and low concentration.

Another interesting result of real-time testing of hot slants buried in subsoil sand media is shown in Figure 15.7 according to [3,4]. The soil surface relief is shown in the top layer, while the hot slants boundary relief is shown in the bottom layer.

Finally, we present an example of the use of UWB RSS for the detection of moving and stationary foreign objects in underwater environments.

15.4.3 Detection of Foreign Objects in Underwater Environments

This is a typical example from a large series of experimental tests carried out in underwater environments (lake, pool, and river) for the detection of foreign objects hidden under the water–air surface

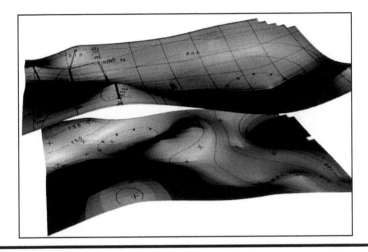

Figure 15.7 View of post-processing data of regular soil layer (top) and the upper boundary layer of the subsoil area filled by hot slants (bottom). (According to Bezrodni, K.P., et al., *Journal of Civilian Construction*, 5, 39–44, 2010; Boltintzev, V.B., et al., *Journal of Radio Electronics*, 1, 39, 2012.)

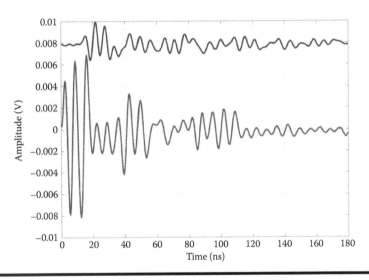

Figure 15.8 The time spread of the received pulse signal without diver (upper trace) and with diver (lower trace) located at a depth of 8 m.

at depths from 3 to 10 m. Thus, the upper trace in Figure 15.8 shows the corresponding radio pulse amplitude variations at a receiver antenna located in a lake 50 m wide and 60 m long, at a depth of 5–8 m. The transmitting antenna was located at the same depth. In the lower trace in Figure 15.8, the same time-pulse amplitude dependence is shown when a diver crosses the virtual line between the receiver and the transmitter, swimming across the middle of the lake at a depth of 8 m.

The corresponding spectra of two events, without and with the diver, are shown in Figure 15.9a and b, respectively.

It is clearly seen from Figures 15.8 and 15.9 that despite a strong multipath due to multiple reflections and scattering from the side contours of the lake and from its bottom, the presence of

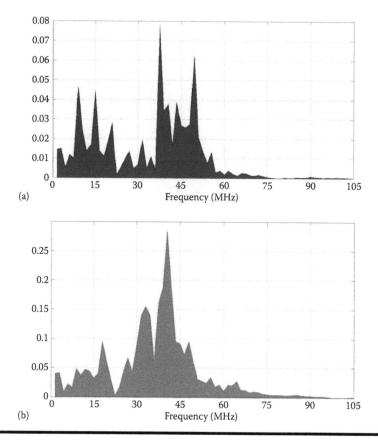

(a)

(b)

Figure 15.9   Spectra of the pulse signal (a) without diver and (b) with diver.

the diver leads to the occurrence of strong signal peaks both in the time domain (Figure 15.8, lower trace) and in the frequency domain (Figure 15.9b).

The same response is given by a stationary metallic scuba cylinder either 20 cm or 30 cm in diameter located at a depth of 5 m at the middle of the pool between the virtual straight line connecting the transmitter and the receiver placed at the opposite sites of the pool. It can be clearly seen from the signal pulse time spread and its amplitude time deviations, presented in Figure 15.10.

The corresponding post-processing data for the imaging of the scuba cylinders, large and small, is shown in Figure 15.11. First, the large and small scuba cylinders were hidden in the water (first left image at the top water layer). In the upper right of the picture, an image obtained during the second experiment, where only a large scuba cylinder was in the water, and then both cylinders were outside the water, are presented. In the upper right of the picture, an image obtained during the second experiment, where only the large scuba cylinder was in the water (denoted as "in") and then it was outside the water (denoted as "out"), is clearly presented.

15.4.4 GPR Experiments for Verification of the Geometrical Optic Model

Finally, to prove the geometrical optic model described in Chapter 14, two actual experiments were carried out, as described in [21]. The performance of an accurate GPR experiment is a complex process that requires knowledge of the subsoil medium at a depth up to 10 m at least and the

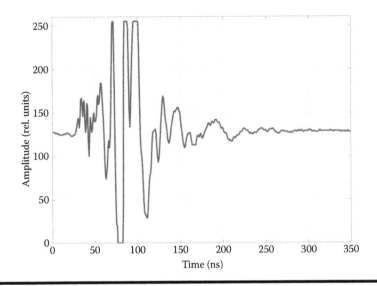

Figure 15.10   Time variations of the received signal amplitude from a metallic cylinder located at the depth of 5 m in the middle of the lake between the source and the detector.

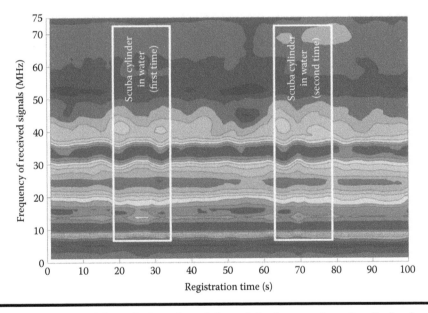

Figure 15.11   Imaging of the cylinders, from left to right: large and small cylinder; large cylinder (without small one); without both cylinders.

use of an object large enough to regain the signals very clearly. Both studies used a GPR with a frequency range from 1 to 200 MHz. The device was completed by different antennas with various frequency ranges available, with a center (carrier) frequency varying from 15 to 150 MHz and sizes in the unfolded form of 1–10 m, accordingly.

The transmitter has the following parameters: a signal voltage of 10 kV, a pulse power of 10 mW, and a pulse duration of 1–20 ns. The transmitter power is regulated by attenuators between

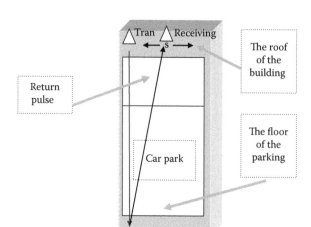

Figure 15.12   General plan of the location.

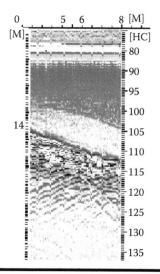

Figure 15.13   Radarogram of the experiment.

0 and 120 dB. The data acquisition and processing program allows real-time combination of GPR scanning and global positioning system (GPS) data, as well as building 3-D imaging.

In the first experiment, the tested signals were recorded after reflection from the floor of an underground car park. The existing garage was in the basement of the house at a depth of 2.5 m (see Figure 15.12). The medium of the experiment was measured quite accurately, and an additional experiment was conducted to compare the results of the simulation according to the geometrical optic model with experimental data. In this experiment, the GPR operated from the roof of the building placed above the underground car park. The possible work area was limited to 8 m. The depth of measurement from the floor of the car park to the transmitting antenna was 14.1 m. Figure 15.12 represents a drawing of the building.

In Figure 15.13, we present the imaging radiogram of the radar received during the experiment.

Figure 15.14 shows the result of calculation of depth L_1 for 15 points that cover the angle range from 16° to 30°. The L_1 is the real depth of the actual bottom floor, whereas the "L_1 calculated by GPR" is the calculated depth L_1 according to the geometrical optic model.

In Figure 15.15, we present the relative error in L_1, as a function of angle β (in degrees).

From the data obtained during measurements and use of the proposed optical approximation model, we can easily calculate the average dielectric coefficient $\bar{\varepsilon}$. The results of its numerical computations and comparison with experimental data are shown in Figure 15.16.

The relatively small error between the simulated and measured data proves the validity of the proposed method in Section 14.3.5, based on geometrical optic [21]. At the same time, the result obtained allows us to improve calculations by decreasing the distance between the antennas.

The second experiment was based on the pulse returns from a train tunnel built at a depth that was not known accurately. It was based on a GPR program and allowed separation between the transmitter and the receiver. Unlike standard GPR operational work, the transmitter remained fixed in one place. In this case, a radar output imaginary picture presents the lines going up and down at a certain angle along the experiment. The possible work area was not limited to 8 m as in the previous experiment. At the same time, the depth of the tunnel was not accurately known,

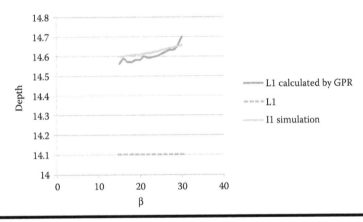

Figure 15.14 Depth of the underground structure L_1 calculated by GPR and L_1 from simulation (both in meters) vs. the angle β (in degrees) compared with the real depth of the buried object L_1.

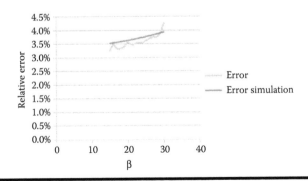

Figure 15.15 Relative error in L_1 estimation, as a function of angle β.

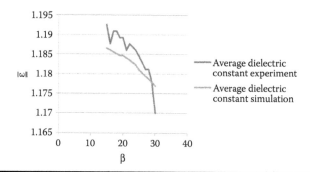

Figure 15.16 Average permittivity $\bar{\varepsilon}$ vs. scattering angle β (in degrees).

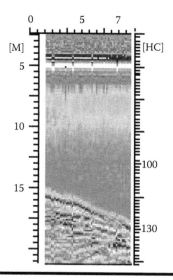

Figure 15.17 Imaging of the subsoil structure regarding the second experiment.

and the depth in relation to the tunnel entrance was measured with GPS. Finally, it was measured at close to 16.5 m.

In Figure 15.17, the corresponding radarogram received during the experiment is presented.

Figure 15.18 shows the results after the calculation of the depth of the tunnel, L_1, for 15 different points. Here, L_1 is the depth of the tunnel roof, and the denoted "L_1 calculated by GPR" is the calculated depth L_1 using the developed geometrical optic model.

In this case, the relative error cannot be calculated, because the accurate depth of the tunnel was unknown, but roughly equal to 16.6 m. We can say that average error changes over the range from 0.2 m to 0.5 m.

From these data, the average permittivity was estimated, and the results of these computations are depicted in Figure 15.19 as a function of the distance between the transmitting and the receiving antennas, L_0 (in meters). It is seen that because, during the second experiment, the depth of the buried object was not accurately measured, we observe wide changes of the tested soil permittivity, which is not so far from the real measured parameter equaling ~4.2 by use of geological methods.

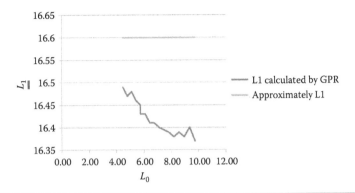

Figure 15.18 **Depth L_1 calculated by GPR and $\underline{L_1}$ from simulation as function of L_0 (all in meters) relative to real L_1.**

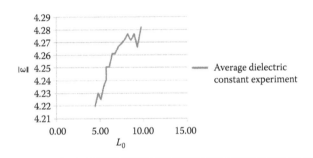

Figure 15.19 **Average permittivity $\bar{\varepsilon}$ as a function of L_0 (in meters).**

These experiments proved the theory developed in the previous sections. Accuracy of calculation can be improved by decreasing the distance between the transmitting and the receiving antenna.

Generally speaking, all the experiments presented in this chapter, along with other numerous examples presented in the bibliography and in [15–21], allow us to outline that ESP/UWB radar and remote sensing systems can be successfully used for the detection and identification of buried objects of various natures, different kinds of minerals, and different constructions, hidden in the subsoil or other material media.

References

1. Cloude, S. R., A. Milne, C. Thornhill, and G. Crips, UWB SAR detection of dielectric targets, *IEE Proceedings on European International Conference on the Detection of Abandoned Land Mines*, Edinburgh, 7–9 October, 114–118, 1996.
2. Jaureguy, M. and P. Borderies, Modeling and processing of ultra wide band scattering of buried targets, *IEE Proceedings on European International Conference on the Detection of Abandoned Land Mines*, Edinburgh, 7–9 October, 119–123, 1996.
3. Bezrodni, K. P., V. B. Boltintzev, and V. N. Ilyakhin, Geophysical testing of injection section of the behind-installed space by method of electromagnetic pulse ultra wide band sounding, *Journal of Civilian Construction* (5), 39–44, 2010 (in Russian).

4. Boltintzev, V. B., V. N. Ilyakhin, and K. P. Bezrodni', Method of electromagnetic ultra wide band pulse sounding of the surface medium, *Journal of Radio Electronics* (1), 39, 2012 (in Russian).

5. Kadava, P. K., Penetration of 1 GHz to 1.5 GHz electromagnetic waves into the earth surface for remote sensing applications, *Proceedings of the IEEE SE Region 3 Conference*, Kiev, Former USSR, 48–50, 1976.

6. Daniels, D. J., D. J. Gunton, and H. F. Scott, Introduction to subsurface radar, *IEE Proc* 135(4), 278–321, 1988.

7. McCann, D. M., D. J. Jackson, and P. J. Fenning, Comparison of the seismic and ground probing methods in geological surveying, *IEE Proc F* 135, 380–390, 1988.

8. Fisher, S. C., R. S. Steward, and M. J. Harry, Processing ground penetrating radar data, *Proceedings of the 5th International Conference on Ground Penetrating Radar*, Kitchener, Canada, 9, 1994.

9. Hamran, S., D. T. Gjessing, J. Hjelmstad, and E. Aarholt, *Ground Penetrating Synthetic Pulse Radar: Dynamic Range and Modes of Operation*. Delft, The Netherlands: Elsevier Science, 1995.

10. Murray, W., C. J. Williams, J. T. A. Pollock, P. Hatherly, and D. Hainsworth, Ground probing radar applications in the coal industry, *GPR '96 Proceedings*, Sendai, Japan, 8, 1996.

11. Unterberger, R. R., Radar and sonar probing of salt, *Proceedings of the 5th International Symposium on Salt*, Hamburg, Northern Ohio Geological Society, 423–437, 1978.

12. Daniels, D. J., *Surface-Penetrating Radar*, London, England: Institute of Electrical Engineers, 1996.

13. *IEE Proceedings on European International Conference on the Detection of Abandoned Land Mines: A Humanitarian Imperative Seeking a Technical Solutions*, Edinburgh, 7–9 October, 1996.

14. Gavrilov, S. P. and A. A. Vertiy, Detection of the cylindrical object buried in dielectric half-space by using wave interference of the two different frequencies, *4th International Conference on Millimeter and Submillimeter Waves and Applications*, San Diego, CA, 5, July 20–23, 1998.

15. Vertiy, A. A., S. P. Gavrilov, and G. Gençay, Microwave tomography systems for investigation of the wave structure, *4th International Conference on Millimeter and Submillimeter Waves and Applications*, San Diego, CA, 5, July 20–23, 1998.

16. Gavrilov, S. P. and A. A. Vertiy, Application of tomography method in millimeter wavelengths band. I. Theoretical, *International Journal of Infrared and Millimeter Waves* 18(9), 1739–1760, 1997.

17. Vertiy, A. A. and S. P. Gavrilov, Application of tomography method in millimeter wavelengths band. II. Experimental, *International Journal of Infrared and Millimeter Waves* 18(9), 1761–1781, 1997.

18. Vertiy, A. A. and S. P. Gavrilov, Modelling of microwave images of buried cylindrical objects, *IJIMW* 19(9), 1201–1220, 1998.

19. Vertiy, A. A. and S. P. Gavrilov, Microwave imaging of cylindrical inhomogenities by using a plane wave spectrum of diffracted field, *Proceedings of the International Conference on the Detection of Abandoned Land Mines*, Edinburgh, 12 October 1998.

20. Vertiy, A. A., S. P. Gavrilov, I. Yoynovskyy, A. Kudelya, V. Stepanuk, and B. Levitash, GPR and microwave tomography imaging of buried objects using the short-term (picosecond) video pulses, *Proceedings of the 8th International Conference on Ground Penetrating Radar*, Gold Coast, Australia, 530–534, 23–26 May 2000.

21. Mejibovsky, M. and N. Blaunstein, Geometric-optical model of radio wave refraction in multilayered sub-soil media and its verification via GPR experiments, *Proceedings of IEEE Workshop on Radar Methods and Systems*, Kiev, Ukraine, 6 pages, September 27–28, 2016.

Index

Milton Keynes UK
Ingram Content Group UK Ltd.
UKHW051949071024
449327UK00026B/2228